inside/out

LESBIAN THEORIES, GAY THEORIES

EDITED BY DIANA FUSS

ROUTLEDGE

NEW YORK AND LONDON

Published in 1991 by

Routledge
An imprint of Routledge, Chapman and Hall, Inc.
29 West 35 Street
New York, NY 10001

Published in Great Britain by

Routledge
11 New Fetter Lane
London EC4P 4EE

Copyright © 1991 by Routledge, Chapman and Hall, Inc.

Printed in the United States of America

ISBN 0-415-90236-3 (HB)
ISBN 0-415-90237-1 (PB)

Library of Congress and British Library cataloging in publication information is available.

Contents

Acknowledgments   v
Inside/Out   1
     Diana Fuss

I   Decking Out: Performing Identities

1   Imitation and Gender Insubordination   13
     Judith Butler

2   Boys Will Be Girls: The Politics of Gay Drag   32
     Carole-Anne Tyler

3   Who Are "We"? Gay "Identity" as Political
     (E)motion (A Theoretical Rumination)   71
     Ed Cohen

4   Seeing Things: Representation, the Scene of
     Surveillance, and the Spectacle of Gay Male Sex   93
     Lee Edelman

II   Cutting Up: Specters, Spectators, Authors

5   Anal *Rope*   119
     D. A. Miller

6   Female Spectator, Lesbian Specter: *The Haunting*   142
     Patricia White

7   A Parallax View of Lesbian Authorship   173
     Judith Mayne

8   Believing in Fairies: The Author and
     The Homosexual   185
     Richard Dyer

III   Zoning In: Body/Parts

9   The Queen's Throat: (Homo)sexuality and the Art
of Singing   205
Wayne Koestenbaum

10   Below the Belt: (Un)Covering *The Well of
Loneliness*   235
Michèle Aina Barale

11   Rock Hudson's Body   259
Richard Meyer

IV   Acting Up: AIDS, Allegory, Activism

12   AIDS in America: Postmodern Governance,
Identity, and Experience   291
Thomas Yingling

13   "All the Sad Young Men": AIDS and the Work of
Mourning   311
Jeff Nunokawa

14   Undead   324
Ellis Hanson

15   Shocking Pink Praxis: Race and Gender on the
ACT UP Frontlines   341
Catherine Saalfield and Ray Navarro

V   Speaking Out: Teaching In

16   Visualizing Safe Sex: When Pedagogy and
Pornography Collide   373
Cindy Patton

17   School's Out   387
Simon Watney

Source Bibliography   405
List of Contributors   425

Acknowledgments

Two years ago, as I attended the Second Annual Lesbian and Gay Studies Conference at Yale University, I was struck by a new level of activity in lesbian and gay scholarship: a degree of heightened productivity fueled by a climate of enthusiasm, passion, anguish, fear, fervor, and general fevered commotion. Out from within that electrifying tumult came the idea for *Inside/Out,* a collection of new essays which would bring together in one volume at least a portion of the work currently being done in a variety of mediums (literature, film, video, music, photography) across a spectrum of theoretical approaches (psychoanalysis, deconstruction, semiotics, discourse theory). Most of the essays are appearing in this volume for the first time: many were initially delivered in conference paper form at either the National Lesbian and Gay Studies Conference or various professional associations in different academic fields, while still other papers were commissioned specifically for this volume. My greatest acknowledgment must certainly go to all of the individual contributors to *Inside/Out* who believed in this project from the very beginning and who generously contributed their most recent work. Many of the contributors also made valuable additions to the source bibliography which concludes this essay collection. In particular, I would like to thank Michèle Barale, Richard Dyer, Richard Meyer, and Carole-Anne Tyler for their excellent and often inspired suggestions. Douglas Crimp, Michael West, and Martha Gever also contributed to the final shape and substance of the bibliography, and I would like to thank them all for their spirit of generosity as well as for the general animation and incitement of their work. I would not have retained my sanity through the two-year compilation and revision of this bibliography were it not for the brilliant library sleuthing of my two research assistants, Jenna Hayward and Lee Talley, whose own invaluable contribution to the volume was supported by the Princeton University Research Council for the Humanities and by the Princeton English Department. I owe a special debt of gratitude to my friends, colleagues, and former colleagues here at Princeton: Eduardo Cadava, Gerry Cadava, Michael Cadden, Adrienne Donald, Emory Elliott, Ellis Hanson, Walter Hughes, Thomas Keenan, Jeff Nunokawa, Lora Romero, Andrew Ross, and Harvey Teres. All of them, in ways I suspect they may not even be aware of (nor wish to take responsibility for), have energized and influenced the production of this collection. It is no small coincidence that so many of the writers who appear in *Inside/Out* have already published or will soon be publishing their own books with Routledge. I would like very much to thank the Routledge editorial staff, and Bill Germano especially, for an unwavering support of this particular book as well as for a demonstrated commitment to the publication of a wide range of scholarship by gay and lesbian authors. Finally, *Inside/Out* is dedicated to one of its contributors, Raymond Navarro, who died after a ten-month battle with AIDS as this book was going to press: *en su memoria.*

Inside/Out

Diana Fuss

The philosophical opposition between "heterosexual" and "homo-sexual," like so many other conventional binaries, has always been constructed on the foundations of another related opposition: the couple "inside" and "outside."[1] The metaphysics of identity that has governed discussions of sexual behavior and libidinal object choice has, until now, depended on the structural symmetry of these seemingly fundamental distinctions and the inevitability of a symbolic order based on a logic of limits, margins, borders, and boundaries. Many of the current efforts in lesbian and gay theory, which this volume seeks to showcase, have begun the difficult but urgent textual work necessary to call into question the stability and ineradicability of the hetero/homo hierarchy, suggesting that new (and old) sexual possibilities are no longer thinkable in terms of a simple inside/outside dialectic. But how, exactly, do we bring the hetero/homo opposition to the point of col-lapse? How can we work it to the point of critical exhaustion, and what effects—material, political, social—can such a sustained effort to erode and to reorganize the conceptual grounds of identity be ex-pected to have on our sexual practices and politics?

The figure inside/outside cannot be easily or ever finally dispensed with; it can only be worked on and worked over—itself turned inside out to expose its critical operations and interior machinery. To the extent that the denotation of any term is always dependent on what is exterior to it (heterosexuality, for example, typically defines itself in critical opposition to that which it is not: homosexuality), the inside/outside polarity is an indispensable model for helping us to understand the complicated workings of semiosis. Inside/outside functions as the very figure for signification and the mechanisms of meaning produc-tion. It has everything to do with the structures of alienation, splitting, and identification which together produce a self and an other, a subject

1

and an object, an unconscious and a conscious, an interiority and an exteriority. Indeed, one of the fundamental insights of Lacanian psychoanalysis, influenced by a whole tradition of semiotic thought, is the notion that any identity is founded relationally, constituted in reference to an exterior or outside that defines the subject's own interior boundaries and corporeal surfaces.[2]

But the figure inside/outside, which encapsulates the structure of language, repression, and subjectivity, also designates the structure of exclusion, oppression, and repudiation. This latter model may well be more insistent to those subjects routinely relegated to the right of the virgule—to the outside of systems of power, authority, and cultural legitimacy. Interrogating the position of "outsiderness" is where much recent lesbian and gay theory begins, implicitly if not always directly raising the questions of the complicated processes by which sexual borders are constructed, sexual identities assigned, and sexual politics formulated.[3] How do outsides and insides come about? What philosophical and critical operations or modes produce the specious distinction between a pure and natural heterosexual inside and an impure and unnatural homosexual outside? Where exactly, in this borderline sexual economy, does the one identity leave off and the other begin? And what gets left out of the inside/outside, heterosexual/homosexual opposition, an opposition which could at least plausibly be said to secure its seemingly inviolable dialectical structure only by assimilating and internalizing other sexualities (bisexuality, transvestism, transsexualism . . .) to its own rigid polar logic?

For heterosexuality to achieve the status of the "compulsory," it must present itself as a practice governed by some internal necessity. The language and law that regulates the establishment of heterosexuality as both an identity and an institution, both a practice and a system, is the language and law of defense and protection: heterosexuality secures its self-identity and shores up its ontological boundaries by protecting itself from what it sees as the continual predatory encroachments of its contaminated other, homosexuality. Of course, any sexual identity, based on the complicated dynamics of object choice, works through a similar defensive procedure. Read through the language of psychoanalysis, sexual desire is produced, variously and in tandem, through acts and experiences of defense, ambivalence, repression, denial, threat, trauma, injury, identification, internalization, and renunciation. Indeed, sexual object choice is not even so "simple" a matter of psychical identifications and defenses; it is also a result of the complex interaction of social conflicts, historical pressures, and cultural prohibitions.

The difference between the hetero and the homo, however, is that the homo becomes identified with the very mechanism necessary to define and to defend any sexual border. Homosexuality, in a word, becomes the excluded; it stands in for, paradoxically, that which stands without. But the binary structure of sexual orientation, fundamentally a structure of exclusion and exteriorization, nonetheless constructs that exclusion by prominently including the contaminated other in its oppositional logic. The homo in relation to the hetero, much like the feminine in relation to the masculine, operates as an indispensable interior exclusion—an outside which is inside interiority making the articulation of the latter possible, a transgression of the border which is necessary to constitute the border as such.

The homo, then, is always something less and something more than a supplement—something less in that it signifies lack rather than addition, and something more in that it signifies an addition to a lack, a lack which, importantly, may not be its own. Recent work on sexual subjectivities has begun to challenge the usual association, prevalent even in some poststructuralist thinking, of the outside (of sexual, racial, and economic others) with absence and lack. This work has begun to recognize that any outside is formulated as a consequence of a lack *internal* to the system it supplements. The greater the lack on the inside, the greater the need for an outside to contain and to defuse it, for without that outside, the lack on the inside would become all too visible.[4]

To protect against the recognition of the lack within the self, the self erects and defends its borders against an other which is made to represent or to become that selfsame lack. But borders are notoriously unstable, and sexual identities rarely secure. Heterosexuality can never fully ignore the close psychical proximity of its terrifying (homo)sexual other, any more than homosexuality can entirely escape the equally insistent social pressures of (hetero)sexual conformity. Each is haunted by the other, but here again it is the other who comes to stand in metonymically for the very occurrence of haunting and ghostly visitations. A striking feature of many of the essays collected in this volume is a fascination with the specter of abjection, a certain preoccupation with the figure of the homosexual as specter and phantom, as spirit and revenant, as abject and undead. Those inhabiting the inside, these essays collectively seem to suggest, can only comprehend the outside through the incorporation of a negative image. This process of negative interiorization involves turning homosexuality inside out, exposing not the homosexual's abjected insides but the homosexual as the abject, as the contaminated and expurgated insides of the heterosexual subject.

Homosexual production emerges under these inhospitable conditions as a kind of ghost-writing, a writing which is at once a recognition and a refusal of the cultural representation of "the homosexual" as phantom Other.

Paradoxically, the "ghosting" of homosexuality coincides with its "birth," for the historical moment of the first appearance of the homosexual as a "species" rather than a "temporary aberration"[5] also marks the moment of the homosexual's disappearance—into the closet. That the first coming out was also simultaneously a closeting; that the homosexual's debut onto the stage of historical identities was as much an egress as an entry; and that the priority or "firstness" of homosexuality, which preceded heterosexuality in Western usage by a startling eleven years,[6] nonetheless could not preempt its relegation to secondary status: all these factors highlight, in their very contradictoriness, the ambiguous operations of ins and outs. "Out" cannot help but to carry a double valence for gay and lesbian subjects. On the one hand, it conjures up the exteriority of the negative—the devalued or outlawed term in the hetero/homo binary. On the other hand, it suggests the process of coming out—a movement into a metaphysics of presence, speech, and cultural visibility. The preposition "out" always supports this double sense of invisibility (to put out) and visibility (to bring out), often exceeding even this simple tension in the confused entanglement generated by a host of other active associations.[7]

To be out, in common gay parlance, is precisely to be no longer out; to be out is to be finally outside of exteriority and all the exclusions and deprivations such outsiderhood imposes. Or, put another way, to be out is really to be in—inside the realm of the visible, the speakable, the culturally intelligible. But things are still not so clear, for to come out can also work not to situate one on the inside but to jettison one from it. The recent practice of "outing," of exposing well-known public figures as closet homosexuals, is (among other things) an attempt to demonstrate that there have been outsiders on the inside all along. To "out" an insider, if it has any effect at all, can as easily precipitate that figure's fall from power and privilege as it can facilitate the rise of other gays and lesbians to positions of influence and authority. Because of the infinitely permeable and shifting boundaries between insides and outsides, the political risks or effects of outing are always incalculable.

Recently, in the academy, some would say that it is "in" to be "out." An avant-garde affinity for the liminal space of the marginal energizes many of those disciplines and programs (Women's Studies, African-American Studies, Multicultural Studies) still routinely denied sufficient funding and support from their home institutions adequate to meet the excess in student demand. Supporters of "Gay Studies," a recently emergent interdisciplinary yet autonomous field of inquiry, must grapple with many of the same issues its predecessors confronted, including the vexed question of institutionalization and the relation of gay and lesbian communities to the academy. The issue is the old stand-off between confrontation and assimilation: does one compromise oneself by working on the inside, or does one short-change oneself by holding tenaciously to the outside? Why is institutionalization over-written as "bad" and anti-institutionalization coded as "good"? Does inhabiting the inside always imply cooptation? (Can incorporation be so easily elided with recuperation?) And does inhabiting the outside always and everywhere guarantee radicality?

The problem, of course, with the inside/outside rhetoric, if it remains undeconstructed, is that such polemics disguise the fact that most of us are both inside and outside at the same time.[8] Any misplaced nostalgia for or romanticization of the outside as a privileged site of radicality immediately gives us away, for in order to idealize the outside we must already be, to some degree, comfortably entrenched on the inside. We really only have the leisure to idealize the subversive potential of the power of the marginal when our place of enunciation is quite central. To endorse a position of perpetual or even strategic outsiderhood (a position of powerlessness, speechlessness, homelessness . . .) hardly seems like a viable political program, especially when, for so many gay and lesbian subjects, it is less a question of political tactics than every-day lived experience. Perhaps what we need most urgently in gay and lesbian theory right now is a theory *of* marginality, subversion, dissidence, and othering. What we need is a theory of sexual borders that will help us to come to terms with, and to organize around, the new cultural and sexual arrangements occasioned by the movements and transmutations of pleasure in the social field.[9]

Recent and past work on the question of sexual difference has yet to meet this pressing need, largely because, as Stephen Heath accurately targets the problem, our notion of sexual difference all too often sub-sumes sexual differences, upholding "a defining difference of man/ woman at the expense of gay, lesbian, bisexual, and indeed *hetero* heterosexual reality."[10] Homosexuality is produced inside the domi-nant discourse of sexual difference as its necessary outside, but this is not to say that the homo exerts no pressure on the hetero nor that this outside stands in any simple relation of exteriority to the inside. Every outside is also an alongside; the distance between distance and proximity is sometimes no distance at all. It may be more accurate to say that the homo, occupying the frontier position of inside out, is neither completely outside the bounds of sexual difference nor wholly inside it either. The fear of the homo, which continually *rubs up against* the hetero (tribadic-style), concentrates and codifies the very real possibility and ever-present threat of a collapse of boundaries, an effacing of limits, and a radical confusion of identities.

In its own precarious position at/as the border, homosexuality seems capable of both subtending the dominance of the hetero and structurally subverting it. Much has been made, in discussions of deconstruction's textual and political efficacy, of the tendency of hierarchical relations to reestablish themselves. Such retrenchments often happen at the very moment of the supposed transgression, since every transgression, to establish itself as such, must simultaneously resecure that which it sought to eclipse. Homosexuality, read as a transgression against heterosexuality, succeeds not in undermining the authoritative position of heterosexuality so much as reconfirming heterosexuality's centrality precisely as that which must be resisted. As inescapable as such a logic might be, it does not diminish the importance of deconstruction in addressing the admittedly stubborn and entrenched hetero/homo hierarchy. That hierarchical oppositions always *tend toward* reestablishing themselves does not mean that they can never be invaded, interfered with, and critically impaired. What it does mean is that we must be vigilant in working against such a tendency: what is called for is nothing less than an insistent and intrepid disorganization of the very structures which produce this inescapable logic. Perhaps what we, as gay and lesbian readers of culture, cannot escape at *this* moment in our histories is an "analysis interminable," a responsibility to exert sustained pressure from/on the margins to reshape and to reorient the field of sexual difference to include sexual differences.

But how do we know when the homo is contributing to the confirmation of the hetero and when it is disturbing it? How can we tell the difference—if we hold to the by no means certain assumption that there is a difference? Questions of epistemology ("how do we know?") enjoy a privileged status in theorizations of gay and lesbian identity. How does one know when one is on the inside and when one is not? How does one know when and if one is out of the closet?[11] How, indeed, does one know if one is gay? The very insistence of the epistemological frame of reference in theories of homosexuality may suggest that we *cannot* know—surely or definitively. Sexual identity may be less a function of knowledge than performance, or, in Foucauldian terms, less a matter of final discovery than perpetual reinvention.[12] The essays in this collection, while not abandoning the demands of the epistemological, nonetheless mark an important shift away from the interrogative mode and towards the performative mode—toward the imaginative enactment of sexual redefinitions, reborderizations, and rearticulations.

"What we need," Foucault writes in "The Gay Science," is "a radical break, a change in orientation, objectives, and vocabulary."[13] While this writer remains suspicious of the faith Foucault places in epistemological "breaks," since such breaks inevitably seem to reassert what they sought to supersede, the call for new orientations, new objectives, and especially new vocabularies is still admittedly a seductive one. It would be difficult, not to say delusionary, to forget the words "inside" and "outside," "heterosexual" and "homosexual," without also losing in this act of willed amnesia the crucial sense of alterity necessary for constituting any sexed subject, any subject as sexed. The dream of either a common language or no language at all is just that—a dream, a fantasy that ultimately can do little to acknowledge and to legitimate the hitherto repressed differences between and within sexual identities. But one can, by using these contested words, use them up, exhaust them, transform them into the historical concepts they are and have always been. Change may well happen by working on the insides of our inherited sexual vocabularies and turning them inside out, giving them a new face.

On the cover of this book is not a face (no attempt was made to select "representative" gay and lesbian bodies, as if such a thing were possible) but a figure, a knot, a figure-eight knot or four knot to be precise. This three-dimensional geometrical domain, constituted by rings and matrices, loops and linkages, is nonetheless embodied, sexualized. The undecidability of this simple topology may be its greatest appeal, for it seems to signify at once an anal, a vaginal, a clitoral, a penile, and a testicular topography. The knot interlaces many orifices, many sites of pleasure, many libidinal economies. It visualizes for us in the very simplicity of its openings and closures, its overs and unders, its ins and outs, the contortions and convolutions of any sexual identity formation.

The figure-eight or four knot is intended as a twist or variation on Lacan's famous Borromean knot which, like several other of his favorite mathematical symbols (the Klein bottle, the Möbius strip), demonstrates how the unconscious itself has neither an inside nor an outside. Like the Borromean knot,[14] the four knot, when pulled inside out, appears as its own mirror image; it is what mathematicians call an "invertible" knot, and so might be glossed in the context of this book as a figure for (sexual) inversion. This invertible, three-dimensional four knot could even be seen as complementary to the more historically weighted and culturally recognizable symbol of identity in gay and lesbian communities, the pink triangle with its sharp angles, its straight undeviating lines, and its solid two-dimensional interior space. I offer it here, however, simply as a kind of shorthand notation for the nodular problems this book seeks to disentangle and to reweave: the entwining of identification and desire, of sexual difference and sexual differences, of heterosexuality and homosexuality, and, finally, of inside and out.

Notes

1. This introduction takes as its focus the probing of the book's title "Inside/Out." For a gloss of the subtitle "Lesbian Theories, Gay Theories" (a reading with which I find myself in substantial agreement), see Judith Butler's contribution to this volume.

2. For the importance of inside/outside in theorizing the psychical constitution of the sexed subject, see Jacques Lacan's "The Mirror Stage" in *Ecrits,* trans. Alan Sheridan (New York and London: W. W. Norton & Company, 1977), 1–7, especially his remarks on the *Innenwelt* and the *Umwelt.*

3. The essays in *The South Atlantic Quarterly* special issue on "Displacing Homophobia," to take one recent example, are linked by a shared concern with the tenuous borders (generic, thematic, ideological, immunological, historical, linguistic) distinguishing insides from outsides. Lee Edelman's "The Plague of Discourse: Politics, Literary Theory, and AIDS" and Robert Caserio's "Supreme Court Discourse vs. Homosexual Fiction" are the pieces perhaps most directly invested in deconstructing the inside/outside binary. See *The South Atlantic Quarterly* 88, no. 1 (Winter 1989).

4. On the question of lack and supplementarity, see Jacques Derrida's *The Truth in Painting,* trans. Geoff Bennington and Ian McLeod (Chicago: Chicago University Press, 1987), 57–59. For an interesting reading of the "spectacle of male lack," and an important revision of Lacan's theorization of castration and subject formation, see Kaja Silverman's "Historical Trauma and Male Subjectivity" in *Psychoanalysis and Cinema,* ed. E. Ann Kaplan (New York and London: Routledge, 1990), 110–27, and her *Male Subjectivity at the Margins* (New York and London: Routledge, forthcoming).

5. This by now famous distinction, of course, belongs to Michel Foucault; see *The History of Sexuality, Vol. I: An Introduction* (New York: Vintage Books, 1980), 43.

6. According to historian Jonathan Ned Katz, homosexuality and heterosexuality were privately coined in 1868 by the nineteenth-century German sodomy law reformer, Karl Maria Kertbeny. "Homosexuality" made its first public appearance in an 1869 appeal for reforming the German sodomy laws, and "heterosexuality" followed

eleven years later in an 1880 published defense of homosexuality. See Katz's "The Invention of Heterosexuality," *Socialist Review* 21, no. 1 (Feb. 1990): 7–34. On this subject of the delayed or secondary emergence of heterosexuality into the public sphere, David Halperin wittily observes that "it came into being, in fact, like Eve from Adam's rib." See Halperin's *One Hundred Years of Homosexuality and Other Essays on Greek Love* (New York and London: Routledge, 1990), 17.

7. "Out" can also signify an end or resolution (outcome; school's out); an excuse, alibi, or means of escape (an easy out); a beyond or surpassing (outdoing); an expiration or exhaustion (outmoded, outdated); a fullness or excessiveness (to deck out or rig out); or an utterance or cry (to call out). The term cannot escape certain contradictory class connotations as well. The phrase "coming out" can refer to a debutante's ceremonious and ostentatious introduction to high society, while the phrase "ins and outs" was coined in the nineteenth century to label the nomadic poor who regularly sought readmission to the workhouse.

8. Very few of Jacques Derrida's works, a corpus to which the present essay is obviously indebted, fail to take up and to work over this classical figure of inside/outside; readers might wish, in particular, to consult the following: "Writing Before the Letter," in *Of Grammatology,* translated by Gayatri Chakravorty Spivak (Baltimore and London: The Johns Hopkins University Press, 1974); Violence and Metaphysics: An Essay on the Thought of Emmanuel Levinas," in *Writing and Difference,* translated by Alan Bass (Chicago: University of Chicago Press, 1987); "Living On: Border Lines," in *Deconstruction and Criticism,* translated by James Hulbert (New York: Seabury Press, 1979); "Plato's Pharmacy" and "The Double Session," in *Dissemination,* translated by Barbara Johnson (Chicago: University of Chicago Press, 1981); *Positions,* translated by Alan Bass (Chicago: University of Chicago Press, 1981); and *The Truth in Painting,* translated by Geoff Bennington and Ian McLeod (Chicago: University of Chicago Press, 1987).

9. For example, any changes in sexual practices prompted by AIDS necessarily creates the conditions and the means for the continuing resocialiation of gay, lesbian, bisexual, as well as heterosexual identities and pleasures.

10. Stephen Heath, "The Ethics of Sexual Difference," *Discourse* 12, no. 2 (Spring/Summer 1990): 132.

11. Michelangelo Signorile, one of the editors of the lesbian and gay magazine *Outweek* and the journalist most frequently associated with the practice of outing, deftly poses the question this way: "how many people must one confide in to be 'out of the closet'?" Signorile adamantly disclaims any responsibility for coining the term "outing," attributing the neologism not to *Outweek* but to *Time*—another example of the way in which the outside can be produced as an effect of the inside. See *Outweek* 46 (May 16, 1990): 40.

12. For a persuasive and powerful reading of identity as performance, see Judith Butler's *Gender Trouble: Feminism and the Subversion of Identity* (New York and London: Routledge, 1990). On the centrality of epistemology in theories of gay identity, see Eve Sedgwick's aptly titled and evocative study, *Epistemology of the Closet* (Berkeley: University of California Press, 1990).

13. I am grateful to D. A. Miller and Michael West for bringing this interview to my

attention and for Michael West's excellent unpublished translation from which I quote here.

14. A Borromean knot is three (or more) interlocked rings which fall apart when one of the links is severed. Lacan uses this particular "matheme" to speak of both the interlaced structure of the symptom as well as the interrelated physical domains of the Symbolic, the Imaginary, and the Real.

I

Decking Out:
Performing Identities

1

Imitation and Gender Insubordination[1]

Judith Butler

> So what is this divided being introduced into language through
> gender? It is an impossible being, it is a being that does not exist, an
> ontological joke. *Monique Wittig*[2]

> Beyond physical repetition and the psychical or metaphysical repeti-
> tion, is there an *ontological* repetition? . . . This ultimate repetition,
> this ultimate theatre, gathers everything in a certain way; and in
> another way, it destroys everything; and in yet another way, it selects
> from everything. *Gilles Deleuze*[3]

To Theorize as a Lesbian?

At first I considered writing a different sort of essay, one with a
philosophical tone: the "being" of being homosexual. The prospect of
being anything, even for pay, has always produced in me a certain
anxiety, for "to be" gay, "to be" lesbian seems to be more than a
simple injunction to become who or what I already am. And in no way
does it settle the anxiety for me to say that this is "part" of what I am.
To write or speak *as a lesbian* appears a paradoxical appearance of
this "I," one which feels neither true nor false. For it is a production,
usually in response to a request, to come out or write in the name of
an identity which, once produced, sometimes functions as a politically
efficacious phantasm. I'm not at ease with "lesbian theories, gay theories," for as I've argued elsewhere,[4] identity categories tend to be
instruments of regulatory regimes, whether as the normalizing categories of oppressive structures or as the rallying points for a liberatory

contestation of that very oppression. This is not to say that I will not appear at political occasions under the sign of lesbian, but that I would like to have it permanently unclear what precisely that sign signifies. So it is unclear how it is that I can contribute to this book and appear under its title, for it announces a set of terms that I propose to contest. One risk I take is to be recolonized by the sign under which I write, and so it is this risk that I seek to thematize. To propose that the invocation of identity is always a risk does not imply that resistance to it is always or only symptomatic of a self-inflicted homophobia. Indeed, a Foucaultian perspective might argue that the affirmation of "homosexuality" is itself an extension of a homophobic discourse. And yet "discourse," he writes on the same page, "can be both an instrument and an effect of power, but also a hindrance, a stumbling-block, a point of resistance and a starting point for an opposing strategy."[5]

So I am skeptical about how the "I" is determined as it operates under the title of the lesbian sign, and I am no more comfortable with its homophobic determination than with those normative definitions offered by other members of the "gay or lesbian community." I'm permanently troubled by identity categories, consider them to be invariable stumbling-blocks, and understand them, even promote them, as sites of necessary trouble. In fact, if the category were to offer no trouble, it would cease to be interesting to me: it is precisely the *pleasure* produced by the instability of those categories which sustains the various erotic practices that make me a candidate for the category to begin with. To install myself within the terms of an identity category would be to turn against the sexuality that the category purports to describe; and this might be true for any identity category which seeks to control the very eroticism that it claims to describe and authorize, much less "liberate."

And what's worse, I do not understand the notion of "theory," and am hardly interested in being cast as its defender, much less in being signified as part of an elite gay/lesbian theory crowd that seeks to establish the legitimacy and domestication of gay/lesbian studies within the academy. Is there a pregiven distinction between theory, politics, culture, media? How do those divisions operate to quell a certain intertextual writing that might well generate wholly different epistemic maps? But I am writing here now: is it too late? Can this writing, can any writing, refuse the terms by which it is appropriated even as, to some extent, that very colonizing discourse enables or produces this stumbling block, this resistance? How do I relate the paradoxical situation of this dependency and refusal?

If the political task is to show that theory is never merely *theoria*, in the sense of disengaged contemplation, and to insist that it is fully political (*phronesis* or even *praxis*), then why not simply call this operation *politics,* or some necessary permutation of it?

I have begun with confessions of trepidation and a series of disclaimers, but perhaps it will become clear that *disclaiming,* which is no simple activity, will be what I have to offer as a form of affirmative resistance to a certain regulatory operation of homophobia. The discourse of "coming out" has clearly served its purposes, but what are its risks? And here I am not speaking of unemployment or public attack or violence, which are quite clearly and widely on the increase against those who are perceived as "out" whether or not of their own design. Is the "subject" who is "out" free of its subjection and finally in the clear? Or could it be that the subjection that subjectivates the gay or lesbian subject in some ways continues to oppress, or oppresses most insidiously, once "outness" is claimed? What or who is it that is "out," made manifest and fully disclosed, when and if I reveal myself as lesbian? What is it that is now known, anything? What remains permanently concealed by the very linguistic act that offers up the promise of a transparent revelation of sexuality? Can sexuality even remain sexuality once it submits to a criterion of transparency and disclosure, or does it perhaps cease to be sexuality precisely when the semblance of full explicitness is achieved?[6] Is sexuality of any kind even possible without that opacity designated by the unconscious, which means simply that the conscious "I" who would reveal its sexuality is perhaps the last to know the meaning of what it says?

To claim that this is what I *am* is to suggest a provisional totalization of this "I." But if the I can so determine itself, then that which it excludes in order to make that determination remains constitutive of the determination itself. In other words, such a statement presupposes that the "I" exceeds its determination, and even produces that very excess in and by the act which seeks to exhaust the semantic field of that "I." In the act which would disclose the true and full content of that "I," a certain radical *concealment* is thereby produced. For it is always finally unclear what is meant by invoking the lesbian-signifier, since its signification is always to some degree out of one's control, but also because its *specificity* can only be demarcated by exclusions that return to disrupt its claim to coherence. What, if anything, can lesbians be said to share? And who will decide this question, and in the name of whom? If I claim to be a lesbian, I "come out" only to produce a new and different "closet." The "you" to whom I come out now has access to a different region of opacity. Indeed, the locus of opacity has simply shifted: before, you did not know whether I "am," but now you do not know what that means, which is to say that the copula is empty, that it cannot be substituted for with a set of descriptions.[7] And perhaps that is a situation to be valued. Conventionally, one comes out *of* the closet (and yet, how often is it the case that we are "outed" when we are young and without resources?); so we are out of the closet, but into what? what new unbounded spatiality? the room, the den, the attic, the basement, the house, the bar, the university, some new enclosure whose door, like Kafka's door, produces the expectation of a fresh air and a light of illumination that never arrives? Curiously, it is the figure of the closet that produces this expectation, and which guarantees its dissatisfaction. For being "out" always depends to some extent on being "in"; it gains its meaning only within that polarity. Hence, being "out" must produce the closet again and again in order to maintain itself as "out." In this sense, *outness* can only produce a new opacity; and *the closet* produces the promise of a disclosure that can, by definition, never come. Is this infinite postponement of the disclosure of "gayness," produced by the very act of "coming out," to be lamented? Or is this very deferral of the signified *to be valued,* a site for the production of values, precisely because the term now takes on a life that cannot be, can never be, permanently controlled?

It is possible to argue that whereas no transparent or full revelation is afforded by "lesbian" and "gay," there remains a political imperative to use these necessary errors or category mistakes, as it were (what Gayatri Spivak might call "catachrestic" operations: to use a proper name improperly[8]), to rally and represent an oppressed political constituency. Clearly, I am not legislating against the use of the term. My question is simply: which use will be legislated, and what play will there be between legislation and use such that the instrumental uses of "identity" do not become regulatory imperatives? If it is already true that "lesbians" and "gay men" have been traditionally designated as impossible identities, errors of classification, unnatural disasters within juridico-medical discourses, or, what perhaps amounts to the same, the very paradigm of what calls to be classified, regulated, and controlled, then perhaps these sites of disruption, error, confusion, and trouble can be the very rallying points for a certain resistance to classification and to identity as such.

The question is not one of *avowing* or *disavowing* the category of lesbian or gay, but, rather, why it is that the category becomes the site of this "ethical" choice? What does it mean to *avow* a category that can only maintain its specificity and coherence by performing a prior set of *disavowals*? Does this make "coming out" into the avowal of disavowal, that is, a return to the closet under the guise of an escape? And it is not something like heterosexuality or bisexuality that is disavowed by the category, but a set of identificatory and practical crossings between these categories that renders the discreteness of each equally suspect. Is it not possible to maintain and pursue heterosexual identifications and aims within homosexual practice, and homosexual identifications and aims within heterosexual practices? If a sexuality is to be disclosed, what will be taken as the true determinant of its meaning: the phantasy structure, the act, the orifice, the gender, the anatomy? And if the practice engages a complex interplay of all of those, which one of this erotic dimensions will come to stand for the sexuality that requires them all? Is it the *specificity* of a lesbian experi-ence or lesbian desire or lesbian sexuality that lesbian theory needs to elucidate? Those efforts have only and always produced a set of con-tests and refusals which should by now make it clear that there is no necessarily common element among lesbians, except perhaps that we all know something about how homophobia works against women—although, even then, the language and the analysis we use will differ.

To argue that there might be a *specificity* to lesbian sexuality has seemed a necessary counterpoint to the claim that lesbian sexuality is just heterosexuality once removed, or that it is derived, or that it does not exist. But perhaps the claim of specificity, on the one hand, and the claim of derivativeness or non-existence, on the other, are not as contradictory as they seem. Is it not possible that lesbian sexuality is a process that reinscribes the power domains that it resists, that it is constituted in part from the very heterosexual matrix that it seeks to displace, and that its specificity is to be established, not *outside* or *beyond* that reinscription or reiteration, but in the very modality and effects of that reinscription. In other words, the negative constructions of lesbianism as a fake or a bad copy can be occupied and reworked to call into question the claims of heterosexual priority. In a sense I hope to make clear in what follows, lesbian sexuality can be understood to redeploy its 'derivativeness' in the service of displacing hegemonic heterosexual norms. Understood in this way, the political problem is not to establish the specificity of lesbian sexuality over and against its derivativeness, but to turn the homophobic construction of the bad copy against the framework that privileges heterosexuality as origin, and so 'derive' the former from the latter. This description requires a reconsideration of imitation, drag, and other forms of sexual crossing that affirm the internal complexity of a lesbian sexuality constituted in part within the very matrix of power that it is compelled both to reiterate and to oppose.

On the Being of Gayness as Necessary Drag

The professionalization of gayness requires a certain performance and production of a "self" which is the *constituted effect* of a discourse that nevertheless claims to "represent" that self as a prior truth. When I spoke at the conference on homosexuality in 1989,[9] I found myself telling my friends beforehand that I was off to Yale to be a lesbian, which of course didn't mean that I wasn't one before, but that somehow then, as I spoke in that context, I *was* one in some more thorough and totalizing way, at least for the time being. So I *am* one, and my qualifications are even fairly unambiguous. Since I was sixteen, being a lesbian is what I've been. So what's the anxiety, the discomfort? Well, it has something to do with that redoubling, the way I can say, I'm going to Yale to be a lesbian; a lesbian is what I've been being for so long. How is it that I can both "be" one, and yet endeavor to be one at the same time? When and where does my being a lesbian come into play, when and where does this playing a lesbian constitute something like what I am? To say that I "play" at being one is not to say that I am not one "really"; rather, how and where I play at being one is the way in which that "being" gets established, instituted, circulated, and confirmed. This is not a performance from which I can take radical distance, for this is deep-seated play, psychically entrenched play, *and this "I" does not play its lesbianism as a role.* Rather, it is through the repeated play of this sexuality that the "I" is insistently reconstituted as a lesbian "I"; paradoxically, it is precisely the *repetition* of that play that establishes as well the *instability* of the very category that it constitutes. For if the "I" is a site of repetition, that is, if the "I" only achieves the semblance of identity through a certain repetition of itself, then the I is always displaced by the very repetition that sustains it. In other words, does or can the "I" ever repeat itself, cite itself, faithfully, or is there always a displacement from its former moment that establishes the permanently non-self-identical status of that "I" or its "being lesbian"? What "performs" does not exhaust the "I"; it does not lay out in visible terms the comprehensive content of that "I," for if the performance is "repeated," there is always the question of what differentiates from each other the moments of identity that are repeated. And if the "I" is the effect of a certain repetition, one which produces the semblance of a continuity or coherence, then there is no "I" that precedes the gender that it is said to perform; the repetition, and the failure to repeat, produce a string of performances that constitute and contest the coherence of that "I."

But *politically*, we might argue, isn't it quite crucial to insist on lesbian and gay identities precisely because they are being threatened with erasure and obliteration from homophobic quarters? Isn't the above theory *complicitous* with those political forces that would obliterate the possibility of gay and lesbian identity? Isn't it "no accident" that such theoretical contestations of identity emerge within a political climate that is performing a set of similar obliterations of homosexual identities through legal and political means?

The question I want to raise in return is this: ought such threats of obliteration dictate the terms of the political resistance to them, and if they do, do such homophobic efforts to that extent win the battle from the start? There is no question that gays and lesbians are threatened by the violence of public erasure, but the decision to counter that violence must be careful not to reinstall another in its place. Which version of lesbian or gay ought to be rendered visible, and which internal exclusions will that rendering visible institute? Can the visibility of identity *suffice* as a political strategy, or can it only be the starting point for a strategic intervention which calls for a transformation of policy? Is it not a sign of despair over public politics when identity becomes its own policy, bringing with it those who would 'police' it from various sides? And this is not a call to return to silence or invisibility, but, rather, to make use of a category that can be called into question, made to account for what it excludes. That any consolidation of identity requires some set of differentiations and exclusions seems clear. But which ones ought to be valorized? That the identity-sign I use now has its purposes seems right, but there is no way to predict or control the political uses to which that sign will be put in the future. And perhaps this is a kind of openness, regardless of its risks, that ought to be safeguarded for political reasons. If the rendering visible of lesbian/gay identity now presupposes a set of exclusions, then perhaps part of what is necessarily excluded is *the future uses of the sign.* There is a political necessity to use some sign now, and we do, but how to use it in such a way that its futural significations are not *foreclosed?* How to use the sign and avow its temporal contingency at once?

In avowing the sign's strategic provisionality (rather than its strategic essentialism), that identity can become a site of contest and revision, indeed, take on a future set of significations that those of us who use it now may not be able to foresee. It is in the safeguarding of the future of the political signifiers-preserving the signifier as a site of rearticulation-that Laclau and Mouffe discern its democratic promise.

Within contemporary U.S. politics, there are a vast number of ways in which lesbianism in particular is understood as precisely that which cannot or dare not *be*. In a sense, Jesse Helms's attack on the NEA for sanctioning representations of "homoeroticism" focuses various homophobic fantasies of what gay men are and do on the work of Robert Mapplethorpe.[10] In a sense, for Helms, gay men exist as objects of prohibition; they are, in his twisted fantasy, sadomasochistic exploiters of children, the paradigmatic exemplars of "obscenity"; in a sense, the lesbian is not even produced within this discourse as a prohibited object. Here it becomes important to recognize that oppression works not merely through acts of overt prohibition, but covertly, through the constitution of viable subjects and through the corollary constitution of a domain of unviable (un)subjects—*abjects,* we might call them— who are neither named nor prohibited within the economy of the law. Here oppression works through the production of a domain of unthinkability and unnameability. Lesbianism is not explicitly prohibited in part because it has not even made its way into the thinkable, the imaginable, that grid of cultural intelligibility that regulates the real and the nameable. How, then, to "be" a lesbian in a political context in which the lesbian does not exist? That is, in a political discourse that wages its violence against lesbianism in part by excluding lesbianism from discourse itself? To be prohibited explicitly is to occupy a discursive site from which something like a reverse-discourse can be articulated; to be implicitly proscribed is not even to qualify as an object of prohibition.[11] And though homosexualities of all kinds in this present climate are being erased, reduced, and (then) reconstituted as sites of radical homophobic fantasy, it is important to retrace the different routes by which the unthinkability of homosexuality is being constituted time and again.

It is one thing to be erased from discourse, and yet another to be present within discourse as an abiding falsehood. Hence, there is a political imperative to render lesbianism visible, but how is that to be done outside or through existing regulatory regimes? Can the exclusion from ontology itself become a rallying point for resistance?

Here is something like a confession which is meant merely to thematize the impossibility of confession: As a young person, I suffered for a long time, and I suspect many people have, from being told, explicitly or implicitly, that what I "am" is a copy, an imitation, a derivative example, a shadow of the real. Compulsory heterosexuality sets itself up as the original, the true, the authentic; the norm that determines the real implies that "being" lesbian is always a kind of miming, a vain effort to participate in the phantasmatic plenitude of naturalized heterosexuality which will always and only fail.[12] And yet, I remember quite distinctly when I first read in Esther Newton's *Mother Camp: Female Impersonators in America*[13] that drag is not an imitation or a copy of some prior and true gender; according to Newton, drag enacts the very structure of impersonation by which *any gender* is assumed. Drag is not the putting on of a gender that belongs properly to some other group, i.e. an act of *ex*propriation or *ap*propriation that assumes that gender is the rightful property of sex, that "masculine" belongs to "male" and "feminine" belongs to "female." There is no "proper" gender, a gender proper to one sex rather than another, which is in some sense that sex's cultural property. Where that notion of the "proper" operates, it is always and only *improperly* installed as the effect of a compulsory system. Drag constitutes the mundane way in which genders are appropriated, theatricalized, worn, and done; it implies that all gendering is a kind of impersonation and approximation. If this is true, it seems, there is no original or primary gender that drag imitates, but *gender is a kind of imitation for which there is no original;* in fact, it is a kind of imitation that produces the very notion of the original as an *effect* and consequence of the imitation itself. In other words, the naturalistic effects of heterosexualized genders are produced through imitative strategies; what they imitate is a phantasmatic ideal of heterosexual identity, one that is produced by the imitation as its effect. In this sense, the "reality" of heterosexual identities is performatively constituted through an imitation that sets itself up as the origin and the ground of all imitations. In other words, heterosexuality is always in the process of imitating and approximating its own phantasmatic idealization of itself—*and failing.* Precisely because it is bound to fail, and yet endeavors to succeed, the project of heterosexual identity is propelled into an endless repetition of itself. Indeed, in its efforts to naturalize itself as the original, heterosexuality must be understood as a compulsive and compulsory repetition that can only produce the *effect* of its own originality; in other words, compulsory heterosexual identities, those ontologically consolidated phantasms of "man" and "woman," are theatrically produced effects that posture as grounds, origins, the normative measure of the real.[14]

Reconsider then the homophobic charge that queens and butches and femmes are imitations of the heterosexual real. Here "imitation" carries the meaning of "derivative" or "secondary," a copy of an origin which is itself the ground of all copies, but which is itself a copy of nothing. Logically, this notion of an "origin" is suspect, for how can something operate as an origin if there are no secondary consequences which retrospectively confirm the originality of that origin? The origin requires its derivations in order to affirm itself as an origin, for origins only make sense to the extent that they are differentiated from that which they produce as derivatives. Hence, if it were not for the notion of the homosexual *as* copy, there would be no construct of heterosexuality *as* origin. Heterosexuality here presupposes homosexuality. And if the homosexual *as* copy *precedes* the heterosexual as *origin,* then it seems only fair to concede that the copy comes before the origin, and that homosexuality is thus the origin, and heterosexuality the copy.

But simple inversions are not really possible. For it is only *as* a copy that homosexuality can be argued to *precede* heterosexuality as the origin. In other words, the entire framework of copy and origin proves radically unstable as each position inverts into the other and confounds the possibility of any stable way to locate the temporal or logical priority of either term.

But let us then consider this problematic inversion from a psychic/ political perspective. If the structure of gender imitation is such that the imit*ated* is to some degree produced—or, rather, *r*eproduced—by imitation (see again Derrida's inversion and displacement of mimesis in "The Double Session"), then to claim that gay and lesbian identities are implicated in heterosexual norms or in hegemonic culture generally is not to *derive* gayness from straightness. On the contrary, *imitation* does not copy that which is prior, but produces and *inverts* the very terms of priority and derivativeness. Hence, if gay identities are implicated in heterosexuality, that is not the same as claiming that they are determined or derived from heterosexuality, and it is not the same as claiming that that heterosexuality is the only cultural network in which they are implicated. These are, quite literally, *inverted* imitations, ones which invert the order of imitated and imitation, and which, in the process, expose the fundamental dependency of "the origin" on that which it claims to produce as its secondary effect.

What follows if we concede from the start that gay identities as derivative inversions are in part defined in terms of the very heterosexual identities from which they are differentiated? If heterosexuality is an impossible imitation of itself, an imitation that performatively constitutes itself as the original, then the imitative parody of "heterosexuality"—when and where it exists in gay cultures—is always and only an imitation of an imitation, a copy of a copy, for which there is no original. Put in yet a different way, the parodic or imitative effect of gay identities works neither to copy nor to emulate heterosexuality, but rather, to expose heterosexuality as an incessant and *panicked* imitation of its own naturalized idealization. That heterosexuality is always in the act of elaborating itself is evidence that it is perpetually at risk, that is, that it "knows" its own possibility of becoming undone: hence, its compulsion to repeat which is at once a foreclosure of that which threatens its coherence. That it can never eradicate that risk attests to its profound dependency upon the homosexuality that it seeks fully to eradicate and never can or that it seeks to make second, but which is always already there as a prior possibility.[15] Although this failure of naturalized heterosexuality might constitute a source of pathos for heterosexuality itself—what its theorists often refer to as its constitutive malaise—it can become an occasion for a subversive and proliferating parody of gender norms in which the very claim to originality and to the real is shown to be the effect of a certain kind of naturalized gender mime.

It is important to recognize the ways in which heterosexual norms reappear within gay identities, to affirm that gay and lesbian identities are not only structured in part by dominant heterosexual frames, but that they are *not* for that reason *determined* by them. They are running commentaries on those naturalized positions as well, parodic replays and resignifications of precisely those heterosexual structures that would consign gay life to discursive domains of unreality and unthinkability. But to be constituted or structured in part by the very heterosexual norms by which gay people are oppressed is not, I repeat, to be claimed or determined by those structures. And it is not necessary to think of such heterosexual constructs as the pernicious intrusion of "the straight mind," one that must be rooted out in its entirety. In a way, the presence of heterosexual constructs and positionalities in whatever form in gay and lesbian identities presupposes that there is a gay and lesbian repetition of straightness, a recapitulation of straightness—which is itself a repetition and recapitulation of its own ideality—within its own terms, a site in which all sorts of resignifying and parodic repetitions become possible. The parodic replication and resignification of heterosexual constructs within non-heterosexual frames brings into relief the utterly constructed status of the so-called original, but it shows that heterosexuality only constitutes itself as the original through a convincing act of repetition. The more that "act" is expropriated, the more the heterosexual claim to originality is exposed as illusory.

Although I have concentrated in the above on the reality-effects of gender practices, performances, repetitions, and mimes, I do not mean to suggest that drag is a "role" that can be taken on or taken off at will. There is no volitional subject behind the mime who decides, as it were, which gender it will be today. On the contrary, the very possibility of becoming a viable subject requires that a certain gender mime be already underway. The "being" of the subject is no more self-identical than the "being" of any gender; in fact, coherent gender, achieved through an apparent repetition of the same, produces as its *effect* the illusion of a prior and volitional subject. In this sense, gender is not a performance that a prior subject elects to do, but gender is *performative* in the sense that it constitutes as an effect the very subject it appears to express. It is a *compulsory* performance in the sense that acting out of line with heterosexual norms brings with it ostracism, punishment, and violence, not to mention the transgressive pleasures produced by those very prohibitions.

To claim that there is no performer prior to the performed, that the performance is performative, that the performance constitutes the appearance of a "subject" as its effect is difficult to accept. This difficulty is the result of a predisposition to think of sexuality and gender as "expressing" in some indirect or direct way a psychic reality that precedes it. The denial of the *priority* of the subject, however, is not the denial of the subject; in fact, the refusal to conflate the subject with the psyche marks the psychic as that which exceeds the domain of the conscious subject. This psychic excess is precisely what is being systematically denied by the notion of a volitional "subject" who elects at will which gender and/or sexuality to be at any given time and place. It is this excess which erupts within the intervals of those repeated gestures and acts that construct the apparent uniformity of heterosexual positionalities, indeed which compels the repetition itself, and which guarantees its perpetual failure. In this sense, it is this excess which, within the heterosexual economy, implicitly includes homosexuality, that perpetual threat of a disruption which is quelled through a reenforced repetition of the same. And yet, if repetition is the way in which power works to construct the illusion of a seamless heterosexual identity, if heterosexuality is compelled to *repeat itself* in order to establish the illusion of its own uniformity and identity, then this is an identity permanently at risk, for what if it fails to repeat, or if the very exercise of repetition is redeployed for a very different performative purpose? If there is, as it were, always a compulsion to repeat, repetition never fully accomplishes identity. That there is a need for a repetition at all is a sign that identity is not self-identical. It requires to be instituted again and again, which is to say that it runs the risk of becoming *de*-instituted at every interval.

So what is this psychic excess, and what will constitute a subversive or *de*-instituting repetition? First, it is necessary to consider that sexuality always exceeds any given performance, presentation, or narrative which is why it is not possible to derive or read off a sexuality from any given gender presentation. And sexuality may be said to exceed any definitive narrativization. Sexuality is never fully "expressed" in a performance or practice; there will be passive and butchy femmes, femmy and aggressive butches, and both of those, and more, will turn out to describe more or less anatomically stable "males" and "females." There are no direct expressive or causal lines between sex, gender, gender presentation, sexual practice, fantasy and sexuality. None of those terms captures or determines the rest. Part of what constitutes sexuality is precisely that which does not appear and that which, to some degree, can never appear. This is perhaps the most fundamental reason why sexuality is to some degree always closeted, especially to the one who would express it through acts of self-disclosure. That which is excluded for a given gender presentation to "succeed" may be precisely what is played out sexually, that is, an "inverted" relation, as it were, between gender and gender presentation, and gender presentation and sexuality. On the other hand, both gender presentation and sexual practices may corollate such that it appears that the former "expresses" the latter, and yet both are jointly constituted by the very sexual possibilities that they exclude.

This logic of inversion gets played out interestingly in versions of lesbian butch and femme gender stylization. For a butch can present herself as capable, forceful, and all-providing, and a stone butch may well seek to constitute her lover as the exclusive site of erotic attention and pleasure. And yet, this "providing" butch who seems *at first* to replicate a certain husband-like role, can find herself caught in a logic of inversion whereby that "providingness" turns to a self-sacrifice, which implicates her in the most ancient trap of feminine self-abnegation. She may well find herself in a situation of radical need, which is precisely what she sought to locate, find, and fulfill in her femme lover. In effect, the butch inverts into the femme or remains caught up in the specter of that inversion, or takes pleasure in it. On the other hand, the femme who, as Amber Hollibaugh has argued, "orchestrates" sexual exchange,[16] may well eroticize a certain dependency only to learn that the very power to orchestrate that dependency exposes her own incontrovertible power, at which point she inverts into a butch or becomes caught up in the specter of that inversion, or perhaps delights in it.

Psychic Mimesis

What stylizes or forms an erotic style and/or a gender presentation—
and that which makes such categories inherently unstable—is a set of
psychic identifications that are not simple to describe. Some psychoanalytic theories tend to construe identification and desire as two mutually
exclusive relations to love objects that have been lost through prohibition and/or separation. Any intense emotional attachment thus divides
into either wanting to have someone or wanting to be that someone,
but never both at once. It is important to consider that identification
and desire can coexist, and that their formulation in terms of mutually
exclusive oppositions serves a heterosexual matrix. But I would like to
focus attention on yet a different construal of that scenario, namely,
that "wanting to be" and "wanting to have" can operate to differentiate mutually exclusive positionalities internal to lesbian erotic exchange. Consider that identifications are always made in response to
loss of some kind, and that they involve a certain *mimetic practice* that
seeks to incorporate the lost love within the very "identity" of the one
who remains. This was Freud's thesis in "Mourning and Melancholia"
in 1917 and continues to inform contemporary psychoanalytic discussions of identification.[17]

For psychoanalytic theorists Mikkel Borch-Jacobsen and Ruth Leys,
however, identification and, in particular, identificatory mimetism,
precedes "identity" and constitutes identity as that which is fundamentally "other to itself." The notion of this Other *in* the self, as it were,
implies that the self/Other distinction is *not* primarily external (a powerful critique of ego psychology follows from this); the self is from
the start radically implicated in the "Other." This theory of primary
mimetism differs from Freud's account of melancholic incorporation.
In Freud's view, which I continue to find useful, incorporation—a kind
of psychic miming—is a response to, and refusal of, *loss*. Gender as
the site of such psychic mimes is thus constituted by the variously
gendered Others who have been loved and lost, where the loss is
suspended through a melancholic and imaginary incorporation (and
preservation) of those Others into the psyche. Over and against this
account of psychic mimesis by way of incorporation and melancholy,
the theory of primary mimetism argues an even stronger position in
favor of the non-self-identity of the psychic subject. Mimetism is not
motivated by a drama of loss and wishful recovery, but appears to
precede and constitute desire (and motivation) itself; in this sense,
mimetism would be prior to the possibility of loss and the disappoint-
ments of love.

Whether loss or mimetism is primary (perhaps an undecidable problem), the psychic subject is nevertheless constituted internally by differentially gendered Others and is, therefore, never, as a gender, self-identical.

In my view, the self only becomes a self on the condition that it has suffered a separation (grammar fails us here, for the "it" only becomes differentiated through that separation), a loss which is suspended and provisionally resolved through a melancholic incorporation of some "Other." That "Other" installed in the self thus establishes the permanent incapacity of that "self" to achieve self-identity; it is as it were always already disrupted by that Other; the disruption of the Other at the heart of the self is the very condition of that self's possibility.[18]

Such a consideration of psychic identification would vitiate the possibility of any stable set of typologies that explain or describe something like gay or lesbian identities. And any effort to supply one—as evidenced in Kaja Silverman's recent inquiries into male homosexuality—suffer from simplification, and conform, with alarming ease, to the regulatory requirements of diagnostic epistemic regimes. If incorporation in Freud's sense in 1914 is an effort to *preserve* a lost and loved object and to refuse or postpone the recognition of loss and, hence, of grief, then to become *like* one's mother or father or sibling or other early "lovers" may be an act of love and/or a hateful effort to replace or displace. How would we "typologize" the ambivalence at the heart of mimetic incorporations such as these?[19]

How does this consideration of psychic identification return us to the question, what constitutes a subversive repetition? How are troublesome identifications apparent in cultural practices? Well, consider the way in which heterosexuality naturalizes itself through setting up certain illusions of continuity between sex, gender, and desire. When Aretha Franklin sings, "you make me feel like a natural woman," she seems at first to suggest that some natural potential of her biological sex is actualized by her participation in the cultural position of "woman" as object of heterosexual recognition. Something in her "sex" is thus expressed by her "gender" which is then fully known and consecrated within the heterosexual scene. There is no breakage, no discontinuity between "sex" as biological facticity and essence, or between gender and sexuality. Although Aretha appears to be all too glad to have her naturalness confirmed, she also seems fully and paradoxically mindful that that confirmation is never guaranteed, that the effect of naturalness is only achieved as a consequence of that moment of heterosexual recognition. After all, Aretha sings, you make me feel *like* a natural woman, suggesting that this is a kind of metaphorical substitution, an act of imposture, a kind of sublime and momentary participation in an ontological illusion produced by the mundane operation of heterosexual drag.

But what if Aretha were singing to me? Or what if she were singing to a drag queen whose performance somehow confirmed her own?

How do we take account of these kinds of identifications? It's not that there is some kind of *sex* that exists in hazy biological form that is somehow *expressed* in the gait, the posture, the gesture; and that some sexuality then expresses both that apparent gender or that more or less magical sex. If gender is drag, and if it is an imitation that regularly produces the ideal it attempts to approximate, then gender is a performance that *produces* the illusion of an inner sex or essence or psychic gender core; it *produces* on the skin, through the gesture, the move, the gait (that array of corporeal theatrics understood as gender presentation), the illusion of an inner depth. In effect, one way that genders gets naturalized is through being constructed as an inner psychic or physical *necessity*. And yet, it is always a surface sign, a signification on and with the public body that produces this illusion of an inner depth, necessity or essence that is somehow magically, causally expressed.

To dispute the psyche as *inner depth*, however, is not to refuse the psyche altogether. On the contrary, the psyche calls to be rethought precisely as a compulsive repetition, as that which conditions and disables the repetitive performance of identity. If every performance repeats itself to institute the effect of identity, then every repetition requires an interval between the acts, as it were, in which risk and excess threaten to disrupt the identity being constituted. The unconscious is this excess that enables and contests every performance, and which never fully appears within the performance itself. The psyche is not "in" the body, but in the very signifying process through which that body comes to appear; it is the lapse in repetition as well as its compulsion, precisely what the performance seeks to deny, and that which compels it from the start.

To locate the psyche within this signifying chain as the instability of all iterability is not the same as claiming that it is inner core that is awaiting its full and liberatory expression. On the contrary, the psyche is the permanent failure of expression, a failure that has its values, for it impels repetition and so reinstates the possibility of disruption. What then does it mean to pursue disruptive repetition within compulsory heterosexuality?

Although compulsory heterosexuality often presumes that there is first a sex that is expressed through a gender and then through a sexuality, it may now be necessary fully to invert and displace that operation of thought. If a regime of sexuality mandates a compulsory performance of sex, then it may be only through that performance that the binary system of gender and the binary system of sex come to have intelligibility at all. It may be that the very categories of sex, of sexual identity, of gender are produced or maintained in the *effects* of this compulsory performance, effects which are disingenuously renamed as causes, origins, disingenuously lined up within a causal or expressive sequence that the heterosexual norm produces to legitimate itself as the origin of all sex. How then to expose the causal lines as retrospectively and performatively produced fabrications, and to engage gender itself as an inevitable fabrication, to fabricate gender in terms which reveal every claim to the origin, the inner, the true, and the real as nothing other than the effects of *drag,* whose subversive possibilities ought to be played and replayed to make the "sex" of gender into a site of insistent political play? Perhaps this will be a matter of working sexuality *against* identity, even against gender, and of letting that which cannot fully appear in any performance persist in its disruptive promise.

Notes

1. Parts of this essay were given as a presentation at the Conference on Homosexuality at Yale University in October, 1989.

2. "The Mark of Gender," *Feminist Issues* 5 no. 2 (1985): 6.

3. *Différence et répétition* (Paris: PUF, 1968), 374; my translation.

4. *Gender Trouble: Feminism and the Subversion of Identity* (New York and London: Routledge, 1990).

5. Michel Foucault, *The History of Sexuality, Vol. I,* trans. John Hurley (New York: Random House, 1980), 101.

6. Here I would doubtless differ from the very fine analysis of Hitchcock's *Rope* offered by D. A. Miller in this volume.

7. For an example of "coming out" that is strictly unconfessional and which, finally, offers no content for the category of lesbian, see Barbara Johnson's deftly constructed "Sula Passing: No Passing" presentation at UCLA, May 1990.

8. Gayatri Chakravorty Spivak, "Displacement and the Discourse of Woman." In *Displacement: Derrida and After,* ed. Mark Krupnick (Bloomington: Indiana University Press, 1983).

9. Let me take this occasion to apologize to the social worker at that conference who asked a question about how to deal with those clients with AIDS who turned to Bernie Segal and others for the purposes of psychic healing. At the time, I understood

this questioner to be suggesting that such clients were full of self-hatred because they were trying to find the causes of AIDS in their own selves. The questioner and I appear to agree that any effort to locate the responsibility for AIDS in those who suffer from it is politically and ethically wrong. I thought the questioner, however, was prepared to tell his clients that they were self-hating, and I reacted strongly (too strongly) to the paternalistic prospect that this person was going to pass judgment on someone who was clearly not only suffering, but already passing judgment on him or herself. To call another person self-hating is itself an act of power that calls for some kind of scrutiny, and I think in response to someone who is already dealing with AIDS, that is perhaps the last thing one needs to hear. I also happened to have a friend who sought out advice from Bernie Segal, not with the belief that there is an exclusive or even primary psychic cause or solution for AIDS, but that there might be a psychic contribution to be made to surviving with AIDS. Unfortunately, I reacted quickly to this questioner, and with some anger. And I regret now that I didn't have my wits about me to discuss the distinctions with him that I have just laid out.

Curiously, this incident was invoked at a CLAGS (Center for Lesbian and Gay Studies) meeting at CUNY sometime in December of 1989 and, according to those who told me about it, my angry denunciation of the social worker was taken to be symptomatic of the political insensitivity of a "theorist" in dealing with someone who is actively engaged in AIDS work. That attribution implies that I do not do AIDS work, that I am not politically engaged, and that the social worker in question does not read theory. Needless to say, I was reacting angrily on behalf of an absent friend with AIDS who sought out Bernie Segal and company. So as I offer this apology to the social worker, I wait expectantly that the CLAGS member who misunderstood me will offer me one in turn.

10. See my "The Force of Fantasy: Feminism, Mapplethorpe, and Discursive Excess," *differences* 2, no. 2 (Summer 1990). Since the writing of this essay, lesbian artists and representations have also come under attack.

11. It is this particular ruse of erasure which Foucault for the most part fails to take account of in his analysis of power. He almost always presumes that power takes place through discourse as its instrument, and that oppression is linked with subjection and subjectivation, that is, that it is installed as the formative principle of the identity of subjects.

12. Although miming suggests that there is a prior model which is being copied, it can have the effect of exposing that prior model as purely phantasmatic. In Jacques Derrida's "The Double Session" in *Dissemination,* trans. Barbara Johnson (Chicago: University of Chicago Press, 1981), he considers the textual effect of the mime in Mallarmé's "Mimique." There Derrida argues that the mime does not imitate or copy some prior phenomenon, idea, or figure, but constitutes—some might say *performatively*—the phantasm of the original in and through the mime:

> He represents nothing, imitates nothing, does not have to conform to any prior referent with the aim of achieving adequation or verisimilitude. One can here foresee an objection: since the mime imitates nothing, reproduces nothing, opens up in its origin the very thing he is tracing out, presenting, or producing, he must be the very movement of truth. Not, of course, truth in the form of adequation between the representation and the present of the thing itself, or

between the imitator and the imitated, but truth as the present unveiling of the present. . . . But this is not the case. . . . We are faced then with mimicry imitating nothing: faced, so to speak, with a double that couples no simple, a double that nothing anticipates, nothing at least that is not itself already double. There is no simple reference. . . . This speculum reflects no reality: it produces mere "reality-effects". . . . In this speculum with no reality, in this mirror of a mirror, a difference or dyad does exist, since there are mimes and phantoms. But it is a difference without reference, or rather reference without a referent, without any first or last unit, a ghost that is the phantom of no flesh . . . (206)

13. Esther Newton, *Mother Camp: Female Impersonators in America* (Chicago: University of Chicago Press, 1972).

14. In a sense, one might offer a redescription of the above in Lacanian terms. The sexual "positions" of heterosexually differentiated "man" and "woman" are part of the *Symbolic*, that is, an ideal embodiment of the Law of sexual difference which constitutes the object of imaginary pursuits, but which is always thwarted by the "real." These symbolic positions for Lacan are by definition impossible to occupy even as they are impossible to resist as the structuring telos of desire. I accept the former point, and reject the latter one. The imputation of universal necessity to such positions simply encodes compulsory heterosexuality at the level of the Symbolic, and the "failure" to achieve it is implicitly lamented as a source of heterosexual pathos.

15. Of course, it is Eve Kosofsky Sedgwick's *Epistemology of the Closet* (Berkeley: University of California Press, 1990) which traces the subleties of this kind of panic in Western heterosexual epistemes.

16. Amber Hollibaugh and Cherríe Moraga, "What We're Rollin Around in Bed With: Sexual Silences in Feminism," in *Powers of Desire: The Politics of Sexuality,* ed. Ann Snitow, Christine Stansell, and Sharon Thompson (New York: Monthly Review Press, 1983), 394–405.

17. Mikkel Borch-Jacobsen, *The Freudian Subject* (Stanford: Stanford University Press, 1988); for citations of Ruth Leys's work, see the following two endnotes.

18. For a very fine analysis of primary mimetism with direct implications for gender formation, see Ruth Leys, "The Real Miss Beauchamp: The History and Sexual Politics of the Multiple Personality Concept," in *Feminists Theorize the Political,* eds. Judith Butler and Joan W. Scott (New York and London: Routledge, forthcoming 1991). For Leys, a primary mimetism or suggestibility requires that the "self" from the start is constituted by its incorporations; the effort to differentiate oneself from that by which one is constituted is, of course, impossible, but it does entail a certain "incorporative violence," to use her term. The violence of identification is in this way in the service of an effort at differentiation, to take the place of the Other who is, as it were, installed at the foundation of the self. That this replacement, which seeks to be a displacement, fails, and must repeat itself endlessly, becomes the trajectory of one's psychic career.

19. Here again, I think it is the work of Ruth Leys which will clarify some of the complex questions of gender constitution that emerge from a close psychoanalytic consideration of imitation and identification. Her forthcoming book manuscript will doubtless galvanize this field: *The Subject of Imitation.*

2

Boys Will Be Girls:
The Politics of Gay Drag

Carole-Anne Tyler

"Girls will be boys and boys will be girls/ It's a mixed up muddled up shook up world except for Lola," the Kinks sang in 1970, asserting that the gay man in drag was the only sane person in a crazy world.[1] That rock group's revaluation of camp and the masquerade is currently shared by many theorists on the left, who advocate it as a postmodern strategy for the subversion of phallogocentric identities and desires. Their now radical chic has made the likes of Dolly Parton and Madonna (and their satin queen or Wanna-Be parodies or imitations) more than chicks with cheek; they have become draped crusaders for the social constructionist cause, catching gender in the act—as an act—so as to demonstrate there is no natural, essential, biological basis to gender identity or sexual orientation. Female impersonation in particular has been theorized as progressive, partly because of the long-standing link between femininity and masquerade in psychoanalysis (going back to Joan Riviere's 1929 essay, "Womanliness as a Masquerade"), and partly because femininity, unlike masculinity, is thought to involve non-phallogocentric ways of relating to the body, to language, to desire, and to others.[2]

But male impersonation, too, has been theorized as transgressive by some, especially by gay and lesbian critics, who have suggested that butch, like fem, role-playing de-natures identity and sexuality, confronting heterosexist essentialism with the artifices of gender and the errant play of desire.[3] Once masculinity is seen as a put-on, mere style, its phallic imposture is exposed as such and so delegitimated, according to proponents of drag. Furthermore, they suggest that because sexuality, like gender, is organized around the phallus in our culture, there can be no escaping phallic effects, no "authentic" non-phallic desires or identities which would originate beyond (or perhaps before) the phallus and its signifiers. Any appeal to such a beyond or before is utopic or essentialist or both and, therefore, suspect as well as impractical. According to this logic, the leather queen and the satin queen are both postmodern pragmatists, deconstructing identity from within so as not to sacrifice desire to an outmoded, purist—and Puritan—essentialism.

Not so long ago camp languished, theorized as the shameful sign of an unreconstructed, self-hating, and even woman-hating, homosexual by gay, feminist, and lesbian feminist critics alike. Now camp has been rehabilitated with a vengeance: not only femininity but even macho masculinity is read as camp and, therefore, radical. Curiously, this theorizing of camp seems camp itself, like a parody of parody (of gender play as subversion). Who is putting on whom—or what—here? If all gender is an act and not the direct expression of a biological essence, what counts as camp and why? And if camp is a parodic distance from an identity theorists once thought it too nearly imitated, what guarantees are there that such a distance is not a difference complicit with phallogocentric hierarchies? When signifiers of identities are free from any anchor in ontology, they can express indirectly— in disguised form—identifications and dis-identifications that may have nothing to do with biology but everything to do with fantasies supporting phallic narcissism.

In fact, the controversy over the meaning of camp reveals as much about the fears and desires of theorists of drag as it does about the fears and desires of impersonators themselves. The narratives into which camp acts are inserted—whether filmic/fictive or factual/theoretical—attempt to close down the open, polyvalent signifiers of drag, fixing them to a signified and in the process, fixing a subject for that signified. Fixed, but not neutered or neutral, that subject uses camp to position him/herself with respect to symbolic castration and what signifies lack. Whether revalued or devalued, camp and its interpretations participate in the reproduction of subjectivity and can be defensive as well as counter-offensive. That is, impersonators and their interpreters say more than they intend to because unconscious as well as conscious impulses motivate their performances, impulses all too often at odds with an acceptance of the radical lack to which all subjects are subject-ed. It is important to read each instance of drag (and its interpretations) symptomatically rather than to insist it is always radical or conservative. In whose eyes is what chic radical? This is the difficult question theorists need to ask themselves when considering the function of camp, which is not a unitary phenomenon, meaning the same thing to everybody.

Inversion

Andrew Ross suggests that after Stonewall camp was an embarrassment to the gay community, the sign of a pre-political gay identity.[4] But other historians of drag have argued that gay and lesbian activists were uncomfortable with it long before then, at least since the 1950s. According to Dave King, both the Daughters of Bilitis and the Mattachine Society disapproved of it and in effect participated in (if only on the margins) the consolidation of a distinction between gender and sexual "deviance" which resulted in the separation of transvestism and transsexualism from homosexuality.[5] The impulse behind the gay and lesbian wish to create such a distinction and the accompanying devaluation of camp was in large part the apparent complicity of the latter with the sexual inversion model of homosexuality, which seems to confuse what Simon Watney labels the two major axes of sexual difference: gender identity and object choice.[6] Sexual inversion theory explains what looks like a homosexual object choice as in effect a heterosexual object choice by labeling the homosexual an "invert" and, therefore, psychically (and perhaps to some degree physically) the opposite sex. Even "third sex" theorists like Magnus Hirschfeld make a similar assumption: the "uranian," like the invert, has the psyche of one gender (or perhaps both) and the body of the other. Thus, if a man desires another man, he must do so as a woman, as Freud explains in an important footnote in *Three Essays on the Theory of Sexuality:*

> In all the cases we have examined we have established the fact that the future inverts, in the earliest years of their childhood, pass through a phase of very intense, but short-lived fixation to a woman (usually their mother), and that, after leaving this behind [in response to castration anxiety], they identify themselves with a woman and take *themselves* as their sexual object. That is to say, they proceed from a narcissistic basis, and look for a young man who resembles themselves and whom *they* may love as their mother loved *them*.[7]

Similarly, if Dora loves Frau K., is it through a masculine identification she makes (perhaps especially with her father).[8] Indeed, among women, "the active inverts exhibit masculine characteristics, both physical and mental, with peculiar frequency and look for femininity in their sexual objects. . . . "[9]

This model has seemed problematic to gays and lesbians because it reinscribes heterosexuality within homosexuality itself, as Judith Butler points out.[10] In doing so, it is unable to account for the apparently "normally" or "correctly" gendered partner in homosexual object choices. If the butch, as a masculine invert, desires the fem for her femininity, then the fem cannot be an invert—so why does she make a homosexual object choice at all? In fact, Freud was willing to admit there was a certain amount of what he described as "ambiguity" about masculine inversion (though, tellingly, not about lesbianism):

> There can be no doubt that a large proportion of male inverts retain the mental quality of masculinity, that they possess relatively few of the secondary characteristics of the opposite sex and that what they look for in their sexual object are in fact feminine mental traits. If this were not so, how would it be possible to explain the fact that male prostitutes who offer themselves to inverts—to-day just as they did in ancient times—imitate women in all the externals of their clothing and behavior? . . . A strict conceptual distinction should be drawn according to whether the sexual character of the *object* or that of the *subject* has been inverted.[11]

Thus, in discussing male homosexuality Freud sometimes presumes the subject of desire to be feminine, in search of a masculine object, and sometimes presumes that subject to be masculine, in search of a feminine object. Though in both cases he explains desire heterosexually, clearly the desire of, rather than for, the gay butch, like that of, rather than for, the lesbian fem, cannot be readily accounted for within an inversion model of regressive identification with the once-desired parent of the opposite sex. Confronting the theoretical impossibility of their existence, gay men asserted men did and could love men as men, while lesbians insisted women did and could love women as women.

Paradoxically, however, the refusal to assimilate homosexuality to heterosexuality as "natural" was consistent with a liberal assimilationist gender politics, like that of the Daughters of Bilitis and the Mattachine Society, whose members argued not for a gay difference but for sameness with respect to "natural" gender identities. Gay men and lesbians, despite their object choices, were really basically just like heterosexual men and women. This is a view which still has a wide currency. It serves, for example, as the basis of one of the common explanations of why the masculinization of gay culture is radical. Martin Humphries relies on it when he asserts, "By creating amongst ourselves [gay men] apparently masculine men who desire other men we are refuting the idea that we are really feminine souls in male bodies."[12] Gregg Blachford also assumes it when he argues that gay macho "may be an attempt to show that masculine or 'ordinary' men can be homosexual too. . . . "[13] A playful extension of the idea occurs in Rita Mae Brown's *Rubyfruit Jungle,* in which it is heterosexuals, not homosexuals, who suffer from gender confusion, as their sexual fantasies of "inversion" reveal.[14] A more serious extension of it would be the belief that transsexualism is only a defense against homosexuality—the logical inverse of inversion theory, which carried to its extreme would assert that homosexuality is really transsexualism. The insistence of gay and lesbian writers on their "straight" gender identity but "deviant" object choice makes homosexuality a matter of sexual rather than gender difference from what culture assumes to be (and legislates as) the norm, heterosexuality.

Eve Sedgwick has pointed out that these two alternative explanations of homosexuality—by gender definitions or sexual definitions—have structured not only how gay identity is understood but also what political alliances through cross-identification seem to make sense.[15] For example, if lesbians stress their gender difference, they might identify with straight or gay men; if they stress their sexual difference, they might identify with straight women or gay men. It seems necessary to add, however, that these explanations structure not only cross-identity or affinity politics but also identities themselves. Clearly, in recent years in the gay movement it has been seen as important to maintain a distinction between gender identity and sexual object choice, even to the point of participating in the consolidation of that distinction, as I have noted above. This has accompanied and evoked a devaluation of camp or drag as a gender confusion from which many gays would distance themselves.

I have suggested elsewhere that such anxiety about being "normal" with respect to gender can be consistent with patriarchal gynephobia when it takes the form of the repudiation of femininity, as when the apparently woman-identified drag queens interviewed on television talk shows and in books like *Men in Frocks* insist they really are men and have no wish to be (mis)taken for women.[16] The emphasis on masculinity in gay macho, therefore, might be a defense against the feminization our culture has persistently linked to homosexuality, just as the hypermasculine activity of male pin-ups, according to Richard

Dyer, or of Thomas Magnum (P.I.), according to Sandy Flitterman-Lewis, or of the hero of the Western, according to Steve Neale, is meant to allay the castration anxiety evoked by the spectacle of the man as spectacle, like a woman, the (homosexual) object of the presumptively male cinematic gaze.[17] Thus John Marshall is right to underline that the association of gender inversion with homosexuality has been used to police masculine and feminine roles, for example, through homophobic questions like, "What are you—a fag?"[18] However, because he privileges sexuality rather than gender when defining gay identity, he does not discuss the misogynist corollary question, "What are you—a girl?"

Though homophobia and misogyny/gynephobia are closely linked in our culture, as Craig Owens indicates, they are not the same thing—which Owens reveals when he suggests it is possible for feminists, like Luce Irigaray, to be homophobic. He, therefore, contradicts himself when he cites Jacques Derrida as authority for the assertion that gay men are not gynephobic because they do not suffer from castration anxiety.[19] It does not follow that because gay men are unafraid of being seen as gay, they are unafraid of being seen as feminine (where femininity signifies castration in a patriarchal fantasmatic) unless gay men "really" are already feminine, and therefore castrated, a possibility ruled out from the moment homophobia and misogyny—or homosexuality and gender inversion—are made disjunct. The fear that homosexuality means a man can be robbed of his virility, articulated as "fact" by Freud in his explanation of Leonardo Da Vinci's homosexuality, may animate homophobia outside the gay community and misogyny within it as well as without.[20]

Misogyny

In fact, the drag queen may bear the brunt of misogyny within the gay male subculture, as the myth of the "homosexual" is debunked by denigrating drag in order to put as much distance as possible between the deviant "role" (the effeminate invert) and the "real thing" (the gay-identified masculine man). The queens in John Rechy's *City of Night* are either tragic or abject, as is Georgette in Hubert Selby, Jr.'s *Last Exit to Brooklyn*.[21] The queens interviewed in *Men in Frocks* are defensive—like Harvey Fierstein's Arnold in the movie *Torch Song Trilogy* (1988), who announces that he is a female impersonator to his soon-to-be-lover Alan with a bravado that suggests he believes he is being provocative if not downright offensive.[22] Indeed, the major premise of the cult hit film *Outrageous!* (1977) is that Robin's (impersonator Craig Russell's) drag is just that, outrageous. "It's one thing to be gay, but drag—"his gay boss tells him at one point, and later fires him for refusing to give it up. Even one of Robin's lovers says, "I don't usually make it with drag queens—none of the guys do."

Such (thinly disguised?) misogyny also haunts some of the most sophisticated theoretical essays when they broach the topic of camp, like Leo Bersani's "Is the Rectum a Grave?" That the piece indulges in misogyny is suggested by one passage which offers a rather disturbingly sexist critique of heterosexism in the media coverage of AIDS:

> TV treats us to nauseating processions of yuppie women announcing to the world they will no longer put out for their yuppie boyfriends unless these boyfriends agree to use a condom. Thus hundreds of thousands of gay men and IV drug users, who have reason to think that they may be infected with HIV, or who know that they are . . . are asked to sympathize with all these yuppettes agonizing over whether they're going to risk losing a good fuck by taking the "unfeminine" initiative of interrupting the invading male in order to insist that he practice safe sex.[23]

Here the women are doubly feminized (as "yupp*ettes*"), even while they are described as having screwed over gay men. Furthermore, it is assumed that for a woman "a good fuck" involves an "invading male," perilously close to the rationales offered for rape ("she really wanted it"). Bersani's justifiable anger against a heterosexist media is unjustifiably directed against women; he fails to offer an analysis of the complex politics of the advertising he critiques, in which gender and class, as well as sexual orientation, are implicated, resorting instead to misogyny.

This misogyny is even more disturbing when Bersani turns to camp:

> The gay male parody of a certain femininity, which as others have argued, may itself be an elaborate social construct, is both a way of giving vent to the hostility toward women that probably afflicts every male . . . *and* could also paradoxically be thought of as helping to deconstruct that image for women themselves. A certain type of homosexual camp speaks the truth of that femininity as mindless, asexual, and hysterically bitchy, thereby provoking, it would seem to me, a violently anti-mimetic reaction in any female spectator. The gay male bitch desublimates and desexualizes a type of femininity glamorized by movie stars, whom he then lovingly assassinates with

his style, even though the campy parodist may himself be quite stimulated by the hateful impulses inevitably included in his performance. The gay-macho style, on the other hand, is intended to excite others sexually, and the only reason that it continues to be adopted is that it frequently succeeds in doing so.[24]

Once again, women are assigned the place of lack (as bitches, actual and potential, in need of the rather violent "help" which drag queens are best equipped to offer them). But here drag queens themselves are also the victims of a misogyny for which Bersani would make them responsible, represented as just as bitchy and narcissistic as the "real thing," r.g.'s ("real girls"), too self-involved to be stimulating anybody else, unlike the altruistic butch.[25] Asserting that neither the "glamorized" movie star nor the queen are desirable (they are "asexual," despite the evidence of star fan clubs and Chicks-with-Dicks phone sex numbers) Bersani condemns them to/for masturbation.

Curiously, the moments of no doubt unconscious misogynistic dis-identification from the feminine and its representatives which the article enacts coexist with an articulated or conscious identification with feminism and even the feminine, or at least "feminine masochism" (as it is called in the Freudian paradigm). Bersani associates the latter with gay male sexuality and asserts it undoes subjectivity itself:

> [T]he self which the sexual shatters provides the basis on which sexuality is associated with power. It is possible to think of the sexual as, precisely, moving between a hyperbolic sense of self and a loss of all consciousness of self. But sex as self-hyperbole is perhaps a repression of sex as self-abolition. It inaccurately replicates self-shattering as self-swelling, as psychic tumescence. If . . . men are especially apt to "choose" this version of sexual pleasure, because their sexual equipment appears to invite by analogy, or at least to facilitate, the phallicizing of the ego, neither sex has exclusive rights to the practice of sex as self-hyperbole. For it is perhaps primarily *the degeneration of the sexual into a relationship that condemns sexuality to becoming a struggle for power.* As soon as persons are posited, the war begins. It is the self that swells with excitement at the idea of being on top. . . . [26]

According to Bersani, it is promiscuous anal sex which results in self-shattering *jouissance,* as he indicates when he asks what could be more threatening to the heterosexist media than "the sexual act [which] is associated with women but performed by men and . . . [which] has the terrifying appeal of a loss of the ego, of a self-debasement?"[27] His conclusion implicitly answers what is really only a rhetorical question: "[I]f the rectum is the grave in which the masculine ideal (an ideal shared—differently—by men *and* women) of proud subjectivity is buried, then it should be celebrated for its very potential for death."[28]

The contradictions are telling. While earlier Bersani seemed to condemn sex outside a relationship as narcissistic, here it is sex in relationships that is narcissistic. In any case, it is not certain all attenuated intersubjective engagements fail to function as "relationships" (presumably Bersani makes this assumption because he believes they are too brief to allow transference and countertransference to develop). Freud stressed the relative stability of the fantasies which structure a subject's psyche and characteristic defenses; there is, therefore, no compelling reason for thinking promiscuity cannot itself be defensive and as much a part of that fantasy life as any other type of object choice. Finally, in a persuasive analysis of T. E. Lawrence's writings, Kaja Silverman demonstrates that masochism is not inconsistent with phallic narcissism and may even be a crucial component of masculinity and leadership in general.[29] In effect, being on the bottom can be a means to being on top.

At one point in his essay Bersani suggests that the ways in which sex politicizes are "highly problematical"; surely this must hold true for psychic as well as cultural politics.[30] If he is right to insist that women, like men, can experience a phallicizing of the ego—and I believe he is, having argued it myself—then he should be willing to concede that promiscuous anal sex is no more a guarantee of the self-shattering death of the subject than is vaginal sex.[31] In fact, in this essay promiscuous anal sex has exactly a phallicizing function, swelling the ego of the theoretical impersonator (as "feminine masochist") at the expense of women. Gay men are the better women, represented as better equipped to undo identity. When the rectum is a grave, the vagina, evidently, is nothing but a dead end.

The Phallic Woman

The gay man in drag in Bersani's essay is sometimes misogynist and sometimes a victim of misogyny, such is the complexity of the play of identification and dis-identification the writing enacts (whatever it articulates). Feminists have too often turned a blind eye to the latter, unable to see that the penis is not the phallus—perhaps not surprising, given that patriarchal culture promotes such a misrecognition, though many feminists have been actively trying to open our eyes to the fact no one has or can have the phallus and the omniscience, omnipotence, and wholeness which it signifies. Feminists have argued that representations of the feminine sustain masculine phallic identities by figuring the lack man repudiates in himself through the regressive defense mechanisms of projection, sadism, voyeurism, and fetishism. In patriarchy, woman serves as the mirror in which man sees himself as whole, the inverse or negative alter ego (at once complement and supplement) he needs to feel complete. According to feminists, the symbolic is therefore really a masculine imaginary, characterized by a phallocentric scopic economy which quite literally en-genders differences that support man's illusion of wholeness through a fantasy of woman's lack.

For many feminists, the gay man in drag is just another example of the gynephobic/misogynist representations of woman which predominate in our culture. Thus, radical lesbian feminist Marilyn Frye states that "gay men's effeminacy and donning of feminine apparel displays no love or identification with women or the womanly." Rather,

> this femininity is affected and characterized by theatrical exaggeration. It is a casual and cynical mockery of women, for whom femininity is the trappings of oppression, but it is also a kind of play, a toying with that which is taboo. It is a naughtiness indulged in . . . more by those who believe in their immunity to contamination than by those with any doubts or fears.[32]

Judith Williamson writes that men in drag undermine "female characteristics" and therefore women because they parody "the feminine form" instead of adopting a "natural" feminine style.[33] And in a similar vein, Erika Munk argues that female impersonators are currently "no more subversive" than whites in blackface were when minstrel shows were popular, while Alison Laurie asserts, "Although women in male clothes usually look like gentlemen, men who wear women's clothes, unless they are genuine transsexuals, seem to imitate the most vulgar and unattractive sort of female dress, as if in a spirit of deliberate and hostile parody."[34] These feminists all assume that camp operates defensively to hold femininity and the lack it signifies at a distance from the man who seems to have adopted it. His femininity is a put-on, not the real thing, signaling he has what women lack: the phallus. The man in drag, they suggest, is the phallic woman.

Psychoanalysts also say that the cross-dresser fantasizes he is a phallic woman. According to them, transvestism is only a special case of fetishism.[35] Like any fetishist, the transvestite fetishizes himself (disavowing his own lack) by fetishizing woman (disavowing her lack, attributing phallic significance to some detail of her appearance). What makes the transvestite different is his wish to wear the fetish himself. It might seem the man in drag has put his identity in jeopardy by confusing the very oppositions which sustain the gendered differences our symbolic legislates: subject/object, active/passive, voyeur/exhibitionist, fetishist/fetish, and, of course, masculine/feminine. However, analysts note, he has feminized himself only in order to "masculinize" (phallicize) himself, attempting to better secure a masculine or phallic and "whole" identity through cross-dressing. The transvestite maintains a distance—and difference—from the feminine (lack) even as he seems to be too close to it for comfort. Masquerading as the phallic woman, he is able to have (the illusion of having) the phallus. "I was in Toronto once, and the only female impersonator they had was a woman," the star of a drag act in *Outrageous!* jokes, thereby revealing why so many feminists have indeed found gay male cross-dressing outrageous, though no laughing matter. For by insisting on their difference from r.g.'s, impersonators can defend themselves against the castration the latter are made to signify. The gay man in drag, like other men in a patriarchal symbolic, may feel whole at woman's expense, since he too can refuse her difference, misrecognizing it as lack and fetishistically disavowing even that.

Andrew Ross has argued that camp is radical because it defetishizes the erotic scenario of woman-as-spectacle.[36] But as Freud points out, the fetishist both worships and castrates the fetish object, romanticizes and reviles it for its differences—differences the fetishist himself invents or makes meaningful (like the "shine on the nose" one of Freud's patients could see on certain women even when others could not).[37] The details that mark an impersonation as such, therefore, function fetishistically. They signal the difference between phallic women and r.g.'s, some of them signifying lack, and others, phallic presence. The transvestite poses the questions, "Is she or isn't she . . . does she or doesn't she . . . ?" and plays with the answer—quite literally (according to analysts transvestic pleasure is narcissistic and masturbatory, mixing object love and identification, a theory transvestite or "tv" porn seems to prove). The routines of drag work to reveal the body beneath the clothes, which is made to serve as the ground of identity.[38] Joking in double entendres, dropping the voice, removing the wig and falsies, exposing the penis—all are made equivalent, and all work to resecure

masculine identity by effecting a slide along a chain of signifiers which
are in a metaphoric and metonymic relationship (in our culture) with
one another and with the transcendental signifier, the phallus (of
course, the butch lesbian could also deploy the signifiers of masculinity
to constitute herself as a phallic woman, though she could not appeal
to her body as ground of her difference from lack).

The pleasure of transvestism may be like that Steve Neale and Paul
Willemen suggest the Western offers, the pleasure of seeing the man
mutilated (castrated) and restored (rendered whole again).[39] It may be
exhibitionistic as well as voyeuristic, inviting identification with rather
than dis-identification from the hero/victim. Feminist film theorists like
Laura Mulvey have associated the transvestic look not with the men
but with the women in the cinema audience, who are said to participate
in film's masculinist perversity (fetishism, voyeurism) vicariously, by
virtue of a never fully resolved bisexuality which allows them to regress
to an earlier, masculine, hysterical identification.[40] But the transvestic
look may be an option for men too where powerful female characters
are concerned, like *Dynasty*'s Alexis Carrington Colby Dexter (Joan
Collins), who serves as a conduit for a gay look, according to Mark
Finch.[41] Such phallic women oscillate between being the subjects and
the objects of the gaze and phallic mastery.

Thus, in one pornographic publication, *Drag Queens,* Lola, "tall,
dark and hung," and Pasha, "the Polynesian Bombshell," are consistently described and imaged as phallic women.[42] Lola has "the right
equipment for either sex . . . [she] loves to play it both ways, and she
knows she's got what it takes to make it work," the first page of copy
reads, and the photos in the magazine back up these claims by drawing
attention both to Lola's breasts and erect nipples and to her generally
semi-erect penis (40). The shots and the writing emphasize fetishism:

> Lola loves to show it all off. The slow striptease is her favorite.
> Wearing lace, nylons, and high heeled shoes, she hides her meaty
> truth. At the right moment, she unveils her cock. The shock is erotic
> and irresistible. Lola is unique! (7)

Lola's (and the magazine's) phallic narcissism is suggested by the many
photos of Lola masturbating and by captions which describe her as
"the seducer of herself, a woman capable of turning herself into a rigid
and throbbing man!" (7) The text makes clear the queen's penis is
king, continually reinscribing patriarchal gender hierarchies, describing Lola's feminine "half" as "turning on the man below," "desir[ing]

to please," "giv[ing] way to the long thick cock," etc. (7,23,11). And
although Lola is never shown having sex with anyone, she is frequently
represented masturbating to pornography in which a black man in
drag (like her) is seen anally penetrating a white man. Even the one
sentence which tells us Lola "knows that she is all woman" begins by
asserting "she's a superstud with breasts" (11). The picture accompanying that text is a low angle shot of Lola in what looks like a fighting
stance, legs apart (framing her penis), one arm drawn back with the
hand clenched into a fist, and an expression on her face that seems to
signify she means to defend her right to the title. If Lola is a woman,
she is one with a very special difference; after all, "she can take her
man where no woman has taken him before" (32). Represented as
active, masterful, and complete, Lola is obviously the phallic woman.

Similarly, when "Virginia Ham" (Arnold/Harvey Fierstein) says to
the (gay) spectators of his drag act—in a deep, masculine voice that
disrupts the effect of femininity his appearance has generated—"You
can't become a dame until you've knelt before a queen," the joke
constitutes her as a phallic woman, invested with an erotic power
denied by Bersani and some of the other writers to whom I have
alluded. Indeed, the humor in drag shows is aggressive and depends
on such distancing effects, which are achieved by the reconfiguration
of the positions of subject/object, active/passive, and even voyeur/
exhibitionist as the woman is revealed to be phallic. A sequence from
Pink Flamingos (1972) is exemplary. It displays the abrupt interruption
of the voyeuristic pleasure of Raymond—and the spectator—in a beautiful woman when she lifts her skirt to reveal her penis. The spectator,
initially aligned by the camera with Raymond, can only laugh insofar
as he refuses to identify with Raymond; otherwise, the joke is on the
spectator too. The transvestite's gesture in this sequence is almost
literally a punch-line, as the look at (not of) a shocked and visibly
displeased Raymond in the reverse shot reveals. The film clearly confronts the male heterosexual viewer at this point; his laughter is a
defensive response to the castration anxiety suddenly evoked and
evaded by making what is literally a transvestic identification with the
phallic woman. These scenes point to the presence of a desire Freud
never discusses when he elaborates on the negative oedipus: the boy's
active, sadistic, and masculine wish to penetrate the father rather than
his passive, masochistic, and feminine wish to be penetrated by him. I
would argue that Freud does not entertain the possibility of such desires
because they undermine the father's alignment with the phallus. It is
another instance of Freud's reinscription of patriarchal heterosexual

norms, as in his discussion of bisexuality, since the father figure is not allowed to have passive, masochistic, and "feminine" desires, just as the mother is not allowed to have active, sadistic, and "masculine" desires.

I am not suggesting that spectators are always encouraged to identify with the man in drag, only that such an identification is possible and may not subvert masculine phallic identities. Of course, it is far more common for distancing effects to be maintained by representing the transvestite as mastered (and lacking) object rather than potent subject of the gaze, which suggests that Marilyn Frye's critique of what she calls the "phallophilia" of gay men and drag is neither fair nor accurate.[43] For example, *The Queens*, a "photographic essay" by George Alpert, is coy about the presence/absence of the penis.[44] There are many shots in which the genitals—and breasts—are fetishistically hidden/revealed by the way the nude or semi-nude subject sits or stands, positions himself with respect to objects in the foreground, or drapes clothing and jewelry across his body. Nevertheless, because the shots are arranged in sequences which generally show the man as a man donning drag, we are never in doubt as to his "true" gender—these "women" really are phallic, if the phallus is the penis.

However, Alpert inscribes them in a photo-narrative of pathos and horror (as "freaks") which effectively prevents our identifying with them on phallic grounds. The book incorporates some series of older "cod" or comic/ugly "dames," whose failure of femininity is suggested by posing and lighting them as "frights," unlike the young "glam" queens included, who are usually not photographed in extreme (microscopic/scientific) close-up or in unflattering lights or poses, and are sometimes even seen in romantic soft focus, like women. But they are also often photographed against or behind doors and windows, sometimes barred, or in corners, suggesting they are trapped by their "perverse" inclinations—and tragically so. The framing sequences in particular help achieve this effect. The first series closes with a close-up of "Baby" looking pensive; on his cheek glistens what appears to be a tear, though it could just be a drop of water left after washing off makeup. The final picture of the last sequence is of "the twins" sadly trying to peer out over the sill or through the frame of what could be a window which partially obstructs their faces; the photo suggests the pain of being caught in "their" world, barred definitively from "ours." This book does not confuse the penis (or at least the queen's penis) with the phallus. It envisions the queen as symbolically castrated, tragically—even horribly—lacking, a point of view which is not necessarily (or only) heterosexist since it is also available to homosexuals (and as I have argued, Bersani resorts to it). In any case, the book is evidence for the inadequacy of phallophilia as a general theory of drag.

Masochism

There is yet another possible response to the phallic woman: masochism. As D. N. Rodowick has pointed out, Mulvey's almost biologizing insistence on aligning the cinematic gaze with masculinity and an active and controlling voyeurism and fetishism blinds her to the possibility of a passive component of vision, one in which the fetishism is masochistic rather than sadistic.[45] As I have already indicated, Freud notes that the fetishist both worships and castrates his fetish and therefore is at once submissive and dominating. Rodowick argues that the male hero/star can be the object of a "feminine masochist" subject's gaze and suggests Mulvey does not draw this conclusion because there seems to be little for feminists to gain by reasserting the link between masochism and femininity.[46] Curiously, Rodowick does not discuss—or even draw— the rather obvious Freudian conclusion, that the gaze directed toward the heroine at those moments when she is most fetishized could be masochistic rather than sadistic, as Mulvey had argued. Nor does he comment on—or take note of—what from a Freudian perspective is rather unusual, though it is an unavoidable consequence of his argument, the fetishizing of the male hero by the masochistic spectator. For Freud, men are fetishists, not fetishes, but Rodowick implies the inverse when he insists on a connection between masochism and fetishism, and masochism and the gaze at (rather than of) the man. Rodowick remains bound by Mulvey's logic: he fails to posit a female fetishism, in which women would be the subjects and men the objects of desires not only masochistic but also sadistic and voyeuristic, and he does not take into account the significance of differences other than that of gender for the gaze, desire, and subjectivity, whether heterosexual or homosexual—differences which may well come into play when the man (rather than the woman) is fetishized.

The image of the (fetishized) phallic woman can indeed solicit a masochistic gaze and pleasure rather than a defensive sadistic voyeurism, according to some recent feminist work. Griselda Pollock argues that one of Dante Gabriel Rossetti's paintings of women, *Astarte Syriaca* (1877), transcends the "repetitious obsessive fetishization" of most of his art in order to represent "a figure before which the masculine viewer can comfortably stand subjected . . . a fantasy image of the imaginary, maternal plenitude and phallic mother."[47] Berkeley Kaite arrives at a similar conclusion about pornographic images of the phallic woman (which feminists have consistently critiqued as sexist and sadistic), asserting that the look at the fetishized woman who looks back— whether that woman's investment with the phallus is "literal" (the tv) or vestiary (the r.g.)—provides the pleasure of the surrender to the penetrating "cut," the moment when the subject is severed from the phallic M/Other and accedes to difference and (a fantasy of) self-possession.[48] And in a series of essays devoted to the topic of masochism itself, Kaja Silverman explores at length the implications of the eroticization of lack and subordination for men, which she suggests disrupts their identification with the phallus by writing the father out of the dominant place and installing the mother in it.[49] Silverman stresses the importance of the conscious, heterosexual, and masochistic fantasy of the male subjects Freud discusses in "A Child Is Being Beaten," which she believes is radical because "it constitutes a 'feminine' yet heterosexual male subject" (Freud himself subordinates it to the unconscious and homosexual fantasy of being beaten by the father).[50] Silverman, like Kaite, associates such radical masochism with "shattering" rather than phallic coherence, and like Kaite and Pollock, with a relation to the phallic M/Other who "precedes" the symbolic, which subordinates her and the child to the father. Thus, Silverman concludes, the male masochist "cannot be reconciled to the symbolic order or to his social identity" because his sexuality is "devoid of any possible productivity or use value."[51]

These are radical claims indeed for a perversion which during the not too distant heyday of the vogue for Sade generated little enthusiasm. In fact, this writing on masochism shares some of the assumptions of that writing on sadism; in particular, that subversion results when woman wields the phallus as whip, and that perversion transgresses the economy of utility, even exposing that economy's veiled structures of eroticized domination.[52] These assumptions require a closer look. I have already suggested that a man's identification with the phallic woman may not be especially radical, since it can reinforce phallic narcissism and that with which it is generally associated, activity and sadism. It would seem, however, that a woman's identification with the phallic woman could be radical because unprecedented. This is the argument Jane Gallop makes when she says the phallic mother undoes the logic of ideological solidarity between phallus, father, power, and man.[53]

But is there really no precedent in our cultural fantasmatic for the phallic woman, in particular, for the phallic mother? In discussing the "Wolf Man" (as well as the taboo on virginity in so-called primitive cultures) Freud himself notes that children sometimes imagine the woman has retained the man's penis after intercourse, becoming phallic by castrating him; this fantasy coexists with the more common—or at least more commonly discussed—theory that the father has wounded or castrated the mother during intercourse.[54] The woman is here phallic on the same terms as the man—and the child (almost always presumed male by Freud)—because somewhere, somehow she has got a penis (or what stands for it). It is, therefore, revealing that Sade's archetypal phallic woman, the eponymous heroine of *Juliette,* explains her desire as a reactive copy of masculine desire: "My lubricity, always modeled after men's whims, never is lit except by fire of their passion; I am only really inflamed by their desires, and the only sensual pleasure I know is that of satisfying all their deviations."[55] When the active, desiring woman still reflects man's desire, the mirrors of the patriarchal imaginary cannot have been shattered.

The fantasy of the phallic mother is perhaps even more common, and is the at least implicit topic of a great deal of feminist writing on the daughter's relation to the mother.[56] This work has focused on the difficulty of difference for the daughter, who cannot quite distinguish herself from her mother in a symbolic which requires that confusion. Woman is theorized as unable to represent lack for herself because she must represent it for men by becoming, through identification, the lost object(s) of desire, principally the mother, in order to ensure man's wholeness. She, therefore, cannot enter the symbolic, too close to the mother whom she is unable to give up or give up being, oscillating between identification and object choice (characteristic of the imaginary) because for her, having nothing to lose, castration poses no "real" threat. The daughter's response to this in-difference of mother and child is paranoia, a defense associated with psychosis and foreclosure of the Name of the Father (and, thus, of symbolic castration). The mother is phallic to the degree that she is invested with the power to free her little girl, that is, to divest herself of her phallus, the child (who has remained in the imaginary mode of "being," rather than "having," the phallus).

This paranoid fantasy is not limited to women. In fact, it is a cornerstone of object-relations theory, for which the boy's accession to masculinity is a problem, rather than the girl's to femininity, as in the Freudian/Lacanian paradigm, which as I have indicated, has trouble keeping the mother and daughter straight—in both senses of the

word—when there are apparently so few inducements to their acceptance of castration and a "feminine" regulation of the "masculine"
libido. Object-relations theorists assume masculinity and femininity
are there from the start, rather than produced through the resolution
of the castration complex and the separation from the mother in which
it results. They suppose a boy is destined for masculinity even though
they postulate he begins in a feminine dependence on—and in-difference from—the mother, who is presumed phallic to the extent that
she is blamed for "his" gender troubles like transsexualism, which
according to well-known expert Dr. Robert Stoller results from too
much mother and too little father.[57] The phallic mother will not let
boys be boys.

Obviously, when the fantasy is paranoid and the in-difference figured
as fearful, it cannot be particularly progressive for women, since it
contributes to the repudiation of femininity that patriarchy already
engenders and it realigns women with the maternal—and the maternal
as a role they can never adequately perform (the phallic mother is at
once castrating and castrated in this fantasy). However, when the
fantasy is of in-difference as pleasurable, or perhaps both painful and
pleasurable, fearful and fascinating, maintaining the subject on the
edge of subject-ion and self-(dis)possession, something potentially
more radical occurs. This is the situation Kaite describes, though she
seems to confuse these two impulses. On the one hand, she argues that
transvestism provides the pleasure of self-dispossession as castration—
and, therefore, the death of desire through the death of the subject,
who lacks a lack in the phallic M/Other, from whom s/he is in-different.
On the other hand, Kaite critiques Francette Pacteau for associating
androgyny with just such a death of desire and subjectivity, which
follows from Pacteau's assertion that androgyny represents the narcissistic desire for wholeness in the phallic M/Other, a wish to be beyond
the lack that motivates desire and so beyond difference itself, including
sexual difference. The tv or androgyne expresses a desire for repression
rather than a repression (or, more properly, foreclosure) of desire,
Kaite asserts.[58]

Kaite wants to retain for transvestism and fetishism the radicality of
a refusal of the symbolic (and its hierarchies of difference and lack,
which makes it, in effect, a masculine imaginary) without giving up
the recognition of castration, difference, and lack accession to the
symbolic is supposed to generate (but does not when that symbolic
promotes an imaginary masculine wholeness at the expense of women).
The contradiction in Kaite's beliefs about fetishism is like that in

the fetishist's own about the mother's phallus and the possibility of achieving wholeness in her (or her displacements): fetishistic disavowal will (not) make him/her whole. The fetishist at once knows and refuses to know his/her lack or castration, his/her self-difference. The perversion has a defensive function, even if it also has a heterocosmic impulse, to employ the expression Silverman uses for the desire for what is here literally a re-vision of the world and its representation of woman as lack.[59] In this, fetishism is like what Julia Kristeva has called abjection, which can re-fashion "his majesty the ego" by storming the fortress in which he reigns, described by Lacan as the "orthopaedic . . . armour of an alienating identity."[60] But the emperor's new clothes threaten to expose him utterly, leaving him defenseless, prey to the psychotic failure of subjectivity itself, by dissolving the defense mechanisms that wall out the phallic M/Other even as they wall him in. For Kristeva, the loss of the subject abjection threatens is not without its liabilities, just as a rigidly defensive ego is also a liability.

Gendering feminine such a tantalizing/terrifying loss reveals the defensive nature of masculinity itself. Silverman says that the beating fantasy Freud discusses, and masochistic fantasies in general, attest to the need to be boys to be girls, so that even the female "feminine masochist" has a masculinity complex, albeit one in which she makes an identification with the homosexual man, wishing to be passive and masochistic rather than active and sadistic. Castration or divestiture, Silverman argues, "can only be realized at the site of male subjectivity because it is there that the paternal legacy is stored" (the woman has nothing to lose).[61] It is the male subject's self-fetishizing phallic imposture which provides him with the signifiers of lack: the penis, but also all that signals the power and privilege accruing to man in a patriarchal culture, such as the woman herself. Man appears to have the phallus by exhibiting what signifies having the phallus, that which is metaphorically or metonymically linked to it; this includes the fetishized M/Other, who "masquerades" as the phallus so that man can "parade" his phallus, the woman he needs to feel complete. In the Lacanian paradigm, man, like woman, only comes into being when "photo-graphed," fixed by the look of the phallic M/Other, who reflects for him an image of wholeness with which he jubilantly identifies.[62] Both man and woman must appear to be subjects—but they only appear to be subjects. Their relations revolve around having or being the phallus for one another, which is never more than appearing to have or be the phallus for the other, who can be duped by the performance.[63]

However, man's fetishistic misrecognition of the organ upon which his identity hangs is legislated by the patriarchal symbolic, so that it seems to be the real thing. The subject who desires to take up the position of being the phallus for the phallic M/Other, the hole in her whole, must be castrated, feminized. This leads to the curious conclusion that only men can become real women (in fact, Moustapha Safouan asserts just that about transsexuals, and something like it is implicit in Bersani's essay).[64] Masochists—and even theorists of masochism—have been duped by the penis once again when they fail to distinguish between it and the phallus, even if such a misrecognition apparently does not serve man's phallic narcissism. Masochistic fantasies may indeed include frequent "scenes" in which the male genitals, the symbol of the man's identification with the father as bearer of the phallus, are beaten or cut off. But this is not necessarily inconsistent with a belief that the phallic mother is phallic because she has castrated the father and retained his penis.

In fact, in a classic essay on transvestism which makes clear its imbrication with masochism, Otto Fenichel notes that passive anal desires directed toward the mother can be elaborated just like those directed toward the father: the little boy can desire to have the mother's baby just as a little girl might desire to have the father's baby.[65] Freud emphasizes that the wish for a child points to an unconscious equation made between the penis and the baby (in which feces and fantasies of anal birth also figure). The daughter's desire to be a (her) mother is an expression of penis envy; what she wants to get from the father is a child/penis/phallus, which according to Freud is why she likes to play with dolls so much.[66] The same, therefore, might be argued about the expectant son, for whom the masochistic sexual relation—like any sexual relation—could effect an exchange of phallus, in which the phallic Other (father or mother) is presumed to have the phallus (baby) to give. A world with such sexual relations would be an inversion but not a displacement of this one, in which the meaning of the phallus and its "privileged" signifiers could remain unanalyzed.

Dragging in Differences

In such a world it would even be possible to turn inside out Luce Irigaray's feminist rereading of Freud on dolls to suggest that if the son plays with dolls it may not express his wish for a phallus like the M/Other's but, rather, his wish for a "feminine" mastery of the mother/child relationship by playing with an image of himself as if he were his own (phallic) mother.[67] Playing with dolls, is, in effect, a variant of what Irigaray calls "mimicry," in which the woman plays with "her" image (the fetishistic masquerade), putting it on so as to signify it is a put on, and can easily be taken off (the woman is also "elsewhere").[68] Irigaray suggests it signifies a distance between woman and her image, a distance not possible in Freudian/Lacanian theory, which associates it only with masculinity (and fetishism and voyeurism). Such a distance is necessary for knowledge, which hinges on dis-identification and difference. Woman cannot know "woman" if she is too close to her image to see it with a critical eye. Transvestic "play" could also be mimicry, in which the son plays with his image like a doll, dressing it up to signal his distance—and difference—from lack. Femininity, like masculinity, could be a defense, a phallic imposture. Because this is possible, a literal castration (as in transsexualism) may not effect a symbolic castration, except to the degree that the latter is complicit with imaginary phallic narcissism, in which the subject appears to have something to lose and, therefore, something to desire. It is the very fact that men can assume femininity (and castration) in order to dis-identify from it (as lack) which has distressed feminists who have discussed drag. Yet the possibility of assuming it to dis-identify from it has excited feminists who theorize a female female impersonation or mimicry. The mimic could know "woman" because she would not have to be her, but she would not have to make a transvestic identification with man in order to have some perspective on her image either. Mimicry provides an alternative to adopting a masculine (and masculinist) point of view, without necessitating a naive idealist or essentialist belief in the ability to access a "genuine" femininity beyond patriarchal feminization and the social construction of gender.

Paradoxically, feminists praise in female female impersonation or mimicry what they condemn in female impersonation or drag: its distancing effects. Such a paradox is symptomatic, but not necessarily of homophobia. Rather, it points to the significance of differences other than those of gender or sexual orientation for camp, differences which have to be "dragged" into drag and its theory. Though in general theorists of mimicry and theorists of drag do not comment on—or apparently even read—the work of the other camp (all puns intended— this is another indication that misogyny and homophobia are disjunct), for better or worse they share many of the same assumptions, strategies, and goals. Both challenge the naturalness of gender and desire as legislated by the symbolic. Both privilege the tactic of assuming an identity as a false identity because for both any identity is an "assumed" or false and alienated identity, unreal, fictional ("masquerade" or "parade" in Lacanian terminology). Style is the wo/man: there is no authentic, "real" self beyond or before the process of social construction. Playing the gender role so as to hold it at a distance foregrounds the fact that it is a role rather than a nature. Both theorists of mimicry and of drag are, therefore, anti-essentialist and deconstructive to the extent that they believe identities must be subverted from within, rather than from some utopic elsewhere purely outside them. "Utopia" means "no place," and there is no place beyond or before our selves where we would be what we "really" are.

Thus Judith Butler explains that drag promotes

> a subversive laughter in the pastiche-effect of parodic practices in which the original, the authentic, and the real are themselves constituted as effects. The loss of gender norms would have the effect of proliferating gender configurations, destabilizing substantive identity and depriving the naturalizing narratives of compulsory heterosexuality of their central protagonists: "man" and "woman." The parodic repetition of gender exposes as well the illusion of gender identity as an intractable depth and inner substance. As the effects of a subtle and politically enforced performativity, gender is an "act," as it were, that is open to splittings, self-parody, self-criticism, and those hyperbolic exhibitions of "the natural" that, in their very exaggeration, reveal its fundamentally phantasmatic status.[69]

Sue-Ellen Case suggests that butch-fem lesbians camp up the fiction of castration, ironizing it, while Jack Babuscio, Richard Dyer, Jeffrey Escoffier, Andrew Ross, and Vivo Russo all discuss drag as a parodic or ironic exaggeration or hyperbolization of gender.[70] These are the very terms and phrases which feminist theorists use when they write about mimicry. To be a mimic, according to Irigaray, is to "assume the feminine role deliberately . . . so as to make 'visible,' by an effect of playful repetition, what was supposed to remain invisible. . . . "[71] To play the feminine is to "speak" it ironically, to italicize it, in Nancy Miller's words; to hyperbolize it, in Mary Ann Doane's words; or to parody it, as Mary Russo and Linda Kauffman describe it.[72] In mimicry, as in camp, one "does" ideology in order to undo it, producing knowledge about it: that gender and the heterosexual orientation presumed to anchor it are unnatural and even oppressive.

It is this very insistence on irony and parody as the difference between the camp or mimic and the man or woman who plays gender straight (in the masquerade or parade)—the anti-essentialist strength of both theories—which also ultimately proves to be their undoing, pointing to an essentialism which inheres in their anti-essentialism, deconstructing by rendering indistinct their significant (signifying) distinctions. For the camp or mimic difference must be visible as such if it is to make a difference in the way gender and sexuality are lived and understood. But if all identities are alienated and fictional, then the distinction between parody, mimicry, or camp, and imitation, masquerade, or playing it straight is no longer self-evident. What makes the one credible and the other incredible when both are fictions? The answer, it seems, are the author's intentions: parody is legible in the drama of gender performance if someone meant to script it, intending it to be there. Any potential in-difference or confusion of the two is eliminated by a focus in the theories on production rather than reception or perception. Sometimes, however, one is ironic without having intended it, and sometimes, despite one's best intentions, no one gets the joke. As Lacan points out, the "real thing" is already a comedy.[73] The specter of heterosexual gender, therefore, haunts both these theories, which manifest (albeit latently) the fear there is no escaping the same old story, one that after all is not very funny. What passes for passing for or impersonating a gender when gender is always already impersonation is symptomatic and must be analyzed.

In camp theory, butch-fem drag is visible as such because of a "gay sensibility," which is invoked to keep straight the difference between gay and heterosexual gender impersonation. One the one hand, it ensures camp is not inversion; on the other hand, it ensures heterosexual masquerade and parade are not camp. This sensibility is an essence which "determines" gay productions in both senses of the word: they are said to express it directly (since camp is conscious, the gay subject's relation with the body is assumed to be unmediated by an unconscious), and it is said to make them gay (though they might not appear as such at first glance). Some theorists, like Babuscio and Russo, explicitly evoke this "gay sensibility" as the ground of camp, explaining that "passing" sensitizes gays and lesbians to both the oppressiveness and artificiality of gender roles.[74] But as Andrew Britton suggests, such a gay essentialism is highly problematic because it is obvious that the experience of homophobic oppression does not necessarily lead to an understanding of it.[75] Gayatri Spivak has made a similar point about oppression in general, arguing that theorists like Michel Foucault are too ready to credit the oppressed with the power to know and articulate their oppression directly when the very fact of oppression can make that impossible, since consciousness itself may be dominated and, indeed, constituted by hegemonic ideology.[76]

Some theorists only implicitly invoke a "gay sensibility," which manifests itself in the difficulty their theories have demonstrating the difference between butch-fem and inversion, on the one hand, and butch-fem and straight gender roles, on the other. It is a difficulty not unlike that apparent in Freudian inversion theory, which as I have pointed out has trouble explaining the desire of the fem for the butch lesbian or, conversely, of the butch gay man for the queen—they are too gay to be straight (to be easily explicable as a variant of heterosexist bisexual/inversion theories of desire).[77] In camp theory, the problem is with the same two roles, which are too straight to be gay (to be easily explicable as parodic gender camping or drag). As Butler, Babuscio, and Oscar Montero note, the butch lesbian or gay queen marks "his/her" impersonation as such through the use of incongruous contrasts, signs of a double gender identity, as well as through what they and other theorists of camp describe as parodic excess (for example, Ross says the queen dresses "over the top" by comparison with r.g.'s).[78] This "excess" is what prevents drag from being mere inversion, signifying a difference from what could be a heterosexual role. It is also necessary to account for camp in which there are no incongruous contrasts and confused gender signs, such as Divine's. After all, when roles are always already unreal, Divine's impersonation cannot appear as such unless he distances himself from the femininity he assumes; his act would only circulate as femininity itself if there were no marked differences from it.

The danger of passing for straight is greatest with the lesbian fem and the gay butch, since their acts do not obviously rely on incongruities, as is revealed in the discursive strategies of two of the most sophisticated and compelling texts on camp, those by Butler and Case. When Butler discusses the play of difference and desire in lesbian camp she argues that the butch does not assimilate lesbianism into heterosexuality (as inversion) because being a woman recontextualizes masculinity through the confusion of gender signs. She says it is exactly this confusion the fem finds desirable: "[S]he likes her boys to be girls."[79] Butler discusses the butch as the subject of gender play but the object of desire, which enables the lesbian to be consistently associated with transvestic subversion. The discussion would not work as well in reverse: the fem's being a woman does not obviously recontextualize femininity, nor does it sound particularly radical to suggest the butch likes her girls to be girls. Yet just a few lines later Butler insists the fem displaces the heterosexual scene as if she embodied the same shifting of sexed body as ground and gender identity as figure that the butch (or queen) does. Similarly, when Case writes that the fem "aims her desirability" at the butch, she inscribes as active a potentially passive fem-ininity so that it can appear as distinct from femininity.[80]

What ultimately makes the fem different from the r.g. for both theorists is that she plays her role for another woman, which is supposed to make it excessive by "recontextualizing" or "reinterpreting" it (an argument which also provides an additional safeguard against butch roles as mere inversion). This is the fem's (or the gay butch's) essential incongruity. But such a notion is based on an essentialist tautology: butch-fem or drag is gender play because it is gay; it is gay and drag because it is gender play. In short, a "gay sensibility" is implicitly invoked to determine in advance what counts as gender play, keeping straight the difference between enlightened drag and unenlightened masquerade or parade. It is perhaps not surprising that the tautology fails to make an essential difference between gay and straight acts, as Lisa Duggan reveals in an article tellingly titled, "The Anguished Cry of an 80's Fem: 'I Want to be a Drag Queen' ": "When lesbians sponsor strip shows, or other fem erotic performances, it is very difficult to 'code' it as lesbian, to make it feel queer. The result looks just like a heterosexual performance, and lesbian audiences don't respond to it as subversively sexual, specifically ours."[81] In fact, the photo of two women in corsets illustrating this article is by a woman who has appeared in tv pornography which has a straight audience; the very same picture—and fantasy—therefore has two different enunciations, one that is heterosexual and masculine, and one that is lesbian.[82] Teresa de Lauretis also notes the difficulty the fem has appearing in most representational contexts today "[u]nless . . . she enters [sic] the frame of vision *as or with* a lesbian in male drag."[83]

Clearly, essentialism can only uneasily inhabit a rigorously anti-essentialist discourse of social constructionism, which argues all gender is an act. But perhaps the most troubling consequence of this homosexual essentialism is its paradoxical reinforcement of the idea that the "authentic" or "natural" self is heterosexual, even as it inverts the hierarchy by proclaiming the "fake" or artificial gay self to be the "better," smarter—more smartly dressed—self, which deconstructs itself by knowing its difference from itself and the gender role it only assumes like a costume. This is to erect the gay self as the upright self, properly non-identical by comparison with the straight self which also, therefore, lacks gay *jouissance*. However, such a use of *jouissance* makes it "stiffen into a strong, muscular image," according to Jane Gallop; it becomes phallic, a sign of "an ego-gratifying identity" in which "fear or unworthiness is projected outward. . . . "[84] Gays and lesbians are no more free from castration anxiety than anyone else, as this defensive maneuver suggests. Like straight men—and women—they can disavow castration, making use of projection and fetishism to that end, including the self-fetishism of phallic imposture which, as I hope I have demonstrated, is not inconsistent with camp. For when roles are already alienated and unreal, the problem may not be how one holds them at a distance but how one responds to that distance. In transvestic drag, it is fetishized: the impersonator assumes a phallic identity through an apparent identification that is, in fact, a dis-identification, signified by the incongruous contrasts and ironic excess s/he sees—and those who share that point of view see—in his or her gender act, which constitute it as camp.

It is also fetishized in mimicry, an understanding of which can help explain how parodic excess is perceived in the fem (and in the gay butch as cowboy, lumberjack, or construction worker). I have argued elsewhere that theories of mimicry reinscribe white, middle-class femininity as the real thing, the (quint)essence of femininity.[85] Indeed, this is implicit in the feminist critiques of drag cited above, which contrast its style as sign of a hostile burlesque with that of a "natural" femininity, whose understated good taste is a sign of the genuine article. If boys will be girls they had better be ladies. A real woman is a real lady; otherwise, she is a female impersonator, a camp or mimic whose "unnaturally" bad taste—like that of the working-class, ethnic, or racially "other" woman—marks the impersonation as such. Miming the feminine means impersonating a white, middle-class impersonation of an "other" ideal of femininity. The mimic flaunts or camps up lack by fetishistically projecting it on to the class, ethnic, or racial other, from whom she distances herself through a dis-identification that takes the form of an apparent identification, as with the impersonator.

Feminist theorists of mimicry distinguish themselves from "other" women even as they assimilate the latter by romanticizing them, assuming the "other" has a critical knowledge about femininity because of her difference from what counts as natural femininity: white, Anglo, bourgeois style. It is only from a middle-class point of view that Dolly Parton looks like a female impersonator; from a working-class point of view she could be the epitome of genuine womanliness. The same can be said of Divine in *Polyester* (1981), whose polyester marks his impersonation as such for those who find it in "unnaturally" bad taste, since Divine never gives any (other) indication he is "really" a man.[86] Mimicry can be distinguished from masquerade because there are significant—signifying—differences between women which white, middle-class feminists fetishistically disavow whenever they talk of "the" feminine, as if it were only one thing.

For some women do "have" the phallus in our culture because it is not just the penis but all the other signs of power and privilege, which stand in a metaphoric and metonymic relation not only to "penis" but also to "white" and "bourgeois"—the signs of a "proper" racial and class identity. Relations between members of different races and classes, like those between genders, therefore, can be imaginary, characterized by fetishism, in which the signs of difference signify phallic lack or wholeness. This is possible because the symbolic is more than a masculine imaginary; it is also a white and bourgeois imaginary, which explains why femininity is able to function defensively, as fetishistic phallic imposture, like masculinity. It also explains the potentially oppressive effects of mimicry—and camp—which constitute the other as what must be repudiated (the inverse complement, a symptom of lack and ignorance) or what can make one whole (the supplement, the phallic M/Other who guarantees one's full self-presence and knowledge). Feminists have shown that talk of a "common humanity" is only a masculinist ruse disguising oppression. They must also acknowledge there is no "common femininity," since despite what women have in common, there are differences between them that make reciprocity and equality difficult. The utopic vision of a femininity fully conscious and free from the effects of castration anxiety has been made possible by an indifference to the significance of differences other than that of gender. The same can be said of relations between gays, which may not be characterized by the perfect reciprocity and equality that Harold Beaver, Craig Owens, and other gay theorists imagine they are.[87]

The Big, Bad Dick

Homosexuality, like femininity, is marked by the effects of castration anxiety. Gay men, like women (including lesbians), are in the symbolic as much as heterosexual men are by virtue of a phallic imposture which they can use to defend themselves from the psychosis with which both homosexuality and femininity have been associated in psychoanalysis since Freud's analysis of Schreber.[88] It is, therefore, important, as Eve Sedgwick points out, for gay theorists to acknowledge the significance of differences within the gay community, differences which may be activated defensively and oppressively in gay relationships and even in gay identities, as I have suggested occurs in camp (which is, in effect, a relationship with an absent "other" as phallic M/Other).[89] A racial and class fetishism can operate in homosexual as well as heterosexual eros, since forms of otherness between men—or women—can have a phallic significance which has all too often been overlooked. Sunil Gupta, Kobena Mercer, Isaac Julien, and Thomas Yingling have written about the potential for the replication of racism in gay relationships through fantasies about the black or Asian man's sex, while Jane Gallop has described a lesbian relationship in which the working-class woman functioned as the phallus for her middle-class lover just as women in general function as the phallus for men.[90] It is these racial and class differences which may come into play in fetishistic masochism so as to give the fantasy a symbolic productivity or use value even when the subject apparently does not reaffirm a phallic identity by identifying with the active, sadistic, phallic mother or father (as Other).

In fact, the fantasy Homi Bhabha locates at the heart of racism, the "primal scene" he claims to derive from Frantz Fanon, centers on a fascinating and fearful interracial rape that could be a permutation of the fetishistic/masochistic beating fantasy analyzed by Freud. In the scene, a little white girl "fixes Fanon in look and word" as she turns from him to identify with her mother, saying, "Look, a negro . . . Mamma, *see* the Negro! I'm frightened. Frightened." Fanon describes the experience as "an amputation, an excision."[91] Its violence is that of a castration, as in the retrospective understanding of the sexual primal scene. In each, subjects take up one of two antithetical positions. One has or lacks color; one lacks or has the penis. But in the racial primal scene's overlap with the sexual primal scene, the other is figured as frighteningly different not because he lacks but because he has the organ, though one which is monstrous.

While Bhabha genders the subject of this drama, Fanon himself does not explicitly mark the sex of the child who speaks of being afraid of him (though later he implicitly does by discussing the white man's fantasy that "his" women are "at the mercy of the Negroes").[92] The fantasy, therefore, could have a white masculine as well as feminine enunciation, just as the beating fantasy has two gendered enunciations. Indeed, Freud's exploration of the effects of the primal scene in his analysis of the "Wolf Man" suggests as much. What the Wolf Man is afraid of is the big, bad dick, symbolized by the well-endowed dream wolves with their overgrown tails.[93] The Wolf Man wants to be loved like a woman by his father, but he fears it means he will be castrated (221, 228). He also wants to be a gentleman like his father and, therefore, different from the maids and male estate workers he imagines are castrated (no doubt because they too seem to have a passive, feminine attitude toward his father), so he cannot afford to be castrated (210, 278–79). Paradoxically, however, his very identification with the father also means he will be castrated, since he believes his mother retains his father's penis after intercourse (279). This fetishistic circuit of pleasure, displeasure, identification, and dis-identification is condensed in the image of the wolves, who represent both the father and the Wolf Man as at once phallic (their tails are big) and castrated (their tales are too big, obvious fakes or prostheses disguising their lack).

At stake in the Wolf Man's castration anxiety fantasies are not only his gender but also his class identity. Peter Stallybrass and Allon White make this clear when they explain why his predilection for debased women like Grusha, his nursery maid, was typical for the bourgeois man of his time:

> The opposition of working-class maid and upper-class male . . . depended upon a physical and social separation which was constitutive of desire. But it was a desire which was traversed by contradictions. On the one hand, the "lowness" of the maid reinforced antithetically the status of the gentleman. . . . But on the other hand . . . she was a figure of comfort and power.[94]

These women represent what had to be repudiated by the middle-class child as s/he grew up: improper dress, manners, speech, and hygiene—all the signs of someone with no class. At the same time, like the fetishized phallic mother, they threatened the bourgeois subject with the return of the lack he had lost. They both shored up and shattered middle-class identity, which accounts for the fearful fascination they exercised.

Though Stallybrass and White do not call it fetishism, that is the term Homi Bhabha uses when discussing the similar psychic mechanism at work in the racial primal scene.[95] He does so because the racial other's real difference remains unsymbolized in the white imaginary, which assimilates the other to the white self by envisioning him (or her) as an alter-ego who (like woman) is just the same as, just the opposite of, or just the right complement and supplement to the white self, whether that other is romanticized (as whole, closer to nature, more fully human) or reviled (as lacking, uncivilized, less than human). Indeed, ambivalence is characteristic of fetishism. While Stallybrass and White focus on the heterosexual rather than homosexual form of the middle-class fascination with the class other, bracketing the Wolf Man's homosexual desires, Jeffrey Weeks documents a gay bourgeois "sexual colonialism," as he describes it, in which " 'working class' equals 'masculine' equals 'closeness to nature' "—for better or worse, as with the racial "primitive other."[96] Clearly, such fetishism can occur in both homosexual and heterosexual relationships, and its effect is the same: class and race differences are reproduced and naturalized.

This fetishism is the type I suggested Rodowick and Mulvey do not address, in which the male hero is fetishized by a cinematic spectator for whom differences other than that of gender have a phallic significance. Such a gaze could be not only fetishistic but also masochistic. Indeed, class and racial differences regularly figure in masochistic fantasies. Silverman describes one in which a man imagines himself a Portuguese prisoner of the Aztecs who is eventually skinned alive, another in which a middle-class woman is beaten by "rough" and "ignorant" working-class women, and yet another in which she is beaten/loved as a male "savage" by a domineering Robinson Crusoe figure.[97] Riviere discusses the case of a (Southern) white woman who fantasizes being attacked by a black man from whom she defends herself by having him make love to her so she can—eventually—turn him over to justice (a scenario remarkably like that in the many popular film versions of *King Kong*).[98] Transvestite pornography often includes stories, sketches, and photos of both men and women who serve a dominatrix as a slave or maid does a mistress.[99] Even the Kinks's domineering queen Lola has "a dark brown voice," a synesthesia suggesting she is black.

What is remarkable about these fantasies is their subjects' fluid shifting not only of gender but also of racial and class identities in ways which simultaneously subvert and sustain phallic identifications complexly articulated through differences in gender, race, and class. It is not always necessary for the masochist (male or female) to fantasize being a man in order to be beaten/loved "like a woman" and so symbolically castrated; there are a number of ways to be divested of the phallus in our symbolic which do not center on the penis as the mark of power and privilege. Phallic divestiture by one means can even be congruent with phallic investiture by another, functioning defensively so as to distinguish the subject from the phallic Other (mother or father) whose (mis)recognition s/he solicits and shares in order to be a subject at all. For example, the transsexual can give up the penis in order to graft on a phallus, undergoing a literal castration which is not a symbolic castration, as I have argued in an analysis of the Renee Richards Story.[100]

Furthermore, the fantasy of the "other" as phallic Other is not necessarily radical, since s/he may be phallic in exactly those terms a sexist, racist, and classist symbolic legitimates, and the fantasizing subject may identify with that position of omnipotence and omniscience, rather than imagine s/he is excluded from it—as occurs in camp and mimicry. Finally, even when the subject does feel excluded from that place, and his/her fetishism is an anxious response to a sense of lack, the object/other remains only a phallic fantasy. S/he does not exist as such: s/he does not exist for the subject (for whom s/he is merely a means to be w/hole), and s/he is not what sh/e seems to be for the subject (since s/he has desires the subject cannot know). Theorists of camp and mimicry have not concerned themselves with the subjectivity of their "others" except as it seems to guarantee their own status as phallic Others (who know what they are up to). The irony in mimicry and camp, therefore, is all too often at the other's expense, a defense against castration anxiety. Thus, while it is perfectly possible to imagine a white male transvestic and camp identification with the heroine in *King Kong*, for example, it would not be particularly progressive for black men, made once again the bearers of the big, bad dick that has figured so prominently in the history of race relations structured by fantasies of miscegenation and all too real lynchings.

Conclusion

Camp (like mimicry) functions complexly by dragging in many differences at once that are all too easily articulated with phallic narcissism in a symbolic which is really a white, bourgeois, and masculine fetishistic imaginary. I have suggested this narcissism needs to be analyzed, its phallic impostures unveiled as such. For that to happen, gay theorists (like feminist theorists) must recognize their positioning in a number of discourses besides those of gender and sexuality and accept difference, including self-difference and lack. While camp may not always facilitate such recognition and acceptance, it is not essentially at odds with it. Indeed, though Zora Neale Hurston's Janie Mae Crawford says, "You got tuh *go* there tuh *know* there," Gayatri Spivak points out that "knowledge is made possible and is sustained by irreducible difference, not identity."[101] The play of identification and dis-identification in drag could be the very condition of autocritique.

I would argue that it does make possible self-criticism for one very fragile moment in *City of Night*, when the first-person hustler narrator briefly accepts his castration by identifying with the beautiful queen

Kathy, whom he understands to be castrated, paradoxically, because she has (rather than lacks) a penis, which prevents her from being a whole (and phallic) woman. His self-knowledge (which promotes our self-knowledge, since we have been asked to identify with him) is revealed in his response to a scene he witnesses in New Orleans during Carnival, when Kathy directs one of the heterosexual male tourists who has come on to her to grope her crotch:

> The man's hand explores eagerly. Kathy smiles fiercely. The man pulled his hand away violently, stumbling back in astonishment. Kathy follows him with the fading eyes. Now Jocko [a hustler friend] smiles too.
> I turn away quickly from the sight. I feel gigantically sad for Kathy, for the dropped mask—sad for Jocko—for myself—sad for the man who kissed Kathy and discovered he was kissing a man.
> Sad for whole rotten spectacle of the world wearing cold, cold masks.

"Minutes later," the narrator says, "my own mask began to crumble": he tells two scores he is not what they think he is, "tough," the opposite from them."[102] In effect, the narrator acknowledges his virile "parade" is a masquerade, a charade of having something valuable to give (the penis as phallus) to those others who can afford to pay for it literally and symbolically (they pay for his services because they can "afford" to be castrated for him, as the Wolf Man could not for his father). He understands that like Kathy he is only a man and not what he must seem to be in the comedy of sexual relations. At that moment, he recognizes sex could be something other than an exchange of the phallus, though he is not quite sure how. But as the rest of the novel reveals, he resumes hustling and refuses the painful knowledge of castration that nevertheless returns to haunt him as the feeling that heaven is unfairly barred to some. The "solution" to anxiety about fetishistic phallic imposture proves to be more fetishism, not surprising, since the symbolic itself legislates the repudiation of lack. Disrupted by camp, the camp moment does not last; misrecognition follows upon recognition, and incredible acts, unfortunately, begin to seem credible once more.

Notes

1. The Kinks, "Lola," *Part One: Powerman, Lola Versus and the Moneygoround* (Burbank: Warner Bros. Records, R56423, 1970).

2. Joan Riviere, "Womanliness as a Masquerade," *Psychoanalysis and Female Sexuality,* ed. Hendrik M. Ruitenbeek (New Haven: College and University Press, 1966), 209–220. I discuss in depth the work on female impersonation in the course of the essay.

3. For example, see Richard Dyer, "Getting Over the Rainbow: Identity and Pleasure in Gay Cultural Politics," *Silver Linings: Some Strategies for the Eighties,* ed. George Bridges and Rosalind Brunt (London: Lawrence and Wishart, 1981), 60–61. I consider the work of others who theorize gay macho as radical later in the essay.

4. Andrew Ross, *No Respect: Intellectuals and Popular Culture* (New York and London: Routledge, 1989), 144.

5. Dave King, "Gender Confusion: Psychological and Psychiatric Conceptions of Transvestism and Transsexualism," *The Making of the Modern Homosexual,* ed. Kenneth Plummer (Totowa: Barnes & Noble Books, 1981), 155–183. See also John Marshall, "Pansies, Perverts and Macho Men: Changing Conceptions of Male Homosexuality," *The Making of the Modern Homosexual,* 150–151; Jeffrey Escoffier, "Sexual Revolution and the Politics of Gay Identity," *Socialist Review* 15, nos. 4–5 (July–October 1985): 126–92, 133–42; Don Mager, "Gay Theories of Gender Role Deviance," *Sub-Stance* 46 (1985); 32–36; and Sue-Ellen Case, "Toward a Butch-Femme Aesthetic," *Making a Spectacle: Feminist Essays on Contemporary Women's Theatre,* ed. Lynda Hart (An Arbor: University of Michigan Press, 1989), 284–286.

6. Simon Watney, "The Banality of Gender," *Oxford Literary Review* 8, nos. 1–2 (1986); 14.

7. Sigmund Freud, *Three Essays on the Theory of Sexuality,* trans. James Strachey (1905; rpt. New York: Basic Books Inc., Publishers, 1975), 11 (footnote added 1910).

8. Sigmund Freud, *Dora: An Analysis of a Case of Hysteria,* trans. James Strachey, ed. Philip Rieff (1900; rpt. New York: Collier Books, 1963), 80–81, 101–2, 133. See also his analysis of lesbianism in "The Psychogenesis of a Case of Homosexuality in a Woman," trans. Barbara Low and R. Gabler, *Sexuality and the Psychology of Love,* ed. Philip Rieff (1920; rpt. New York: Collier Books, 1963), 133–59.

9. Freud, *Three Essays,* 11.

10. Judith Butler, *Gender Trouble: Feminism and the Subversion of Identity* (New York and London: Routledge, 1990), 54–55, 60–61.

11. Freud, *Three Essays,* 10.

12. Martin Humphries, "Gay Machismo," *The Sexuality of Men,* ed. Andy Metcalf and Martin Humphries (London and Sydney: Pluto Press, 1985), 84.

13. Gregg Blachford, "Male Dominance and the Gay World," *The Making of the Modern Homosexual,* 200.

14. Rita Mae Brown, *Rubyfruit Jungle* (New York: Bantam Books, 1977), 202–3, 206.

15. Eve Kosofsky Sedgwick, "Across Gender, Across Sexuality: Willa Cather and Others," *The South Atlantic Quarterly,* 88, no. 1 (1989): 53–61.

16. Carole-Anne Tyler, "The Supreme Sacrifice? TV, 'TV,' and the Renée Richards Story," *differences* 1, no. 3 (1989): 162 (I discuss talk shows at length in the article); Kris Kirk and Ed Heath, *Men in Frocks* (London: GMP Publications, Ltd., 1984). This is a history of gay male drag which relies extensively on interviews; many of the interviewees state that they do not wish to be mistaken for women—see, for example, Boy George, 112, and Frank Egan, 128.

17. Richard Dyer, "Don't Look Now," *Screen* 23, nos. 3–4 (1982): 61–73; Sandy Flitterman-Lewis, "Thighs and Whiskers: The Fascination of 'Magnum, P.I.,' " *Screen* 26, no. 2 (1985): 42–58; Steve Neale, "Masculinity as Spectacle: Reflections on Men and Mainstream Cinema," *Screen* 24, no. 6 (1983): 2–16.

18. Marshall, "Pansies," 153–54.

19. Craig Owens, "Outlaws: Gay Men in Feminism," *Men in Feminism*, ed. Alice Jardine and Paul Smith (New York and London: Methuen, 1987), 220; 219.

20. Sigmund Freud, *Leonardo Da Vinci,* trans. A. A. Brill (1916; rpt. New York: Vintage Books, 1944), 88.

21. John Rechy, *City of Night* (New York: Grove Press, 1963); Hubert Selby, Jr., *Last Exit to Brooklyn* (1957; rpt. New York: Grove Press, 1986).

22. Sometimes the interviewees in *Men in Frocks* are defensive about their masculinity, as I indicated above; sometimes they are defensive about their femininity and discuss the denigration of queens in the gay community—see, for example, Terri Frances, 110, and Rebel Rebel, 120.

23. Leo Bersani, "Is the Rectum a Grave?" *October* 43 (Winter 1987): 202–3.

24. Bersani, 208.

25. The transvestic slang, "r.g." ("real girl"), is useful for suggesting that even the "real thing" needs to be written in quotation marks, since she is only a product of certain gender codes which privilege the body as essential ground of gender identity. These are codes the transvestite contests but also uses, if the impersonation is fetishistic, involving an apparent identification with femininity which is, in fact, a dis-identification, through an appeal to the body beneath the clothes as sign of the truth of gender. I discuss this double strategy later in the essay. See Judith Butler, *Gender Trouble,* for a deconstructive critique of the ontology of the body.

26. Bersani, 218.

27. Bersani, 220.

28. Bersani, 222.

29. Kaja Silverman, "White Skin, Brown Masks: The Double Mimesis, or With Lawrence in Arabia," *differences* 1, no. 3 (1989): 3–54.

30. Bersani, 206. See also Diana Fuss, who notes in *Essentially Speaking* (New York and London: Routledge, 1989) that simply being gay does not guarantee political activism, 101.

31. Carole-Anne Tyler, "The Feminine Look," *Theory between the Disciplines: Authority/Vision/Politics,* ed. Martin Kreiswirth and Mark Cheetham (Ann Arbor: Univ. of Michigan Press, 1990), 191–212. See also "The Supreme Sacrifice?"

32. Marilyn Frye, *The Politics of Reality: Essays in Feminist Theory* (Trumansburg: The Crossing Press, 1983), 137.

33. Judith Williamson, *Consuming Passions: The Dynamics of Popular Culture* (London: Marion Boyars, 1986), 47–54.

34. Erika Munk, "Drag: 1. Men," *Village Voice,* 5 Feb., 1985, 91; Alison Lurie, *The Language of Clothes* (New York: Random House, 1983), 258.

35. The classic psychoanalytic essay on transvestism is Otto Fenichel, "The Psychology of Transvestism," *Psychoanalysis and Male Sexuality,* ed. Hendrik M. Ruitenbeek (1930; rpt. New Haven: College and University Press, 1966), 203–10. Fetishism is discussed in Sigmund Freud, "Fetishism," *Sexuality and the Psychology of Love,* 214–19, and in Jacques Lacan and Wladimir Granoff, "Fetishism: The Symbolic, the Imaginary and the Real," *Perversions,* ed. Sandor Lorand (New York: Gramercy Publishing, 1956), 265–76. See also Kaja Silverman, *The Acoustic Mirror: The Female Voice in Psychoanalysis and Cinema* (Bloomington and Indianapolis: Indiana University Press, 1988), 1–42, and Carole-Anne Tyler, "The Feminine Look," 201–10.

36. Ross, *No Respect,* 159.

37. Freud, "Fetishism," 219; 214.

38. Annette Kuhn suggests something similar about films with cross-dressers, which she argues offer the promise of a multiplicity of gender relations but tend to renege on it ultimately by exposing the body beneath the clothes as the "truth" of gender. See her *The Power of the Image: Essays on Representation and Sexuality* (New York and London: Routledge & Kegan Paul, 1985), 56–57.

39. Neale, "Masculinity as Spectacle," 8–10; Neale discusses Willemen on 8.

40. Laura Mulvey, "Afterthoughts on 'Visual Pleasure and Narrative Cinema' Inspired by *Duel in the Sun,*" *Feminism and Film Theory,* ed. Constance Penley (New York and London: Routledge, 1988), 70–72.

41. Mark Finch, "Sex and Address in 'Dynasty,' " *Screen* 27, no. 6 (1986): 24–42.

42. *Drag Queens* 4, no. 3 (1986): 2. References immediately following are cited in the text.

43. Frye, *The Politics of Reality,* 128–51.

44. George Alpert, *The Queens* (New York: Da Capo Press, Inc., 1975).

45. D. N. Rodowick, "The Difficulty of Difference," *Wide Angle* 5 (1982): 7–9. The text Rodowick critiques is the influential essay by Laura Mulvey, "Visual Pleasure and Narrative Cinema," *Feminism and Film Theory,* 57–68.

46. Rodowick, 9.

47. Griselda Pollock, *Vision and Difference: Femininity, Feminism, and the Histories of Art* (London and New York: Routledge, 1988), 153.

48. Berkeley Kaite, "The Pornographer's Body Double: "Transgression is the Law," *Body Invaders: Panic Sex in America,* ed. Arthur and Marilouise Kroker (New York: St. Martin's Press, 1987), 158. I have used the term "phallic M/Other" because the place of phallic omnipotence and omniscience can be filled by the fantasy of the phallic mother or the primitive father, since neither is imagined to be subject to castration. I will suggest later in the essay that the phallic Other may

appear to have the phallus by virtue of his/her class or racial difference as well as because of his/her gender, since such differences signify lack or having with respect to the power and privileges which accrue to the phallic subject. Women are not the only ones who do not exist except as a phallic fantasy in the symbolic.

49. Kaja Silverman, "Masochism and Male Subjectivity," *Camera Obscura* 17 (1988): 36. See especially this essay for the subversiveness of masochism, but see also her "White Skin, Brown Masks," and "Masochism and Subjectivity," *Framework* 12 (1981): 2–9.

50. Silverman, "Masochism and Male Subjectivity," 57.

51. Silverman, 58.

52. For discussions of the literature on Sade, see Jane Gallop, *Intersections: A Reading of Sade with Bataille, Blanchot and Klossowski* (Lincoln: University of Nebraska Press, 1981), and Angela Carter, *The Sadeian Woman and the Ideology of Pornography* (New York: Harper Colophon Books, 1978).

53. Jane Gallop, *The Daughter's Seduction: Feminism and Psychoanalysis* (Ithaca: Cornell University Press, 1982), 117.

54. Sigmund Freud, "From the History of an Infantile Neurosis," *Three Case Histories,* trans. James Strachey, ed. Philip Rieff (1918; rpt. New York, Collier Books, 1963), 256, 278; "The Taboo of Virginity," *Sexuality and the Psychology of Love,* 76–78.

55. Quoted in Gallop, *Intersections,* 57.

56. Two excellent, representative essays are Mary Ann Doane, *The Desire to Desire: The Woman's Film of the 1940s* (Bloomington and Indianapolis: Indiana University Press, 1987), 123–54, and Jane Gallop, *The Daughter's Seduction,* 113–30.

57. Robert Stoller, *Presentations of Gender* (New Haven: Yale Univ. Pres, 1985).

58. Kaite, "Pornographer's Body," 164.

59. Silverman, "Masochism and Male Subjectivity," 62.

60. Jacques Lacan, *Ecrits: A Selection,* trans. Alan Sheridan (1949; rpt. New York: W. W. Norton and Company, 1977), 4–5. Julia Kristeva writes about abjection in *The Powers of Horror: An Essay on Abjection,* trans. Leon Roudiez (New York: Columbia University Press, 1982).

61. Silverman, "Masochism and Male Subjectivity," 62.

62. Jacques Lacan, *The Four Fundamental Concepts of Psychoanalysis,* trans. Alan Sheridan, ed. Jacques-Alain Miller (New York: Norton, 1978), 104.

63. Jacques Lacan, "The Meaning of the Phallus," *Feminine Sexuality,* trans. Jacqueline Rose, ed. Jacqueline Rose and Juliet Mitchell (New York: Norton, 1982), 83–85.

64. Moustapha Safouan, "Contribution à la psychanalyse du transsexualisme," *Scilicet* 4 (1983): 150–52.

65. Fenichel, "The Psychology of Transvestism," 214–215.

66. Sigmund Freud, *New Introductory Lectures on Psychoanalysis,* trans. James Strachey (1933; rpt. New York: W. W. Norton and Company, 1965), 113.

67. Luce Irigaray, *Speculum of the Other Woman,* trans. Gillian Gill (Ithaca: Cornell University Press, 1985), 73–80.

68. Luce Irigaray, *This Sex Which Is Not One*, trans. Catherine Porter (Ithaca: Cornell University Press, 1985), 76.

69. Butler, *Gender Trouble*, 146–47.

70. Sue-Ellen Case, "Toward a Butch-Femme Aesthetic," 287, 291–92; Jack Babuscio, "Camp and the Gay Sensibility," *Gays and Film*, ed. Richard Dyer (New York: New York Zoetrope, Inc., 1984), 41, 44, 47–49; Richard Dyer, "Getting Over the Rainbow," 60–61; Jeffrey Escoffier, "Sexual Revolution," 140–41; Andrew Ross, *No Respect*, 162; Vito Russo, "Camp," *Gay Men: The Sociology of Male Homosexuality*, ed. Martin Levine (New York: Harper & Row, Publishers, 1979), 205.

71. Irigaray, *This Sex Which Is Not One*, 76.

72. Nancy Miller, "Emphasis Added: Plots and Plausibilities in Women's Fiction," *PMLA* 96 (1981): 38; Mary Ann Doane, "Film and the Masquerade—Theorising the Female Spectator," *Screen* 23, nos. 3–4 (1982): 82; Mary Russo, "Female Grotesques: Carnival and Theory," *Feminist Studies/Critical Studies*, ed. Teresa de Lauretis (Bloomington and Indianapolis: Indiana University Press, 1986), 217, 224; Linda Kauffman, *Discourses of Desire: Gender, Genre, and Epistolary Fictions* (Ithaca: Cornell University Press, 1986), 294–95, 298.

73. Lacan, "The Meaning of the Phallus," 84.

74. Babuscio, "Camp and the Gay Sensibility," 41 (and throughout); Russo, "Camp," 208.

75. Andrew Britton, "For Interpretation: Notes Against Camp," *Gay Left* 7 (1978–1979): 12.

76. Gayatri Spivak, "Can the Subaltern Speak?," *Marxism and the Interpretation of Culture*, ed. Cary Nelson and Lawrence Greenberg (Urbana and Chicago: University of Illinois Press, 1988), 273–76.

77. Once again, I want to stress that this is a problem for theory, and not necessarily for real people.

78. Butler, *Gender Trouble*, 123; Babuscio, "Camp and the Gay Sensibility," 41; Oscar Montero, "Lipstick Vogue: The Politics of Drag," *Radical America* 22, no. 1 (1988): 40–41; Andrew Ross, *No Respect*, 162.

79. Butler, *Gender Trouble*, 123.

80. Case, "Toward a Butch-Femme Aesthetic," 294; see 291 for the assertion that playing the gender roles between women recontextualizes them and "foregrounds" them as myths.

81. Lisa Duggan, "The Anguished Cry of an 80's Fem: 'I Want to be a Drag Queen,' " *Out/Look* 1, no. 1 (1988): 64.

82. See "A Touch of Class in the Hourglass," *Reflections* 9, no. 1 (1986): 21–29, which features Annie Sprinkle (and other women) in corsets (Sprinkle first appears solo on 22).

83. Teresa de Lauretis, "Sexual Indifference and Lesbian Representation," *Theatre Journal* 40, no. 2 (1988): 177.

84. Jane Gallop, "Beyond the *Jouissance* Principle," *Representations* 7 (1984): 114.

85. Tyler, "The Feminine Look."

86. Both Case and Ross note that class differences may be a factor in camp, but neither elaborates on the observation or makes it as central to camp as I am suggesting it is. See Case, "Toward a Butch-Femme Aesthetic," 286, and Ross, *No Respect,* 146.

87. Harold Beaver. "Homosexual Signs (*In Memory of Roland Barthes*)," *Critical Inquiry* 8, no. 1 (Autumn 1981): 113–14; Craig Owens, "Outlaws," 228; see also my discussion above about the implication for egalitarianism of a subjectivity free from castration anxiety, as Owens (and, he maintains, Derrida) assume homosexuality to be, 219. With regard to the question of the radicality of camp, Bersani (in "Is the Rectum a Grave?") points out that a distinction must be made between its effects on the gay couple, who may not have subversive intentions, and its effects on heterosexuals, 207. While I believe any politics of consciousness is suspect—as I hope to demonstrate here, the effects, not the intentions, of camp are what count—Bersani's statement does at least suggest the importance of context. Andrew Britton also notes the importance of context (in "For Interpretation") when he says that subversion is not intrinsic to a phenomenon but to its context, its reception, 12.

88. Sigmund Freud, "Psychoanalytic Notes Upon an Autobiographical Account of a Case of Paranoia (Dementia Paranoides)," *Three Case Histories* (1911; rpt.), 103–86.

89. Sedgwick, "Across Gender, Across Sexuality," 54–55.

90. Sunil Gupta "Black, *Brown,* and White," *Coming on Strong: Gay Politics and Culture,* ed. Simon Shepherd and Mick Wallis (London: Unwin Hyman, 1989), 163–79; Kobena Mercer and Isaac Julien, "True Confessions," *Ten.* 8, no. 22 (no date): 4–9; Thomas Yingling, "How the Eye is Caste: Robert Mapplethorpe and the Limits of Controversy," *Discourse* 12, no. 2 (1990): 3–28; Jane Gallop, "Annie Leclerc Writing a Letter with Vermeer," *The Poetics of Gender,* ed. Nancy Miller (New York: Columbia University Press, 1986), 137–56. I discuss Gallop's essay in "The Feminine Look," 207–8.

91. Homi Bhabha, "The Other Question: Difference, Discrimination, and the Discourse of Colonialism," *Literature, Politics, and Theory: Papers from the Essex Conference, 1976–1984,* ed. Francis Barker et al. (New York and London: Methuen, 1986), 163.

92. Frantz Fanon, *Black Skin, White Masks* (New York: Grove Press, 1967), 157. The child's fear of the black man is described on 112.

93. Freud, "History of an Infantile Neurosis," 213, 216. References immediately following are cited in the text.

94. Peter Stallybrass and Allon White, *The Politics and Poetics of Transgression* (Ithaca: Cornell University Press, 1986), 156.

95. Bhabha, "The Other Question," 159.

96. Jeffrey Weeks, "Inverts, Perverts, and Mary-Annes: Male Prostitution and the Regulation of Homosexuality in England in the Nineteenth and Early Twentieth Centuries," *Journal of Homosexuality* 6, nos. 1–2 (1980–1981): 121–22.

97. Silverman, "Masochism and Male Subjectivity," 55; 60; 61.

98. Riviere, "Womanliness as a Masquerade," 212.

99. For example, see *Reflections,* cited above.

100. Tyler, "The Supreme Sacrifice?."

101. Zora Neale Hurston, *Their Eyes Were Watching God* (1937; rpt. New York: Harper & Row Publishers, 1990), 183; Gayatri Chakravorty Spivak, *In Other Worlds: Essays in Cultural Politics* (New York and London: Methuen, 1987), 254.

102. Rechy, *City of Night,* 341.

3

Who Are "We"?
Gay "Identity" as
Political (E)motion
(A Theoretical Rumination)
Ed Cohen

> But the problem is, precisely, to decide if it is actually suitable to place oneself within a "we" in order to assert the principles one recognizes and the values one accepts; or if it is not, rather, necessary to make the future formation of a "we" possible, by elaborating the question. Because it seems to me that the "we" must not be previous to the question; it can only be the result—and necessarily the temporary result—of the question as it is posed in the new terms in which one formulates it.[1]   *Michel Foucault*

> I have always known that I learn my most lasting lessons about difference by closely attending to the ways in which the differences inside me lie down together.[2]   *Audre Lorde*

Being a gay academic living near the intellectual enclaves of New York City, I've been going to a lot of "gay and lesbian studies" discussions recently and it's been a somewhat unsettling experience. On the one hand, I enjoy the potential for conviviality and comradery that these occasions provide: most of the time getting together with a group of intellectual dykes and faggots to talk about interesting issues seems like a pleasant if not always worthwhile endeavor. On the other hand, I often leave these meetings wondering how these people ended up in the same room with each other, thinking it's a miracle that any mutual understanding exists, and trying to figure out what in the world we have in common. It's this last part that especially gets to me. I mean, I'd like to have the feeling—as one reading group participant recently characterized his feeling about gay bars in the 1970s—that gay and lesbian studies was a place where we didn't have to explain to anyone "who we are." However my visceral response belies this characterization: the more often I find myself at these collocations, the more often the nausea in my stomach seems to tell me that "I" have no idea "who 'we' are."

To some extent this anxious recollection is simply a confession of my own (academic?) neurosis: groups are very difficult and often very scary places for me precisely because I have a tendency to fear losing my "self" in them. Yet I believe there's more to my anxiety than just personal aversion. It seems to me that there is something particular about groups self-reflexively organized under the rubrics "gay" and "lesbian" which provokes my dis-ease. I find that there is something about the sameness desired by these categories which makes "the differences inside me" (to abuse Audre Lorde's phrase) jump up from where they have been "lying down together" and start running around my intestinal tract. In the midst of this internal struggle between sameness and difference, it becomes difficult to align myself with a "gay" collectivity, especially when the categories around which that collectivity asserts its coherence put my "self" out of alignment. So, although the assumption that "we" constitute a "natural" community because we share a sexual identity might appear to offer a stable basis for group formations, my experience suggests that it can just as often interrupt the process of creating intellectual and political projects which can gather "us" together across time and space. By predicating "our" affinity upon the assertion of a common "sexuality," we tacitly agree to leave unexplored any "internal" contradictions which undermine the coherence we desire from the imagined certainty of an unassailable commonality or of incontestable sexuality. Hence we almost inevitably render ourselves vulnerable to personal and political crisis whenever such putative certainty is destabilized from within the body, the psyche, the collectivity, or the polity. It is my sense that in unproblematically hinging "our" personal/group identity upon idealized notions of sexuality and the body, the aggregation of "gay" and "lesbian" as epistemological, social, and political categories frequently occludes the very difficulties *that both bring us together and keep us at odds* time and time again—i.e., the force of "our" difference(s).

Now this insight is certainly not news. As John D'Emilio has illustrated in his wonderful account of American gay and lesbian politics, "identity" and "difference" have simultaneously served as the crux and the crisis for most gay and lesbian organizing in this country.[3]

Indeed, the paradoxical interplay between them underscores the nominal instability engendered by using the mobile and contradictory pairing identity/difference as the theoretical basis for articulating the collective actions of lesbians and gay men. For, while some would try to constitute "identity" as the ground for claiming larger social inclusion (e.g., we are the same as everybody else and hence should not be treated differently), others would use "difference" as a strategy to interrupt the hegemony of dominant social/sexual arrangements (e.g., we are different and our difference will resist those practices that try to make us the same). Concomitantly and conversely, those holding the former position often seem intent on policing the boundaries of "difference" (as the periodic attempts to exclude S/M or intergenerational erotic practices from "proper" gay or lesbian identity attest), while those espousing the latter frequently abjure possible slippages between categories of "identification" (as the periodic vilifications of "bisexuals," "closet cases," and, more recently, "lesbians who sleep with men" suggest). Appearing ubiquitously in the self-representations offered by American gay and lesbian movements since the late 1950s, the apparently "natural" opposition (re)produced between "identity" and "difference" illuminates the historical constraints that circumscribe both how social/sexual agents are imagined in "our" gay American culture and how they are articulated within, by, and as processes of change.

In a recent article arguing for the "political utility" of using ethnicity as a model for "gay identity," Steven Epstein attempts to mediate between these apparently oppositional positions by foregrounding the historical necessity of the paradox itself:

> How do you protest a socially imposed categorization, except by organizing around the category? Just as blacks cannot fight the arbitrariness of racial classifications without organizing *as blacks,* so gays could not advocate the overthrow of the sexual order without making their gayness the very basis of their claims.[4]

In framing his question in terms of a collective response to an externally organized repressive force, Epstein assumes the monovocalizing authority of "socially imposed categorization" and thus defines resistance primarily as negation, as "fighting back." However, the very expression of his assumption belies its validity: neither the nominations "black" nor "gay" were products of the dominant culture but rather both were the political self-affirmations of marginal (or as I prefer, ec-centric) movements. Moreover, the implied isomorphism between the "arbitrariness of racial categorizations" and the "sexual order" elides the complex processes of social differentiation that assign, legitimate, and enforce qualitative distinctions between "types" of individuals. Here the explicit parallel drawn between "race" and "sexuality," familiar to so many polemical affirmations of (non-racial) identity politics, is meant to evoke an underlying and apparently indisputable common sense that naturalizes this particular choice of political strategy almost as if the "naturalness" of racial "identity" could confer a corollary stability upon the less "visible" dynamics of sexuality. Unfortunately, by focusing the political and cultural effects of racial differentiation upon "*blacks*" instead of upon the diverse practices that naturalize the bodies of African-Americans as perhaps the foremost signifiers/bearers of "race" in U.S. history, the rhetorical strategy itself unwittingly reinforces the very "arbitrariness of racial classification" that it intends to decry. It collapses the diverse points of intersection *and* opposition between African-American individuals and organizations into the apparently homogeneous distinction, "blackness," thereby effacing—for its presumably white audience—the ongoing struggles by and between African-Americans about the category itself.[5]

By relying on the assumption that the political efficacy of "blackness" is uncontestably self-evident (because "written" on bodies?), Epstein symmetrically appeals to "gayness" as a unifying difference that can and should organize a "sexual identity" politics. However, since neither "race" and "sex" nor "ethnicity" and "gender" are isomorphic social matrices, he depends upon the metonymic force of his analogy to sustain the legitimacy of his claims. Thus, he uses "blackness" to hypostatize "gayness" (here subsuming the unmarked "lesbian") as a self-evident category of social differentiation rather than inquiring into what makes "gayness" "gay." Although the point here is semantic, it is not entirely academic. To the extent that Epstein suggests that the goal of "gay" politics is the "overthrow of the sexual order"—that is, of the imputed mechanism behind "socially imposed ['sexual'] categorization"—it seems imperative to ask whether a gay and lesbian identity politics is the most effective rubric for organizing individuals whose shared concerns include the radical refiguring of what Gayle Rubin succinctly labels the "sex/gender system."[6] Conversely, there are many people who claim the nominations "gay" and "lesbian" as positive self-descriptions who would not affirm such a "radical" politics as their own. Are they then not to be accorded membership in "our" community? "our" movements? And what of individuals who chose to situate their activities as gay men, lesbians, bisexuals, transvestites, S/M radicals, paedophiles, butch/fem women, or fem/butch men, in what may not be seen as primarily sexual arenas— as many lesbians and gay men of color or working-class or ethnic gay men and lesbians have undertaken to do?

Although these questions are not taken up by Epstein's analysis, they are not unknown to it either. Hence, in his conclusion, he fleetingly notes the liabilities which inhere in the exclusive potential that he imagines as "gay 'ethnic' politics":

> . . . it seems clear enough that the gay movement will never be able to forge effective alliances with other social movements unless it can address the inequalities that plague its internal organization. In this light it is worth noting a peculiar paradox of identity politics: *while affirming a distinctive group identity that legitimately differs from the larger society, this form of political expression simultaneously imposes a "totalizing" sameness within the group: It says, this is who we "really are."* A greater appreciation for internal diversity— on racial, gender, class and even sexual dimensions—is a prerequisite if the gay movement is to move beyond "ethnic" insularity and join with other progressive causes.[7] (my emphasis)

This hasty caveat in the final paragraphs of an otherwise lengthy and painstaking argument signals the problems of including "difference" within "identity politics." Indeed, as the passage all too quickly shifts from its concern with the possibility of moving between "alliance" and "identity" (defined here as the legitimation of difference) to its concern about the " 'totalizing' sameness within the group," it underscores the extent to which the "peculiar paradox of identity politics" renders difficult precisely those kinds of inquiry that would open into a *politics that would take as both* its process and its goal *the interruption of those practices of differentiation that (re)produce historically specific, asymmetrical patterns of privilege and oppression.* Therefore, by relegating questions of "internal diversity" to an afterthought that follows only in the wake of the consolidation of "identity," Epstein's argument illustrates the almost inevitable privileging of sameness over difference and of goals over processes that has characterized the "gay" enactments of "identity politics" in America.

My point in undertaking this protracted and admittedly nitpicking interpretation of a few sentences from Epstein's article is not to vilify his analysis; indeed, the reason I choose to focus on his text here is because I find it to be such a well-considered, thought-provoking, and highly concerned piece of writing. Rather I am trying to suggest that no matter how sensitively we go about it, "identity politics" has great difficulty in affirming difference(s). Or more accurately, as Diana Fuss has recently demonstrated, identity politics is predicated on denying the difference that is already there in "the same." Drawing on Heidegger's and Derrida's critiques of the metaphysical heritage of Western epistemologies, Fuss lucidly observes: "To the extent that identity always contains the specter of non-identity within it, the subject is always divided and identity is always purchased at the price of the exclusion of the Other, the repression or repudiation of non-identity."[8] This evocation of identity's exclusive "price" foregrounds what Derrida characterizes as the "violence" inhering in classical philosophical oppositions:[9] if identity presupposes the "fixing" of difference (in the sense of both repairing it and pinning it down), then the fixation on identity reiterates a painful process that simultaneously excludes and exacerbates "non-identity." Although some might aver that this philosophical consideration mystifies the vernacular usage intended by the advocates of "identity politics," I believe that such a distinction is hard to maintain. For, from the moment it enters the vernacular, the historical traces of this metaphysical paradox seem to be embedded in all personal/political articulations of "identity" as a qualitative definition of human individuation.

In an essay sketching out the trajectory by which Western conceptualizations of identity (e)merged as "identity politics" in the U.S. during the 1960s, Philip Gleason indirectly alludes to this problem of epistemological embedding. He notes that as Enlightenment thinkers sought to challenge earlier theological paradigms which explained human "difference" (both inter- and intra-species) as an epiphenomenon of the "soul," they adopted a term that had previously been used technically in algebra and logic to characterize the problematic distinction/relation between "body" and "mind."[10] "Identity" provided an effective way of understanding the sameness of what was concomitantly being constituted as difference (body/mind) precisely because it mobilized the idealizing effects derived from earlier philosophical and mathematical (con)texts. Moreover, the idealization worked simultaneously in two directions so that just as "mind" came to signify the transcendental qualities of reason which enabled this self-reflexive undertaking (most infamously illustrated by Descartes's *cogito*), "body" served to naturalize the essential and autonomous unity of the thinking being. Hence John Locke's famous explanation in his *Essay Concerning Hu-*

man Understanding (1690) predicates "identity" as an enduring quality of the person on the enduring sameness of "the body":

> Identity of the same Man consists . . . in nothing but a participation of the same continued Life, by constantly fleeting Particles of Matter, in succession vitally united to the same organized Body. He that shall place the identity of man in anything else, but like that of other animals, in one fitly organized body, taken in any one instant, and from thence continued, under one organization of life, in several successively fleeting particles of matter united to it, will find it hard to make an embryo, one of years, mad and sober, the same man, by any supposition, that will not make it possible for Seth, Ismael, Socrates, Pilate, St. Austin, and Caesar Borgia to be the same man.[11]

As Locke's definition suggests, "identity" evokes the "sameness" of human differentiation *across time* by collapsing the processes of (self-)transformation *through time* into an unchanging and highly idealized notion, "the same organized Body." This dehistoricizing gesture correspondingly organizes a matrix of intelligibility and visibility which produces the idealized body as both the ground and the guarantee for making qualitative distinctions between "kinds" of human beings. The rhetorical effect of this somatic idealization is to support the more wide reaching and perhaps historically significant inference that if one's "identity" presupposes the "sameness" of one's somatic differentiation, then conversely one's somatic difference(s) must "naturally" define the "sameness" of one's "identity."

Since the social significance attributed to somatic signifiers of difference has provided the source for so many of our received notions about human "types" (sexual, racial, class, ethnic, generational, etc.), it may now be useful to go a bit further to consider how political assertions of "identity" necessarily reiterate the reification of human bodies as "natural invariants" which such typologies have both engendered and been engendered by. For, as the Canadian political theorist C. B. Macpherson illustrates in his now classic analysis, liberal democratic discourse—which implicitly if not explicitly underwrites almost all historical claims of "identity" movements to "individual" rights in this country—is predicated on a set of fundamental assumptions about the disposition of bodies as they mark out the locus of the self. In Macpherson's famous formulation, Western political discourse is circumscribed by a tradition of what he calls "possessive individualism" in which individuals are defined primarily as proprietors of their fleshly incarnations, who are consequently entitled to rights only as the owners of themselves:

> . . . seventeenth-century individualism contained [a] central diffi-
> culty which lay in its possessive quality. Its possessive quality is
> found in the conception of the individual as essentially the proprietor
> of his own person or capacities, owing nothing to society for them.
> The individual was seen neither as a moral whole, nor as a part of
> a larger social whole, but as owner of himself. The relation of
> ownership, having become for more and more men [sic][12] the criti-
> cally important relation determining their actual freedom and actual
> prospect of realizing their full potentialities, was read back into the
> nature of the individual.[13]

While Macpherson focuses his interpretation upon the utility which this formulation of human individuation has had for the social legitima-tion (naturalization) of bourgeois political economy, his insights also suggest an important corollary. If human beings are imagined as ex-isting in an essentially proprietary relation to themselves, they are constituted simultaneously as possessors and possessions of them-selves, thereby reproducing the isomorphic dissection of mind/body which the concept of "identity" seeks to reconcile. This dichotomous positioning then organizes a "technology of the self"—to appropriate Foucault's phrase—in which and through which the bourgeois individ-ual comes to understand its "identity" as what is "proper" to it, i.e., its possessive relation to itself. Yet since what is specifically designated as "property" in this relation is the body and its labor ("every Man has a *Property* in his own Person. This no body has any Right to but himself. The *Labour* of his Body, and the *Work* of his Hands, we may say are properly his"[14]), somatic materiality implicitly becomes the unchanging human ground upon which an identity can be both erected and possessed. In this process of self-construction, then, the slippage between bodies as property and the properties of bodies comes to overdetermine what Macpherson felicitously terms "the nature of the individual." Thus, as the body comes to define the proper locus of human individuation, its (somatic) properties are increasingly utilized in order to legitimate the interpretation of social differences as "natural."[15]

Not surprisingly, the dissemination of this schema for imagining somatic ("biological") individuation as the basis for organizing and enforcing social gradients coincides with the "deployment of sexuality" that Foucault describes as emerging in 18th-century Europe. In Foucault's account, "sexuality" names a complex nexus of "concrete arrangements"[16] which include sexuality "in the body as a mode of specifying individuals."[17] "The notion of sex," he suggests, "made it possible to group together, in an artificial unity, anatomical elements, biological functions, conducts, sensations, and pleasures, and it enabled one to make use of this fictitious unity as a causal principle, an omnipresent meaning, a secret to discover everywhere."[18] Foucault's objective in asserting this "counter-intuitive" position is to break apart the "artificial unity" naturalized by the apparent singularity of somatic differentiation—i.e., by the assumption that most bodies can be unproblematically distinguished as unique and that the genital configurations which appear at birth (and presumably endure throughout a lifetime) are essential signifiers of this distinctiveness. In so doing, he seeks to problematize the "dense web" of power relations woven between these points of "natural" difference and thereby to interrupt the power/knowledge [*pouvoir/savoir*] nexus that maintains them as "true." Foucault argues that as sexuality came to signify something about "the truth" of one's person, it situated what was called "the body" within a constellation of emerging medical, biological, pedagogical, anthropological, sexological, sociological, and economic discourses and, conversely, mapped these discursive frames onto and into the historical concatenations of particular somatic events ("anatomical elements, biological functions, conducts, sensations, and pleasures").

While Foucault avoids offering causal explanations for the emergence of "sexuality" as a "form of power [which] applies itself to immediate everyday life, which categorizes the individual, marks him [sic] by his own individuality, *attaches him to his own identity,* imposes a law of truth on him which he must recognize and which others have to recognize in him"[19] (my emphasis), he correlates this emergence with the positive self-affirmations of the European middle classes starting in the mid-eighteenth century:

> With this investment of its own sex by a technology of power and knowledge which it had itself invented, the bourgeoisie underscored the high political price of its body, sensations and pleasure, its well-being and survival. . . . It provided itself with a body to be cared for, protected, cultivated and preserved from the many dangers and contacts, to be isolated from others so that it would retain its differential value. . . .[20]

The idealized, "healthy" body, Foucault suggests, formed the basis for legitimating a "political ordering of life" insofar as it "naturally" impressed the individual within aggregations such as "population" and "the life of the species." Hence, the affirmation of the middle-class body served to progressively link an affirmation of (species) life to a specific, political investment in life, an investment that concomitantly legitimated the continued (re)production of bourgeois Europeans' privilege by casting it as an effect of the "healthier" body. It is this affirmative principle that Foucault characterizes as "dynamic racism," depicting it as the "bud" which would bear the "fruits" of nineteenth-century imperialism.[21] What Foucault's analysis suggests, then, is that sexuality operates as a powerful "game of truth"[22] which "categorizes the individual, marks him by his own individuality, [and] attaches him to his own identity" insofar as it makes a disparate set of power relations knowable as qualities of (human) life and (re)produces the stable, "sexed" body as the "essential" metonym for this configuration.

When he undertook what Maria Daraki calls his "journey to Greece"[23] at the end of his life, Foucault seemingly moved away from this focus on "sexuality" per se in order to illuminate the "arts of existence" through which "men [sic] not only set themselves rules of conduct, but also seek to transform themselves, to change themselves in their singular being, and to make their life an oeuvre that carries certain stylistic criteria."[24] Classical Greek (fourth-century BCE) and Graeco-Roman (second-century CE) cultures provided Foucault with the domain for his inquiry into the "techniques of the self" which organize the "relationship of self with self and the forming of oneself as a subject."[25] Although chronologically discontinuous with his earlier inquiries, Foucault's last writings interestingly interrupt the assertion of a "natural" equivalence between a singular, "sexed" body and an "identity" precisely by problematizing the unitary conception of human individuation and instead depicting the "relationship of self with self" as a *practice of transformation and change*. Indeed, in as much as Foucault characterized "the general theme of [his] research" as "not power, but the subject,"[26] his last two books significantly pose the question of the "self" as a *dynamic interaction* among heteronomous elements comprising an often conflicted field of intelligibility, regulation, exclusion, and creation. By situating his historical inquiry prior to the inscription/incarnation of (somatically defined) individuation as "identity," Foucault seems to move purposely outside "modern" political discourses in order to recast "politics as an ethics."[27] This "return" to ethics leads Foucault to foreground the practices through which we (aesthetically, ethically, and politically) constitute our relations to ourselves and to each other in order to "ask politics what it has to say about the problems with which it [is] confronted."[28] He thereby underscores the necessity for exploring how the practices of political action inflect those processes that engender different, relational "selves."

If we accept the assessment that this genealogical coincidence between "sexuality" and "identity" is the effect of a "modern" Western regime of power which implicates human bodies in and as the sites of its discursive (re)production, then how are we to understand the consequences of a politics that grounds itself in/on a "sexual identity"? Or, in other words, to the extent that "sexuality" and "identity" are both predicated upon a constellation of power relations that naturalize their own historical contingency by making themselves knowable as fixed qualities of somatic differentiation, what limitations do the political articulations of "sexual identity" unwittingly import? In her exciting new book *Gender Trouble*, Judith Butler entertains questions such as these in order to challenge the assumption that feminism's status as an "identity politics" is comfortably grounded on the stability of the "self-evidently" differential category, "woman." Framed by the attempts within feminism over the last fifteen years to interrupt the painful exclusions experienced by "different" women, Butler's analysis seeks to elucidate why the political invocations of "woman" seem to have systematically engendered not identity but dissent. For Butler, part of the problem lies in the recognition that what Epstein characterized as the "totalizing' sameness within the group" simultaneously conditions a " 'totalizing' sameness" within the individual. By circumscribing people (here specifically women) within gender categories, the political invocations of sexual identity mask the complex and often contradictory processes of social differentiation that produce "gender" as a "naturally" distinguishing signifier of human "identity."

> If one "is" a woman, that is surely not all one is; the term fails to be exhaustive, not because a pregendered "person" transcends the specific paraphernalia of its gender, but because gender is not always constituted coherently or consistently in different historical contexts, and because gender intersects with racial, class, ethnic, sexual and regional modalities of discursively constituted identities. As a result, it becomes impossible to separate out "gender" from the political and cultural intersections in which it is invariably produced and maintained.[29]

Rather than imagining "gender" as the social and historical significance derived from a pre-given, unchanging, anatomical "sex," Butler suggests that we need to begin to rethink gender as the accreted effects of specific cultural practices that give differential meaning to individual bodies: "Gender is the repeated stylization of the body, a set of repeated acts within a highly rigid regulatory frame that congeal over time to produce the appearance of substance, of a natural sort of being (33)." In offering this "performative" interpretation of gender as a "stylized repetition of acts" (140), Butler believes that she can obviate the ways that

> identity categories often presumed foundational to feminist politics, that is, deemed necessary to mobilize feminism as an identity politics, simultaneously work to limit and constrain in advance the very cultural possibilities that feminism is supposed to open up.(147)

Thus, instead of presupposing an "essential" (biological) difference as the ground for a (political) "sexual identity" which then must subsequently come to terms with the significant differences among those who have already been defined as "essentially" the same, Butler's analysis suggests that it is more effective *politically* to understand (qualitative) differences—whether "essential" or not—as historical effects and to devise political practices that "affirm the local possibilities of intervention through participating in precisely those practices of repetition that constitute identity and, therefore, present the immanent possibility of contesting them (147)." Such local interventions would presumably be better able to address the complex relations among, between, and within individuals who are engendered by the multiple, overlapping, and indeed contradictory effects of socially (re)produced differentials and gradients precisely because they would take these effects as both *the points and processes of intervention.*

Given my own crisis about "gay" identity—which may also be a good, old-fashioned "identity crisis"—perhaps it's not surprising that much of Butler's analysis seems congenial to me. To imagine genders as sets of performative effects shifts the focus of my political and personal imagination away from the mechanisms that institute "socially imposed categorizations" [30] to the practices that organize the processes of social differentiation/identification. In so doing, this conceptualization foregrounds the recognition that power relations are not monolithically imposed from "outside" but locally circulated everywhere, thereby opening the possibility for thinking change not as cataclysmic and hence (temporally) distant but rather as omnipresent and hence ongoing. If the ways genders get thought can be displaced from "inside" bodies onto those practices that organize how specific individuals move through, apprehend, and change their life-contexts, then gender politics entails the organization and (re)production of critical enactments that at once defamiliarize and destabilize those processes through which the differentiating forms of "difference" are naturalized.

For me, however, there is also a twofold problem with Butler's politically proscriptive account of the complex practices and processes that engender these culturally and historically specific forms. On the one hand, in its attempt to rethink "agency" so that it is "constituted" in terms of "construction," it obviates any concern with what brings individuals together to effect changes in the social imagination/organization of their shared life-world, implicitly portraying collective action as "simply" voluntaristic. On the other hand, in its focus on "rethinking [the] subversive possibilities for sexuality and identity within the terms of power itself,"[31] it fails to explore how the concatenations of local "strategies of subversive repetition" crystallize into new constellations of relationship and position, i.e., how they cohere as "movements." Actually, as far as I can tell both of these are probably the "same" problem—that is, the problem of what the theory defines as the ground of the "same." For, while Butler assiduously abjures any recourse to an essentializing model of gender that is predicated on the ontological or metaphysical priority of the body, she does so precisely by invoking a parallel somatic idealization: "the body is not a 'being,' but a variable boundary, a surface whose permeability is politically regulated, a signifying practice within a cultural field of gender hierarchy and compulsory heterosexuality."[32] By attempting to move gender out of the "depths" of bodies, Butler collapses bodies onto the "surface" of discourse reiterating the classic Cartesian mapping of mind onto/over body that inscribes individuation as "identity." As a consequence, while her endeavor to de-essentialize the "biological" ground of sexual sameness aspires to open up possibilities for exploring the complexity of how genders are embodied, it unfortunately forecloses this exploration by evacuating somatic practices, rendering "the body" as a "conceptual problem."

Given Butler's preference for feminist formulations garnished with French Freud, it's not surprising that her "problematic"—to use Foucault's framing—figures "the body" as "a variable boundary," "a surface," and a "signifying practice." For by displacing somatic materiality and intelligence onto/into discursive processes, Butler reiterates the founding psycho/somatic contradictions of psychoanalysis, contradictions that Lacan sought to resolve by dissolving the (e)motions of embodied experience in the diaspora of language. Yet, as Marcia Ian has recently suggested, this "Cartesian fetishization of language and image" radically circumscribes the locus of "lived experience" so that the productive (political) differences bodied forth by somatic individuation are elided by the totalizing "difference" of signification.[33] Dissolved into discourse, post-Lacanian (political) "subjects" are (imagined to be) subjected to and the subjects of "effects" that are accreted metonymically across intersecting and interrupting terrains of signification; concomitantly, "they" are inscribed in a theoretical practice that evacuates embodied (e)motion from the "space" of its inquiry. How individuals come together to act for change, how these actors are changed by their activities, and how these acts and actors crystallize as movements cannot be adequately imagined if the powerful effects *felt* by acting subjects are "theoretically" disappeared. Thus, rather than simply opening up feminism's cultural possibilities, Butler's critique of "identity politics" simultaneously imposes its own limits and constraints by idealizing the "difference" that "the body" makes to "identity" politics.

Of course, it is always possible to find contradictions like these within any philosophical text. This is the "game of truth" that deconstruction teaches us to engage in: an intellectual hide and seek for hidden metaphysical presumptions. However, I'm playing this game here not to challenge Butler's analysis on epistemological grounds, but instead to tag it for failing—in a bad paraphrase of Stephen Heath's now infamous bon mot—"to risk metaphysics."[34] You see, I *feel* there *is* something "different" about the body: I *believe* feeling is the difference that bodies make, a difference that *moves* people to action. As far as I can tell, political movements are engendered by personal and political (e)motions that impel people—in the parlance of the old "New Left"—to put their bodies on the line. If we want to consider what it is that moves people to act together often in the face of manifest danger or violence in order to transform their collective life-worlds, then we must begin to take seriously the notion that political movements cohere only to the extent that they express and make meaningful the shared *feeling and knowledge* that things ought to and can become different than they are—i.e., to the extent that they touch and move people who touch and move each other. Ironically for identity politics, these shared feelings often frustrate the crystallization of an "identity" that is sometimes thought to be its precondition precisely because they provide the possibility for experiencing one's "own" body not as the site of (self-)differentiation but as the medium for creating transpersonal contiguities. Indeed, it would seem that any "movement" which predicates itself on an "identity" dooms itself to fragmentation in so far as it preempts the possibility of being moved by and/or beyond the (somatic) differences presupposed in the very "identity" that it defines. By advocating an understanding of political movements as embodied processes, then, I want to suggest both that bodies do make a (political) difference and that difference is often a matter of (e)motion.[35]

In thinking about political (e)motion as it touches gay men and lesbians, I have been moved by Minnie Bruce Pratt's stirring autobiographical essay, "Identity: Skin Blood Heart."[36] Here Pratt's account of her life oscillates between the parochial Alabama where she spent her WASP childhood and pre-political college years enmeshed in the embodied racist history of the American South; the intellectual Research Triangle, North Carolina, where she lived her increasingly politicized years of marriage and motherhood—until her (political/personal) relationship to herself and to others was radically transformed by her (sexual) relationships with other women; and the urban Washington, D.C., where her experiences as a white, Southern, Christian lesbian mother with a Northern Jewish lover living in a predominantly Black neighborhood of a predominantly Black Mid-Atlantic city provoke her acute reflections on the global implications of racism, sexism, anti-Semitism, and class. Appropriately, Pratt's essay arises from the effects of her own somatic movements: her awareness of her "self" as she walks the streets of her neighborhood initiates an intellectual trajectory that will carry her both back into the past (her own, "ours," America's, the world's) and forward into the future (which her writing of this memoir hopefully helps change) in order to highlight the traces which "our" history inscribes through the bodies of those who move within its time and space:

> . . . when I walk out in my neighborhood, each speaking-to another person has become fraught, for me, with the history of race and sex and class; as I walk I have a constant interior discussion with myself, questioning how I acknowledge the presence of another, what I know or don't know about them, and what it means how they acknowledge me. It is an exhausting process, this moving from the experience of the "unknowing majority" (as Maya Angelou called it) into consciousness. It would be a lie to say this process is comforting.[37]

Pratt's rumination on the exhausting *process* of becoming aware of the personal/political difference that differences make foregrounds the importance of understanding "who we are" not as a standing still but as a moving, as a speaking to and a being spoken to, as a being touched by and as a touching. With her perambulations through the city, through the past, and through the text, she illustrates the laborious and often painful creativity needed to engender these narrative fragments about her "identity" while simultaneously displaying the gaps and fissures, the cracks and wounds, that rend this construct even as— or before—it is imagined. The places and people and buildings and stories that run together in Pratt's "autobiography" reveal her "self" as multiple sets of relationships—with herself, her parents, her children, her lover, her friends, her husband, her childhood community, her college cohort, as well as with people on the streets, buses, and trains of D.C., in the supermarkets, in the governments, and in the other nations of the world—relationships whose consanguinity almost necessarily exceed the constraints of representational spaces. As Biddy Martin and Chandra Talpade Mohanty have recently observed of this essay,

> one of the most striking aspects of "Identity: Skin Blood Heart" is the text's movement away from the purely personal, visceral experience of identity suggested by the title to a complicated working out of the relationship between home, identity and community that calls into question the notion of a coherent, historically continuous, stable identity and works to expose the political stakes concealed in such equations.[38]

In working to enact its own significance, Pratt's writing shows itself as an always incomplete and always being completed construction of "identity"—"construction" here underscoring the sense, as Marcia Ian has recently suggested, that the world is both made and made up. Drawing upon the therapeutic project that framed Freudian psychoanalysis, Ian characterizes "construction" as an intersubjective process that impinges upon and transforms people's somatic, psychic, and social "reality":

> A construction unites image and interpretation, symbol and history, icon and narrative in a conception which moves its audience to "complete and extend the construction"; it is in this sense that construction adds to the richness of its perceiver's life by leaving him or her not "untouched." Being touched in this sense makes it possible for individuals "to give up repressions (using the word in its widest sense) belonging to early development and to replace them by reactions of a sort that would correspond to a psychically mature

condition." If a discourse which acknowledges the extent to which
it is constructed can do for a society what psychoanalytic construction can do for an individual, then it matters what "bits" we add to
the construction always in process around us, what values we endorse in our critical writing, whether we are sexist, elitist, unfeeling,
sentimental, or otherwise backward.[39]

If Pratt's construction of reality leaves me "not untouched," if it inspires me to "complete and extend the construction" here, it is precisely
because her narrative demonstrates the insufficiency of "identity" as a
paradigm for *knowing and feeling* one's way through the world. In her
relentless "self"-questioning, Pratt illustrates how the self "always
already" includes others whom we touch and by whom we are touched.
Using the trope of movement to splay out the apparent self-contain-
ment of her body, "Skin Blood Heart," across the dimensions of time
and space, Pratt's writing resists the eponymous fiction "identity" as
that which militates against construction of a world where racism,
sexism, class oppression, homophobia, and anti-Semitism no longer
touch us:

> I'm trying to learn how to live, to have the speaking-to extend
> beyond the moment's word, to act so as to change the unjust circum-
> stances that keep us from being able to speak to each other; I'm
> trying to get a little closer to the longed-for but unrealized world,
> where we each are able to live, but not by trying to make someone
> less than us, not by someone else's blood or pain: yes, that's what
> I'm trying to do with my living now.[40]

What Pratt's wandering teaches, then, is that the "living now" that
bodies forth possibilities for future transformations is itself a movement. Across, within, and through time and space, we trace out the
trajectories of our (e)motions, always crossing and being crossed,
touching upon and being touched by the (e)motions of others. In this
mobile and transformational life-context, "affection" (which may or
may not be "sexual desire") becomes one of a number of impelling
forces that move us to realign, interrupt, or alter our trajectories,
challenging us to join with, observe, deny, ignore, or resist the movements that are coalescing within and around us.

Coda

So where, then, do these ruminations leave/lead "us"? How does
my dis-ease about "identity" move away from the constraints and

fragmentation that I fear it produces? Why does my belief that the body matters more than can be said make a personal/political difference? To tell the truth, I don't know. Quite possibly because it is not a matter of "knowing." At least not for me. At least not for now. And yet I hope that there is something here which may be of use to someone besides my "self." I hope that there is something in this "construction" that will touch and move those who (will) touch and move me. But these hopes are not directed towards those who are "the same as" me. They are not intended as extensions or confirmations of my "identity." Rather they are part of the political (e)motion that characterizes how my "gayness" moves me. In this regard I have been profoundly influenced by Michel Foucault's admonition that

> we must be aware of . . . the tendency to reduce being gay to the questions: "Who am I?" and "What is the secret of my desire?." Might it not be better if we asked ourselves what sort of relationships we can set up, invent, multiply or modify through our homosexuality? The problem is not trying to find out the truth of one's sexuality within oneself, but rather, nowadays, trying to use our sexuality to achieve a variety of different types of relationships. And this is why homosexuality is probably not a form of desire, but something to be desired. We must therefore insist on *becoming* gay, rather than persist in defining ourselves as such.[41]

Foucault's suggestion that instead of defining ourselves as "gay" or "lesbian" we attempt to create ourselves as "becoming" such seems to offer an important advantage for imagining how to use "personal" (e)motions to engender political movements that validate the power of personal/political affect(ion)s. For if we can begin to gather together on the basis of constructions that "we" are constantly and self-consciously in the process of inventing, multiplying, and modifying, then perhaps "we" can obviate the need for continuing to reiterate the fragmenting oscillations between identity and difference that have been the legacy of post 1960s progressive politics.

As far as I can tell, the problem with "movements" based on "identity" is that by seeking change on the basis of a concept which is itself unchanging, they will almost inevitably and painfully contradict themselves. This is not to say that contradiction is wrong or bad, only that it confounds "identity" and as such qualifies the efficacy of groups organizing under this rubric. Indeed, part of what I would like to suggest is that by incorporating ("self"-)contradictions into the processes of political transformation as moments/sites of possibility, movements may be able to consciously affirm the political significance of their own complex (e)motions rather than be driven, and riven, by the struggle to "fix" identity. Such a validation of collective process as political practice would then encourage the imagination and creation of new skills that would allow us to think simultaneously about the trajectory and the quality of political (e)motions rather than dissecting these apart as body/mind, ends/means, or identity/difference. This possibility seems especially important when we are considering political collectivities that seek to affirm the validity of eccentric "sexual" relationships, since after all our affect(ion)s are what bring us together anyway.

When I told my friend Elizabeth that I was working on an essay about "gay" politics called "Who Are 'We'?" she laughed at me. "That's great," she chortled, "and who are 'you' to write this piece?" Now we're good friends, so I understood her comment as a gentle rebuke to my ego, which does sometimes tend towards having the subtlety of a steamroller; however, her comment has lingered with me throughout the months that I have been ruminating over this text, prodding me to keep asking myself why I want this title. The answer I come back to again and again is contained in the relation between the epigraphs that I chose when I started to write:

> But the problem is, precisely, to decide if it is actually suitable to place oneself within a "we" in order to assert the principles one recognizes and the values one accepts; or if it is not, rather, necessary to make the future formation of a "we" possible, by elaborating the question. Because it seems to me that the "we" must not be previous to the question; it can only be the result—and necessarily the temporary result—of the question as it is posed in the new terms in which one formulates it.   *Michel Foucault*

> I have always known that I learn my most lasting lessons about difference by closely attending to the ways in which the differences inside me lie down together.   *Audre Lorde*

For me, the significance of these quotations lies in the ensuing question that they evoke: *How can we affirm a relational and transformational politics of self that takes as its process and its goal the interruption of those practices of differentiation that (re)produce historically specific patterns of privilege and oppression?* "I" certainly don't have the answer, but I do believe that if we begin to ask the question this way "we" might become differently.

Notes

1. Michel Foucault, "Polemics, Politics, and Problematizations: An Interview with Michel Foucault," *The Foucault Reader,* ed. Paul Rabinow (New York: Pantheon, 1984), 385.

2. Audre Lorde, *A Burst of Light* (Ithaca, New York: Firebrand Books, 1988), 117–18.

3. John D'Emilio, *Sexual Politics, Sexual Communities: The Making of a Homosexual Minority in the United States, 1940–1970* (Chicago: University of Chicago Press, 1983).

4. Steven Epstein, "Gay Politics, Ethnic Identity: The Limits of Social Constructionism," *Socialist Review* 17, no. 3/4 (May/August 1987): 19.

5. Audre Lorde has eloquently formulated this problem in her most recent book of essays:

> I see certain pitfalls in defining Black as a political position. It takes the cultural identity of a widespread but definite group and makes it a generic identity for many culturally diverse peoples, all on the basis of a shared oppression. This runs the risk of providing a convenient blanket of apparent similarity under which our actual and unaccepted differences can be distorted or misused. This blanket would diminish our chances of forming genuine working coalitions built upon the recognition and creative use of acknowledged difference, rather than upon the shaky foundations of a false sense of similarity. (67)

From another perspective, Howard Winant considers the political implications of "post-modern racial politics" in "Postmodern Racial Politics in the United States: Difference and Equality," *Socialist Review* 20, no. 1 (January 1990): 121–47. Also see Diana Fuss's discussion of essentialism in African-American literary theory in *Essentially Speaking: Feminism, Nature and Difference* (New York: Routledge, 1989), 73–96.

6. Gayle Rubin, "The Traffic in Women," *Towards an Anthropology of Women,* ed. Rayna Reiter (New York: Monthly Review Press, 1975).

7. Epstein, "Gay Politics," 47–48.

8. Fuss, *Essentially Speaking,* 103.

9. Jacques Derrida, *Positions,* trans. Alan Bass (Chicago: University of Chicago Press, 1981), 41.

10. Philip Gleason, "Identifying Identity: A Semantic History," *Journal of American History* 69, no. 4 (March 1983): 911.

11. John Locke, *Essays Concerning Human Understanding* (London: George Bell and

Sons, 1892), 462–63. The O.E.D. uses the first sentence of this quotation as its example of "identity" as it qualifies the character of human individuation.

12. While Macpherson is using the generic "man" here to designate humans generally, his analysis would have been considerably enhanced had he understood the gendered implications of this assertion. In my book, *Talk on the Wilde Side: Towards a Genealogy of Male Sexualities* (New York: Routledge, forthcoming), I attempt to flesh out the ways that bourgeois masculinity in England during the late 18th and early 19th centuries was imagined precisely as the supreme embodiment of "possessive individualism," an embodiment which conversely worked to circumscribe the parameters of "normal masculinity."

13. C. B. Macpherson, *The Political Theory of Possessive Individualism* (Oxford: Oxford University Press, 1962), 3.

14. John Locke, *Second Treatise in Two Treatises of Government,* ed. Peter Laslett (Cambridge: Cambridge University Press, 1960), sec. 27.

15. Although it occurs in an entirely different context, Derrida's meditation in "White Mythology" on the movements between "property," "properties," and "the proper"—to which I would add, apropos of post-Enlightenment bourgeois culture, "propriety"—suggests to me here that what is "of essence" in the imagination of Western subjectivity is the fixing of the living human body as "soma"—i.e., as a corpse. Quite a scary notion of "fixing," I feel/fear. See Jacques Derrida, "White Mythology," *Margins of Philosophy,* trans. Alan Bass (Chicago: University of Chicago Press, 1982), 207–72.

16. Michel Foucault, *The History of Sexuality Vol. 1,* trans. Robert Hurley (New York: Vintage, 1980), 140.

17. Foucault, *History,* 47.

18. Foucault, *History,* 154.

19. Michel Foucault, "The Subject and Power," *Michel Foucault: Beyond Structuralism and Semiotics,* eds. Hubert Dreyfus and Paul Rabinow (Chicago: University of Chicago Press, 1982), 211.

20. Foucault, *History,* 123.

21. Foucault, *History,* 123.

22. Foucault, *The Use of Pleasure,* trans. Robert Hurley (New York: Vintage, 1985), 6.

23. Maria Daraki, "Michel Foucault's Journey to Greece," *Telos* 67 (Spring 1986): 87–110.

24. Foucault, *Pleasure,* 10–11.

25. Foucault, *Pleasure,* 6.

26. Foucault, "Subject," 209.

27. Foucault, "Polemics," 375.

28. Foucault, "Polemics," 385.

29. Judith Butler, *Gender Trouble: Feminism and the Subversion of Identity* (New York and London: Routledge, 1990), 3. References immediately following are cited in the text.

30. Epstein, "Gay Politics," 19.

31. Butler, *Gender Trouble,* 30.

32. Butler, *Gender Trouble,* 139.

33. Marcia Ian, "Two's Company, Three's a Construction: Psychoanalysis and the Failure of Identity" (paper delivered at the Rutgers Center for Historical Analysis, New Brunswick, New Jersey, February 6, 1990).

34. Heath's precise words are "the risk of essence may have to be taken." See "Difference," *Screen* 19, no. 3 (Autumn 1978): 99.

35. There is a part of me which fears that in my advocacy of re-problematizing the knowing/feeling distinction, I am simply attempting to redress an imbalance that has plagued me ever since adolescence, when I became painfully aware that my feelings for other men and boys were a "problem" and as a consequence I retreated into the acceptability of intellectual—if not biblical—"knowledge." However, I am taking the risk of seeming "overly naive" here in affirming the importance of theorizing "(e)motion" because I believe that my experience, rather than being anomalous, is at once personal and political, individual and collective.

36. Minnie Bruce Pratt, "Identity: Skin Blood Heart," *Yours in Struggle: Three Feminist Perspectives on Anti-Semitism and Racism,* E. Bulkin, M. B. Pratt, and B. Smith (Brooklyn, New York: Long Haul Press, 1984), 10–63.

37. Pratt, "Identity," 12.

38. Biddy Martin and Chandra Talpade Mohanty, "Feminist Politics: What's Home Got to Do with It?," *Feminist Studies/Critical Studies,* ed. Teresa de Lauretis (Bloomington: Indiana University Press, 1986), 195.

39. Ian, "Two's Company," 21.

40. Pratt, "Identity," 13.

41. Michel Foucault, "Friendship as a Lifestyle: An Interview with Michel Foucault," *Gay Information* 7 (Spring 1981): 4. Translation modified.

4

Seeing Things: Representation, the Scene of Surveillance, and the Spectacle of Gay Male Sex

Lee Edelman

In 1810 an angry London mob attacked a group of men who were being taken to the pillory after having been convicted of assault with the intent to commit sodomy in the back room of a Vere Street pub. As Louis Crompton observes in *Byron and Greek Love,* the journalistic reports detailing the violence wreaked by the thousands who participated in this scene prompted Louis Simond, a French visitor to England, to make the following notation in the journal he kept: "We have just read in all the newspapers a full and disgusting account of the public and cruel punishment on the pillory of certain wretches convicted of vile indecencies. I can conceive of nothing more dangerous, offensive, and unwise, than the brutality and unrestrained publicity of such infliction. The imagination itself is sullied by the exposition of enormities, that ought never to be supposed to exist."[1]

These comments repudiate the virulence of the mob, but only by suggesting that such scenes of brutality make evident the brutalizing effects on the populace of any public discourse on sexual relations between men—effects that cannot be avoided even when such discourse is generated to make possible the prosecution of "wretches" who commit "vile indecencies." The horrifying spectacle of the riotous mob pelting the manacled convicts with, as one contemporary account reported, "mud, dead cats, rotten eggs, potatoes, and buckets filled with blood, offal, and dung,"[2] does not argue, in the passage from Simond, against the criminalizing of sodomitical relations, but functions, instead, as a displaced image of the interdicted sexual act: it figures forth, in other words, the infectious indecency of sodomy itself by reading the atrocities committed by the crowd as yet another effect of the "indecencies" that brought those "wretches" to the pillory in the first place. Such a sentiment was by no means unusual, of course; homosexuality, or more precisely, the bias toward sodomitical relations, already had assumed, by the time Simond wrote, its extraordinarily potent, though phobically charged, position within the signifying conventions of the West. It had already come to be construed, that is, as a behavior marked by a transgressive force that could be reproduced, not merely designated, by naming or discussing it. For it constituted, more than an assault upon the flesh, an assault upon the logic of social discourse, an assault so extreme that not only one's morals but even one's "imagination" could be sullied by the "exposition of enormities, that ought never to be supposed to exist."

It is worth pausing to consider the significance attached to this scandal of supposition in which horror and violent denial seem indissociable from the discursive representation of homosexuality itself. What wound, after all, can the scene of sodomy inflict to make its staging, if only in the space of the imagination, so dangerous to effect, and what within that scene has such power to implicate—and, by implicating, to sully—that such a scene, or even the possibility of such a scene, ought properly to be disavowed? Framed in these terms this scandal of supposition may begin to take shape in relation to the process whereby psychoanalysis articulates the constitution of masculine subjectivity: a process that centers on the crisis of representation through which the subject acquires knowledge of sexual difference. The sexual supposition that Simond would disallow may suggest, then, not only the undecidable question of presence or absence that inheres in any fetishistic supposition or belief, but also the male subject's normative interpretations or narrative accounts of sexual difference: the suppositions with which he responds to the "law" of castration and his retroactive understanding of what Freud defines as "the primal scene." I want to examine that scene and its framing in *From the History of an Infantile Neurosis*—Freud's analysis of the Wolf Man, as his patient has subsequently come to be known—both because that case engages explicitly the question of sexual supposition and because it does so by invoking the representation of a sodomitical encounter.

Let me be clear about my purpose at the outset, however: I aim neither to privilege nor to repudiate the psychoanalytic paradigm; rather, I hope to read its relationship to the inscriptions of sodomy in the primal scene as a response to the sodomitical implications of the scene of psychoanalysis itself. For that reason, along with Freud's account of the primal scene as one in which the supposition of homosexuality is embedded, I want to examine, if only briefly, passages from a number of other texts that suppose the scene of sodomy between men: passages from John Cleland's *Memoirs of a Woman of Pleasure,* Tobias Smollett's *Adventures of Peregrine Pickle,* and Jacques Derrida's *The Post Card.* In each case a presumptively heterosexual spectator's unobserved surveillance of a sexual encounter between men occasions certain narrative and tropological effects that operate in Freud's case history as well; but rather than construing the Freudian analysis as a master-discourse with which to illuminate the more explicitly literary passages, or, alternatively, using the literary passages to deconstruct Freudian psychoanalysis, I want to observe how in each of these texts homosexuality comes to signify as a distinctively literary or rhetorical operation in its own right. Though read differently at different historical moments, the inscription of homosexuality within a sodomitical scene proves scandalous in all of these quite different texts not because it occupies a position *outside* the rules of social discourse, but precisely because it operates from *within* those rules to suggest the instability of positioning that is sexuality itself.

Perhaps it is appropriate to try to make clear the direction from which I want to come at these issues by noting that the problem I want to address is the problem, at least in part, of how one comes at a problem: from what direction, that is, one approaches it and in what position one chooses to engage it. Freud's metapsychological theories, after all, repeatedly articulate a structural return to a trauma occasioned by an earlier event that has no existence *as a scene of trauma* until it is (re)presented—or (re)produced—as a trauma in the movement of return itself. His theories, in this way, define a psychic experience in which the most crucial and constitutive dramas of human life are those that can never be viewed head on, those that can never be taken in frontally, but only, as it were, approached from behind. As Mary Ann Doane has recently observed, "The psychical layer Freud designated perception-consciousness is frequently deceived, caught from behind by unconscious forces which evade its gaze."[3]

Not for nothing, therefore, in his analytic (re)construction of the Wolf Man's primal scene, does Freud propose that the sexual encounter observed (or fantasized) by the Wolf Man in his infancy involved his parents in what Freud envisions as an act of coitus *a tergo;* for along with the other ways in which this interpretation serves Freud's purpose, such a posture conveniently allegorizes both the retroactive understanding whereby the primal scene will subsequently generate its various effects, and the practice of psychoanalysis itself to the extent that it approaches experience from behind through the analyst's efforts to replicate the distinctive logic of the unconscious.[4] Psychoanalysis, in other words, not only theorizes about but also operates by means of the (re)construction or reinterpretation of earlier experiences in ways that evoke the temporal logic distinctive of deferred action; and as a result of what Laplanche and Pontalis describe as the "unevenness of its temporal development," human sexuality constitutes the most significant arena in which the effects of deferred action, or *Nachträglichkeit,* come into play.[5] With this theory psychoanalysis refuses any unidirectional understanding of the temporality of psychic development; instead, it questions the logic of the chronological and the determinate relationship of cause and effect. If temporal revisions and inversions, then, mark the production of psychoanalytic narrative, the very articulation of psychoanalytic logic can be construed in terms of metalepsis, the rhetorical substitution of cause for effect or effect for cause, a substitution that disturbs the relationship of early and late, or before and behind.[6] And nowhere is this metaleptic structure—a structure I propose to discuss as "(be)hindsight" so as to figure its complicitous involvement in the sodomitical encounter—more evident than in Freud's theorization of the Wolf Man's primal scene.

Perhaps it is not irrelevant, then, to remind ourselves that the Wolf Man, in his earliest psychoanalytic transferences, believed that Freud himself desired to "use [him] from behind."[7] At the time that he made this comment, of course, the Wolf Man did not have access to what Freud would "uncover" as his primal scene—a scene in which, according to Freud, the Wolf Man observed at first hand what being used from behind entailed. Indeed, in Freud's formulation of it, the primal scene itself can never be recollected or brought forward into consciousness but only, at best, pieced together during the analytic process: "scenes, like this one in my present patient's case, which date from such an early period and exhibit a similar content, and which further lay claim to such an extraordinary significance for the history of the case, are as a rule not reproduced as recollections, but have to be divined—constructed—gradually and laboriously from an aggregate of indications."[8] Thus the supposition or construction of the primal scene is the effect of the analyst's interpretation of symptoms that subsequently will be determined to have been, themselves, effects of that constructed scene; this disarticulation of temporal logic in what I have chosen to call "(be)hindsight" exemplifies the metaleptic structure of the psychoanalytic hypothesis, especially when the trope of metalepsis is considered, as Marquerite Waller has aptly phrased it, as a "rhetorical moebius loop."[9]

Now what distinguishes the moebius loop, of course, is the impossibility of distinguishing its front from its back, a condition that has, as I have already implied, an immediate sexual resonance; but that indistinguishability bespeaks as well a crisis of certainty, a destabilizing of the foundational logic on which knowledge as such depends. Thus if *From the History of an Infantile Neurosis,* in its elaboration of the primal scene, enacts a psychoanalytic method as metaleptic as the moebius loop, the self-questioning hesitancy with which Freud responds to his own positing of that scene betrays the effects of the moebius loop's epistemological disruptions; for no other case history testifies so powerfully to the psychoanalyst's inability to decide where to position himself with regard to his theoretical insights. As Nicholas Abraham and Maria Torok observe in discussing Freud's analysis of the Wolf Man: "Polemical in its explicit purpose, it also reflects another debate, that of the author with himself. Throughout this stirring account and within the meanderings of the theoretical discussion, attentive readers will sense a doubt—it is Freud's doubt regarding his own statements."[10] Indeed, throughout the case history of the Wolf Man the insistence of such doubt reflects Freud's deep anxiety that the primal scene occupying the very center of his analysis may prove to be only an illicit supposition of something that ought never to be supposed to exist.

Certainly the audacity of the scene Freud calls forth might justify such an anxiety: that the parents of a one-and-a-half-year-old boy—a boy who was suffering at the time from malaria—would engage in sexual relations three times while the child rested in the same room— let alone that those relations would feature penetration from behind— and that all of this would take place around five o'clock on a summer afternoon, represents, within its discursive context, so sensational an erotic vision that Freud must initially defend his construction by flatly denying that there is anything sensational in this scenario at all: "On the contrary," he writes, "such an event would, I think, be something entirely commonplace and *banal*" (38). Later, however, in an addition to the manuscript, when he undertakes to reconsider the primal scene's "reality," Freud proposes that prior to his dream of the wolves, the child may have witnessed "not copulation between his parents but copulation between animals, which he then displaced on to his parents" (57). Freud goes on to acknowledge that with this supposition "the demands on our credulity are reduced. We need no longer suppose that the parents copulated in the presence of their child (a very young one, it is true)—which was a disagreeable idea for many of us" (58). That Freud designates here as straining credulity what he first described as banal, that he now presents as a "disagreeable idea" what he first called "entirely commonplace," bespeaks the ambivalence of his position and the extent of what Abraham and Torok describe as his "doubt regarding his own statements."

Now Freud himself offered a provocative insight into the nature of such doubt and the etiology of such ambivalence in a letter written in another context to Lou Andreas-Salomé. "Your derivation of the phenomenon of doubt," he tells her, "is too intellectual, too rational. The tendency to doubt arises not from any occasion for doubt, but is the continuation of the powerful ambivalent tendencies in the pregenital phase, which from then on become attached to every pair of opposites."[11] In this Freudian genealogy, the doubt that attaches to such binary oppositions as cause and effect, or before and behind, represents the carrying forward of an ambivalence associated with the oral and anal stages of libidinal organization, stages in which, as Freud puts it, "it is . . . a question of *external* and *internal*. What is unreal, merely a presentation and subjective, is only internal; what is real is also there *outside*."[12] This description appears in Freud's essay on negation, or *Verneinung,* the psychic defense he employs in denying that the erotic spectacle he initially proposed as essential to the primal scene exceeds in any way the merely commonplace and banal. Freud's subsequent ambivalence, his expression of doubt about the status of the scene as either internal or external, imagined or real, bears the traces, therefore, of a pre-genital survival according to his own analysis; and since the mobilization of that doubt seeks to expel or cast out an anxiety about the ontological condition of the most, as it were, *fundamental* theoretical construct at work in his reading of the Wolf Man, it carries more specifically the psychic inscription of the anal-erotic organization.[13]

It is all the more significant, therefore, that anal-erotic fixation and the tendency toward doubt that it is said to produce figure centrally in the Wolf Man's neurosis as Freud construes it in this case history. After all, Freud attempts to account not only for the Wolf Man's predilection for heterosexual relations in which he penetrates his partner from behind, but also for the patient's inability to move his bowels without an enema administered by a male attendant. Freud attributes to this anal fixation, moreover, the skepticism with which the Wolf Man first resisted his spiritual indoctrination into Christian piety. Freud sees in this questioning of orthodox belief the Wolf Man's desire to perpetuate his infantile erotic attachment to his father in the face of the overwhelming uncertainties and doubts occasioned by the dream of the wolves that

Freud interprets as signaling the analysand's deferred understanding of the primal scene. These doubts find expression, tellingly enough, in the Wolf Man's need to determine whether or not Christ "had a behind" (63) and consequently experienced the necessity of defecation. "We catch a glimpse," Freud goes on to declare, "of [the Wolf Man's] repressed homosexual attitude in his doubting whether Christ could have a behind, for these ruminations can have had no other meaning but the question whether he himself could be used by his father like a woman—like his mother in the primal scene" (64); his doubt, that is, expresses an anxiety about his own desire to be used from behind—a desire whose fulfillment seems now necessarily to subject him to the law of castration. But we only "catch a glimpse" of this structure by coming at the primal scene itself through "(be)hindsight," and Freud's interrogation within this case history of his belief in the theoretical insights he produces by approaching the scene from this direction takes shape at once as a resistance to, and an unwitting reinscription of, the disorienting confusion between outside and inside, real and imagined, analyst and analysand in the articulation of the primal scene. Freud, to put it another way, tries to distance his method from the anal-eroticism he identifies as characteristic of the Wolf Man by casting doubt upon the coitus *a tergo* that Freud himself had initially envisioned in his approach to the primal scene through analytic "(be)-hindsight"; but that very doubt, however tendentiously it seeks to differentiate Freud's eros from the Wolf Man's, only reenacts the doubt or skepticism that Freud has already specified as an index of the Wolf Man's anal-eroticism. Freud's ambivalence about the vision of penetration from behind generates, in consequence, a certain defensiveness about the status of his own analytic hypothesis—a defensiveness that may tell us a great deal about the danger posed by the vision of the sodomitical scene.

For Freud exposes himself at his most self-protective when he responds, in a section of *From the History of an Infantile Neurosis* that he sets aside for just this purpose, to suggestions that what he labels as primal scenes are not "real occurrences" with a historical basis in the experience of the infant, but only "products of the imagination, which find their instigation in mature life" and thus constitute nothing more than phantasies that "owe their origin to a regressive tendency" (49). While acknowledging that such a "regressive tendency . . . [is] regularly confirmed by analysis" (53), and even going so far as to take credit for having been the one to identify such tendencies in the first place,[14] Freud denies that the theory of psychoanalysis demands that the primal scene be read as a mere retroactive phantasy. Defending his belief in the reality of such scenes, he argues instead that the early outbreak of the Wolf Man's obsessional neurosis demonstrably "limits the regressive part of the causation" and "brings into full view the portion of it which operates in a forward direction" (55).

What Freud, I would argue, feels called upon to limit in relation to this critical scene is a particular reading of the metaleptic structure that marks psychoanalysis as a coming from behind; he cannot allow the primal scene that he still views here as real and central to the course of the Wolf Man's neurosis to be interpreted as merely a *phantasmatic* effect of the effects it is alleged to have produced. He needs, instead, to affirm the possibility of its operation in a "forward direction"—an operation that Freud wants to "bring into full view" in the context of a case that will, if successful, "give a clear picture of this position of things" (55). Freud's defense of his theory of the primal scene thus depends upon his ability to "bring into full view" a "clear picture" of the "forward direction" of the effects produced by the primal scene, a scene that itself can only be constructed metaleptically, put together *a posteriori*, through the "aggregate indications" of those effects themselves. To complicate further the "clear picture" Freud would offer, the "forward direction" of the scene's effects must be viewed in the context of an erotic scene whose thematic content explicitly focuses on the question of what can or cannot be viewed, and on the specific positions that the actors must occupy in order for the observer to be able to view specific "things" without obstruction; it is a scene, therefore, that permits a "clear" view only when the act of intercourse at its center does not take place in a "forward direction" but occurs, instead, from behind. Only thus, after all, is it possible for the spectator to gain visual access to what later will register as the signifying presence of the father's penis in relation to what at that point will be construed as the problematical absence of the mother's, an absence that will be attributed, metaleptically, to the mother's submission to the father's desire.

Freud performs in this passage an elaborate dance of forward and backward, before and behind—not a fox-trot, but a Freudian Wolf-trot perhaps; and the rigorous confusion that characterizes this attempt to present a "clear picture of [the] position of things," expresses his concern that the mere envisioning of this scene, with its spectacular representation of penetration from behind, may color or call into question the position of the analyst—or even of psychoanalysis itself—in relation to the man on the analyst's couch. For the primal scene, as

Freud reconstructs the perspective of the infant at the moment he observes it,[15] activates the pre-genital supposition "that sexual intercourse takes place at the anus" (78). Thus in the first instance the primal scene is always perceived as sodomitical, and it specifically takes shape as a sodomitical scene between sexually undifferentiated partners, both of whom, phantasmatically at least, are believed to possess the phallus. In a sense, then, the primal scene as Freud unpacks it presupposes the imaginative priority of a sort of proto-homosexuality, and it designates male heterosexuality, by contrast, as a later narcissistic compromise that only painfully and with difficulty represses its identification with the so-called "passive" position in that scene so as to protect the narcissistically invested penis from the fate that is assumed to have befallen the penis of the mother.[16] Insofar as the participants in the primal scene are as yet undifferentiated sexually to the infant who observes them—both, that is, in the logic of Freudian theory, are seen as phallic—it is small wonder that he has little difficulty in experiencing an identification with each of their positions; but insofar as that scene must thereafter bear traces of sodomitical phantasy and homosexual desire, it is small wonder that Freud has great difficulty indeed in allowing himself or his psychoanalytic practice to be implicated in the scene at all. The "(be)hindsight" of psychoanalysis produces a correspondence too close for comfort.

One pragmatic reason for such discomfort becomes apparent when Freud responds to the charge that the primal scene is not only a retroactive phantasy, but a phantasy whose origin must be attributed to the analyst rather than to the analysand. He ventriloquizes this line of reasoning as follows: "what is argued now is evidently that they are phantasies not of the patient but of the analyst himself, who forces them upon the person under analysis on account of some complexes of his own" (52). The supposition or imagining of the sodomitical scene so destabilizes the division between real and imagined, external and internal, patient and analyst, that the psychoanalyst's imagining of the scene itself can be read as a figural enactment of that scene: for the analyst is now subject to representation as one who "forces" himself surreptitiously "upon the person under analysis," imposing himself, like the unconscious, in a way that evades the patient's gaze. He is accused, that is, at bottom, of wanting to "use [his patient] from behind" not only by the Wolf Man in his early imaginary or transferential relation to the analyst, but also by real, external critics of psychoanalysis as he practices it.

This charge, to which Freud's text responds as it is leveled by such contemporaries as Jung and Adler, has received more recent formulation in an essay by Stanley Fish. "Freud reserves to himself," Fish argues, " . . . the pleasure of total mastery. It is a pleasure that is intensely erotic, . . . affording the multiple satisfactions of domination, penetration, and engulfment."[17] Though Fish identifies, correctly in my view, Freud's implication in the primal scene's coitus *a tergo,* neither pleasure nor mastery seems adequate as a description of his response to that implication. Rather, the fancy rhetorical footwork he performs in an effort to keep the forward and backward directions of psychoanalytic operations and sexual encounters from corresponding too exactly suggests the precariousness of his relation to a scene that cannot be viewed without wounding the non-homosexually identified spectator who is positioned to observe it. After all, as Freud himself understands, no possible response can dissuade his accusers from reading the primal scene as a phantasy that reveals the analyst's psychological "complexes," his own "perverse" desires. "On the one side," he notes with resignation, "there will be a charge of subtle self-deception, and on the other of obtuseness of judgment; it will be impossible to arrive at a decision" (53).

If the supposition of the primal scene calls forth this radical indeterminacy that threatens to put the analyst in the position of the patient, that same indeterminacy more famously informs Freud's final remark concerning the ontological status of the scene itself: "I intend on this occasion," he declares, in a passage added after he had finished the manuscript of his text, "to close the discussion of the reality of the primal scene with a *non liquet*" (60), that is, with a legal determination that the evidence is insufficient. But the Latin phrase thus appropriated by the law means literally "it is not clear," and this denial of clarity thus marks a return of the optical metaphor always at issue in the thematics of the primal scene. By affirming a lack of clarity in the perspective from which he would undertake to view or "catch a glimpse" of that theoretically indispensable scene, Freud situates himself unresolvedly before the very *analytic* scene in which the Wolf Man's primal scene was metaleptically constructed. His acknowledgment, in other words, of a conceptual opacity within the scene of psychoanalysis, an opacity that betokens a node of resistance internal to the *theorization* of the primal scene, reenacts the resistance of the Wolf Man, after his "recognition" of castration, to his spectatorial involvement in the primal scene as originally construed. In each case, a sexual theory undergoes revisionary rearticulation in order to protect the theorist from implication in the spectacle as he initially envisioned it.

Thus the Wolf Man's sexual theory, as Freud argues, at the moment he witnessed the primal scene, centered on his identification with the pleasure derived from (what he took to be) the penetration of the anus, a "penetration" that should be read as describing both the act of penetrating and the act of being penetrated. This double identification allowed him imaginatively to inhabit the positions of both his mother and his father in the spectacle of coitus *a tergo;*[18] but that theoretical positioning was psychically rewritten with the dream that insisted on castration as the price of gratifying what Freud defines as the patient's "homosexual enthusiasm" (78). And the dream that marks (and/or effects) this theoretical revision crucially features a reassignment of spectatorial positions as well, so that the child who viewed the primal scene (and in the process experienced the pleasure of multiple erotic identifications) dreams that he himself has now become the *object* of observation (and consequently experiences the paranoid fear that he must suffer for his earlier experience of spectatorial satisfaction). Similarly, the psychoanalyst whose theory makes the primal scene visible within the theater of analysis in order to "give a clear picture" of how psychological trauma can sneak up from behind, belatedly redefines as a "disagreeable idea" the coitus *a tergo* that he first described as "entirely commonplace and *banal."* The theorist who sought to produce a "clear picture" produces, in response to the criticism of analysts who would turn his own methods against him and make him the object of their professional gaze, a theory in which the anxious-making "picture" of the primal scene must not be made too clear; for as the analytic scene and the primal scene uncontrollably collapse into one another, Freud can only conclude with a *non liquet,* declaring his inability to specify with any clarity the meaning of either one.

This inability testifies to the destabilization of definitional barriers and to the undoing of the logic of positionality effected by the sodomitical spectacle; it thus makes possible the identification of Freud with the infant who observes and identifies with both participants in the primal scene. It puts the Freud, that is, who fails to resolve the theoretical status of the primal scene in the position he imagines the infant occupying *within* that scene itself, a position from which real and imagined, inside and outside, active and passive are so deeply and inextricably interwoven that he simultaneously identifies with positions that only later become mutually exclusive (op)positions. I would argue that this disorientation of positionality is bound up with the danger historically associated in Euro-American culture with the spectacle or representation of the sodomitical scene between men, and that this can be demonstrated by attending to the ways in which the logic of spatio-temporal positioning insistently marks our culture's framing of homosexual relations.

I mean by this something more than the fact that we are accustomed to using a metaphorics of "in" or "out" to measure an aspect of lesbian and gay political identity; I mean something that can be approximated more closely by noting that modern masculinist heterosexual culture conceptualizes lesbian and gay male sexuality in terms of a phallocentric positional logic, insistently (and dismissively) articulating lesbianism as a form of extended, non-productive foreplay and gay male sexual relations as a form of extended, non-productive behind-play. The scene of sodomy comes to figure, therefore, both a spatial disturbance in the logic of positions and a temporal disturbance in the logic essential to narrative development. In "Jenny Cromwell's Complaint Against Sodomy" (1692), the complainant, for example, looks back to a time "When Britains did encounter face to face/ And thought a back stroke trecherous and base"; but that lost time of "homely joys," was, as Jenny Cromwell tells us, before the "Reformation/ Turned all things Arsy-versy in the nation."[19] As this poem makes explicit, the practice of sodomy is construed as exemplifying a logic of reversal with widespread and uncontrollable implications—implications that reenact a "sodomitical" disturbance of temporal (and therefore narrative) positionality that threatens to reduce the play of history to the finality of an endgame.

Such disarticulations of positional logic find concise expression in a passage from John Cleland's *Memoirs of a Woman of Pleasure,* a novel in which Fanny Hill, that memorable woman of pleasure herself, celebrates all manner of erotic experience with the single and noteworthy exception of male-male sexual relations. Forced unexpectedly to amuse herself in a roadside "publick-house," Fanny discovers a "paper patch" concealing an opening in the moveable partition that divides her room from the one adjoining it. Piercing the patch with a needle, she manages to spy upon "two young sparks romping . . . in frolic, and innocent play."[20] Before long, however, their play turns amorous, and Fanny is able to discover, as she knowingly puts it, "what they were" (158); for theirs, in Fanny's significant phrase, is a "project of preposterous pleasure" (157). I focus on this phrase in particular because it signally condenses the disturbance of positionality that is located in and effected by the sodomitical scene; sodomy, that is, gets figured as the literalization of the "preposterous" precisely insofar as it is interpreted as the practice of giving precedence to the posterior and thus as confounding the stability or determinacy of linguistic or erotic positioning. Not surprisingly, this defiance of the order of meaning articulated through relations like before and behind—a defiance like that inherent in the very structure of the moebius loop—dominates Fanny's interest in the sexual spectacle played out before her, especially when she focuses on the erection sported by the young man being penetrated from the rear. "His red-topt ivory toy, that stood perfectly stiff," she scientifically notes, "shewed, that if he was like his mother behind, he was like his father before" (158).

The figural logic at work in this sentence must not pass unremarked, for the categories designated by "like his mother" and "like his father" bear a heavy conceptual burden. If Fanny's magnetized attention to the young man's "red-topt ivory toy" seems to specify exactly what she means in describing him as "like his father before," there remains, nonetheless, an element of opacity when she likens him to "his mother behind." Consider, for instance, that the syntax here allows as a perfectly proper interpretation of this sentence that the young man who, when seen from before, is like his father *when seen from before,* is simultaneously, when seen from behind, like his mother *when seen from behind;* the sentence, that is, could be construed to assert that where his penis represents a phallic endowment comparable in kind to that of his father, his buttocks represent a posterior endowment comparable in kind to that of his mother. But the sentence, as most readers of Cleland intuit, seems to signify something else instead: that the man who, from the front, is like his father from the front, is also, from the back, like his mother *from the front.* The sodomite, therefore, like the moebius loop, represents and enacts a troubling resistance to the binary logic of before and behind, constituting himself as a single-sided surface whose front and back are never completely distinguishable as such.

In order to bring fully into focus, however, the meaning of this metaphoric equation of the young man's anus and the mother's vagina, it is useful to remember that before and behind not only identify spatial positions, but gesture toward temporal relations as well. Psychoanalysis, of course, posits castration as the event that effects the temporal logic whereby what was perceived as phallic "before" becomes feminine "behind." Indeed, as Freud writes with specific reference to the Wolf Man's pathogenic dream, the eroticism associated with the posterior or the "behind" has, for men, a deep-seated relation to their emergent understanding of female sexuality in the wake of the castration complex:

We have been driven to assume that during the process of the dream he understood that women are castrated, that instead of a male organ they have a wound which serves for sexual intercourse, and that castration is the necessary condition of femininity; we have been driven to assume that the threat of this loss induced him to repress his feminine attitude toward men, and that he awoke from his homosexual enthusiasm in anxiety. Now how can this comprehension of sexual intercourse, this recognition of the vagina, be brought into harmony with the selection of the bowel for the purpose of identification with women? Are not the intestinal symptoms based on what is probably an older notion, and one which in any case completely contradicts the dread of castration—the notion, namely, that sexual intercourse takes place at the anus? (78)

Obedient to the law of castration—the law that plays out the fort/da logic of presence and absence so that "before" and "behind" can elaborate a sequencing of loss into a coherent narrative that offers itself as the basis for the binary organization of all logic and all thought[21]— the male here must repudiate the pleasures of the anus because their fulfillment allegedly presupposes, and inflicts, the loss or "wound" that serves as the very definition of femaleness. Thus the male who is terrorized into heterosexuality through his internalization of this de- termining narrative must embrace with all his narcissistic energy the phantom of a hierarchically inflected binarism always to be defended zealously. His anus, in turn, will be phobically charged as the site at which he traumatically confronts the possibility of becoming "like his mother," while the female genitalia will always be informed by their signifying relation to the anal eroticism he has had to disavow—a relation underscored by the Wolf Man's reference to the vagina as the female's "front bottom" (25).[22]

The scandal of the sodomitical scene, therefore, as Cleland has Fanny describe it, derives from its repudiation of the binary logic implicit in male heterosexualization and from its all too *visible* dismissal of the threat on which the terroristic empire of male heterosexuality has so effectively been erected. For the sodomite, after all, to be "like his mother behind" and *still* to be "like his father before," is apparently to validate the sexual theories and the libidinal cathexes of the infant as he observes the primal scene. Playing out the possibility of multiple, non-exclusive erotic identifications and positionings, the spectacle of sodomy would seem to confirm precisely those infantile sexual specula- tions that the male, coerced by the bogey of castration, is expected to have put behind him. It threatens to bring out of the closet, that is, the realization that the narcissistic compromise productive of male heterosexuality, the sacrifice of "homosexual enthusiasm" to defend against the prospect of castration, might not have been necessary after all. Indeed, the sodomitical spectacle, when viewed from this perspective, cannot fail to implicate the heterosexual male situated to observe it since it constitutes an affront to the primary narrative that orients his theory of sexuality. From such a vantage point it generates a response that can be interpreted as the negative counterpart or inversion, as it were, of fetishism and the fetishistic oversteeming of the object: for if the problem engaged in the fetish is that of affirming a belief in presence over and against the knowledge of loss, the problem produced by the scene of sodomy is that of affirming a belief in loss over and against the knowledge of presence. In order to uphold the law of castration, the male homosexual must be cut off from the social prerogatives associated with maleness, signified by the penis, precisely because the vision of male-male sodomy shows that the penis has *not* been cut off as castration should demand. Its presence in the order of anatomy must be transformed into an absence in the order of culture, thus complying with the logic of the signifying processes that derive from the articulation of sexual difference through the agency of castration. The sodomitical scene, in consequence, must be overwritten with a code, one essentially legislative, that effects a psychic translation of "to have" into "to have not."

The disappropriation of "proper" relationship in the episode narrated in Cleland's novel extends, therefore, beyond the two men whom Fanny subjects to her surveillance until it encompasses Fanny herself as an observer of that scene. In this regard it is important to bear in mind Nancy K. Miller's suggestion that Fanny must be viewed as "a male 'I' in female drag."[23] While this is true throughout the novel, the sodomitical encounter calls forth a particularly insistent thematic emphasis on the reversal of gender roles and expectations and the concomitant destabilization of binary logic for Fanny as an observer of the spectacle as well as for the two young men more actively involved. Fanny's very spectatorial position, for example, confers upon her the power to see without becoming an object of scrutiny herself—a power culturally coded as the prerogative of the heterosexual male—and it places her in the position associated in the Freudian scenario with the analyst or the unconscious, a position from which she can come upon the sodomitical spectacle from behind. And as she gains access to this spectacle by appropriating a male-coded position in the erotics of vision, she achieves that position by figuratively enacting the male role in a heterosexual script: by piercing, that is, the paper patch on the wall, a sort of textual hymen, with the bodkin or needle she carries, thereby revealing a hole or "flaw" (157) in the partition allowing intercourse between the two rooms. Moreover, as one last instance of sodomy's power to implicate those stationed to observe it, when Fanny indignantly determines to "raise the house" upon the "miscreants" whose "preposterous pleasure" has shown her that they don't know which end is up, she catches her foot unexpectedly on some "nail or ruggedness in the floor," which "fl[ings] [her] on [her] face with such violence, that [she] f[alls] senseless to the ground" (159). Lying unconscious—face down, bottom up—on this suddenly unreliable ground, Fanny embodies the instability of positioning that radiates out from the sodomitical scene and demonstrates that it was not without reason that Cleland named her Fanny after all.

A similar dissemination of reversals could be traced in the sodomitical episode recounted by Smollett in *The Adventures of Peregrine Pickle*. When Peregrine's companion, Pallet, observes an Italian count making amorous overtures to a sleeping German baron, he is "scandalized" by "such expressions of tenderness," and, becoming "conscious of his own attractions, [and] alarmed for his person" he flees the room and "put[s] himself under the protection" of the novel's eponymous hero, explaining to Peregrine the particulars of the "indecency" he has so distressingly observed.[24]

> Peregrine, who entertained a just detestation for all such abominable practices, was incensed at this information; and stepping to the door of the dining-room where the two strangers were left together, saw with his own eyes enough to convince him, that Pallet's complaint was not without foundation, and that the baron was not averse to the addresses of the count. Our young gentleman's indignation had well nigh prompted him to rush in, and take immediate vengeance on the offenders but, considering that such a precipitate step might be attended with troublesome consequences for himself, he resisted the impulse of his wrath, and tasked his invention with some method of inflicting upon them a disgrace suited to the grossness of their ideas. (242)

Despite his indignation at the "grossness" of this sodomitical vision, Peregrine dares not intervene for fear of "troublesome consequences to himself"—for fear, in other words, that any intervention, even if only to enact his revenge on the practitioners of vice, will lead to his being implicated in the "grossness" of the scene. But the very fact of his being prevented from intervening in this way identifies in itself his implication in the disturbances of positionality this spectacle effects; it demonstrates, that is, how his sexual authority has been challenged by a sight that imposes upon the male a disturbing "conscious[ness] of his own attractions" and thus an awareness of his susceptibility to being taken as a potential sexual object instead of an active sexual subject. Peregrine's implication in the sodomitical scene's disruption of gender-coded oppositions, however, is only reinforced by the strategy he adopts in order to vent his "wrath." Wary of taking action himself, he arranges for his landlady, described as "a dame of remarkable vivacity," to step into the next room in the belief that she is carrying a message to its occupants.

> The lady very graciously undertook the office, and entering the apartment, was so much offended and enraged at the mutual endearments of the two lovers, that instead of delivering the message with which she had been entrusted, she set the trumpet of reproach to her mouth, and seizing the baron's cane, which she found by the side-table, belaboured them both with such eagerness of animosity, that they found themselves obliged to make a very disorderly retreat, and were actually driven down stairs, in a most disgraceful condition, by this exasperated virago. . . . (243)

If Peregrine, after witnessing the spectacle of male-male love, is effectively unmanned by his inability to take action, the landlady becomes all the more martial and virile as she sounds the trumpet of battle, wields the baron's cane, and forces the two male lovers to make a "disorderly retreat." And as if to signal that the landlady's transformation into an animated "virago"—literally, her transformation into a simulacrum of a man—has not put an end to the logical disturbances produced by the sodomitical scene, Peregrine and Pallet celebrate the punishment of the amorous "offenders" by attending a masquerade that night, with Pallet in full female drag.

In each of these passages the scene of sodomy between men exposes the impossibility of establishing the distance necessary to secure an "uncontaminated" spectatorial relation to that scene. The spectatorial position is destabilized, however, not because the scene is so alien or remote, but precisely because the vision of male-male sodomy looks uncannily familiar: as familiar, that is, as the primal scene that in Freudian theory only belatedly undergoes heterosexualization. Since gay male sexual relations thus threaten to disseminate what might be described as a generalized sodomitical effect—threaten, that is, to effect a contagious disturbance of positional logic—it should come as no surprise that the sodomitical passages in both these eighteenth-century texts should have been expurgated after their initial publication. Like Freud or Fanny or Peregrine, after all, the heterosexually identified reader has too much at stake in such an encounter with or representation of the sodomitical scene.

Just what that stake is may be illuminated from a different historical direction by catching a glimpse of one last spectator catching a glimpse of sodomy between men. In the section of *The Post Card* titled "Envois," Jacques Derrida, producing what he suggests may be a "satire of epistolary literature"[25]—a satire, that is, of a genre that includes *The Memoirs of a Woman of Pleasure*—focuses much of his attention on a medieval drawing of Plato and Socrates that he claims to have noticed on a post card in the gift shop at Oxford's Bodleian Library. Tellingly, his espial of the post card takes place, as Derrida recounts it, while he himself is being spied on and made a participant in a scene; for at the moment when his eye first falls upon the image of the two philosophers in the drawing, he has the sense that his companions, Jonathan Culler and Cynthia Chase, whom he imagines as having anticipated and arranged for this discovery, were, as he writes, "observing me obliquely, watching me look. As if they were spying on me in order to finish the effects of a spectacle they had staged (they have just married more or less)" (16). Thus it is as a third party in the company of newlyweds staging a "spectacle" before him—a spectacle in which he finds himself both conscripted and implicated—that Derrida encounters an image that represents philosophy's primal scene; perhaps it is not coincidental, then, that he reads the image on the post card as a graphic depiction of penetration from behind. "I see *Plato* getting an erection in *Socrates'* back," he writes, "and see the insane hubris of his prick, an interminable, disproportionate erection . . . slowly sliding, still warm, under *Socrates'* right leg" (18). For Derrida, as for Cleland and Smollett and Freud, this scene plays out a vertiginous reversibility of positions, specifically of the spatio-temporal positions on which Western philosophy rests: "Socrates, the one who writes—seated, bent over, a scribe or docile copyist, Plato's secretary, no? He is in front of Plato, no, Plato is *behind* him" (9).

This reversal of priority between Socrates and Plato extends its metaleptic reach across the whole of Western history so that Derrida can insist not only that "S. is P., Socrates is Plato, his father and his son, therefore the father of his father, his own grandfather and his own grandson" (47), but also, as the references to grandfather and grandson suggest through their evocation of *Beyond the Pleasure Principle,* that Freud too has a part to play in this unorthodox genealogy, this narrative of a temporality articulated otherwise: "as-I-show-in-my-book it is then Plato who is the inheritor, for Freud. Who pulls the same trick, somewhat, on Plato that Plato pulls on Socrates. This is what I call a catastrophe" (28). Catastrophe, "an overturning and inversion of relations" (22), as Derrida describes it, the condition of being "Arsy-versy" as in "Jenny Cromwell's Complaint," names for Derrida the deconstructive logic not only of the primal scene, but also of writing and philosophy as they are construed in the Western tradition: "S. does not see P. who sees S., but only (and here is the truth of philosophy) only *from the back.* There is only the *back,* seen from the back, in what is written, such is the final word. Everything is played out in *retro* and *a tergo*" (48). Thus for Derrida, as for Western philosophy, the sodomitical spectacle constitutes the primal scene of writing;[26] philosophy—and psychoanalysis as an offshoot of philosophy—ceaselessly elaborates itself by turning its back on its origin, only to turn back, through that very gesture, to the origin it seeks to deny.

This means, as I see it, something more than what Stanley Cavell, for instance, apparently intends when he writes, in an essay titled (by coincidence?) "Postscript (1989)": "I am from time to time haunted— I rather take it for granted that this is quite generally true of male heterosexual philosophers—by the origin of philosophy (in ancient Greece) in an environment of homosexual intimacy."[27] What haunts Derrida is not just (whatever "just" in this case might mean) the homophobic, homosocial, homoerotic, and homosexual relations that endlessly circulate within—and as—"the philosophical tradition"; at issue for him is the irreducibility of both sodomy and writing to a binary logic predicated on the determinacy of presence or absence—a binary logic that Derrida defines as intrinsic to "phallogocentrism [which] is articulated on the basis of a determined situation (let us give this word all its imports) in which the phallus *is* the mother's desire to the extent that she does not have it."[28]

Casting doubt on the analytico-philosophical "system of the symbolic, of castration, of the signifier, of the truth" ("Le facteur," 444), Derrida engages a structure of rigorously *in*determinate situations (and I give that word all its imports) that Freud, in a sentence cited earlier in part and offered now in its entirety, might gloss in the following way: "The tendency to doubt arises not from any occasion for doubt, but is the continuation of the powerful ambivalent tendencies in the pre-genital phase, which from then on become attached to every pair of opposites that dresent [sic] themselves." If the logic of paired opposites generated through castration's institution of sexual difference supplants a pre-genital ambivalence—which is to say, an overdetermined multiplicity of identifications—that makes such distinctions as inside or outside, imagined or real, problematic, it is important to note that only by adopting the perspective of castration can castration be seen as the "opposite" of pre-genital ambivalence. Castration, that is, represents itself as the *knowledge* of antithetical positioning and thus positions itself in opposition to the indeterminancy of the primal scene; it does so, moreover, by constituting itself as the very *principle* of paired opposites, as the truth of "truth" as the either-or determination of presence or absence.

Yet in the passage quoted in the previous paragraph from Freud's letter to Lou Andreas-Salomé, the word rendered indeterminate through a "typographical" error in the English translation as published—and published in association with the Institute of Psycho-Analysis—is, suggestively, the word "present" itself. The "present" has thus been absented from this translation of the Freudian text through a Derridean "catastrophe," a sodomitical inversion or overthrow; "erroneously" positioned with its bottom up, the "p" has effected a sudden multiplication of its identity, has come out of the closet of typography in the disturbing drag of a "d."[29] In the context of *The Post Card*'s argument it is difficult not to speculate on the significance of this transformation; if "S. is P." according to Derrida, surely it is fair to meditate on this dislocation of "p" by "d": *P*lato, *p*hilosophy, *p*hallogocentrism, and *p*sychoanalysis *d*isarticulated by *D*errida and *d*econstruction? The fortifications of the *p*resent shown not to be a "fort" after all but a "*da*"? In this translation of the letters circulated between Freud and Lou Andreas-Salomé, letters that in many ways echo those included in Derrida's "Envois,"[30] the word "present" cannot present itself; it is defeated or deferred by a letter. Thus writing, performing a sodomitical reversal, gestures toward the persistence of a "pre-genital" indeterminacy that the law of castration would deny through institutionalized categories of present and not present. The *différance* of the *p*resent figured by the "p" with its bottom up allegorizes the insistence of the *b*ehind (another inversion: "p" as "b"?) in the very act of making present. Thus both philosophy and psychoanalysis insist on coming back to the back, returning to the behind that is always at the forefront of the "dresent": "Before all else it is a question of turning one's back," as Derrida observes, "[o]f turning the back of the post card (what is *Socrates'* back when he turns his back to *Plato*—a very amorous position, don't forget—? this is also the back of the post card: as we remarked one day, it is equally legitimate to name it recto or verso). . . . To turn one's back is the analytic position, no?" (178).

Such reversals, inversions, or conflations of (putative op)positions recur throughout Derrida's writing and mark the organization of his text; hence the "Envois," which designates a concluding passage in poetry or prose, is located at the front of *The Post Card,* a text in which Derrida has written, "I owe it to you to have discovered homosexuality" (53). What this means, of course, has everything to do with the figuration of sodomy in terms evocative of the (il)logical structure of the moebius loop, the (il)logic that dislocates such spatio-temporal "situations" as "pre" and "post," or before and behind. For sodomy and writing insist on the (il)logical possibility that what is behind can also, and properly, come before: "In the beginning," as Derrida phrases it, "in principle, was the post" (29). If we can say of such an observation that it is, to be precise, "preposterous," we can add that what makes it "preposterous" also makes it precisely—and even "in principle"—sodomitical.

Perhaps, too, we can understand better, in relation to this principle of the preposterous, why Louis Simond might have feared the imagination's susceptibility to being "sullied by the exposition of enormities, that ought never to be supposed to exist." The (il)logic by which exposition exposes its implication in such enormities, the (il)logic by which narrative produces the "crime" that it apparently only reports, the (il)logic of metalepsis that locates the cause as the effect of its effects, is, after all, an (il)logic that refutes all possibility of defining clear identities or establishing the security of fixed positions. It discovers, instead, within the either-or logic that Freud, *as a heterosexual man,* enshrines as the law of castration, the scandalous presence of another logic, the sodomitical (il)logic of the primal scene that comes always both before and behind it. Thus for Cleland and Smollett, Simond and Derrida, as for countless others who intervene more oppressively in the politics of discursive practices, any representation of sodomy between men is a threat to the epistemological security of the observer—whether a heterosexual male himself or merely heterosexual-male-identified—for whom the vision of the sodomitical encounter refutes the determinacy of positional distinctions and compels him to confront his too clear implication in a spectacle that, from the perspective of castration, can only be seen as a "catastrophe."

Notes

This essay was first presented, in a shorter form, at the 1989 conference on Lesbian and Gay Studies held at Yale University. Joanne Feit Diehl, D. A. Miller, and, as always, Joseph Litvak read versions of this essay and offered valuable support and advice.

1. Louis Crompton, *Byron and Greek Love: Homophobia in 19th-Century England* (Berkeley: University of California Press, 1985), 169.

2. *Trying and Pilloring of the Vere Street Club* (London: J. Brown, 1810), cited in Crompton, *Byron and Greek Love,* 166.

3. Mary Ann Doane, "Veiling over Desire: Close-ups of the Woman," *Feminism and Psychoanalysis,* ed. Richard Feldstein and Judith Roof (Ithaca: Cornell University Press, 1989), 105. Similarly, Kaja Silverman, in her excellent essay "Too Early/ Too Late: Subjectivity and the Primal Scene in Henry James," notes that the Freudian model of the psyche in *The Interpretation of Dreams* "rests precisely upon the possibility of forward and backward movement between the unconscious and the preconscious/conscious system" (*Novel* 21 [Winter/Spring 1988]: 149). Silverman touches on a number of issues related to those that I am examining here. Although she uses Freud as the source of a psychic model that she then applies to James, her account of James's inscriptions of anality can itself be "turned around" upon Freud. In any case, despite its differences from mine, her project constitutes an important source for anyone working toward the possibility of re-envisioning the primal scene.

4. See, for instance, Freud's remark in *From the History of an Infantile Neurosis:* "Of the physician's point of view I can only declare that in a case of this kind he must behave as 'timelessly' as the unconscious itself, if he wishes to learn anything or to achieve anything," in *The Standard Edition of the Complete Psychological Works of Sigmund Freud,* ed. James Strachey (London: The Hogarth Press, 1955), Vol. 17, 10. All subsequent references to this case history will be given in the text.

5. J. Laplanche and J.-B. Pontalis, *The Language of Psychoanalysis,* trans. Donald Nicholson-Smith (London: The Hogarth Press, 1983), 112.

6. Though his focus is quite different from mine, Jonathan Culler provides an excellent discussion of metaleptic narrative structures, and frames them briefly in terms of Freud's analysis of the Wolf Man, in "Story and Discourse in the Analysis of Narrative," *The Pursuit of Signs: Semiotics, Literature, Deconstruction* (Ithaca: Cornell University Press, 1981), see especially 172–82.

7. Quoted in Peter Gay, *Freud: A Life for Our Time* (New York: W. W. Norton & Co., 1988), 287.

8. Freud, *From the History of an Infantile Neurosis,* 51. See also his earlier assertion that "these scenes from infancy are not represented during the treatment as recollections, they are the products of construction" (50–51).

9. Marguerite Waller, "Academic Tootsie: The Denial of Difference and the Difference It Makes," *Diacritics* 17, no. 1 (Spring 1987): 2.

10. Nicholas Abraham and Maria Torok, *The Wolf Man's Magic Word: A Cryptonymy,* trans. Nicholas Rand (Minneapolis: University of Minnesota Press, 1986), 2.

11. Sigmund Freud, *The Letters of Sigmund Freud and Lou Andreas-Salomé*, ed. Ernst Pfeiffer, trans. William and Elaine Robson-Scott (London: The Hogarth Press and the Institute of Psychoanalysis, 1972), 77.

12. Sigmund Freud, "Negation," *The Standard Edition of the Complete Psychological Works*, Vol. 19 (1961), 237.

13. Stanley Fish has persuasively read this case history as an "allegory of persuasion" (938) in his essay, "Withholding the Missing Portion: Power, Meaning and Persuasion in Freud's 'The Wolf-Man,' " *Times Literary Supplement*, August 29, 1986, 935–38. He too focuses on Freud's anal-erotism, though he sees its inscription not in Freud's manifestations of uncertainty or doubt, but in his management of information, his withholding and then delivering of crucial interpretive details at strategic moments in his narrative. Fish's insights have been valuable to me in formulating my reading, though I am primarily interested in reading the discursive logic of Freud's positioning in relation to the primal scene, a logic of which Freud is not the master and which bears a determining relation to the discourse of homosexuality, while Fish undertakes to examine Freud's rhetoric as a sign precisely of his insistent mastery over the reader, however much that rhetoric may have its "sources in his deepest anxieties" (938).

14. "I was the first—a point to which none of my opponents have [sic] referred—to recognize both the part played by phantasies in symptom-formation and also the 'retrospective phantasying' of late impressions into childhood and their sexualization after the event," *From the History of an Infantile Neurosis*, 103, n. 1.

15. The use of the masculine pronoun here is intended to signify that my reading of the primal scene, like Freud's, focuses on an experience whose implications are emphatically affected by gender. In the case under discussion here, the gender of the subject in question is male.

16. The primal scene, to put this another way, always starts as the mobilization of libidinal energies that will be defined, after the fact, as homosexual; the scene only later becomes heterosexualized, and that heterosexualization induces the horror and anxiety that the Wolf Man experiences in his pathogenic dream.

17. Fish, "Withholding the Missing Portion," 938.

18. It should be recalled that Freud insists that the infant signals this dual libidinal identification by passing a stool and interrupting his parents' lovemaking with a scream. Reading this activity as a "sign of [the infant's] sexual excitement," Freud argues that it "is to be regarded as characteristic of his congenital sexual constitution. He at once assumed a passive attitude, and showed more inclination towards a subsequent identification with women than with men" (81).

19. "Jenny Cromwell's Complaint Against Sodomy," cited in Dennis Rubini, "Sexuality and Augustan England: Sodomy, Politics, Elite Circles and Society," *The Pursuit of Sodomy: Male Homosexuality in Renaissance and Enlightenment Europe*, ed. Kent Gerard and Gert Hekma (New York: Harrington Park Press, 1989), 381.

20. John Cleland, *Memoirs of a Woman of Pleasure*, ed. Peter Sabor (New York: Oxford University Press, 1985), 157. All subsequent references to this work will be given in the text.

21. In the psychic economy of the heterosexualized male, the *narrative* of castration, however frightening its content, achieves a fetishistic, recuperative status to the

extent that its explanatory coherence domesticates the violence that it thematizes. It becomes, in effect, a primal screen to obscure the primal scene. Jacques Derrida offers a related observation in "Le facteur de la vérité": "In this sense castration-truth is the opposite of fragmentation, the very antidote for fragmentation: that which is missing from its place has in castration a fixed, central place, freed from all substitution" (*The Post Card: From Socrates to Freud and Beyond,* trans. Alan Bass [Chicago: University of Chicago Press, 1987], 441; all subsequent references to this work will be given in the text).

22. Eve Kosofsky Sedgwick provides a powerful reading of such figurations in "A Poem is Being Written," *Representations* 17 (Winter 1987): 110–136. In particular, she analyzes the significance of the fact that in colloquial discourse "women's *genital* receptivity is described as 'ass,' as in 'a piece of' " (129).

23. Nancy K. Miller, " 'I's' in Drag: The Sex of Recollection," *The Eighteenth Century* 22, no. 1 (1981): 53.

24. Tobias Smollett, *The Adventures of Peregrine Pickle,* ed. James L. Clifford (New York: Oxford University Press, 1964), 242. All subsequent references to this work will be given in the text.

25. This phrase appears in the "letter" printed on the back cover of *The Post Card.*

26. Throughout *The Post Card* and particularly in the "Envois," Derrida elaborates a theory of textual rivalry within the philosophical tradition that echoes Harold Bloom's formulations of literary revisionism and the anxiety of influence. Derrida suggests, for example, that "In compromising Socrates Plato was seeking to kill him, to eliminate him, to neutralize the debt while looking as if he were taking on the entire burden. In *Beyond* . . . , precisely on the subject of Aristophanes' discourse, Freud starts it all over, he forgets Socrates, erases the scene and indebts up to Plato" (146). This implies the need to reconsider the Bloomian scenario of Oedipal rivalry in relation to a sodomitical scene that presents a more complicated network of anxieties, identifications, and desires.

27. Stanley Cavell, "Postscript (1989): To Whom It May Concern," *Critical Inquiry* 16 (1990): 256.

28. Derrida, "Le facteur de la vérité," *The Post Card,* 480.

29. This can be seen by paying attention to the serifs of the letters "p" and "d" in the text. It is worth adding that both Freud and Derrida provide justifications in their writings for taking errors of transcription, typing, or typesetting seriously. See, for instance, Derrida, "Du Tout," *The Post Card,* 513–15; an important discussion of typographical distortions and Freud's relation to the Wolf Man can be found in Maria Torok, "Afterword: What is Occult in Occultism? Between Sigmund Freud and Sergei Pankeiev Wolf Man," *The Wolf Man's Magic Word: A Cryptonomy.*

30. Compare for instance the recurrent anxieties about the reliability of the post in both collections. Freud writes, "Let us hope that the postal authorities will not continue to be unfavourably disposed toward us. My lost letter contained all the details that were meant for you better than I can repeat them today" (*Sigmund Freud and Lou Andreas-Salomé: Letters,* 148); Derrida writes, "Hound them at the post office. Does the search go through them? No, I will never rewrite it, that letter" ("Envois," 57). Or compare Freud's comment that "not every arrow reaches its mark" (172) with Derrida's famous assertion, "A letter can always not arrive at its destination" ("Le facteur," 444).

II

Cutting Up:
Specters, Spectators, Authors

Figure 1. Production still for Rope.

5

Anal *Rope*

D. A. Miller

I have nothing at all on my mind, but I've too many things under my behind.   *Charlotte's Web.*

Rope Trick

The technical originality of Alfred Hitchcock's *Rope* has been so little neglected by serious-minded criticism that the latter may be considered almost definitively shaped by a ritual of recounting and assessing the director's desire to do the film, as he put it, "in a single shot," or at any rate, as nearly without benefit of montage as the state of the art allowed in 1948, when a camera only held ten minutes' worth of film. Yet this technicist bias has proven to be curiously distracted by the very shooting technique on which it elects to concentrate. For one thing, contrary to all reasonable expectations, it has hardly managed to generate a single accurate account of the technique in question. Again and again, for instance, we are told that each shot in *Rope* runs to ten minutes, whereas the shots range variously from roughly three to nine minutes; or that Hitchcock blackened out the action every time he changed cameras, though only five of *Rope*'s ten cuts are managed this way. It is as though *Rope* criticism aimed less at a description than a correction of Hitchcock's experiment, for whose irregularities and inconsistencies there is substituted a programmatic perfection that better supports the dream of a continuous film (not yet to mention whatever wishes might find fulfillment in that dream) than Hitchcock's actual shooting practice. Furthermore, *Rope* criticism has surprisingly little good to say of this technique, even when it speaks of nothing but. Only unconsciously, in its lapses and inaccuracies, does it aim at

119

indulging and protecting the fantasy of a film without cuts; its conscious concern is to diminish this fantasy to, precisely, a one-shot-thing. However much one might admire or be intrigued by the experiment in *Rope*, "nevertheless," as François Truffaut puts the characteristic disavowal in his interview with Hitchcock, "weighing the pros and cons—and the practices of all the great directors who have considered the question seem to bear this out—it is true that the classical cutting techniques dating back to D. W. Griffith have stood the test of time and still prevail today."[1] The evidence of a compelling, but meaningless device (a paradox writ large in the debate over the role of technique in Hitchcock's work as a whole) is as familiar as the accompanying denunciations of mass culture's tendency to degrade formal experimentation to the status of a gimmick. But it is never simply enough, here or elsewhere, to observe the gimmick structure, or to identify it as that which elicits technicist accounts and at the same time betrays them into an all but self-acknowledged pointlessness. Far from ever truly installing a site of non-meaning (which the denunciation of formalism, like the embrace, cannot help affirming), the gimmick only exploits the idea of such a site in relation to specific meanings whose production is felt to need obscuring. The gimmick arrests attention, but only in the process to relax the demands put on it by an ostentatiously unworthy object. In the case of *Rope*, Hitchcock himself has been more than happy to trivialize his formal experiment; his urgency may be measured, in the Truffaut interview, by the inevitably worried criterion of normality that presides over his retraction, and by the oddly—to the point of being contradictorily—assorted excuses he offers for himself. "I undertook *Rope* as a stunt; that's the only way I can describe it. I really don't know how I came to indulge in it. . . . I got this crazy idea to do it in a single shot. When I look back, I realize that it was quite nonsensical because I was breaking with my own theories on the importance of cutting and montage" (179–80). Yet what is at first an incomprehensible freak later becomes a mere semblance of aberration, beneath which a reassuring orthodoxy has merely mistaken its identity: "This film was, in a sense, precut. The mobility of the camera and the movement of the players closely followed my usual cutting practice. In other words, I maintained the rule of varying the size of the image in relation to its emotional importance within a given episode" (180). In the end, Hitchcock adopts a somewhat more forgiving third position (responding to Truffaut's suggestion that *Rope* represents an inevitable moment in his career, just as inevitably superseded): "As an experiment, *Rope* may be forgiven, but it was definitely a mistake when I insisted on applying the same techniques to *Under Capricorn*" (184). What emerges through these shifts of defense (*I don't know how I came to do it—I didn't really do it at all—it wouldn't matter if I only did it once*) is less a gratuitous technique, than an attempt, undertaken for reasons whose remoteness the shifts are there to insure, to render it such. In rejecting *Rope* as a stunt, Hitchcock does not break with his exclusive preoccupation during the filming (when in the course of numerous exhausting retakes James Stewart is said to have complained that what was being rehearsed was not the players, but the camera[2]) so much as he continues to consider *Rope*'s technique the only thing that matters about the film, even if, on this retrospection, it doesn't matter much. The stunt may no longer be valued, but it retains all its old centrality in Hitchcock's refusal to depart from a technicist perspective on the film as though there were—so that there appear to be—no others.

If Hitchcock's own single-minded attention to technique thus signals a strategy for dismissing the consequence of everything else, Truffaut's fidelity to that closure of concern helps specify what the strategy happens to target. "Since Alfred Hitchcock deals solely with the technical aspects of *Rope*," he writes in the interview, "a brief description of the story is sufficient for our purposes":

> All the action takes place on a summer evening in a New York apartment. Two young homosexuals strangle a school friend just for the thrill of it and conceal his body in a chest in the very room in which his parents and fiancée are expected for a cocktail party. Among the guests is their former school teacher. As the party is in progress, their attempt to impress their mentor leads them to disclose bits of truth, which he eventually pieces together. Before the evening is over, he will discover the body and turn the two young men over to the police. (179; "college" corrected to "school")

For all the announced succinctness, one word here appears almost sumptuously extraneous: homosexual.[3] Every other element in the summary is furnished on the direct evidence of what we hear or see in the film. Yet in this sense, the homosexuality of the protagonists, never either visually displayed (with a kiss) or verbally disclosed (by a declaration), is simply not in the story at all. In an account that is attempting to reduce the story to its most abbreviated articulation, their homosexuality must seem at once a remarkable and a remarkably pointless piece of information. Certainly, no apparent use is ever found for it in the hit-and-run summary that having encountered "two young homosexuals" at the start recurs only to "two young men" in the end, and for which itself no use is ever found. It is as though Truffaut—in this typical of *Rope*'s other critics—were as determined to acknowledge homosexuality as to prevent it from entering into an eventual understanding of the film. Unlike Hitchcock in the interview, he does not thus repress the homosexual theme, if that means utterly refusing to address it, so much as he constructs it into *a homosexuality of no importance*. Yet where homosexuality is concerned, the sophistication that has learned how to drop the subject in passing must be just as suspect as the balder mode of panic that would simply drop the subject, period. In a culture where variously sharp excitements (sexual and phobic, of bodies and minds, in women as well as men) greet the mere nomination of the subject, a truly offhand reference to male homosexuality must hardly be credible, least of all from a heterosexual-identified man whom the category has likely served half his life to bully into good behavior. Were such a thing possible, moreover, it would amount to so spectacular an achievement as still to belie any claim to casualness. The heavy silence surrounding homosexuality requires explanation no less than the featherweight fussing over technique.

Rope has in fact been famous for two things: not just its technique, but also the fact that it seems to be about "two young homosexuals." Yet these two things have stimulated criticism in quite opposite, if equally unfruitful ways. On one hand, *Rope* criticism (including Hitchcock's own) indulges the appeal and propagates the repulsiveness of the film's technique with a loquacity as little embarrassed by hermeneutic obligation as by fear of monotony. Concerning the narrative homosexuality, on the other hand, it affects a bored indifference that seldom goes beyond a brief banalizing acknowledgment à la Truffaut, as though to suggest that the idea and image of men kissing, sucking, fucking one another, were altogether devoid of the fascination that, on the contrary, the problems of the mobile camera may be taken for granted to hold in abundance. I have of course been implying that if technique is considered a more engrossing question than the critical results even begin to warrant, and homosexuality a less interesting one that can plausibly be the case, the reason is that both questions have been unconsciously but definitively crossed with one another, so that technique acquires all the transgressive fascination of homosexuality, while homosexuality is consigned to the status of a dry technical detail. To the exact extent that an interest in technique phobically bespeaks a *desire for* homosexuality, homosexuality is shown hardly to exist—

or if it does exist, not to matter. This is why the interest in technique, missing its desire—*made* in missing its desire, can only prattle, equally incapable of comprehending its declared object, or of declaring a comprehensible project; why neither the technique nor the fascination it undeniably exerts can be understood apart from the derisory (at least, derided) theme of male homosexuality; why, therefore, this theme needs to be better laid open than a non-gay-identified criticism—whose well-exercised will-to-tautness in this department must keep it from noticing Hitchcock's own—has been content to do.

Trouble with Connotation

Let us begin by raising a question that is presupposed in the common judgment that Brandon and Philip are two young homosexuals, but that the usual summary delivery of this judgment keeps from being put—namely, how do we think we know? It bears repeating that whatever information is conveyed in a phrase like "two young homosexuals" cannot be learned by viewers empirically, on the evidence of their senses. Though by their cursory mention of it critics seem to imply that the protagonists' homosexuality is as plain to see as its proofs may go without saying, homosexuality is in fact extensively prevented from enjoying any such obviousness not only, of course, by the famously hardass Production Code in force at the time of the film's making, which strictly forbade the display and even denomination of homosexuality, but also, more diffusely, by the cultural surround of legal, social, psychic, and aesthetic practices (the last including those of spectatorship) that tolerate homosexuality only on condition that it be kept out of sight.[4] While, despite that no one does, one surely *could* furnish a wide-ranging abundance of evidence for homosexual meaning in *Rope*, starting with the post-coital nuances of the dialogue between Brandon and Philip after the murder ("How did you feel—during it?" "I don't remember feeling much of anything—until his body went limp, and I knew it was over, then I felt tremendously exhilarated"), all that any of it would ascertain is how completely *Rope*'s representation of homosexuality has been consigned to connotation—that is to say, following Roland Barthes, to a kind of secondary meaning "whose signifier is itself constituted by a sign or system of primary signification, which is denotation."[5]

Now, defined in contrast to the immediate self-evidence (however on reflection deconstructible) of denotation, connotation will always manifest a certain semiotic insufficiency. The former will appear to be telling us, as Barthes says, "something simple, literal, primitive: something *true*," while the latter can't help appearing doubtful, debatable, possibly a mere effluvium of rumination (stereotypically, the English professor's) fond of discovering in what must be read what need not be read into it.[6] The dubiety, being constitutive, can never be resolved. On one hand, connotation enjoys, or suffers from, an abiding deniability. To refuse the evidence for a merely connoted meaning is as simple—and as frequent—as uttering the words "But isn't it just. . .?" before retorting the denotation. On the other, this maneuver is so far betrayed by the spirit of irritation, willfulness, and triumphalism in which it is infallibly performed, that it ends up attesting not just to the excesses of connotation, but also to the impossibility of ever really eliminating them from signifying practice. On the front page of the *New York Times*, for instance, I read that an earthquake has destroyed "the quirky charms" of San Francisco.[7] If, bringing the queers out from the closet of quirkiness, I catch the reporter's wistful lamentation sustaining his not necessarily unconscious vindictive satisfaction, as if over the punishment finally visited upon Sodom, this reading will seem as extravagant as the rejection of its possibility must be disingenuous. In probably more deliberate and certainly more systematic fashion, *Rope* exploits the particular aptitude of connotation for allowing homosexual meaning to be elided even as it is also being elaborated. In a first step, the connotation is broached: Brandon tells Janet, who needs to make a call, that the telephone is "in the bedroom," to which she replies, lubriciously intoning the phrase, "How cozy." Her remark seems less well explained by any supposed breach of decorum in making use of the telephone where one sleeps than by the implication that more than one person, of no more than one sex, must sleep there. In a second step, however, the connotation is contradicted: Mrs. Wilson the housekeeper later directs David's aunt Mrs. Atwater to the same phone, "down the hall, to your left, dear—the *first* bedroom."[8] Or again, step one: Brandon has no girlfriend—he may be homosexual. Step two: Brandon had a girlfriend once—he may not be. Notice that the contradiction, itself registered as no more than a connotation, does not exactly dispel suspicion (Mrs. Wilson is arguably covering for her "boys," and the relegation of Brandon's heterosexuality to the past might be taken to open, not close, the question of his present orientation); it simply reinforces the undecidability that keeps suspicion just that, a thing never substantiated, never cleared.

Until recently, homosexuality offered not just the most prominent— it offered the only subject matter whose representation in American mass culture appertained exclusively to the shadow kingdom of connotation, where insinuations could be at once developed and denied, where (as with the mafioso who alleged he wasn't there and if he was, was asleep) one couldn't be sure whether homosexuality was being meant at all, but on the chance it was, one also learned, along with the codes that might be conveying it, the silence necessary to keep about their deployment. In this sense, the cultural work performed by *Rope*, toiling alongside other films (e.g., *Laura*, Hitchcock's own *Notorious*) and other cultural productions (the advice column, the muscle magazine), consists in helping construct a homosexuality held definitionally in suspense on no less a question than that of its own existence—and in helping produce in the process homosexual subjects doubtful of the validity and even the reality of their desire, which *may only be, does not necessarily mean,* and all the rest.

Yet if connotation, as the dominant signifying practice of homophobia, has the advantage of constructing an essentially insubstantial homosexuality, it has the corresponding inconvenience of tending to raise this ghost all over the place. For once received in all its uncertainty, the connotation instigates a project of confirmation. In cases where nothing prevents what is connoted from being denoted as well, confirmation is easily provided—or the fact that it could be dispenses with the need for it: who requires a bank statement to be convinced of the affluence connoted by the apartment Brandon and Philip inhabit, the clothes they wear, the style of life they lead? But when, with homosexuality as with nothing else, what is connoted may not be denoted, whoever would establish a given connotation can only support it through other connotations equally precarious.—*Brandon and Philip live together with no mention of girlfriends.—But that doesn't necessarily mean. . .—They also went to a boys' prep school.—But that doesn't prove. . .* Needing corroboration, finding it only in what exhibits the same need, with no better affordance for meeting it, connotation thus tends to light everywhere, to put all signifiers to a test of their hospitality. Pushing its way through the Text, it will exploit the remotest contacts, enter into the most shameless liaisons, betray all canons of integrity—like an arriviste who hasn't arrived, it simply can't stop networking. (For if unprovable, connotation can at least be probable, by virtue of an accumulation, a redundancy of notations.) If a case for the homosexuality of Brandon and Philip were ever actually made, therefore, we should find homosexual meaning inevitably tending, via connotation's limitless mobility, to recruit every signifier of the text.[9]

One straightforward thematic consequence of such tendency would be the implicit homosexualization of almost all the other male characters in the story as well. For if the homosexual suggestion is first dropped in conversation between Brandon and Philip about the murder, surely a hairpin or two must also fall on the "murder" "victim" David, whose name this context endows with a "Michelangelesque" reference, and whose mother (who according to his father won't let her son grow up) joins Brandon's own, equally solicitous, to cut a single figure in the usual etiology. (From a Barbara Pym novel: "—He strikes one as the kind of person who would have a mother.—Well, everybody has or had a mother. But I see just what you mean.") And if on David, then why not—via the same associative logic of connotation—on Kenneth, too, who the script maintains is "often mistaken" for "his best friend"? Why not on the bachelor pedagogue Rupert himself, to whose magisterial *influence*, as Wilde might put it, all four boys submitted when they were together at school—the very kind of school, in fact, that is popularly considered a seminary of male homosexual activity? The homosexual atmosphere is hardly alleviated by the appearance of Janet, of whom in any case Arthur Laurents's script focuses as little and with as little interest on the character, as Hitchcock's camera does on the body. On the contrary, Janet's hysteria, apparent even to herself, seems to complement male homosexuality, almost as though two kinds of heterosexual blockage were each being meant to explain the other. Less frigid, Janet might have been the "right woman" to cure Brandon; less gay, he could have administered Charcot's prescription for what ails her. And while the fact that as girlfriend she has been passed from Brandon to Kenneth to David grants all three men an ostensible heterosexuality, it does so by making suspiciously intense the homosocial bond between boyfriends.

In this perspective, where the conventional assumption of the classical detective story that *anyone might have committed the murder* at once conveys and culpabilizes a universal potential for homosexuality in men, Rupert's last speech may be seen as an attempt to quarantine the pandemic of homosexual signification.

> Brandon, Brandon, until this very moment, this world and the people in it have always been dark and incomprehensible to me, and I've tried to clear my way with logic and superior intellect. And you've thrown my own words right back in my face, Brandon. You were right to—if nothing else, a man should stand by his words. But you've given my words a meaning that I never dreamed of. And you've tried to twist them into a cold logical excuse for your ugly

murder. Well, they never were that, Brandon, and you can't make them that. There must have been something deep inside you from the very start that let you do this thing. But there's always been something deep inside me that would never let me do it and that would never let me be a party to it now . . . Well, I don't know what you thought or what you are, but I know what you've done: you've murdered. You've strangled the life out of a fellow human being who could live and love as you never could—and never will again.

Rupert's aim is to evoke a clear, quasi-intuitive opposition between homosexuality and something else, something that could be thought of as its other, with the murderers accused on one side of the divide and their victim, as well as their executioner, himself, comfortably excused on the other. Yet his very effort to decide the matter willfully discloses, if not the impossibility of doing so, the sleight of hand that must make such decision factitious in every sense except as *la raison du plus fort*. David, he says, "could live and love as you never could— and never will again." The insinuation is unusually clear, or would be were it not for this odd parapraxis: if Brandon and Philip could *never* live and love like David, it can hardly follow that they never will live and love like him *again*. Rupert's syntax here has conflated two separate propositions—"David could live and love as you never could and never will"; and "though David could live and love as you never could, unfortunately, thanks to you two, he never will again"—with the result of perpetuating the boundary confusion supposedly being straightened out. Rupert's own immunity is more decisively established by the synergism of two tactics, of which the first is a manifest stupidity and the second an equally unconcealed violence. "You've given my words a meaning that I never dreamed of. And you've tried to twist them into a cold logical excuse for your ugly murder. Well, they never were that, Brandon, *and you can't make them that*." While the last claim might seem almost feeble-minded, as though Rupert had quite forgotten that his pedagogy liked to feature such dicta as "murder is a crime for the masses, a privilege for the elite," it nonetheless enjoys considerable power, of the kind that grows out of the barrel of a gun, which the man of "logic and superior intellect" is flourishing as he speaks. Whatever Rupert may think he is saying or doing, his speech goes to show that, when homosexuality is entrusted to the totalizing, tantalizing play of connotation, the only way to establish the integrity of a truly other subject position is performative; by simply declaring that one occupies such a position and supporting the declaration with a strong arm.

Yet even after Rupert's speech has achieved the theoretical restoration of the male heterosexual subject, and the report of his gun, summoning the police, will insure the practical disposal of the male homosexual one, the charged atmosphere of *Rope* never quite dissipates. To this residual tension, the formal correlative is the kind of coda that the film appends onto the resolution of the story. Rupert having fired moves back from the window to a chair where he will keep Brandon and Philip under watch until the police arrive. For a full half-minute, the camera prolongs its gaze on the inverted triangle that the three men form, Rupert at the apex interposed between Brandon and Philip at the corners of the base. With no narrative justification to cover it, remarkable for no more apparent reason than that it has been thus pointedly and protractedly remarked, the moment belongs to what Hitchcock criticism is fond of calling pure cinema. Yet as with other displays of virtuosity in Hitchcock (such as most famously the shower sequence of *Psycho*), its imposing formality offers the profoundest inscription in the viewer of the psycho-sexual themes that, as mere themes, might seem to be left behind. The moment, I mean, is eerie not just in the sense that one doesn't know what to make of it, but also in the sense that one rather does. Strangely, or so some might still like to say, the exigencies of constructing the "good" male subject have ultimately brought Rupert, and with him, the viewing subject whom the camera puts almost in his place, to a heterosexuality configured entirely in terms of men, and whose only necessary content is not a desire for women, but the negation of the desire for men. In the homo-/hetero- opposition thus defined, homosexuality provides the marking term, whose presence or absence is wholly determining for what lies on *both* sides of the virgule. For a normal-seeming contrast, consider the end of *Strangers on a Train*, where Guy's approach by a fellow train passenger recalls his ferroviary encounter with homosexual, homosexualizing Bruno at the beginning; but this time around Guy is accompanied by his newlywed wife, with whom, not before throwing our way a legibly arch complicitous glance, he moves to another compartment. For all that even now Guy does not cease to be in flight from homosexual threat (or temptation), yet his possession of a woman who substantiates his heterosexuality allows both the flight and the threat to be played in the register of light comedy. Rupert, however, if not a gay bachelor, remains a confirmed one, and unlike Guy's, his heterosexuality amounts to nothing but a *non-homosexuality*; as such, it is always and only engaged in rejecting a determination that thus can't fail to determine it. By the end of *Strangers*, homosexuality has been

relegated to a distant (or rather, distanced) point in the genealogy of
the heterosexual subject who, if he hasn't evolved beyond it, has at any
rate run away from it. At *Rope*'s end, far less tritely, it is precisely the
developed heterosexual subject who is most definitively implicated in
a structure of homosexual fixation, a notion that accordingly proves
to have perhaps as little to do with gay men as penis envy does with
women.

Trouble with Denotation

"Even if the Hays Office had allowed the homosexual element to
unfold its full peacock's fan," Raymond Durgnat writes in a gro-
tesquely candid passage on *Rope*, "the temptation would have been
considerable to have substituted a pathological explanation for a moral
soul-fight or for intimations of the moral issues involved in the adoption
of homosexual positions to begin with. *This may seem to be expecting
too much*, but if we are considering the proposition of whether *Rope*
is a masterpiece and whether Hitchcock is a moral master, . . . then
too much is what one would expect to find" (emphasis added).[10] It is
hard for a reader of these lines to attend to their declared preference
for an anti-gay moralism over an anti-gay pathology, even if this small
point in gay-bashing etiquette is accorded all the moment that Durgnat
thinks it has, when a certain syntactical slackness is opening his writing
up to another, more interesting possibility: for what, may we ask, is
"this" that one must not expect because one might well expect it, and
that is never unambiguously claimed by any one antecedent, but is
attracted variously to the *intimations* of the moral issues, to the *temptation* to substitute a pathological explanation for them, and even, perhaps especially, to the condition of that temptation in the *unfolding of
the homosexual element*? The Hays Office may be responsible for
censoring this element, if only most immediately, but it is Durgnat
himself who imagines unfolding—in a sense, must already have un-
folded—what we shall eventually see how aptly he calls "its full peacock's fan."

Connotation, we said, excites the desire for proof, a desire that, so
long as it develops within the connotative register, tends to draft every
signifier into what nonetheless remains a hopeless task. Hence the
desire assumes another, complementary form in the dream (impossible
to realize, but impossible not to entertain) that connotation would quit
its dusky existence for fluorescent literality, *would become denotation*.

Every discourse that speaks, every representation that shows homosexuality by connotative means alone will thus be implicitly haunted by the phantasm of the thing itself, not just in the form of the name, but also, more basically, as what the name conjures up: the spectacle of "gay sex." Whenever homosexuality is reduced to epistemology, to a problem of *being able to tell*, this will-to-see never fails to make itself felt; excepting rare gay-affirmative contexts that disarm its assaultiveness or suspend its shame, neither does it ever fail to be disguised or disclaimed, in a variety of strategems ranging from the lip-smacking "disgust" of the moral majoritarian to the fuller-mouthed "sympathy" of the would-be fellow traveler.

Even the script of *Rope*, subject to a censorship traditionally cleverer at discovering verbal innuendoes than visual ones, goes some way to articulating a viewer's desire for an explicitation of gay material. When Rupert says "I don't know what you are," his words perhaps imply that *someone* knows full well. And when Brandon tells his guests of a Sunday morning in the country when "across the valley the church-bells were ringing and in the yard Philip was doing likewise to the necks of two or three chickens," his punning (to which the propensity at least one early modern sexologist was prepared to include among the homosexual's supposed symptoms[11]) alerts us to the more resonant twist on *choking the chicken*, old adolescent slang for masturbation. But of course the most sustained evocation of the possibility of such explicitation occurs at the level of the image. Sometimes this image, through an attenuation of depth perception, is able to suggest that Brandon and Philip are actually touching, holding, or leaning against one another, when they are only occupying parallel spatial planes. More often and simply, it is content to capture the couple in less egregious, but also less disputable infractions of the codes governing male homosocial space. In their tight framing by the camera, for instance, Brandon and Philip always seem to be standing too close to one another, and what is already a transgression of the normally enforced boundaries between men's bodies promotes the fantasy that these boundaries will be even further breached—as indeed they twice are toward the end of the film: first, in the violent quarrel between the murderers, where the choreography of their bodies relies prominently on Hollywood conventions of romantic embrace; and second, in the struggle between Rupert and Philip for the gun that tends to disappear under a show of passionate and prolonged hand-holding.

Not just more constant, the visual teasing is also more charged than the verbal kind. At least outside certain practices of dirty talk, words are hardly identical with the "gay sex" that they may only signify or designate; but no sooner do we enter the visual field of relations between looks, or between bodies, or between looks and bodies, than the *sign* of "gay sex" tends in some degree to become an *index* of it. A-man-standing-too-close-to-another signifies homosexual behavior by being an instance of it. If this instance does not quite qualify as "gay male sex," it entertains closer, more nearly causal connection to gay male sex than is supposed by the arbitrariness of the sign. In effect, then, we are continually put in the position of being *just about to see* what we are waiting for; and the desire for the spectacle of gay male sex is intensified accordingly into that pleasurably (because all but unpleasantly) prolonged state of expectation we call suspense.

What affines this suspense to panic, at least within the film's homophobic (not quite to say heterosexual) male perspective, involves the possibility of continuity, even coincidence between the sight that the viewer is looking to see and the very act of his looking to see it. For perhaps the most salient index to male homosexuality, socially speaking, consists precisely in how a man looks at other men. "If he looks into another man's eyes for even a microsecond longer than it takes to make socially acceptable eye contact," *Cosmopolitan* bluntly admonishes the Janets of the world, "beware. Heterosexual men do not do it."[12] But how does any viewer grasp that look except by *looking at it in turn*? And when during this second look would its socially acceptable epistemological task leave off and a reprehensible erotic fascination begin to take over? Particularly in the case of the homophobic male viewer supposed by the film, what would prevent this second look from being effectively assimilated to the first look that it is the means to catch? With those tight close-ups imposing a scrutiny of Brandon and Philip as intimate and intense as their own of each other, and putting men who stand too close to one another too near us as well, Hitchcock's camera deliberately awakens the paranoid suspicion that, where homosexuality is concerned, the sense of sight no longer operates at or by a distance, and the object beheld may penetrate, capture, and overwhelm the beholder's body consciousness like a smell, say the rankness of a body in heat (Janet to Brandon: "*You* smell dreamy") or the fetor of a cold decomposing cadaver. No less busily than *Rope* excites a desire to see, it inspires a fear of seeing; the object of voyeuristic desire is precisely what must not catch the eye.

Yet how might a desire to see what one is afraid to look at ever be gratified? Or how might a fear of what one can't stop desiring ever be allayed? The classic solution to both questions, of course, lies in *the closet*, which not only alleviates the trouble with connotation, by confining an otherwise totalizing homosexuality to a local habitation, but also relieves the trouble with denotation, by making this homosexuality visible only as a structure of occultation. Though the entire plot of *Rope* is oriented toward the moment when the cassone or chest in the center of the living room will be opened, once the moment arrives, instead of disclosing whatever evidence might be furnished, if only symbolically, by the sight of David's "dead" body, the camera merely provides the viewer with a close-up of the cassone lid, while Brandon is saying, "Go ahead and look. I hope you like what you see." Indeed I do, we may imagine the implied viewer responding to this address, inasmuch as I want to see, precisely, *that I don't have to look*: that is the paradox of the closet, insofar as the term is understood to refer to a homophobic, heterosexual *desire* for homosexuality, and not merely a homophobic, heterosexual *place* for it. If the paradox is somewhat statically represented by the cassone, it is much more energetically performed at the level of technique, where the dynamic of homosexual meaning so far described may be seen to determine every main aspect of the film's famous "stunt."

Notwithstanding Hitchcock's retrospective dismissal of this stunt as "breaking with [his] own theories of cutting," it remains the case that, if some of his most suspenseful effects depend on a spectacular art of montage, others are produced within and through prolonged single shots. Take the example of suspense that the director himself offers from *Young and Innocent* (1937):

> Towards the end of the picture the young girl is searching for the murderer, and she discovers an old tramp who has seen the killer and can identify him. The only clue is that the man has a nervous twitch of the eyes.
>
> So the girl dresses up the old tramp in a good suit of clothes and she takes him to this big hotel where a thé dansant is in progress. There are lots of people there, and the tramp says, "Isn't it ridiculous to try to spot a pair of twitching eyes in a crowd of this size."
>
> Just then, right on that line of dialogue, I place the camera in the highest position, above the hotel lounge, next to the ceiling, and we dolly it down, right through the lobby, into the big ballroom, and past the dancers, the bandstand, and the musicians, right up to a close-up of the drummer. The musicians are all in blackface, and we stay on the drummer's face until his eyes fill the screen. And then, the eyes twitch. *The whole thing was done in one shot.* (114; emphasis added)

The thrill effect here promotes and depends on the fantasy of a camera powerful enough to bring into being what it is looking for simply by virtue of looking for it. For as Hitchcock has conceived the scene, it is not as though the camera simply happens to catch the drummer in the act of blinking; on the contrary, the drummer seems to blink in response to a gaze, evidently the camera's, that is fixed on his own in a kind of staring contest ("We stay on [his] face"). Within this fantasy, of course, the camera's gaze must remain steady, unbroken by any cut; for if the camera eye ever permitted itself to blink, as it were, it might possibly miss the twitch of the drummer's in that very second—or perhaps, the contest being thus forfeited to the drummer, his eye might not be compelled to twitch at all. In *Rope*, too, the camera sustains a similarly provocatory expectancy by its extreme unwillingness to shut its eye, as though it were refusing to take the even the slightest chance of failing to be on hand, when the act it is waiting for should eventually occur.

Or if. The same fantasmatic vigilance that would keep the camera from missing out on the spectacle of "gay male sex" might prevent it from taking place. The camera-voyeur that patiently waits for "it" to happen also wears the hat of the camera-cop whose presence on the scene will ensure that "it" won't happen at all, and whose unremitting surveillance will therefore go to show that "it" doesn't exist. The terms of this ambivalence become particularly visible at the moments when, the loading camera having run out of film, a break in continuity is unavoidable. As is well known, at such times Hitchcock masks the cut (alternatively: shows he is masking it) by focusing close up on a dark object that motivates a blackout during which the camera may be reloaded. In every case, however, the blackout is motivated by more than the exigency of a technical *gageure*. Of the five cuts managed in this way, four seize the occasion offered by a man's backside (Brandon's, Kenneth's), while the fifth makes use of the cassone just as Rupert is opening it. Reinforcing the visual cueing, the dialogue that accompanies it evokes now the desire to see David ("She seems to be missing David—as a matter of fact I'm beginning to miss him myself"), now the dread of seeing him ("you'd like David to walk in"; "no, that would be too much of a shock"), as though, in addition to advancing the literal concerns of the narrative, it were announcing the fantasmatic prospect of the "gay male sex" we have been waiting to see. Thus contextualized, the blackouts come as proof positive that there is nothing to see, unless of course what is laid bare, through the imperfections of the joins, is the structure of the join itself, hence the very operation of the closet.

The Full Peacock's Fan

If there had been something to see instead of this operation, however, what might it have been? I have so far pretended to speak of the spectacle of "gay male sex" as though both what it consists in and why what it consists in should be phobogenic, if only to the non-gay-identified male spectator who is the film's first address, were questions too obvious to require answers. In fact, of course, no less important a consideration than how the implied spectator imagines he knows about gay male sex in *Rope* is what he imagines he knows in knowing this. What *is* gay male sex, according to the film? Of all the body parts, positions, and practices that the term may be thought to encompass, around which in particular does *Rope* fantasmatically entwine itself? and by what logic might these form a basis for producing the implied spectator's recoil?

The first four blackouts bespeak almost an eagerness to be revealing in this regard. When the camera closes in on the backside of a man's suit only to reward thus intensified expectation with blank darkness, one is invited to imagine that the camera's itinerary has been blocked, or what comes to the same thing, *would otherwise have continued*— and how otherwise but, with a kind of x-ray vision, from behind the gorgeously tailored suit (*superbement coupé*, as a French critic put it[13]) through the cleft of the buttocks all the way to the perforation of the anus itself, whose cavital darkness would in any case make no difference between an interrupted itinerary and one that had reached its proper destination? Under cover of these blackouts, two things get "hidden." One is the popularly privileged site of gay male sex, the orifice whose sexual use general opinion considers (whatever happens to be the state of sexual practices among gay men and however it may vary according to time and place) the least dispensable element in defining the true homosexual. The other is the cut, for whose pure technicity a claim can hardly be sustained at so overwhelmingly halluci-natory a moment, even if the script didn't link the word with a body wound of irreducible symbolic importance. ("It's nothing; it's just a little cut," says Philip of his bleeding hand; everybody knows better.) Moreover, these two things, by seeming to come in place of one an-other, configure one and the same thing: the anus is a cut, and vice versa. The most immediate reason for wanting to hide the cut, then, is that it is imagined to be a penetrable hole in the celluloid film body; and though there are countless obvious and ordinary reasons for wanting to hide the anus, it is hidden here *as what remains and reminds of a cut.*

Recall how regularly, in the child's fantasy that Freud calls the primal scene, sexual intercourse between the parents takes place from behind—or in other words, for all the child knows of anatomy, "at the anus," where the mother's penis, somehow lost, perhaps severed, in this very aggression, is supposed to have been.[14] This "sodomitical scene," as Lee Edelman frankly styles it, "presupposes the imaginative priority of a sort of proto-homosexuality, and it designates male heterosexuality, by contrast, as a later narcissistic compromise that only painfully and with difficulty represses its identification with the so-called 'passive' position . . . so as to protect thereby the narcissistically invested penis from the fate that is assumed to have befallen the penis of the mother."[15] The same reason, however, that qualifies the anus to provoke castration anxiety in the male subject, as evincing on his own body anatomo-fantasmatic potential for his being—even anatomo-fantasmatic proof of his having been—in the mother's place, keeps such anxiety from being altogether controlled in the classic recognized manner, namely, by means of a fantasy about the body of what the subject is comforted to construe as the *opposite* sex. For even if his success in confining this sex (socially as well as psychically) to the castration attributed to it in the primal scene were far less problematic than is ever demonstrably the case, his anus would remain to raise, on his own male person, the very possibility (of being fucked and so forth) that, with all the force of binary opposition, he had projected onto *her* vagina. Accordingly, he requires another binarism to police the difference between man and woman as, by the back door, it reenters to make a difference within man. So it is that, with a frequency long outlasting the formative years, however particularly striking then, straight men unabashedly *need* gay men, whom they forcibly recruit (as the object of their blows or, in better circles, just their jokes) to enter into a polarization that exorcises the "woman" in man through assigning it to a class of man who may be considered no "man" at all. Only between the woman and the homosexual together may the normal male subject imagine himself covered front and back.

Thus doubly aligned with this subject's heterosexualization (as what most brutally enforces it), castration anxiety may not finally be all that anxiogenic. For while such anxiety no doubt occasions considerable psychic distress, neither in the long run can it fail to be determined by the knowledge that it enjoys the highest social utility in tending to confirm heterosexual male identity in a world where, if this precious, but precarious identity is not exactly rewarded, the failure to assume it is less ambiguously punished. At the point where castration anxiety is taught to anticipate its redeeming social value, it immediately carries ultimate reassurance; its normalizing function allows it to be not just thought, but even lived, as normal itself. That point has been more than reached in the cultural production that, down to its underwear ads, is engaged in the routine propagation of such normalizing anxiety right and left. Perhaps more than any other figure, Hitchcock suggests the distinctive service that is performed by the thriller under this administration. In educing castration anxiety as the affective correlative to a suspense that is always framed by the reassuring prospect of its own resolution, he does more—or less—than dispel the anxiety; he stimulates what is considered, though insatiable, a healthy appetite for it, as for what will eventually ensure the proper formation of the romantic heterosexual couple.

Yet it almost seems as though the necessity of again and again having to produce a castration complex came to reabsorb much of the anxiety that is thus drained from the complex per se. In *North by Northwest*, for instance, a film that more plainly than any other by Hitchcock indicates how *repetitiously* castration anxiety attests to its manifest destiny in fashioning the norm couple,[16] all that saves the anxiety from seeming orgiastically overproduced is the evidence going to show that, for establishing this couple, or at any rate its male half, even infinite draughts of such anxiety would be no more than required. The almost delirious proliferation of Roger Thornhill's adventures, despite the virtual uniformity of their psychological significance, suggests that there can never be generated enough castration, or enough castration anxiety, or enough comfort in castration anxiety, to meet the abyssal needs of the male heterosexuality whose achievement, at no time altogether safe or stable, stands in place of resolution as ambiguously as the film's last image of a train entering, but also disappearing, into a tunnel.

Under such circumstances, castration easily slides from being the property of the woman or the homosexual to providing the badge of the heterosexual identity that these abjected figures are necessary to constructing. Hence, Hitchcock's ex post facto pronouncements on *Rope* assimilate his "usual cutting practice" to a normality, and taint his "crazy idea" to forego this practice with a perversity, that are both more than technical. Nor need one have waited until the Truffaut interview for this opposition, which is first built, by technical as well as thematic means, into the film itself. Though the fact is seldom acknowledged (and when it is, always disavowed), Hitchcock only camouflages the reel changes in the camera when they fall within the eventual formation of a single reel on the projector; between reels on the projector, he makes no attempt to conceal the severance.[17] Not one, but two principles for managing the cut are deployed in *Rope*, and given that the projector accommodates approximately twice the amount of film that the camera can carry, they operate by regular turns.[18] According to the one, for which *Rope* is famous, the cut vanishes at a man's erotized backside; by the rule of the other— however ignored, presiding over an equal number of breaks in the film's continuity—the cut is not only shown, but shown as being to the patron or props of what, if this weren't precisely what is here at issue, would be called normal male desire (to Rupert twice; to Janet and Mrs. Wilson once apiece). Only to the extent that they are *seen* can the cuts at a man's backside promote a heterosexualizing castration anxiety. Insofar as they succeed in making themselves invisible, and thus alternative to the "usual cutting practice" whose heterosexual orientation is here so unusually trenchant, then homosexuality would be characterized not by a problematics of castration, but on the contrary by an exemption from one.

To this possibility, the film's fifth and final blackout—on the cassone just as having opened it Rupert looks inside—brings an illumination of its own. With little in the ostensible narrative or its generic conventions to forbid displaying the corpse (everything in both the one and the other seeming almost a positive warrant for just such a climax), so curious a censorship can only find its explanation along whatever pathways of symbolic signification allow David's body to be considered *obscene*—and so to be kept offscreen. What invisible but hardly unimaginable sites on this body would obscenity accordingly invest? "Murdered" from behind, the body would no doubt show or signify the penetrated, penetrable anus—or would do so if once again a cut did not phobically intervene. Inasmuch as David is a victim of asphyxiation, moreover, another "secret" to be disclosed with the opening of the cassone is that the stiff within has a hard on.[19] "Show me a gay corpse," the film would almost thus be saying, "and I'll show you a happy homosexual," as though the cheerless view commanded by a boy in the band were somewhat contradicted by the more animated sight of a boy *en bandant*. Yet shocking though his visibly sexualized anus or penis might be judged, either image *by itself* would readily allow David's body—even acknowledged as homosexually active—to confirm the primacy of male heterosexual scenography. Identified with his *tool*, David would be the "man" thus outfitted for fucking; identified with his *hole*, he would be the "woman" who gets fucked for the reason, or with the result, that she has no such tool. Far more disconcerting than the evidence of a penetrated anus or an erect penis is the prospect of their copresence on the same male body. Whether as a simple refusal or a more elaborate attempt at regulation, *Rope*'s conflicted technique is in no small degree responsive to this disorienting spectacle, whose versatility—not unlike the rope that now dangles and tautens like a penis and now encircles and tightens like a sphincter—one is baffled to know, precisely, how to take. David's erection, for instance, would arise as a condition of being fucked, not of fucking: though his penis might still come, this would no longer be by virtue of its going anywhere. And if, in relinquishing its purposefulness, his erection would no longer amount to anything of greater consequence than a pleasure, it could scarcely while remaining itself shrink to anything of less: or in other words, quite simply, being fucked could no longer *be seen* to entail castration.

So, together with a fear of castration, *Rope* braids an oddly compatible fear of the negation of castration. Since castration motors the compromise that is struck by (and in large measure *as*) male heterosexuality, it is only ostensibly concealed in what is better understood as a publicity campaign. (In technicist terms, whether by "a sudden acceleration in the acting pace after the join," or by "incomplete blacking out," or because "the actor or the camera just misses the position necessary for perfect masking of the frame," all four attempts to mask the cut behind a man's back are "spoiled."[20]) But the negation of castration, to the extent that it proposes a more disturbing sense in which this compromise will have exacted *a needless renunciation*, is better hidden in the structure of *Rope*, where, technically speaking, none but the last camera changeover—the one at the cassone lid—is "completely successful" in feigning a continuity from which nothing can appear to have been omitted.[21] Thus rigorously secreted, the pressure of so all but intolerable a possibility tends to renew the psychic investment in castration, whose incessant propaganda in turn contributes to helping the pressure operate under cover. Small wonder that Rupert, who has long since divined David's fate, is furious with fright when he actually sees David's body, or that having seen it, he must reorient his own body according to the polarities (front/back = penis/anus = fuck/be fucked = see/be seen = man/woman = straight man/gay man) that the spectacular beauties of the full peacock's fan will have confounded. For even after he has done shooting out the window, with the police on the way and himself incontestably armed for standing guard until their arrival, his uneasy glance backward announces the necessity of one last piece of work, which is, ingloriously enough, to sit down: as though only from a place where his ass is covered might he identify with so total a prick as the camera that has never managed— or is it, has managed never?—to leave Brandon and Philip and David alone.

Notes

Varia: (a) Raul Companioni and I once amused ourselves by imagining how, taking shelter, or pretending to take shelter, under the video equipment he let me use during my research, I might dedicate this essay to him, "through whose good offices I learned most of what I know about *Rope*." That together we could be thus *easily* amused is not the least affluent source of my attachment to his memory. (b) "Anal *Rope*" was first presented, through the invitation of Teresa de Lauretis, during the conference she organized on "Queer Theory" at the University of California, Santa Cruz, in February 1990. Peter Bowen, William Cohen, Christopher Craft, Douglas Crimp, David Dryden, Lee Edelman, Casey Finch, Christopher Friden, Richard Meyer, Leland Monk, William Nestrick, Jeff Nunokawa, Mary Ann O'Farrell, and Craig Rubano were exceedingly helpful in the preparation of the text. (c) Of my many viewings of *Rope*, let me recall one that took place at the Bridge Theater in San Francisco, where I was exhilarated to witness—and even, in the company of my friend Ben, somewhat to demonstrate—how thoroughly the comfort of the gay couples in the audience succeeded in dating the film's treatment of homosexuality. (d) Alfred Hitchcock began the filming of *Rope* on January 22, 1948—by what we call coincidence, meaning an event that is impossible to consider *just* a coincidence, also the day I was born: almost as though *Rope* were wound by some malevolent fairy as part of a spell to ensure that—for how many years?—its outdated date would remain my own.

1. François Truffaut, *Hitchcock*, trans. n.s., revised edition (New York: Simon & Schuster, 1985), 184. Further references to this work will be given parenthetically in the text.

2. Donald Spoto, *The Dark Side of Genius: The Life of Alfred Hitchcock* (Boston: Little, Brown, 1983), 306.

3. In the French text the unassimilated character of this disclosure is even more pointed: "Deux jeunes hommes, homosexuels, étranglent, etc." (*Hitchcock/Truffaut* [Paris: Editions Ramsay, 1983], 149).

4. Even "after Stonewall," this principle does not cease determining mass culture's representational practice, in which homosexuality, though obviously a less infrequently cited phenomenon, has hardly therefore become a more visible sexuality. The recent television biography of Rock Hudson, considered and considering itself daring for bringing up homosexuality at all, offers a case in point. Notwithstanding that the film piously denounces the necessity of the Hollywood closet, at whose door it implies that Hudson's many personal troubles may be laid, yet it continues to respect every classic decorum of that necessity in its own compulsion to append a "beard" to Hudson's face by several times requiring that he embrace his wife, while forbidding him even once to kiss another man.

5. Roland Barthes, S/Z, trans. Richard Miller (New York: Hill & Wang, 1974), 7.

6. Barthes, S/Z, 9.

7. Craig Wolff, "Night, Not Despair, Falls Over a Shaken City," *New York Times*, October 18, 1989.

8. Robin Wood, who has also observed this contradiction, puts the point of it thus: "It's not simply that *Rope* cannot tell us that the two men sleep together; it also cannot tell us clearly that they *don't*, since that would imply that they might" ("The Murderous Gays: Hitchcock's Homophobia," *Hitchcock's Films Revisited* [New York: Columbia University Press, 1989], 351).

9. A recent magazine article purporting to assist heterosexual women in the AIDS-related task of identifying "bisexual" men offers these clues: "Women should . . . be cautious of men in certain careers. Bisexuals (and gays) are prevalent in such narcissistic businesses as the theatre, fashion, the beauty industry, art and design, and fitness. Many bisexuals are also attracted to the helping professions: medicine, social work, counseling. Some bisexual husbands seek jobs that involve travel. . . .These profession include the travel industry, import/export, and any work, such as law and consulting, that involves out-of-town clientele. Bisexuals also like to work in hotels, restaurants, and other places where they earn cash tips. . ." (Susan Gerrard and James Halpin, "The Risky Business of Bisexual Love," *Cosmopolitan* [October 1989]: 205). Observe how, under the pressure of establishing a homosexuality that can only be ascertained circumstantially, the initial category of "certain careers" is gradually enlarged to the point where, of all careers from which the magazine's target reader might choose her lover (short of submitting to an unthinkable *déclassement*), the paradigm is saturated. Accordingly, what begins as practical advice to women who would resist their possible victimization ends in a paranoid fantasy in which they are more needful of help than ever, and less likely to get it.

10. Raymond Durgnat, *The Strange Case of Alfred Hitchcock* (Cambridge: MIT Press, 1974), 205.

11. In *L'Uranisme: Inversion sexuelle congénitale* (1895), Marc-André Raffalovich isolates what he calls paradoxomania as an important factor in Oscar Wilde's "anti-natural genital vocation"; quoted in Sherwood Williams, "The Gay Science: Paradox and Pathology in Wilde and Melville" (unpublished manuscript).

12. Gerrard and Halpin, "The Risky Business of Bisexual Love," 204.

13. Jean-Pierre Coursodon, "Le Désir attrapé par la corde," *Cinéma* 311 (November 1984): 28. Brilliant with such aperçus, this study of *Rope* has the additional rare merit of being willing to engage the erotics of technique in the film. According to Coursodon, the blatant formalism of the *plan continu* (in keeping with a screenplay that has nothing to tell except an utterly pointless murder) advertises the perverse workings of a desire that dispenses with the credibility of any attempt to motivate it. To which account, however, my own will be seen to imply the following reservation. Insofar as the generality of desire, even perverse desire, faithfully transposes the abstraction of technique, Coursodon's argument must perpetuate the phobic dehomosexualization that is sedimented in such abstraction, and in doing so must fail to consider how—and how particularly—a certain motiveless-ness might be motivated.

14. Sigmund Freud, *From the History of an Infantile Neurosis* ["The Wolf Man"], in *The Standard Edition of the Complete Psychological Works of Sigmund Freud*, ed. James Strachey, 24 vols. (London: The Hogarth Press and the Institute of Psycho-Analysis, 1953–74), 17:78.

15. Lee Edelman, "Seeing Things: Representation, the Scene of Surveillance, and the Spectacle of Gay Male Sex," 101 in this volume.

16. See Raymond Bellour, "Le Blocage symbolique," *Communications* 23 (1975): 235–350.

17. V. F. Perkins, *"Rope" Movie* 7 (February—March 1963): 11.

18. *Rope*'s ten cuts may be schematized as follows:

    1: unhidden, to David's strangulation;

    2: hidden, by Brandon's back;

    3: unhidden, to Janet;

    4: hidden, by Kenneth's back;

    5: unhidden, to Rupert;

    6: hidden, by Brandon's back;

    7: unhidden, to Mrs. Wilson;

    8: hidden, by Brandon's back;

    9: unhidden, to Rupert;

    10: hidden, by the cassone lid.

    #2–9 represent an orderly oscillation between the apparently continuous and the unmistakably cut, thematized as an opposition between homo- and heterosexuality, but the system is oddly framed by #1 and #10, not least because the latter two cuts present the same (homosexual) thing, David's "dead" body, and because, in violation of one of the thriller's cardinal laws, the less reticent, more graphic variant seems to come first.

19. As viewers of *The Trouble with Harry* hardly need to be told, Hitchcock is perfectly capable of displaying a corpse, even without benefit of hanging, in full erection. The paradox offered by the early image of Harry's lifeless but aroused body gets elaborated in the various courtship narratives engendered through the process of burying him. In *Rope*, not dissimilarly, at the same time as the cassone serves as a grave, it also designates the site of an unbridled eroticism. (To Brandon's favorite story of the bride who on her wedding night locked herself in a chest, Janet, freshly engaged to David, replies: "I don't think I'll get *that* playful.") It will be seen, however, that David's erection points to something at once more specific and more specifically troubling than the general link between eroticism and death.

20. Perkins, *"Rope,"* 11.

21. *"Rope,"* 11.

6

Female Spectator,
Lesbian Specter:
The Haunting
Patricia White

Feminism has shaped contemporary film studies in a fundamental fashion. Nevertheless it has become increasingly apparent that discussions of critical issues such as desire, identification, and visual and narrative pleasure do not automatically encompass the lesbian subject. The dominance of the heterosexual concept of "sexual difference" as term and telos of feminist inquiry has impoverished not only the study of specific film texts, but also the very theorization of female subjectivity. In this essay I attempt to trace the ghostly presence of lesbianism in classical Hollywood cinema on the one hand, and in feminist film theory on the other, through the reading of two texts in which a defense against homosexuality can be detected.

Genre and Deviance

What have been considered the very best of "serious" Hollywood ghost movies—*Curse of the Cat People* (1944), *The Uninvited* (1944), *The Innocents* (1961) (fig. 1), and Robert Wise's 1963 horror classic *The Haunting* to name a few, are also, by some uncanny coincidence, films with eerie lesbian overtones. Masquerading as family romance, these films unleash an excess of female sexuality which cannot be contained without recourse to the super-natural. To be more explicit, in the case of *The Haunting*, female homosexuality is manifested in the character of Claire Bloom. Regrettably though perhaps understandably eclipsed by two films Wise directed just before and after *The Haunting*, namely *West Side Story* and *The Sound of Music*, the film will maintain

Figure 1.

its place in cinematic history for two reasons. First, it is one of the few Hollywood films that *has* a lesbian character. Claire Bloom appears as what is perhaps the least objectionable of sapphic stereotypes—the beautiful, sophisticated, and above all predatory lesbian. Although not herself a fashion designer, her wardrobe is by Mary Quant; she has ESP, and she shares top billing with Julie Harris, a star who from her film debut in *The Member of the Wedding* through her incongruous casting as James Dean's love interest in *East of Eden*, to her one-woman-show as *The Belle of Amherst*, has insistently been coded "eccentric." The second reason for which *The Haunting* is remembered is its effectiveness as a horror film. Like its source, Shirley Jackson's *The Haunting of Hill House*, the movie is adept in achieving in the spectator what Dorothy Parker on the book jacket calls "quiet, cumulative shudders."[1] At least one reliable source pronounces *The Haunting* "undoubtedly the scariest ghost movie ever made."[2] It is clear that reason number two is related to reason number one—for *The Haunting* is one of the screen's most spine-tingling representations of the disruptive force of lesbian desire.

Though the alliance of horror with lesbianism may leave one uneasy, it should be pointed out that the horror genre has been claimed by film criticism as a "progressive" one on several grounds. Concerned with the problem of the normal, it activates the abnormal in the "threat" or the figure of the monster. Linda Williams has noted a potentially empowering affinity between the woman and the monster in classic horror films, without exploring the trope of the monster as lesbian. The omission of any mention of lesbian desire is all the more striking given her thesis: "it is a truism of the horror genre that sexual interest resides most often in the monster and not the bland ostensible heroes," or, "clearly the monster's power is one of sexual difference from the normal male."[3]

The horror genre manipulates codes specific to the cinema—camera angles that warp the legibility of the image and the object of the gaze; framing that evokes the terror of what-lies-beyond the frame; sound effects that are not diegetically motivated; unexplained point-of-view shots that align the spectator with the monster—for effect and affect.

In *The Haunting* the two female leads, both "touched by the super-natural" (as it were), are invited to take part in a psychic experiment in a haunted New England mansion. As explicitly deviant women, they are asked to bear witness to an other power, an alternative reality. They join their host Dr. Markway (Richard Johnson), the pompous anthropologist turned ghost-buster, and the wisecracking future heir

Figure 2.   Left to right: Claire Bloom, Russ Tamblyn, Julie Harris, Richard Johnson

to the house, Luke (Russ Tamblyn), who is skeptical of any unusual "goings-on" (fig. 2).[4] A truly terrifying sojourn with the supernatural at Hill House leaves the Julie Harris character dead due to unnatural causes and the spectator thoroughly shaken.

Secret Beyond Theory's Door

The lesbian specter can also be said to haunt feminist film theory, and in particular to stalk the female spectator as she is posited and contested in that discourse. The "problem" of female spectatorship has taken on a dominant and in a sense quite puzzling position in feminist film theory, which in some instances has denied its very possibility. Laura Mulvey herself, reading her widely read "Visual Pleasure and Narrative Cinema," in an essay called "Afterthoughts on 'Visual Pleasure and Narrative Cinema' " explains: "At the time, I was interested in the relationship between the image of woman on the screen and the 'masculinization' of the spectator position, regardless of the actual sex (or possible deviance) of any real live movie-goer."[5] This parenthetical qualifier, "(or possible deviance)," is one of the few references to sexual orientation in the body of film theory. Yet within the binary stranglehold of sexual difference, lesbianism is so neatly assimilated to the "masculinization of the spectator position" as to constitute an *im*possible deviance. In asserting the female spectator's narcissistic over-identification with the image; in describing her masculinization by an active relation to the gaze; or in claiming that the fantasy of the film text allows the spectator to circulate among identifications "across" gender and sexuality, feminist film theory seems to enact what Freud poses as the very operation of paranoia: the defense against homosexuality.[6] Female spectatorship may well be a theoretical "problem" only insofar as lesbian spectatorship is a real one.[7]

In *The Desire to Desire: The Woman's Film of the 1940s* Mary Ann Doane addresses female spectatorship in relation to the film gothic, a (sub)genre which she aptly designates the "paranoid woman's film." Doane argues that the figuration of female subjectivity in the woman's film plays out the psychoanalytic description of femininity, characterized in particular by a deficiency in relation to the gaze, a metonymy for desire itself. Within this framework "subjectivity can . . . only be attributed to the woman with some difficulty,"[8] and "female spectatorship . . . can only be understood as the confounding of desire" (13)—or at most as the desire to desire.

The gothic subgenre has a privileged status within Doane's book, corresponding to its ambiguous position within the woman's film genre. Related to the "male" genres of film noir and horror "in [its] sustained investigation of the woman's relation to the gaze," the gothic is both an impure example of the woman's film and a "metatextual" commentary on it (125–26). The "paranoid woman's film" is inadvertently privileged in another sense. For, via Freud's definition of paranoia, the specter of homosexuality makes a rare appearance in the text. The process by which it is exorcised is intimately bound up with Doane's definition of female spectatorship.

Paranoia and Homosexuality

In *The Desire to Desire*, Doane devotes to the gothic two chapters entitled: "Paranoia and the Specular" and "Female Spectatorship and Machines of Projection," offering a compelling analysis of the genre to which my reading of *The Haunting* is indebted. Yet despite a lengthy discussion of the psychoanalytic description of paranoia, she qualifies Freud's identification of paranoia with a defense against homosexuality as the "technical" definition of the disorder (129). Freud himself was "driven by experience to attribute to the homosexual wish-phantasy an intimate (perhaps an invariable) relation to this particular form of disease."[9] The relevance of homosexuality to the discussion of paranoia and to the content of film gothics returns as the "repressed" of Doane's argument:[10]

> Yet, there is a contradiction in Freud's formulation of the relationship between paranoia and homosexuality, because homosexuality presupposes a well-established and unquestionable subject/object relation. There is a sense in which the very idea of an object of desire is foreign to paranoia. (129–30)

Homosexuality, it appears, is foreign to the definition of paranoia that Doane wishes to appropriate to describe the gothic fantasy. "Because Freud defines a passive homosexual current as feminine, paranoia, whether male or female, involves the adoption of a feminine position." This assimilation of homosexuality to the feminine effectively forecloses the question of the difference of lesbianism when Doane later turns to Freud's "Case of Paranoia Running Counter to the Psychoanalytical Theory of the Disease."[11] In this case, which is said to run "counter" to psychoanalytic theory on the point of homosexual desire, the fantasy which Freud ultimately uncovers as confirmation of his hypothesis (the homosexual wish betrayed by the discovery of a same-sexed persecutor) is read by Doane as the female patient's "total assimilation to the place of the mother." Desire is elided by identification. Doane writes that

> the invocation of the opposition between subject and object in connection with the paranoid mechanism of projection indicates a precise difficulty in any conceptualization of female paranoia—one which Freud does not mention. For in his short case history, what the woman projects, what she throws away, is her sexual pleasure, a part of her bodily image. (168)

In forming a delusion as defense against a man's sexual advances and breaking off relations with him (whether this shields a defense against a homosexual wish is here immaterial), the woman is seen to be throwing away her pleasure.

For Doane homosexuality is too locked into the subject/object dichotomy to have much to do with paranoia. Femininity represents a default in relation to the paranoid mechanism of projection—"what [the woman spectator] lacks . . . is a 'good throw' "[12]—precisely because the woman cannot achieve subject/object differentiation. The "contradiction" between homosexuality and paranoia, and the "precise difficulty" inherent in female paranoia are related by a series of slippages around a central unspoken term, lesbianism.

"Homosexuality" appears in Doane's text only furtively; female subjectivity is its central focus. Yet, remarkably, it is an account of "lesbian" desire that is used to summarize Doane's position on female spectatorship:

> The woman's sexuality, as spectator, must undergo a constant process of transformation. She must look, as if she were a man with the phallic power of the gaze, at a woman who would attract that gaze, in order to be that woman. . . . The convolutions involved here are analogous to those described by Julia Kristeva as "the double or triple twists of what we commonly call female homosexuality": " 'I am looking, as a man would, for a woman'; or else, 'I submit myself, as if I were a man who thought he was a woman, to a woman who thinks she is a man.' " (157)

Doane has recourse to what only Kristeva could call "female homosexuality" to support a definition of female spectatorship that disallows homoeroticism completely—lesbianism and female spectatorship are abolished at one "twist." Female subjectivity is analogous to female homosexuality which *is* sexuality only insofar as it is analogous to male sexuality. The chain of comparisons ultimately slides into actual delusion: "a woman who thinks she is a man." In what seems to me a profoundly disempowering proposition, the very possibility of female desire as well as spectatorship is relinquished in the retreat from the ghost of lesbian desire. As we shall see, a similar path is traced in *The Haunting*.

A House Is Not Her Home

> An evil old house, the kind that some people call haunted, is like an undiscovered country waiting to be explored. . .

The male voice-over—Dr. Markway's—with which *The Haunting* opens, will have, for some viewers, an uncanny resonance with a description of woman as "the dark continent." This connection between signifiers of femininity and the domicile is unsurprising; in cinema it appears in genres from the western to the melodrama. Mary Ann Doane cites Norman Nolland and Leona Sherman's version of the gothic formula as, simply, "the image of woman-plus-habitation."[13] It is the uncanny house that the heroine is forced to inhabit—and to explore.

Freud's essay on the uncanny draws on the literary gothic, particularly the work of E. T. A. Hoffman. In it he associates the sensation with the etymological overlap between the definitions of the uncanny, *das Unheimliche*, and its apparent opposite *das Heimliche* (literally, the homey, the familiar), ultimately identifying this convergence with "the home of all humans," the womb.[14] The woman provokes the uncanny; her experience of it remains a shadowy area.

In the threatening family mansions of the gothic, or in *The Haunting*'s evil old Hill House, a door, a staircase, a mirror, a portrait are never simply what they appear to be, as an image from Fritz Lang's "paranoid woman's film" *Secret Beyond the Door* (fig. 3) illustrates. The title sums up the enigma of many of these films, in which a question about the husband's motives becomes an investigation of the house (and of the secret of a woman who previously inhabited it). In *Secret Beyond the Door*, the husband is an architect whose hobby is "collecting" rooms in which murders have occurred, one of which is the heroine's bedroom.

Hill House, too, reflects the obsessions of its builder, we are told. "The man who built it was a misfit. . . . He built his house to suit his mind. . . . All the angles are slightly off; there isn't a square corner in the place." Visitors become lost and disoriented, doors left ajar close unnoticed. The film's montage exploits this as well, disorienting the spectator with threatening details—a gargoyle, a door knob, a chandelier—and unexplained camera set-ups and trick shots. Yet as a house that is "literally" haunted, Hill House poses another secret beyond its doors, one of which the architect himself is unaware. Hill House is "uncanny" *for the woman*; it is a projection not only of the female body, but also of the female mind, a mind which, like the heavy oak doors, may or may not be unhinged. An ad slick for the film (fig. 4) uses the image of a female figure trapped in a maze. Architectural elements are integrated into the title design. Thus the aspect of the house, its gaze, are crucial in the film, as they were even for the novelist who, Shirley Jackson's biographer tells us, "plowed through architecture books and magazines" for a picture of the perfect house

Figure 3.   Joan Bennett, Secret Beyond the Door *(1948).*

Figure 4.

before writing her tale, only to find out that her great grandfather, an architect, had designed it.[15]

Robbers, Burglars, and Ghosts

The relationship between the representation of woman and the space of the house is not, Teresa de Lauretis tells us in her reading of Jurij Lotman's work on plot typology, a coincidence or simply a generic requirement of the literary or film gothic. De Lauretis analyzes Lotman's reduction of plot types to a mere two narrative functions: the male hero's "entry into a closed space, and emergence from it. . . ." Lotman concludes that

> inasmuch as closed space can be interpreted as "a cave," "the grave," "a house," "woman" . . . entry into it is interpreted on various levels as "death," "conception," "return home" and so on; moreover all these acts are thought of as mutually identical.[16]

And de Lauretis sums up: "the obstacle, whatever its personification, is morphologically female and indeed, simply, the womb."[17] The sinister slippage in the chain of designations from grave to house to woman lends a narrative progression to Freud's uncanny. Given the collapse of "woman" onto the space rather than the subject of narrative, and given the identification of heterosexuality *qua* conception with the very prototype of narrative progression, it is no wonder that the lesbian heroine (and her spectatorial counterpart) are so difficult to envision.

Insofar as the cinema rewrites all stories according to an Oedipal plot, when the woman is the hero of a gothic such as *Rebecca* (1940), her story is told as the female Oedipus.[18] Her conflicting desires for the mother and for the father are put into play only to be "resolved" as the mirror image of man's desire. De Lauretis proposes that as the story unfolds the female spectator is asked to identify not only with the two poles of the axis of vision—feminist film theory's gaze and image—but with a second set of positions, what she calls the figure of narrative movement and the figure of narrative closure. Of this last, de Lauretis writes that

> The female position, produced as the end result of narrativization, is the figure of narrative closure, the narrative image in which the film, as [Stephen] Heath says, 'comes together.' "[19]

Figure 5.

We can recognize the "narrative image" as fundamentally an image of heterosexual closure, or, in Lotman's equation, death.

It is in relation to the narrative work of classical cinema defined as the playing out of space (the house, the grave, the womb) as the very image of femininity that I wish to situate the story of *The Haunting*. It is an exceptional Hollywood film that would frustrate the hero's "entry into a closed space" and stage a story of deviant female subjectivity, of the *woman's* return home as a struggle with the topos of the home. Here (fig. 5) an "image of woman-plus-habitation" illustrates this difficulty.

The Haunting tells not the story of Theodora (Claire Bloom's character) but of Eleanor (Julie Harris's character), a woman whose sexuality—like that of the heroine of *Rebecca*—is latent, not necessarily, not yet, lesbian. Her journey is articulated as female Oedipal drama almost against her will, and is resolved, with her death, as a victory of, exactly, the house and the grave (perhaps the womb). "Now I know where I am going, I am disappearing inch by inch into this house," she finally recognizes. My reading of the film will attempt to trace the "haunting" of Hill House as it shifts between homosexuality and homophobia.

The Haunting as ghost film dramatizes not the lesbian's "deficiency in relation to vision" as feminist film theory would characterize femininity, but a deficiency in relation to visibility or visualization—in *The*

Haunting we never see the ghost but we do see the lesbian. Which is not to say that we "see" lesbian sexuality. *The Haunting* is "not a film about lesbians"; it is (pretends to be) about something else. I would consider "something else" to be a useful working definition of lesbianism in classical cinema.[20] For it is precisely the fact that the "haunting" is unseen, that there are no "special effects," that renders *The Haunting* the "ultimate" ghost film.

> Robbers, burglars and ghosts, of whom some people feel frightened before going to bed. . .all originate from one and the same class of infantile reminiscence. . . . In every case the robbers stood for the sleeper's father, whereas the ghosts corresponded to female figures in white nightgowns.[21]

What is immediately striking in Freud's reading is the dissymmetry between the referents of the two dream symbols. Burglars and robbers stand quite definitively for the father; ghosts are a figure of—a figure. Not "the mother," perhaps a governess, a nurse, or a sister. . . (fig. 6).

"Scandal, Murder, Insanity, Suicide"

Dr. Markway's voice-over resumes after the opening credits of *The Haunting*. The story of Hill House as Dr. Markway envisions it— literally en-visions it, for his narration is accompanied by a bizarre flashback/fantasy sequence—is the story of female death. The mansion, built by one Hugh Crain "ninety-odd—very odd" years ago, is the site of the deaths of four women, which are enacted for us: his two wives, his daughter Abigail who lived to old age in the house, and her paid companion. This prologue sequence supplies us with a surplus of cinema's "narrative image"—female scandal, suicide, murder, and insanity—*before* the drama even begins to unfold. It is as if all the visual power of cinema (surpassing even Dr. Markway as narrator) is amassed to contain the threat that "whatever" it is that haunts Hill House poses.

Dr. Markway hides his interest in the supernatural under the guise of science; his true object of study, like that of Freud, another "pseudo" scientist, is deviant femininity. He designates one room of the house the "operating room"—"that is, the center of operations," he reassures his female guests. Suave, paternalistic, Dr. Markway is yet somehow lacking in relation to the law—or at least the laws of Hill House. (In contrast is Theodora's ESP, which affords her privileged knowledge of

Figure 6. Women in white.

"the haunting" and of Eleanor. She's thus a better analyst as well.) Dr. Markway admits, when asked to reveal the laws of psychic occurrences, "you'll never know until you break them." His laughably inadequate readings of the goings on in Hill House: "I have my suspicions"; his lectures on the preternatural (that which will some day come to be accepted as natural); his efforts to measure the cold spot; become more and more readable as fumbling attempts to explore the "undiscovered country" of female homosexuality. In this light his disclaimer on the supernatural, "don't ask me to give a name to something which hasn't got a name" is also a disclaimer to knowledge of "the love that dares not speak its name." He rejects the word "haunted" preferring "diseased," "sick" and "deranged," pathologizing, anthropomorphizing and, I would argue, lesbianizing the haunted house.

When his version of the story of Hill House includes the proclamation: "It is with the young companion that the evil reputation of Hill House really begins" we are prepared, indeed invited, to speculate what the scandal attached to the companion might be. It is onto the fates of the four female characters/ghosts, most crucially that of the companion who is extraneous (subordinate) to the nuclear family, that Eleanor Lance maps her "Oedipal" journey, her crisis of desire and identification.

As narrativity would demand, she starts out in the place of the daughter. Yet she is a grown-up daughter, a spinster, who leaves her family home—her mother has recently died, and as the maiden aunt she lives in her sister's living room—to return home to Hill House. Eleanor and Theodora are the remaining two of a select company of persons "touched" by the supernatural who were invited by Dr. Markway in the hopes "that the very presence of people like yourselves will help to stimulate the strange forces at work here." The doctor's interest in Eleanor's case is sparked by her childhood "poltergeist experience"—a shower of stones that fell on her house for three days. Eleanor at first denies—"I wouldn't know" (about things like that)— what her brother-in-law calls the "family skeleton," the secret of "what [her] nerves can really do." In the internal monologue accompanying her journey to the house (a voice-over that recurs throughout the film, giving the spectator an often terrifying access to her interiority) Eleanor refers to herself as "homeless." She has never belonged within the patriarchal home and its family romance. Her "dark, romantic secret" is her adult attachment to her mother, which she angrily defines as "eleven years walled up alive on a desert island." Eleanor is thrilled at the prospect of "being expected" at her destination; for the first time something is happening to *her*. More is "expected" of her than she dreams . . .

Things That Go Bump in the Night

When Eleanor arrives at Hill House she is relieved to meet one of her companions. "Theodora—just Theodora," Claire Bloom's character introduces herself to Eleanor, immediately adding, "The affectionate term for Theodora is Theo." "We are going to be great friends, Theo," responds Eleanor, whose affectionate name "Nell" Theo has already deduced by keen powers of extrasensory perception which are exercised most frequently in reading Eleanor's mind.[22] "Like sisters?," Theo responds sarcastically (fig. 7). Theo recommends that Eleanor put on something bright for dinner, sharing with her the impression that it is a good idea always to remain "strictly visible" in Hill House. On their way downstairs, they encounter their first supernatural experience, with Eleanor shouting, "Don't leave me, Theo," and Theo observing, "It wants you, Nell." After they have joined the others Eleanor proposes a toast: "I'd like to drink to companions." Theo responds with obvious pleasure and the camera moves in to frame the two women. "To my new companion," replies Theo with inimitable, elegant lasciviousness. The toast, like their relationship, alas, remains unconsummated, for Eleanor continues—"except I don't drink."

Eleanor clearly is the "main attraction" of both the house and Theo, each finding in her what Theo calls "a kindred spirit" (fig. 8). The film, resisting the visualization of desire between women, displaces that desire onto the level of the supernatural, Theo's seduction of Eleanor onto the "haunting."

The process whereby the apparition of lesbian desire is deferred to the manifestation of supernatural phenomena is well illustrated by a sequence depicting the events of the first night spent by the company in Hill House. Theo accompanies Eleanor to the door of her bedroom, and invites herself in, under the pretext of arranging Eleanor's hair. Although Eleanor refuses Theo's advances, the women end up in bed together anyway, but not according to plan (fig. 9). Eleanor, realizing with a mixture of relief and anxiety that she is alone, locks her door ("Against what?," she muses) and drifts off to sleep. A shot of the exterior of the house and a dissolve to a shot from the dark interior at the base of the main staircase are accompanied by a faint pounding which rises in volume. Eleanor stirs and, half-asleep, knocks in response

Figure 7. *"Like sisters?"*

Figure 8.   A kindred spirit.

Figure 9.

on the wall above her bed: "All right, mother, I'm coming." When
Theo calls out to her in fear, Eleanor realizes her mistake and rushes
into Theo's adjoining room. Huddled together in Theo's bed throughout the protracted scene, the women face off an unbearably loud
knocking which eventually comes to the door of the bedroom. Finally
the sound fades away, and Eleanor runs to the door when she hears
Luke and the doctor in the hall. The men enter, explain they had been
outside chasing what appeared to be a dog, and ask whether anything
has happened. The women burst into laughter, and after catching their
breath, sarcastically explain that something knocked on the door with
a cannonball. Luke remarks that there isn't a scratch on the wood-
work—"or anywhere else," and the doctor soberly intones: "When we
are decoyed outside, and you two are bottled up inside, wouldn't you
say that something is trying to separate us?" The sequence ends with
ominous music and a close-up of Theo.

The knocking that terrorizes the women takes up an element of the
film's prologue—the invalid Abigail pounds with her cane on the wall
to call the companion who fails to come, sparking malicious town
gossip that she had somehow or other murdered her mistress. At this
point in the film we are already aware that Eleanor harbors guilt about
her own mother's death; what this scene makes explicit is the exact
parallel, down to the knocking on the wall that Eleanor later admits
she fears she may have heard and ignored on the fatal night, which
puts Eleanor in the position of "companion" *vis-à-vis* her own mother.

> When a wife loses her husband, or a daughter her mother, it not
> infrequently happens that the survivor is afflicted with tormenting
> scruples . . . which raise the question whether she herself has not
> been guilty through carelessness or neglect of the death of the beloved
> person. No recalling of the care with which she nursed the invalid,
> no direct refutation of the asserted guilt can put an end to the
> torture . . .[23]

Freud concludes in *Totem and Taboo* that a repressed component of
hostility toward the deceased is the explanation for these reproaches,
and similarly for the "primitive" belief in the malignancy of spirits of
dead loved ones: the *projection* of that hostility is feared aggression
from the dead. Projection is also a technique of those suffering from
paranoia who are "struggling against an intensification of their homosexual trends." In paranoia, Freud tells us, "the persecutor is in reality
the loved person, past or present."[24]

Eleanor's psychosexual history is similar to that of the subject of Freud's "Case of Paranoia Running Counter to the Psychoanalytical Theory of the Disease" a thirtyish woman living with her mother who forms a paranoic delusion to defend herself against the attentions of a man. In both cases, the loved person, then, the persecutor, is the mother. Much has been made in film theory of the form the patient's delusion took in this case: that of being photographed, sparked by an "accidental knock or tick" which she hears while visiting the man in his apartment. The visual and the auditory, the camera and the click are the two registers of which the cinema is composed, rendering it analogous to paranoid projection.[25] The noteworthy point of Freud's case history is his reading of the instigating cause of the delusion: "I do not believe that the clock ever ticked or that any noise was to be heard at all. The woman's situation justified a sensation of throbbing in the clitoris. . . . There had been a 'knocking' of the clitoris." "In her subsequent rejection of the man," Freud concludes, "lack of satisfaction undoubtedly played a part."[26]

The knock recurs in this scene from *The Haunting* with the force of a cannonball (proportionate to the force of Eleanor's repression, manifested before in the violence of her "poltergeist" experience) and intervenes precisely at the moment of a prohibition against homosexual desire. It is a knocking which on the manifest level can be read as the ghost of Abigail looking for a companion, or on a latent level as the persecution of Eleanor by her own mother in conjunction with her taking of a new lover. (That is, Theo. If we are reluctant to read this as a quasi-love scene I offer as anecdotal support the fact that, despite its centrality, it was cut from the version I saw on TV.) Like Freud, the men do not believe there had been any noise at all. Love between women is considered unspeakable; it is inaudible; and it doesn't leave a scratch. I do not contend that the laughter Theo and Eleanor share over the men's ignorance is irrecuperable; indeed the scene most literally transforms homosexuality into homophobia—replacing sexuality with fear. When the doctor pompously acknowledges that "something" is separating the girls from the boys in Hill House, he resolves to take precautions. "Against what?," Eleanor asks, naively, for the second time in this sequence. For the camera tells us it is Theo, someone, not some thing, who separates the doctor and Eleanor.

The next morning Eleanor awakens a little too excited by her first experience of the "supernatural." Over breakfast, her hair arranged in a new style, she claims to be "much more afraid of being abandoned or left behind than of things that go bump in the night." This does not

Figure 10.   The heterosexual embrace.

appear to be entirely true, for her feeling of excitement is accompanied by her turning away from Theo as potential love object and towards the doctor, whose paternalistic interest in her Theo calls unfair. When asked what *she* is afraid of, Theo responds, "of knowing what I really want." Her words make Eleanor uncomfortable on several levels. Eleanor misreads her own desire, as I suspect some feminist film critics would, as desire for the man, i.e., the father. Theo's attitude toward her demeaning rival is manifested with knowing sarcasm, telling Eleanor she "hasn't the ghost of a chance." A still image (fig. 10) freezes in a perverse embrace Eleanor's relationship to the doctor. Actually, he has just caught her as she is about to fall backwards over the railing. She had been staring up at the turret, and in a rapid zoom from the point of view of the tower window, she has been virtually pushed by the camera, the house itself, and the implied gaze of a (female) ghost. Eleanor's turning towards the father smacks indeed of "a defense against a homosexual wish," and she literally begins to see Theo as a persecutor. The very forcefulness of this defense supports a reading of the night of knocking as a seduction scene.

More than Meets the Eye

The defense against homosexuality is mirrored on the level of the film's enunciation; when the supernatural events of the second night

Figure 11. A family portrait.

bring the women together, the cinematic apparatus emphatically separates them. The women are sleeping in beds pushed next to each other. Dr. Markway (taking precautions) has advised the women to move in together. ("You're the doctor," Theo responds). When Eleanor wakes to mysterious sobbing noises she holds on tightly to Theo's hand. She finally manages to turn on the light and the camera pans rapidly to Theo on the opposite of the room. Eleanor, horrified, realizes it was not Theo's hand she was holding but that of some ghostly companion. It is not the "supernatural" alone that is responsible for this mean trick. The cinema itself renders the women's physical contact (albeit merely handholding) impossible. For we know that Theo's bed is not on the other side of the room. A cinematically specific code—and a disruptive one at that, the swish pan—intervenes to separate the two women from each other and to render the viewer complicit.

In a scene that encapsulates the "Oedipal" drama of Hill House and thus the conflict over Eleanor's proper identification, the cinema works *with* the supernatural in allowing a lesbian reading. The four guests literally find their "family portrait" in a massive group statute meant to represent St. Francis curing the lepers, who are all female (fig. 11). The women notice that the statue seems to move when they look away, a classic "uncanny" effect. Luke remarks that the configuration reminds him of a family portrait of the historical inhabitants of Hill House, Hugh Crain looming above his wives, his daughter, the companion, and a dog. Theo maps the current group onto the statue and thus onto the original group, designating Eleanor as the companion, herself, tellingly, as the daughter "—grown up," the doctor as Hugh Crain, and Luke, the ostensible Oedipal hero, as the dog. Luke, startled, indicates with a glance at the women that he has finally caught on to Theo's sexual orientation, commenting that "more than meets the eye" is going on in Hill House. This phrase, denoting lesbianism, applies equally to the supernatural events of *The Haunting*. Yet, immediately after the group leaves the room, "more" meets the eye of the spectator—the camera zooms into two of the female figures, which seem to have moved so that one clutches the other's breasts. This privileged view is a cinematic flourish, and a key to a reading, implicating Eleanor in a lesbian embrace through the figure to which she corresponds, and suggesting that the female forces of Hill House are beginning to close in on her.

"You're the monster of Hill House," Eleanor finally shouts at Theo, several scenes later, coming closer to the truth than she knows. It is at the culmination of this scene: "Life is full of inconsistencies, nature's mistakes—you for instance," that Mrs. Markway, consistently, makes her entrance. Coming to persuade her husband to give up his nonsense, she embodies the missing element of the family portrait, marking the futility of Eleanor's attempt to identify herself with that position. In another still (fig. 12), the psychic importance of the mother to Eleanor is represented by her subordination to Mrs. Markway.

The materialization of the wife at this point in the film seems to be part of the process whereby cinema—like the house itself, which calls Eleanor home through literal writing on the wall—demands its tribute of the heroine. On this "final" night of Eleanor's stay, she imagines she has killed off the wife/mother when Mrs. Markway, because of her skepticism, becomes "deranged" by Hill House, and disappears from her room—the nursery, Abigail's room, "the cold rotten heart of Hill House," that had remained locked before opening spontaneously on the night of her arrival. Mrs. Markway then appears unexpectedly to scare Eleanor (ultimately to scare her to death) on two additional occasions.

First she interrupts Eleanor's intense identification with the place of the companion's suicide, the library. Eleanor's haunting by the wife is quite logically played out over the architecture of the house, which is fantasmatically inflected with Eleanor's own psychic history. Eleanor sums up her subjective crisis: "So what if he does have a wife, I still have a place in this house. I belong." As Eleanor runs through the

Figure 12.   Mrs. Markway materializes.

Figure 13.   The library door.

house, she is frightened by her own reflection; we hear loud creaking and crashing, and the image rocks. She thinks, "the house is destroying itself, it is coming down around me." Eleanor had been unable to enter the library before, overpowered by a smell she associates with her mother (fig. 13), but tonight she seems to be called there; the *unheimlich* is transformed to the *heimlich*. Eleanor climbs the library's spiral staircase as if induced by the camera which makes the dreamlike ascent before her. The companion had hung herself from the top of the staircase, and the camera had prefigured these later ascents in the prologue's enactment of this death: "I've broken the spell of Hill House. I'm home, I'm home," Eleanor senses. The doctor "rescues" her when she reaches the top, yet just as she turns to descend, Mrs. Markway's head pops into the frame through a trap door above. Eleanor faints, and the screen fades to black.

It is now that the doctor, futilely, decides to send Eleanor away from Hill House. For he misrecognizes (as an hallucination) her recognition of the wife. Yet for once she has actually *seen* something that we, importantly, also see. She is terrorized, at the very moment of her identification with the companion, by the apparition of the heterosexual role model, the wife. Eleanor comprehends the displacement of her Oedipal drama (the substituting of herself for the mother) by the inverted drama of Hill House (the wife's substitution for Eleanor in relation to the house's desire). "I'm the one who's supposed to stay. She's taken my place." And Eleanor dies, ironically, literally in the wife's place.

For the "narrative image" figured in the film's prologue—the death of Hugh Crain's first wife—her lifeless hand falling into the frame, after her horse rears, "for no apparent reason"—is now offered as the "narrative image" of the film. The shot is repeated exactly after Eleanor's car crashes into the very same tree, her hand falling into the frame. The first wife died before rounding the corner that would have given her the gothic heroine's first glimpse of the house; Eleanor cannot leave the gaze of Hill House.

She crashes, apparently, to avoid hitting Mrs. Markway, who, for the second time, suddenly runs across her path. Mrs. Markway appears as the agent of a deadly variant of heterosexual narrative closure. Eleanor is not allowed to live or die as the companion; incapable of living as the wife, she is tricked into dying in her place.

But, being a ghost film, *The Haunting* goes beyond the image of death. The final image is properly the house—the grave, woman?— accompanied by Eleanor's voice-over (or rather the voice of Eleanor's ghost) echoing these words from the opening narration: "Whatever walked there, walked alone." Prying the "narrative image" from its Oedipal logic and usurping the authoritative male voice-over, Eleanor transforms the words: "We who walk here, walk alone." Eleanor finally belongs—to a "we" that we know to be feminine and suspect might be lesbian, "we who walk alone," and the house belongs to her. The "haunting" exceeds the drive of cinema to closure, actually using the material codes of cinema, the soundtrack, to *suggest* something else.

The Haunting exceeds the woman's story as female Oedipal drama enacted, Tania Modleski demonstrates, in a gothic like *Rebecca*. In that genre the protagonist's search for the "secret" of a dead woman is facilitated (or impeded) by a key figure, an older, sometimes sinister female character variously the "housekeeper," the "nurse," or in some other capacity a "companion" to the dead woman. These roles are truly a gallery of the best of lesbian characters in classic cinematic history. Played by the likes of Judith Anderson (Mrs. Danvers in *Rebecca*, fig. 14) or Cornelia Otis Skinner (*The Uninvited*, fig. 15) they are a compelling reason for the young woman, recently married and suspecting it might have been a mistake, to realize that it *was* one. I have discussed the centrality of the companion in the psychic history of Hill House, and will venture that the companion function provides

Figure 14. *Fontaine, Anderson in* Rebecca.

Figure 15. *Cornelia Otis Skinner, far right, in* The Uninvited.

a mapping and an iconography of female homosexuality throughout the gothic genre. In *The Haunting* a crucial transformation has taken place with the manifest appearance of lesbianism. The representation of the dead woman, the object of the heroine's desire ("Rebecca" as precisely unrepresentable in that film), and the function of the companion, converge in the figure of Theodora, who is emphatically not the mother.

The Canny Lesbian

If the nameless heroine of *Rebecca* oscillates between the two poles of female Oedipal desire—desire for the mother and desire for the father—Mrs. Danvers sets the house on fire and dies with it, joining the ghost of Rebecca which, as Modleski reads it, "haunts" her.[27] And if Eleanor's trajectory sums up these two variants, Theo grows up— like Abigail, the daughter before her, and lives to tell of the terrors of Hill House. In developing a feminist film theory which would incorporate Theo, we might recall the model of spectatorship she offers in the film. Telepathy, to lesbians and gay men as historical readers and viewers, has always been an alternative to our own mode of paranoic spectatorship: "Is it really there?" The experience of this second sight involves the identification of and with Theo as a lesbian. As for *The Haunting*, it's a very scary movie, even a threatening one. As the TV movie guide recommends, "See it with a friend."[28]

Or, perhaps, a "companion."

Notes

My thanks to Eric Hickson and Teresa de Lauretis for their invaluable comments and suggestions. I also want to thank Cynthia Schneider for her intelligent criticism, her encouragement and companionship.

1. Shirley Jackson, *The Haunting of Hill House* (New York: Penguin Books, 1959; repr. 1987).

2. Michael Weldon, *The Psychotronic Encyclopedia of Film* (New York: Ballantine, 1983), 307.

3. Linda Williams, "When the Woman Looks," in *Re-Vision*, ed. Mary Ann Doane, Patricia Mellencamp, and Linda Williams (Frederick, MD: University Publications of America and the American Film Institute, 1984), 87. The fact that the horror genre is not one traditionally associated with female audiences is nicely illustrated by Williams: "Whenever the movie screen holds a particularly effective image of

terror, little boys and grown men make it a point of honor to look, while little girls and grown women cover their eyes or hide behind the shoulder of their dates" (83). The representation of the female gaze within the film, however, is a primary device of horror. As Mary Ann Doane reads Williams' argument: "Female scopophilia is a drive without an object ... what the woman actually sees, after a sustained and fearful process of looking, is a sign or representation of herself displaced to the level of the nonhuman." *The Desire to Desire* (Bloomington: Indiana University Press, 1987), 141–42. Doane's remarks on the horror film are made within her discussion of the film gothic, a genre which does address a female spectator, and with which *The Haunting* shares an affiliation.

4. As one contemporary reviewer summarized the doctor's thesis: "The occurrences, according to Markway, are 'brought on by the people whom they affect,' " pointing to the similarity among theories of neurosis, homosexuality, and "haunting" which I will exploit later. *Film Quarterly* (Winter 1963/4): 44–46. The review focuses on the specifically filmic means by which Wise achieves the terrifying effects of *The Haunting*. The film's press book recounts how Wise was posed with the problem of how to film "nothing," and how he devised an ingenious effect for filming a "cold spot," thereby allying the director with the doctor.

5. Laura Mulvey, "Afterthoughts on 'Visual Pleasure and Narrative Cinema' Inspired by *Duel in the Sun* (King Vidor, 1946)," *Framework*, nos. 15/16/17 (1981): 12.

6. "In all these cases a defence against a homosexual wish was clearly recognizable at the very centre of the conflict which underlay the disease." Sigmund Freud, "On the Mechanism of Paranoia" (1911), in *General Psychological Theory* (New York: Collier Books, 1963), 29.

7. The appearance of the special issue of *Camera Obscura* on "The Spectatrix," 20–21 (May–September 1989), edited by Janet Bergstrom and Mary Ann Doane, signals the continued vigor of these debates. National surveys and a host of individual responses to a series of questions on the theorization and relevance of female spectatorship offer a great deal of information on scholars' research. However, the forum of the survey discouraged the participation of key figures in feminist film theory, most notably Teresa de Lauretis and Tania Modleski.

8. Doane, *The Desire to Desire*, 10. Subsequent references are cited in the text.

9. Freud, "On the Mechanism of Paranoia," 29.

10. For instance the important, lesbian-coded character of Mrs. Danvers is barely mentioned in Doane's discussion of *Rebecca*.

11. Sigmund Freud, "A Case of Paranoia Running Counter to the Psychoanalytical Theory of the Disease" (1915), in *Sexuality and the Psychology of Love* (New York: Collier Books, 1963), 97–106.

12. Thus "throwing away her pleasure" describes the process of female spectatorship: " ... to possess the image through the gaze is to become it. And becoming the image, the woman can no longer have it. For the female spectator, the image is *too* close—it cannot be projected far enough. ... What she lacks, in other words, is a 'good throw' " (168–69).

13. Norman N. Holland and Leona F. Sherman, "Gothic Possibilities," *New Literary History* 8, no. 2 (Winter 1977): 279, cited in Doane, 124.

14. Sigmund Freud, "The 'Uncanny' " (1919) in *Art and Literature*, ed. Albert Dickson (Harmondsworth: Penguin, 1985), 335–76.

15. Judy Oppenheimer, *Private Demons: The Life of Shirley Jackson*. (New York: Ballantine, 1988), 226.

16. Jurij M. Lotman, "The Origin of Plot in the Light of Typology," cited in Teresa de Lauretis, *Alice Doesn't: Feminism, Semiotics, Cinema* (Bloomington: Indiana University Press, 1984), 118.

17. De Lauretis, *Alice Doesn't*, 119.

18. Tania Modleski, " 'Never To Be Thirty-Six Years Old': *Rebecca* as Female Oedipal Drama," *Wide Angle 5*, no. 1 (1982): 34–41, reprinted in *The Women Who Knew Too Much: Hitchcock and Feminist Theory* (New York and London: Methuen, 1988), 43–56. See also de Lauretis, *Alice Doesn't*, 51–55, for a reading of Modleski's article.

19. De Lauretis, *Alice Doesn't*, 140. The notion of "narrative image" is a complex one to which the present discussion cannot do justice. Heath's introduction of the concept had only the suggestion of the overdetermined association with femininity which de Lauretis traces so convincingly. He defined the narrative image as "a film's presence, how it can be talked about, what it can be sold and bought on . . . in the production stills displayed outside a cinema, for example." *Questions of Cinema* (Bloomington: Indiana University Press, 1981), 121. For instance, lesbian and gay supporting characters are evicted from the narrative image, from reviews, from plot summaries, from the images on posters. The production stills included in the present context are examples from a film whose narrative image is unrepresentable.

20. Vito Russo notes the homophobic tendency to claim gay-themed movies are about "something else" in his *The Celluloid Closet: Homosexuality in the Movies* (New York: Harper and Row, 1981), 126. Yet a standard of "coming out"—the search for the overt, fully realized representation of homosexuality (particularly if the standard is arguably a masculine one) can lead to reductive readings of actual films, as is the case in Russo's discussion of *The Haunting*:

> Unconscious lesbianism is its own punishment . . . for Claire Bloom's neurotic Greenwich Village lesbian in *The Haunting* (1963). She gets her psychosexual jollies by hugging Julie Harris and blaming it on ghosts. But she is not predatory; she is just out of life's running. She professes no interest in actively seducing either Harris *or an attentive Russ Tamblyn.* The lesbianism is entirely mental, and her sterility leaves her at a dead end. . . . Lesbianism is rendered invisible because it is purely psychological. *And since most lesbians were invisible even to themselves,* their sexuality, *ill-defined in general,* emerged onscreen as a wasted product of a closeted lifestyle. (158; emphasis added).

I perceive the Bloom character as, on the contrary, very well adjusted, and I read the very "invisibility" of lesbianism in the film as a strategy of representation. Parker Tyler writes, "it might seem to both readers of the novel and viewers of the film . . . that lesbianism had a role in drawing these unusual ladies closer in the frightening, macabre situation to which they commit themselves and where they must 'cling' to each other." *Screening the Sexes: Homosexuality in the Movies* (New York: Holt, Rinehart and Winston, 1972), 190.

21. Sigmund Freud, *The Interpretation of Dreams* (New York: Avon Books, 1965), 439.

22. The spectator/auditor is also able to "read Eleanor's mind" through the voice-over device, although sometimes Theo seems to have access to Eleanor's unconscious thoughts and desires, as well as to effects of the "haunting" signified to the spectator by other visual and auditory cues.

23. Sigmund Freud, *Totem and Taboo* (New York: Vintage Books, 1946), 80.

24. Freud, "A Case of Paranoia. . .," 99.

25. See Doane, *The Desire to Desire*, 123.

26. Freud, "A Case of Paranoia. . .," 109.

27. Modleski, *The Women Who Knew Too Much*, 51. In the later version of her essay, Modleski makes explicit the lesbian element with the addition of this phrase, "the heroine continually strives . . . to win the affections of Mrs. Danvers *who seems herself to be possessed, haunted, by Rebecca and to have a sexual attachment to the dead woman.*"

28. Leonard Maltin, ed., *Leonard Maltin's TV Movies & Video Guide* (New York: Signet, 1989), 444.

7

A Parallax View of
Lesbian Authorship

Judith Mayne

Diane Kurys's 1983 film *Coup de foudre (Entre Nous)* has a devoted following among many lesbians, despite—or perhaps also because of— the fact that the allusions to lesbianism occur from within the securely defined boundaries of female bonding and friendship.[1] Two women, Léna (played by Isabelle Huppert) and Madeleine (played by Miou-Miou), living in post-World War II provincial France discover an attraction for each other (an attraction that is definitely erotic though never explicitly sexual) and eventually leave their husbands to live together. As was widely publicized at the time of the film's release, the friendship of the two women has a strong autobiographical signifi-cance, for it corresponds to the experience of Kurys's own mother. At the conclusion of the film, when Léna (Kurys's mother) asks Michel (Kurys's father, played by Guy Marchand) to leave, their daughter— i.e., the fictional representation of Kurys herself—is seen watching them. Over the final shot of the film, of Madeleine walking with the children on the beach, a title appears, a very literal authorial signature: "My father left at dawn. He never saw my mother again. It's now been two years since Madeleine died. I dedicate this film to the three of them."[2]

The sudden appearance of the author's signature, within the child's point of view, situates the enigma of the women's relationship in the ambiguous world of childish perception. All of Kurys's films are marked by the connection between storytelling and a female bond that wavers between the homosocial and the homoerotic. Somewhat surprisingly, perhaps, that connection is most strongly marked and articulated in what appears to be, on the surface, the film that departs the most sharply from the distinctly female world central to Kurys's

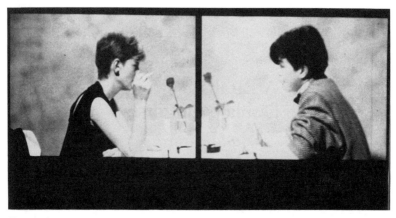

Figure 1.

first three films (*Diablo Menthe [Peppermint Soda], Cocktail Molotov,* and *Entre Nous*). In *A Man in Love (Un Homme amoureux)* [1987], the plot centers upon a young actress, Jane (played by Greta Scacchi) whose affair with a narcissistic American movie star, Steve Elliot (played by Peter Coyote) is interwoven with her relationship with her mother (played by Claudia Cardinale) who suffers from and eventually dies of cancer.

While the film follows Jane as its central protagonist, it is not until approximately two-thirds of the way through the film that her voice emerges, quite literally, as the voice of the film, through voice-over commentary. The voice-over is the major component of the film's self-mirroring quality; in the concluding scenes, Jane begins writing a text entitled "A Man in Love." The first appearance of the voice-over occurs immediately after a scene in which Jane, in bed with her lover Steve, speaks—seemingly at his request—a fantasy of lesbian lovemaking. Hence, the conditions of the emergence of the female narrator's voice are bound up, narratively, with the lesbian fantasy, a fantasy which offers, within the logic of the film, the possibility of combining two spheres otherwise separate—heterosexual passion, on the one hand, and the mother-daughter bond, on the other.

Some aspects of Kurys's films offer significant revisions of the components of narrative cinema—such as the re-writing of the boys' school scenario (central to two classics of French film history, Jean Vigo's *Zéro de conduite* and François Truffaut's *The 400 Blows*) in her first feature film, *Diablo Menthe (Peppermint Soda)*; or the exchange of looks between the two women in *Entre Nous*. The self-representation of Kurys (in *Peppermint Soda* and *Entre Nous* in particular), and the representation of female authorship, are far more problematic in the present context, for they consistently evoke and dispel lesbianism simultaneously. Put another way, the "lesbianism" affiliated with Kurys's signature is so framed by the duality of heterosexuality on the one hand, and the maternal bond on the other, that female authorship is foregrounded but not significantly reframed or retheorized outside of that duality.

However, if the popular reception of Kurys's *Entre Nous* by lesbian audiences is any indication, then the film lends itself to the same kind of reading as Barbara Smith offered of *Sula*, a reading based, that is, on the permeable boundaries between female bonding and lesbianism.[3] This is not to say that *Entre Nous* has been defined in any simple way as a "lesbian film." Indeed, whether Kurys's film is appropriately described as a "lesbian film"—permeable boundaries notwithstanding—has been a matter of some debate among lesbians. In a letter to the editors of *Gossip*, a British lesbian-feminist journal, Lynette Mitchell criticizes two essays published in the journal which represent *Entre Nous* as "an unequivocally lesbian film."[4] Mitchell notes that in the film, "the two women are shown admiring each other's bodies and at one point in the film they exchange a swift kiss, but this could just as easily be an expression of deep physical affection as erotic desire."[5] In any case, if *A Man in Love* offers the theory (and *Entre Nous* the practice), then the lesbianism evoked in Kurys's work is not only fully compatible with, but also fully dependent upon, heterosexual fantasy and maternal connections. Put another way, lesbianism is simultaneously a limit and a horizon of female narration and authorship.

In some oddly similar ways, lesbianism is also a limit and a horizon for contemporary feminist work on the female subject. Two of the most common and persistent threads of this work have been, first, the theorizing of a double position for women, as both inside and outside of patriarchal culture, and second, a staging of what is by now a classic fixture of feminist theory, the encounter between so-called American empiricism and French theory. While feminist theories of the subject and of subjectivity are often criticized by lesbians and women of color for being inattentive to the difference that marginalities make, it's not altogether accurate, at least not in the case of lesbianism, to describe the apparent indifference as an absence.

Consider, for example, the by-now notorious dismissal in Toril Moi's *Sexual/Textual Politics* of American black or lesbian feminist criticism: "Some feminists might wonder why I have said nothing about black or lesbian (or black-lesbian) feminist criticism in America in this survey. The answer is simple: this book purports to deal with the theoretical aspects of feminist criticism."[6] Moi proceeds to explain that black and lesbian literary critics are as controlled by the limits of empirical criticism as their straight white sisters; while they may have political importance, their work is theoretically—well, theoretically retarded. Moi does note, however, that these " 'marginal feminisms' ought to prevent white middle-class First-World feminists from defining their own preoccupations as universal female (or feminist) problems."[7] By the conclusion of her own book, even this vapid concession—from which the term "heterosexual" is, in any case, conspicuously absent—is forgotten. That lesbian criticism doesn't have too much importance—political or otherwise—is demonstrated by Moi's elevation of Julia Kristeva as a model of theoretical feminism, with no mention of the extent to which Kristeva's theorizing establishes the lesbian as bad object, and no consideration that this might be a problem for her feminist usefulness.[8]

This isn't to say that Moi is representative of all feminist explorations of the French-American encounter and the contradictory status of the female subject. Nancy K. Miller, for instance, has noted that Moi "manages to collapse each side of the American/French divide with an astonishing lack of concern for the bodies (and positions) under erasure."[9] Indeed, Miller's own work is far less invested in the simple dualities of simple-minded American feminism versus smart French theory. But here, lesbianism also acquires an implicit function, one defined far more in terms of the pole of attraction (in contrast to the pole of repulsion in Moi's account). In the introduction to her book *Subject to Change*, Miller notes that "[i]t may also be that the difference of another coming to writing requires an outside to heterosexual economies."[10] While the term "lesbian" is not used to describe the utopian female communities which figure so prominently in Miller's analyses of women's fiction, the language used is quite evocative of much lesbian writing, and Miller's own reading of Adrienne Rich with Roland Barthes can be read as an attempt both to acknowledge lesbian writing and to redefine the intersections between homosexuality and feminism. Thus, while Miller's avoidance of the term "lesbian" has more to do with the desire to avoid a perilous opposition of "lesbian" and "heterosexual" than to dismiss lesbian possibilities, one is left with a conception of female space with distinct, yet distinctly unspecified, lesbian contours.

Moi dismisses while Miller is more inclusive. However, if the specter of lesbianism does not necessarily haunt feminist theories of the subject, lesbianism has had a signifying function by virtue of its very status as "other"—whether untheoretical other, in Moi, or utopian other, in Miller. It is commonly assumed—and frequently euphemized through phrases like "radical feminism"—that a politically informed lesbian subjectivity participates in the naive affirmation of self, the unproblematic articulation of agency, and the most common refrain of all, essentialism, taken to be characteristic of "American feminism."

Many lesbian filmmakers have engaged with the redefinition and reconceptualization of the cinema, and in so doing have challenged the implicit oxymoron of "lesbian theory" that haunts so many feminist explorations of the subject. But why, one might ask, define these projects in terms of *authorship*, particularly given the suspicious reputation it has acquired—much like lesbianism itself, one might add—for harboring idealized, untheorized defenses of the fictions of identity? Furthermore, within the context of cinema studies, the very notion of authorship is far more evocative of traditional, patriarchal film criticism than even is the case in literary studies, for instance. To be sure, throughout the history of contemporary film studies, there have been calls to rethink and retheorize authorship, from Claire Johnston's insistence in 1973 that *auteurism* and feminism could function compatibly, to Kaja Silverman's recent critique of feminist film theorists whose ostensible dismissal of the film author is accompanied by the return of a desire for unproblematized agency.[11] Nonetheless, the revision of the concept of authorship has not been a high priority in film studies.

The need to bring authorship into a discussion of lesbian representation is evidenced by a significant body of films in which the filmmaker herself is written into the text, although not in ways that match the common, easy equation between authorial presence and the fictions of identity. There are some lesbian films where this does occur as an affirmative and self-revelatory gesture—Barbara Hammer's celebrations of lesbian love come immediately to mind. But a far more provocative feature of contemporary lesbian filmmaking is the articulation of lesbian authorship as a critical exploration of the very components of subjectivity—self/other relations, desire, and—where lesbianism provides the most crucial challenge to theories of the subject—the relationship between the paradigms of gender and agency, e.g., the presumed identity between activity and masculinity, passivity and femininity. Chantal Akerman's 1974 film *Je tu il elle*, for instance, is saturated with an authorial presence that explores the possible alignments of the pronouns of its title, and Akerman attempts nothing less than the rewriting of the cinematic scenario that prescribes formulaic relations between those terms along the lines of heterosexual symmetry. Or, to take a related but different example, Ulrike Ottinger has written herself into her films as cameo performances. From the flashback appearance as the dead lover, Orlando, of the title character of *Madame X* to a drunken passerby in *Ticket of No Return*, these appearances revise substantially the assumed equation between authorial fictions and heterosexual oedipal narratives.[12]

Midi Onodera's *Ten Cents a Dance (Parallax)* (1985) is a short (30 minutes) film, divided into three sections (in the catalogue of *Women Make Movies*, the film is described as a kind of "*Je tu il elle* in miniature"). Like other explorations of lesbian representation, *Ten Cents a Dance* is less concerned with affirmative representations of lesbian experience than with explorations of the simultaneous ambivalence and pressure of lesbianism with regards to the polarities of agency and gender. This could of course be taken to mean that the film is, because less "explicitly" lesbian in its focus, less lesbian, period. Indeed, the status of *Ten Cents a Dance* as a "lesbian film" has been crucial to its reception.

For *Ten Cents a Dance* has had a controversial reception history. At the Tenth Annual Lesbian/Gay Film Festival in San Francisco in 1986, for instance, Onodera's film was shown last on a program entitled "Lesbian Shorts," with four other films. By all accounts, the film precipitated something close to a riot, with a considerable portion of the audience booing the film and demanding its money back. If the letters devoted to the screening which later appeared in *Coming Up!*—a San Francisco gay/lesbian newspaper—are representative of the controversy, then *Ten Cents a Dance* was indicative of—to borrow a phrase from B. Ruby Rich—a crisis of naming in lesbian filmmaking.[13] For how could this film, two-thirds of which is devoted to the representation of gay men and heterosexuals, possibly be called a "lesbian film," and advertised as such? More specific criticisms were made as well—that unsafe sex was depicted between the two men, for instance, and that the lesbian scene included a heterosexual woman. The Board of Directors of Frameline, the organizers of the festival, responded that *Ten Cents a Dance* ". . . was not only by a lesbian, but was strongly pro-lesbian, despite a scene by two gay men and a straight couple having sex" (sic).[14] The exhibition context required the charge of "not a lesbian film" to be countered with "not only a lesbian film, but a pro-lesbian film." But the reception of the film speaks to a larger issue about lesbian representation, concerning precisely the relationship between lesbianism and the contradictory subject theorized within contemporary feminist theory.

Each section of *Ten Cents a Dance* is concerned with a different configuration of sexual desire and language. A split screen is used throughout, so that the two players in every scene are divided from each other. In the first section, two women, while waiting for (or just having finished) dinner in a Japanese restaurant, discuss whether or not they will have a sexual relationship. In the second section, shot from a high angle, two men have sex with each other in a public restroom. And in the final section, a man and a woman engage in phone sex. The use of the split screen creates a wide angle effect, since the top and bottom of the frame are masked, and the two screens appear as if "projected" against a black background, with a dividing line between them. Each scene in Onodera's film captures a sense both of pleasurable duration—depending, of course, upon how you define "pleasure"—and of uncomfortable pauses.

The title of Onodera's film cites the Rodgers and Hart song about a hostess at the Palace Ballroom who sells dances to "Fighters and sailors and bow-legged tailors . . . butchers and barbers and rats from the harbor." The song is a cynical lament, full of bitter resignation and desperation. The most obvious "match" to the song is the third section of the film, and it would be easy to argue that Onodera equates heterosexual sex with the pathos of sex for sale. But in this respect, *Ten Cents a Dance* has an ambiguous quality—it suggests simultaneously the difference and the analogy between different sexualities. For all of the participants in the film enact rituals of erotic connection and distance.

In any case, the title of the film also reminds us that "Ten Cents a Dance," is not to be taken so literally: the addition of "Parallax" in parentheses, over the right screen, can be read in relationship not only to each of the participants in the respective couples, but in relationship to the distinction between straight and gay, gay and lesbian, male and female as well. If the difference between two points of view allows the "apparent displacement of an observed object" (as the dictionary says), then the "parallax" of Onodera's title refers quite obviously to the way in which lesbian and gay readings take citation and replacement as central strategies. More specifically, the "parallax" view of *Ten Cents a Dance* is evocative of Joan Nestle's insistence—speaking of the difference between "replication" and "resistance" in the appropriation of butch and fem styles—that lesbians "should be mistresses of discrepancies, knowing that resistance lies in the change of context."[15]

Undoubtedly the doubled screen is the most striking visual figure of discrepancy in *Ten Cents a Dance*. The split screen suggests a number of cinematic precedents, such as the stereoscope card—a doubled image which, when viewed at the proper distance, creates the illusion of depth. Other uses of the split screen come to mind as well. In *Pillow Talk* (1959), for instance, split screens are used extensively to juxtapose the telephone conversations of Doris Day and Rock Hudson, frequently with contrasting pink and blue color schemes—which Onodera adapts in her red and blue portrayal of heterosexual phone contact. If the third section of the film is the one most obviously informed by classical Hollywood conventions, all three sections play upon the edges of the frame, particularly in their contrasting functions of reiterating the markers separating the two women (the rose) and rendering oblique the restroom wall and glory hole that separate and connect the two men.

In all three instances, the two views are juxtaposed to disrupt the seamless fit between the participants in sexual dramas. The relationship between the two screens in each section acquires the contours of simultaneous connection and separation. The screen surfaces are figures of permeability and division at the same time. Far from serving as the unproblematized ground for the image, the screen in *Ten Cents a Dance* becomes a site of tension. This occurs by the doubling of the screens, and by the relationship between the two edges that never quite touch. In addition, the interplay of screen and frame makes the film's representation of sexuality more a question of what is screened, in both senses of the term, than what is unproblematically visible. In the first and last sections of the film, of course, sexual talk obscures the sexual act, but even in the second section of the film, it is the threshold between the two men which is foregrounded far more than sexual acts themselves.

In her recent essay on lesbian representation and Sheila McLaughlin's film *She Must Be Seeing Things*, Teresa de Lauretis distinguishes films like McLaughlin's, which produce "modes of representing that effectively alter the standard frame of reference and visibility, the conditions of the visible, what *can* be seen and represented" (a description which obviously applies to *Ten Cents a Dance*), from those which provide "sympathetic accounts . . . without necessarily producing new ways of seeing or a new inscription of the social subject in representation."[16] In the latter category, de Lauretis includes films like *Desert Hearts* and *Lianna*. Mandy Merck has described *Desert Hearts* as "steeped in the heterosexual tradition of the active pursuit of the reluctant woman," and goes on to cite a series of rigid dichotomies which structure the film—those of class and geography, for instance.[17]

Such dichotomies have more than a passing relationship with *Ten Cents a Dance*, particularly insofar as the first section of the film is concerned. Merck notes that in *Desert Hearts*, the "brunette is to blonde as active is to passive" dichotomy appears as a stock feature of the genre of the lesbian romance. Dark-haired Onodera casts herself in the role of the "experienced lesbian" having relationship talk with a blonde woman whom she had considered "essentially straight" (the experienced lesbian versus the experimenting heterosexual is another typical opposition described by Merck). Yet Onodera cites the dichotomies in order to disrupt them and suspend them simultaneously. For by casting herself, an Asian woman, in the role of the active pursuer, Onodera reverses one of the most common Western representations of Asians, male or female, as passive and obedient. But that such a reversal cannot function in any simple way as an alternative is made clear in the last section of the film, where the woman assumes the active role, but one which reinforces her own position as sexual commodity. More crucially, the oppositions thus cited never attain narrative or sexual resolution—or rather, only attain resolution by displacement and suspension.

But this displacement and suspension engages a risk, for by focusing on two women talking, *Ten Cents a Dance* could be seen as affirming the popular stereotype that lesbians talk about relationships while men have sex—whether with women or with each other. In other words, *Ten Cents a Dance* could be read as affirming lesbianism as, if not asexual, then at least pre-sexual, or, in the language of much contemporary psychoanalytic theory, as pre-oedipal, as a recreation of the mother-child bond. However, what seems to me most crucial in this representation of lesbian sexuality is the way it is framed—not so much in terms of the scene itself, but rather in relationship to the sexual rituals that surround it.

In the essay mentioned above, Teresa de Lauretis is critical of the tendency, in much writing about lesbianism and feminism and the female subject, to conflate identification and desire. The so-called pre-oedipal, mother/daughter bond can only be regarded as the foundation for lesbianism if the desire *for* another woman is subsumed to the desire to be (like) a woman. As de Lauretis puts it, there is a "sweeping of lesbian sexuality and desire under the rug of sisterhood, female friendship, and the now popular theme of 'the mother-daughter bond.' "[18] Implicit in such accounts is a definition of heterosexuality as mature, adult, and symbolic, whether such accounts are "straight" or symptomatic—e.g., really the ways things are, or really the way things are under patriarchy. And heterosexual intercourse becomes the norm against which other sexualities are classified as deviant.

Interestingly in Onodera's film, the possessors of the most explicit (though not completely visible) *sex* are not the heterosexuals but the gay men, and the closest thing to a sexual referent in the film is oral sex, not intercourse. Indeed, orality is one of the sexual common denominators of the film, whether through conversation, smoking ciga-rettes, or sexual acts. Heterosexual intercourse is thus displaced from its status as the standard of sexuality against which all others are compared. The three sections of the film become, rather, sexual con-figurations in which orality—so long considered a major attribute of the regressive, narcissistic, homosexually inclined individual (male or female)—figures across the dividing lines of different sexualities.

As de Lauretis suggests, the conflation of desire and identification, and the attendant relegation of lesbianism to the pre-sexual stage serves to reinforce what are ultimately homophobic definitions. At the same time, however, the definition of lesbianism as an extension of female bonding or mother love is one to which many lesbians have been drawn. Within contemporary lesbianism, there are competing definitions of what lesbianism is, from the most intense form of female and feminist bonding (as theorized by Adrienne Rich in her controversial lesbian continuum),[19] to a sexuality that is distinctly different from heterosexu-ality, whether practiced by men or women. The ironic signature which Midi Onodera brings to her performance—understood here both in terms of her role and the entire film—suggests both of these simultane-ously.

In the first section of the film, Onodera is both the "experienced" lesbian discussing the possibility of an intimate relationship with a woman, and an Asian-Canadian having dinner in one of the most popularized Western clichés of Asia, a restaurant. In other words, she appears to occupy a position of some authority. But Onodera defines authorship so as to expose its fictions as well as its desires. For the position that she occupies, on the right side of the screen, is taken up by a gay man engaging in anonymous sex in the next section, and a woman offering phone sex in the last part of the film. Given the extent to which anonymity and sex for sale are defined, in much lesbian writing, as symptomatic of either male sexuality or heterosexuality, the affiliation between Onodera's position and those of the man and the woman in the subsequent scene brackets any simple notion of lesbian desire as isolated from other forms of sexual desire.

At the same time, of course, the lesbian scene *is* different than the other two, with more emphasis on conversation and the erotics of the look—the latter serving a particularly ironic function, given the extent to which the look has been defined in much feminist film theory as the province of the heterosexual male's possession of the woman. Onodera's ambiguous role in the film, as both author and actor, and as both like and unlike gay men and heterosexuals, thus suggests that the lesbian author is defined as both complicit in and resistant to the sexual fictions of patriarchal culture, and that lesbian irony holds competing definitions of lesbianism up to each other, while refusing to collapse one into the other.

Notes

1. Thanks to Chris Lymbertos, who provided me with information about the reception of *Ten Cents a Dance*; and Laura George, Lucretia Knapp, and Terry Moore, who read this essay at various stages and offered encouragement.

2. "Mon père est parti au petit jour. Il n'a plus jamais revu ma mère. Madeleine est morte il y a maintenant deux ans. A eux trois, je dédie ce film."

3. Barbara Smith, "Towards a Black Feminist Criticism," *Conditions* 2 (1977): 25–44.

4. See Sibyl Grundberg, "Deserted Hearts: Lesbians Making it in the Movies," *Gossip* 4 (no date): 27–39; Lis Whitelaw, "Lesbians of the Mainscreen," *Gossip* 5 (n.d.): 37–46.

5. Lynette Mitchell, "Letter," *Gossip* 6 (n.d.): 11–13.

6. Toril Moi, *Sexual/Textual Politics* (London and New York: Methuen, 1985), 86.

7. Moi, *Sexual/Textual Politics*, 86.

8. See Judith Butler, *Gender Trouble* (New York and London: Routledge, 1990); Teresa de Lauretis, "The Female Body and Heterosexual Presumption," *Semiotica* 67, nos. 3–4 (1987): 259–79; Elizabeth Grosz, *Sexual Subversions: Three French Feminists* (Winchester, Massachusetts: Unwin Hyman, 1989); Kaja Silverman, *The Acoustic Mirror: The Female Voice in Psychoanalysis and Cinema* (Bloomington: Indiana University Press, 1988).

9. Nancy K. Miller, *Subject to Change: Reading Feminist Writing* (New York: Columbia University Press, 1988), 21, n. 16.

10. Miller, *Subject to Change*, 10.

11. Silverman, *Acoustic Mirror*, 209.

12. I discuss at length Akerman's *Je tu il elle* and Ottinger's *Ticket of No Return* in

chapter four of my book, *The Woman at the Keyhole: Feminism and Women's Cinema* (Bloomington: Indiana University Press, 1990).

13. B. Ruby Rich, "The Crisis of Naming in Feminist Film Criticism," *Jump Cut* 19 (1979): 9–12.

14. "Lesbian (?) Short Raises Storm of Controversy at Lesbian Gay Film Festival," *Coming Up!* 11 (August 1986): 5.

15. Joan Nestle, "The Fem Question," *Pleasure and Danger: Exploring Female Sexuality*, ed. Carole S. Vance (Boston: Routledge and Kegan Paul, 1984), 236.

16. Teresa de Lauretis, "Film and the Visible" (Paper delivered at the *How Do I Look?* Conference, New York City, October 1989), 2.

17. Mandy Merck, "Dessert Hearts," *The Independent* 10, no. 6 (1987): 16.

18. De Lauretis, "Film and the Visible," 31.

19. Adrienne Rich, "Compulsory Heterosexuality and Lesbian Existence," *Powers of Desire: The Politics of Sexuality*, eds. Ann Snitow, Christine Stansell, and Sharon Thompson (New York: Monthly Review Press, 1983), 177–205.

8

Believing in Fairies:
The Author and The Homosexual

Richard Dyer

A student once said of me to a colleague, "Of course, Richard doesn't believe in authors—unless the author is a woman." He or she might have added "black" or "lesbian/gay," and it was an acute remark. I'll happily teach *The Searchers* (John Ford) as a John Wayne movie about race, but as soon as it's *Dance, Girl, Dance* (Dorothy Arzner) or *Car Wash* (Michael Schultz) I'm wanting students to worry about whether you can tell they were directed by a woman and a black person, respectively, and how, and whether it matters. (Note already, however, the discrepancies: Ford is banished as Ford, but Arzner and Schultz come back as woman and black; then there's the whiteness of Arzner, the maleness of Schultz, the white maleness of Ford, the sexualities of all three . . .) Equally most of my writing has been about images and representations, texts and readers, yet I have just finished a book on films made by lesbians and gay men,[1] a book posited, that is, on the notion that it does make a difference who makes a film, who the authors are. In this essay I want to think through some of the implications of what that student observed, relating it to a further apparent paradox, a commitment to lesbians and gay men and an acceptance that being lesbian/gay is "only" a social construction. I do this through an account of some of the problems and discoveries I had writing the book just mentioned.

The project was haunted by two politically and theoretically dubious figures: the author and the homosexual. Worries about these figures are most easily authorized by reference to the formulations of two homosexual theorists, Roland Barthes's pronouncement of the death of the author and Michel Foucault's labeling of the homosexual as a social construction. These texts crystallized wider intellectual and political misgivings about both figures, misgivings that I shared.

As far as the author is concerned, reference to him/her in the study of the arts privileged the individual over the social and in practice privileged heterosexual, white, upper-/middle-class male individuals over all others. Texts were often treated, at worst, as illustrations of the author's biography, at best as the expression of his inner life, flying in the face of both the evident discrepancy between most authors' persons and their texts and also the vast range of public functions cultural production performs. In the interpretation of texts, the author was used as a means of fixing and giving weight to particular interpretations, rather than acknowledging the multiplicity of meanings and affects that readers generate from texts. In short, the author was an authority concept, anti-democratic in its triumphant individualism, a support of existing social divisions, hostile to public discourses, and resistant to the creativity of the reader.

The homosexual, when treated as a universal figure in human societies, also posed problems of authority, if by contrast one saw him/her as a social construction, a personality type characteristic of and probably unique to modern Western societies. Work that sought to establish the continuity of lesbian/gay identity across time and culture seemed to be imposing the way lesbian/gay sexuality is for "us" now upon the diversity and radical differences of both the past and "other" (non-white, Third World) cultures and often eliding the differences between lesbians and gay men. The notion of the homosexual seemed to buy into the very operation of power through the regulation of desire that lesbian/gay politics and theory were supposed to be against. It also seemed to sail too close to the wind of the kind of biological etiologies of homosexuality that had been used against same-sex relations and, by holding up a model of what we inexorably are, to deprive of us of the political practice of determining what we wanted to be.

This last misgiving gives the social constructionist position its political edge over the apparently more inspiring universalist positions on homosexuality. While the latter seem to have more immediate political power to mobilize people round an identity apparently rooted in an essential human type, social constructionism returns control over same-sex sexuality to those who live it. It does this by identifying the fact that the latter are not those currently in control of it and indicating the cases and ways in which they are or can be. Those cases and ways include forms of cultural production—but one can have no concept of socially specific forms of cultural production without some notion of authorship, for what one is looking at are the circumstances in which counter-discourses are produced, in which those generally spoken of and for speak for themselves.

I want here to suggest some of the ways in which I tried to work with a model of the author and the homosexual that takes on board the misgivings indicated above. I'll begin by sketching this model and suggesting the ways in which it is useful in trying to conceptualize lesbian/gay cultural production before looking at the ways I found it helpful in the historical analysis of lesbian/gay films and the ways in which the model itself informs and animates many of the texts of those films themselves.

I'm not sure that I ever believed (since I left school) in either the author or the homosexual in quite the way attacks on them presented them.[2] If believing in authorship (in film) means believing that only one person makes a film, that that person is the director, that the film expresses his/her inner personality, that this can be understood apart from the industrial circumstances and semiotic codes within which it is made, then I have never believed in authorship. If believing in lesbians and gay men means believing that they/we have existed as particular kinds of persons at all times and in all places, that what they/we have been like has been pretty much the same in ditto, that being lesbian/gay automatically gives one a particular way of looking at the world and expressing that, then I have never believed in fairies. I sometimes underestimate the extent to which anyone at all believes either in authors or gays and lesbians in those ways, and am brought up sharp by people's readiness to credit a shot in a film to the director's sexual life or to assume that all lesbians identify with the Amazons and all gay men love Judy Garland. But I also think professional intellectuals are inclined to overestimate the extent to which those who went before them thought such things.

Not believing in sole and all-determining authorship does not mean that one must not attach any importance whatsoever to those who make films and believing that being lesbian/gay is a culturally and historically specific phenomenon does not mean that sexual identity is of no cultural and historical consequence. The model I worked with was of multiple authorship (with varying degrees of hierarchy and control) in specific determining economic and technological circumstances, all those involved always working with (within and against) particular codes and conventions of film and with (within and against) particular, social ways of being lesbian or gay. The model is general but none of its particulars are; they always had to be worked out in each case.

In this perspective both authorship and being lesbian/gay become a kind of performance, something we all do but only with the terms, the discourses, available to us, and whose relationship to any imputed self doing the performing cannot be taken as read. This may be a characteristically gay (I hesitate to claim lesbian/gay) perception, since for us performance is an everyday issue, whether in terms of passing as straight, signaling gayness in coming out, worrying which of these turns to do, unsure what any of that has to do with what one "is." If the perception is gay, however, I am not arguing that the author-as-performer model applies only to lesbian/gay authorship—it's just that our social position tends to make us rather good at seeing authorship like that. All authorship and all sexual identities are performances, done with greater or less facility, always problematic in relation to any self separable from the realization of self in the discursive modes available. The study of (gay/lesbian) authorship is the study of those modes and the particular ways in which they have been performed in given texts.

This model of authorship as performance hangs onto the notion of the author as a real, material person, but in what Janet Wolff terms a "decentered" way.[3] In other words, it still matters who specifically made a film, whose performance a film is, though this is neither all-determining nor having any assumable relationship to the person's life or consciousness. What is significant is the authors' material social position in relation to discourse, the access to discourses they have on account of who they are. For my purposes, what was important was their access to filmic and lesbian/gay sub-cultural discourses. In other words, because they were lesbian or gay, they could produce lesbian/gay representations that could themselves be considered lesbian/gay, not because all lesbians or gay men inevitably express themselves on film in a certain way, but because they had access to, and an inwardness with, lesbian/gay sign systems that would have been like foreign languages to straight filmmakers.

There are two advantages to retaining authorship in this form. One is that it allows one to have a notion of lesbian/gay cultural production without having to locate that notion only in the way the text is read or else only in the peculiarities of the text itself. I have nothing against either of these approaches for a full understanding of lesbian/gay culture. Neither the Amazons nor Judy Garland were "meant" to be figures in lesbian or gay culture, but they are and it is proper to analyze them as such.[4] However, we will miss much lesbian and gay cultural production if we restrict ourselves to what fits in with our own codes and conventions of lesbian/gay culture. Equally, some works may have textual properties pretty well unique to lesbian/gay cultural production—the campiness of Jack Smith's films, perhaps, or the clitoral celebrations of Barbara Hammer's—but such cases are unusual and often hard to make; if the poor old text alone has to bear the burden of being lesbian/gay, one will come up with few lesbian/gay texts.

Let me illustrate the last point in a way that will, I hope, also indicate why I think it matters. While I was thinking about this piece, I happened to hear a performance of Tchaikovsky's *Pathétique* Symphony on the radio. I had not heard it for quite a while, but it reminded me that virtually the first thing I ever did which could be construed as gay studies was while I was still in secondary school, when I gave a talk entitled, can you believe it, "The Sick Genius of Tchaikovsky." Then (1964) certainly I did talk about the beautiful tragic cadences of the *Pathétique* as an emanation of Tchaikovsky's inner despair at being a queer. Listening to it again, I still felt one could hear that feeling, though now I might choose to write about it in terms of constructions of queerness and self-hate. It would be hard, however, to argue that one can hear that feeling because of something about the melodic structures and orchestration of the *Pathétique* that could only embody a specifically homosexual despair. You can hear the homosexual feeling by putting together what you know of the circumstances of queerdom of the time with those sounds. This is different from simply choosing (as with camp) to make a cultural artifact work within a particular cultural register; there is warrant to hear the *Pathétique* in a homosexual way and it gives one a particular kind of pleasure, that of fellow feeling, a pleasure of particular political importance to minority or marginalized people.[5]

There is another reason why there is some value in hanging on to authorship in some form. Jean-Paul Sartre once aphorized (of a perhaps rather obscure French poet), "Valéry is a petit-bourgeois intellectual, no doubt about it. But not every petit-bourgeois intellectual is Valéry."[6] In other words, it tells you a lot, where an author is socially placed (in my terms, what discourses she/he has access to) but it still doesn't tell you everything. It doesn't tell you how a woman with no experience of filmmaking, in a production team under the control of a highly patriarchal man, is able to come up with a film as subtle and affirmative as *Mädchen in Uniform*, or how a 17-year-old boy in his parents' house one weekend can make a film as sophisticated and fascinating as *Fireworks*. Placing will tell you a lot about both cases: Leontine Sagan was a theater director who had trained in traditions stressing the use of light and performance, both crucial to the subtlety and affirmation of *Mädchen in Uniform*; Kenneth Anger had knocked about Hollywood and knew some of the film students at USC, whence the sophisticated and fascinating mix of extravagant and avant-garde elements in *Fireworks*; both lived in periods and places of lively lesbian and gay culture—but if all that were so clear an explanatory model, why were there not many more *Mädchens* and *Fireworks*? The very specific contribution of the key authors need not be the starting point or an explain-all, but it is often needed if one is to give a full account of how a lesbian/gay film came into being and why it took the form it did.

Treating authorship as multiple, hierarchical, performed within material and semiotic circumstances, turned out to be revealing as well as conceptually and politically necessary. It focused attention on the contradictoriness and impurity of the work I was looking at and it suggested the way in which these films were partly *about* authorship, or rather than authorship, claiming images one produces as one's own, is often what is at stake for lesbian/gay authors/identities. This section looks at the first of these points.

I took it as a starting point that the films I was looking at, as all cultural artifacts, are not culturally pure, that is, are not lesbian/gay films uncontaminated by straight norms and values. Equivalent issues have been much debated in relation to both women's and black writing. Elaine Showalter and Nancy Miller, among others, have discussed the problem of conceptualizing the position of the woman writer and are equally uneasy with ideas of an *écriture féminine* existing outside of the language women share with men and with any assumption that writing in that language is the same for women as for men. Similarly, the work of Henry Louis Gates, Jr. and others has tried to steer a path between approaches to African-American literature that seek to affirm only one side of that appellation, making it either purely African or only American.[7] Likewise, lesbian/gay cultural production must be understood to take place within, and to be a struggle about, both the cultures of the mainstream and lesbian/gay subcultures. (The latter are themselves in large measure a handling and rehandling, sometimes to the point of unrecognizability, of the former, nor do the cultures of the mainstream learn nothing from lesbian/gay cultures.)

This situation is perhaps particularly sharp with lesbian/gay film production, since lesbian/gay sub-cultures are especially clandestine (often illegal), despised and indirect, and filmmaking requires a scale of financial investment and technological know-how that means it is seldom left in the control of persons from socially subordinated groups. Because of all this, I took it as given that I would have to look, for instance, at the norms of the cycle of (straight) sex education films of which *Anders als die Anderen* (1919) was a part; or the conventions of the avant-garde that fed into U.S. underground cinema and the work of Anger, Smith, Warhol, and others; or the developments in documentary that underpinned the talking heads movies of gay liberation. The whole history is complex—there was also, to varying degrees, a lesbian/gay input to the shaping of all the film traditions involved—but teasing out the interplay, the within and against, of lesbian/gay sub-cultural discourses and the relevant available filmic discourses was a point of departure. What I was less prepared for was the importance of considering the actual personnel who made the films, in terms of who among them did have access to lesbian/gay discourse from a lesbian/gay social position.

This was less of an issue, less problematic, in my later groupings (the U.S. underground, the cultural feminism of the seventies, the films made under the banner of lesbian and gay movements), but with my earliest studies, on the two Weimar films, *Anders als die Anderen* and *Mädchen in Uniform* (1931), and on *Un Chant d'amour* (1950), things were less clear-cut. Neither of the Weimar films was directed by someone we know to have been gay or lesbian, but I felt I had to include them, chiefly because prima facie they felt so lesbian/gay-authored. To be true to my "by" criterion I had to hunt for the lesbian-gay author, identify both who had access to lesbian/gay discourses and who had control, and in what way, over the films' textual properties. *Chant* presented a different issue, raised by the question mark over the relative importance of the two main gay men involved in its making, Jean Genet and Jean Cocteau, who performed in almost antithetical gay sub-cultural modes. In all three cases, looking in detail at these issues uncovered something of the power play of (lesbian/gay) cultural production and helped to draw attention to and clarify the contradictory pulls in the films themselves. Let me say a little more about each case to illustrate this.[8]

Anders als die Anderen was directed by Richard Oswald and co-scripted by him and Magnus Hirschfeld, the leader of the most established gay rights organization of the time, the Scientific Humanitarian Committee. Oswald was an established director and producer working for his own successful production company and specializing in both tales of the fantastic and what were known as *Aufklärungsfilme* (enlightenment films), dealing with social, and especially sexual, issues from a perspective of liberal tolerance. There is no reason to suppose he was gay.

The in-put of these two authors to different aspects of the film draws attention to and accounts for the oddness of this compaigningly "positive" work which nonetheless contains strongly "negative" feelings. *Anders* intersperses a narrative causal chain of love, blackmail, suicide, and resolve to fight to change the law with lectures (by Hirschfeld) about both homosexuality and the law. The lecture elements are unequivocally positive about homosexuality, even if there are many quarters in which they would not find favor today (with, for instance, their interest in the biological basis of homosexuality and their roll call of the great and the good lesbians and gay men of the past) and these are the elements most obviously controlled, authored, by Hirschfeld. The narrative elements are more equivocal. There is no doubt that the central love relationship (between a violinist, Paul, and his pupil, Kurt) is to be celebrated, and Kurt's determination to avenge Paul's suicide to be applauded. Yet the *Aufklärungsfilm* genre constructs the issues it deals with, here homosexuality, as problems, the story places the cause of Paul's downfall in his visit to a gay bar where he picks up a rough-trade blackmailer, and the casting (notably of Conrad Veidt as Paul) and lighting bring in the tragic-sinister tones of the fantastic. In other words, in those elements that it is more likely Oswald controlled (simply by virtue of know-how), a rather different message about homosexuality comes across.

There is a further ironic twist to this. The "positive" homosexual relationship shown in the film is that between Paul and Kurt, one with definite overtones of the "Greek" love widely canvassed at the time, which was often equivocal about whether such eroticism involved genital acts. Although by no means politically straightforward, it certainly drew on discourses of respectability and manliness that were current in the period. It was not Hirschfeld's view of homosexuality, which tended more towards ideas of a Third Sex and was much more rooted in the ghetto culture of the time. This culture, and its androgynous denizens, is depicted in the film, but as the embodiment of unequivocal genital desire and resultant blackmail. In other words, in terms of narrative and imagery, the province of the experienced producer/director Oswald, the gay discourses exalted and denigrated by the film run counter to those generally favored by Hirschfeld in his work. Far from presenting an unproblematic, unified image of homosexuality, the fragments of *Anders als die Anderen* indicate that what it means to be homosexual is always contested, within and without the cultures of homosexuality.

The case of *Mädchen in Uniform* is just as tricky in a different way.

It was directed by Leontine Sagan, but under the "artistic supervision," as the credit puts it, of Carl Froelich. He was a well-established film director who had moreover set up the company to produce *Mädchen* (which had been a hit as a play under different titles in Leipzig in 1930 and Berlin in 1931); Hertha Thiele, who played the part of Manuela, remembered him as being very much the boss on set. Neither he nor Sagan were, so far as we know, gay/lesbian. Of the key personnel involved, only Christa Winsloe was. She had written the original play (the second production of which had been directed by Sagan) and co-scripted (with a man, F. D. Andam) the film. However this is complicated, even before we relate the script to the film itself. In 1930 (that is, at the time of the production of the first play version, in which the element of lesbianism was almost entirely absent), Winsloe was still married. It was only in the next few years that she began to live openly as a lesbian and not until 1935 and her short story "Life begins" that she wrote a work directly exploring lesbian life. In other words, *Mädchen* was written at a time of identity transition in Winsloe's life. This does not throw into question the validity of considering her a lesbian author—we cannot require that authors are card-carryingly out to themselves and the world—but it does mean that we have to be careful in how we understand *Mädchen*'s lesbianism, in how we relate it to prevalent discourses of lesbianism.

This problem is highlighted when we learn that it is only in the film that Manuela (the pupil in love with the teacher, Fräulein von Bernburg) does not kill herself and that this decision was Froelich's (on the grounds of taste). In other words, what seems to be the most triumphantly affirmative aspect of the film in relation to lesbianism cannot be credited to the only person we can reasonably presume was a lesbian among the key personnel. Yet the evidence of the film suggests we have a different case from that of *Anders*. Froelich was a far from liberal director, whose other films show sympathy with the authoritarianism that *Mädchen* attacks and who was perfectly happy working under the Nazis (who condemned *Mädchen* for its decadence). Nevertheless, despite all that, *Mädchen in Uniform* undoubtedly celebrates lesbianism. Can we turn to Sagan to account for this?

Although we have no clear evidence of who made what directorial decisions, it does seem the case that the elements that most carry the celebration of lesbianism in the film are performance and lighting, elements that derive as much from theatrical as cinematic tradition. If Sagan might have had to follow Froelich's lead in relation to camera angles and editing, say, then she would surely have had the confidence and authority to control performance and lighting, especially as she had so successfully directed those in the Berlin production of the play. But still, we have no reason to consider Sagan lesbian. She was, however, of course, a woman.

It would be wrong to credit all women, and therefore Sagan, with special sympathy for lesbians and we have no evidence of what her attitude was. What we can argue, gingerly, is that the film is directed (especially performances and lighting) within the cultural codes of the "feminine," valuing especially softness, diffuseness, delicacy, and roundness, and representing hardness and straightness as oppressive to women. This "femininity" (noted by many critics, notably the doyenne of Weimar film historians, Lotte Eisner) is of a piece with the construction of lesbianism in the central relationship in the film, in two ways. First, the relationship is represented through delicate looks and touches, and through the suffused light that envelops both partners (unlike the contrast of lighting often found in the representation of heterosexual couples, sharp for him, soft for her); second, the structure of the relationship is seen to be identical with that of mother-daughter, pupil-teacher relationships. Indeed, one could posit (though there is no warrant for this either way) that for Sagan it was only that, and critics have often suggested the film is not about lesbianism but about a young girl longing for her mother (which she is, among other things)—but seeing the mother-daughter bond as the ideal form of relationships for women and thus as the very foundation of lesbianism was a widely held view in the period. In other words, Sagan's "feminine" direction enriches and heightens the lesbianism of the film without necessarily being intended to, because it is in line with contemporaneous constructions of lesbianism.

The argument I have just elaborated can be made along similar lines about a number of other films I looked at, notably Maya Deren's *At Land* and many of the women's documentaries of the seventies. The former contains imagery suggestive of lesbianism in the context of a predominantly heterosexual exploration of consciousness, the latter often present lesbianism as part and parcel of women's liberation from male definitions. All are based in a perception of continuity between femininity, or womanhood, and lesbianism. A similar argument for men would be hard to make, because male gay identity has more often been constructed as oddly placed in relation to masculinity, seen as either departing from it towards effeminacy or else as play-actingly exaggerating it in clonedom.

Analysis of who exactly was and was not gay or lesbian among those who made *Anders* and *Mädchen* illustrates the problems of identifying and making sense of gay and lesbian authorship in contexts in which straight people had most control, and the consequences this has for the texts produced. *Un Chant d'amour* is different in that no one questions that the two authors at issue, Jean Genet and Jean Cocteau, were both gay. The argument is about whether it is of any importance to mention Cocteau. For many years it was widely intuitively felt that it was relevant, until the producer Nicos Papatakis in an interview said that Cocteau had had no influence. We do not need to doubt Papatakis, either his veracity or his memory, to open the question up again. The intuitive sense that there is something Cocteau-ish about the film should be respected. Considering the authorial circumstances may account for it and draw attention to the rather different constructions of homosexuality at work in the film.

It may well be the case that Cocteau did not intervene by actively making suggestions, but he and Genet were extremely close at this period (ex-lovers and mutually involved in various artistic ventures), Cocteau was present almost every day at the shooting, was an established filmmaker and an embodiment of a certain tradition of playful, rarefied literary homo-eroticism. Genet, on the other hand, had never made a film and came from an underground, provocatively homosexual culture. It is hard to believe that Cocteau's charisma and cinematic know-how are of no significance in approaching *Chant* and indeed they may account for why the film, though it does have a great deal in common with Genet's other work, is also in certain respects unlike it. While unequivocally gay (unlike Cocteau's own work), it is much less radically perverse than the novels and plays. It does have the characteristic Genet play upon beauty and sordidness, sexuality and spirituality, but in Genet's other work these elements are always felt simultaneously and ambiguously (does he exalt the perverse or bring low the holy?), whereas in *Chant* there are passages, most notably chiaroscuro, abstracted love-making scenes and sequences of lovers in a wood, which are untouched by the sordid or perverse, in a way that is more Cocteau than Genet. Focusing on the mix of Cocteau and Genet as authors in *Chant* accounts for the way the film has something for everyone, delighting those who generally find Genet sordid and self-oppressive as well as those who find him exciting and subversively perverse (to say nothing of those who find Cocteau silly and evasive as well as those who find him subtle and sublime).

My central concern in the book was with the available and utilized filmic and lesbian/gay discourses, but picking over authorship down to its particulars in the way just described also allowed me to bring out in quite a concrete way the realities of power and contradiction in lesbian/gay cultural production. However, constructs of authorship were not only useful for me, they were also part of the *raison d'être* of these films, and in terms of the very misgivings theorists had about it.

The idea of authority implied in that of authorship, the feeling that it is a way of claiming legitimacy and power for a text's meanings and affects, is indeed what is at issue in overtly lesbian/gay texts. They are about claiming the right to speak as lesbian/gay, claiming a special authority for their image of lesbianism/gayness because it is produced by people who are themselves lesbian/gay. They do this in different ways; their doing so reintroduces the problem of the social construction of homosexuality; and they also often indicate that they know something of that problem.

I was focusing on films made by people known to be, in whatever the parlance of their day, lesbian/gay, and which dealt directly with homosexuality as subject matter. What was at stake in such texts was in part the act of producing lesbian/gay images that were owned by those who made them as being about themselves, an act with obvious parallels to the strategy of coming out so central to lesbian/gay politics. This marking of authorship could be achieved in various ways.

In film the burden of evident author(iz)ing of the text most readily falls to those on screen. The lesbian or gay man filmed speaking about being lesbian/gay, to an audience or to camera, is the clearest statement of a lesbian/gay person owning what they say on film. Hirschfeld's appearance in *Anders als die Anderen* is one of the few early examples; the talking heads films of the seventies, including the marathon *Word is Out*, are perhaps the most familiar. Documentary footage—in lesbian/gay bars in *Anders*; in the COC club in Amsterdam in *In dit teken* (1949); at the meetings, demos, and get-togethers that fill lesbian/gay documentaries of the seventies—also generally implies by the way it is filmed a consent to have been filmed and hence an owning of that consequently circulating identity.[9]

Less easy to make clear in film is the lesbian/gay identity of the filmmaker(s). There are a fair number of examples of texts which draw attention to their maker, sometimes just in credit sequences, more often in other ways. Quite common is the use of filmmaker's voice interrogating the imagery: Jan Oxenburg reflects on the contrast between her father's home movies of her as a child and her own footage of lesbian gatherings in *Home Movie*; Curt McDowell describes the process, and his feelings about it, of picking up straight men and getting them to undress and masturbate for the camera in *Loads*. Others are still more elaborate: Susana Blaustein assembles people from her past and discusses on camera their reactions to her lesbianism in *Susana*; Barbara Hammer frequently includes herself in shot filming, reflected in a mirror, say, or her hand or feet coming into the frame.

More often though, it is the context that indicates lesbian/gay author-ship/authority, or at any rate heavily implies it. Coverage in the gay press has facilitated this, but even without that coverage something in the context may effect it. Genet and Cocteau were well known as gay writers. The underground tradition stemming from the forties was in general based on a model of the individual author expressing his/her individuality on film, so that anything in the films, including homosex-ual imagery, was to be read as issuing from the author's self. The cultural feminist cinema of the seventies was part of a political-artistic milieu which insisted on the connection between the artist and her work. Films explicitly promoting lesbian/gay liberation one pretty well assumes were made by lesbian/gay people. The same is true of gay male pornography, though the recent development of lesbian-made lesbian pornography cannot make that assumption and achieves its lesbian identity perhaps in its imagery and construction (though it might be hard to distinguish this from straight male porn out of context) and certainly through its marketing in lesbian magazines and networks, in gay and women's bookshops.

All these examples claim authorship, but the circumstances which make that claim possible and the nature of the consequent authority differ. At one end, as it were, there is the deliberate, promotional presence of the self-declaring lesbian or gay man. The clearest example is *In dit teken*, because it is an advertisement for the COC and as such more or less says, "we are homosexual people, come and join us." This is also implicit in the talking heads films, though what there is to join is rather more amorphous (the films often keeping quiet their base in the sexual political movements) and there is sometimes another address, a message of "accept us," mixed in. At the other end, the makers of films such as *Fireworks* or *Twice a Man* (Gregory Markopoulos) might very well aver that these are not gay films, they are Anger or Markopoulos films—but it is precisely in so fiercely claiming them in individual terms when that individual is himself gay that they become, at any rate, films evidently authored by gay men. Somewhere between these two variants of the lesbian/gay author-text relationship comes cultural feminist cin-ema, explicitly grounded in the experience and vision of the particular women making the films but wishing to affirm the collective, trans-individual dimension of that experience and vision.

All these examples in their different ways are claiming the authority to speak—as representatives of homosexuality, as lesbian/gay individuals, as embodiers of lesbian community. What they are also often doing is attempting to fix identity: in the first and last case, they are (or can appear to be) attempts to freeze a certain construction of lesbian/gay identity and claim it as definitive; in the case of the second, they assert the individual as the source of authority. As has been said of coming out in general, in the very act of claiming, in the face of denial, the right to speak, these films are stemming the flux of identity. In countering the malignant distortions of the mainstream media, stating either "this is how we are" or "this is how I am," they seem to deny the historically contingent, provisional, incomplete, and socially determined nature of being lesbian/gay. What is fascinating about so much of lesbian/gay film, however, is the degree to which some kind of awareness of this problem is apparent, either in the form of challenges to the work or as a feature of the work itself.

Gay/lesbian films, when they are not insistently individualistic, do, implicitly or explicitly, claim to speak for and on behalf of gay men and/or lesbians. This claim has always been vulnerable to criticism, in two forms. The first is that the claim to representativeness often turns out to be socially restricted: lesbian/gay films that are really only about the boys, others that are overwhelmingly white and middle-class. This criticism does not question the notion of lesbian/gay identity itself and the response to it has usually been to open up the representation, to recognize the importance of statements from non-white, non-middle-class lesbians and gay men, to make general films as socially inclusive as possible.

The second criticism is that the representative gay/lesbian identities shown exclude the majority of lesbians and gay men even when they are sensitive to other social differences. Lesbian cultural feminism has perhaps been given the toughest time on this score. I know many women who define themselves as lesbian and lead very out, open lesbian lives who cannot relate at all to the vaginal and nature/spirit iconography of lesbian cultural feminist cinema. This iconography, rooted as it is in notions of the ahistorical and archetypal, constructs a vision of "authentic" lesbianism in which many lesbians do not recognize themselves, a source of often bitter resentment. Certainly I had a problem in writing about this work, and not just as a man, but because of an irreconcilable contradiction between the implications of (literal) lesbian universality in the films and an approach (like mine) which stresses cultural-historical specificity and wants to celebrate this work as a particular construction of lesbian identity.

The criticism of the claim to represent lesbian/gay identity or a lesbian/gay self has not only come from outside the films themselves. A peculiarly sharp awareness of the debatability of lesbian/gay identity is central to many of them. I have already suggested that one can see within films such as *Anders, Mädchen*, and *Chant* intimations of competing lesbian/gay identities, but this is not really because the films themselves foreground them. However a tendency to do just that, to disrupt any implication that lesbian/gay identity is unified, unchanging, or natural, is found in many of the films, as in so much gay/lesbian culture.

The underground film tradition, for instance, is much more complex in relation to authorship and identity than I have so far indicated.[10] While the earlier films (Anger, Markopoulos), and later ones following on from them, do operate with a notion of self-expression, what characterizes this most repeatedly is a notion of the fragmentation of self, often a source of anxiety, generally only healed by reference, in Anger especially, to transcendent forces. Moreover, this impulse within the underground was displaced by the mid-sixties by the approach of filmmakers such as Jack Smith and Andy Warhol. Here the filmmaker is either present as highly artificial performer (Smith) or absent from the text, though known as a self-consciously one-dimensional celebrity (Warhol). In other words, through various strategies, the idea of self-expression (and fragmentation) has given way to something like self-performance. Everything is superficial, playing lesbian/gay is presented as a particular way of carrying on.

Again, lesbian, women's, and gay liberation cinema always had another dimension to it aside from presenting affirmative images of who we are. The impulse to do the latter stemmed from an awareness of how "we" were/are constructed in the media in general. Talking heads documentaries sought to provide alternative images to that dominant construction, but other films wanted to deconstruct mainstream media constructions. The process of doing so proved more perplexing than early gay liberation theory had anticipated, because it became clear, once you started dealing with those constructions, that they were not in any simple sense "untrue." They might be distortions of the truth, but there was something in them, and even something we often found attractive. For instance, it might be inaccurate of straight movies and television to make out that all gay men are screaming queens and that that is something frightful to be, but plenty of gay men do enjoy a good scream. Lesbian/gay cinema had to take on board the fact that lesbian/gay cultures and identities are themselves impure, made against but nonetheless with available and dominant imagery.

Films that examined the imagery of lesbian/gay identity were thus not straight in any sense of the word. *Comedy in Six Unnatural Acts, Madame X—eine absolute Herrscherin*, and *Outrageous!*, Lionel Soukaz's provocative examinations of pornography and pedophilia, and much of the new lesbian and gay film work all fit this description. Even apparently straightforward films like *Desert Hearts* and *Parting Glances* are surprisingly ironic and self-conscious about how to represent lesbians and gay men. They take imagery to bits without rejecting it, they work it without endorsing it. They are, I guess, postmodern, but a postmodernism rooted in a sub-cultural, and largely politicized, tradition which has always known, at least part of the time, the importance, nay inescapability, of performance.

Lesbian/gay culture has always had for the sake of political clarity to include assertions of clear images of lesbian/gay identity, but it has also always carried an awareness of the way that a shared and necessary public identity outstrips the particularity and messiness of actual lesbian/gay lives. We have felt a need to authorize our own images, to speak for ourselves, even while we have known that those images don't quite get what any one of us is or what all of us are. So too, whether as filmmakers or historians of film, we go on believing in those fairies, the author and the homosexual, *because* we know that they are only ("only"!) human inventions.

Notes

I should like to thank Diana Fuss, Janice Radway, and especially Hilary Hinds and Jackie Stacey for their help in the preparation and writing of this essay.

1. *Now You See It: Studies on Lesbian and Gay Film* (New York and London: Routledge, 1990).

2. For a bracing exposition of the distortions of (film) anti-authorship, see V. F. Perkins, "Film Authorship: the Premature Burial," *CinemAction!* (forthcoming).

3. Janet Wolff, *The Social Production of Art* (London: Macmillan, 1981).

4. See, respectively, Judy Grahn, *Another Mother Tongue: Gay Words, Gay Worlds* (Boston: Beacon Press, 1984), and Richard Dyer, *Heavenly Bodies: Film Stars and Society* (London: Macmillan, 1986).

5. I have not dealt any further with the political importance of claiming authorship, a point discussed in relation to women and authorship by, among others, Christine Battersby in *Gender and Genius* (London: The Women's Press, 1989) and Pam Cook in "The Point of Self-Expression in Avant-Garde Film," in *Theories of Authorship*, ed. John Caughie (London: Routledge & Kegan Paul, 1981), 271–81. Gay/lesbian cultural history is not only concerned, like feminist and black work,

with bringing to light those who have been actively neglected by tradition, but also with making visible the lesbian/gay sexuality of already familiar artists (in a sense, outing them) or showing that their already known sexuality matters. On this last point, see the introduction to a recent collection on lesbian/gay writing edited by Mark Lilly, *Lesbian and Gay Writing* (London: Macmillan, 1990).

6. Jean-Paul Sartre, *Search for a Method* (New York: Vintage, 1968): 56.

7. See Elaine Showalter, "Feminist Criticism in the Wilderness," in *The New Feminist Criticism*, ed. Elaine Showalter (New York: Pantheon Books, 1985), 243–70; Nancy K. Miller, "Changing the Subject: Authorship, Writing, and the Reader," in *Feminist Studies/Critical Studies*, ed. Teresa de Lauretis, (London: Macmillan, 1988), 102–21; and Henry Louis Gates, Jr. (ed.), *Black Literature and Literary Theory* (New York and London: Methuen, 1984).

8. Fuller details of all the films discussed in this article may be found in my *Now You See It: Studies in Lesbian and Gay Film*. More detail yet on the Weimar films may be found in my "Less and More than Women and Men: Homosexuality and Weimar Cinema," *New German Critique* no. 51 (Fall 1990): 5–60.

9. See Thomas Waugh, "Lesbian and Gay Documentary: Minority Self-Imaging, Oppositional Film Practice, and the Question of Image Ethics," in *Image Ethics: The Moral Rights of Subjects in Photography, Film and Television*, ed. Larry Gross, John Stuart Katz, and Jay Ruby (New York: Oxford University Press, 1988), 248–72.

10. This is explored more fully in my "Lesbian/gay Identities in US Underground Film," in *The Journal of Homosexuality: Homosexuality, Which Homosexuality?: Literature and Art*, ed. Marty van Kerkhof (forthcoming).

III

Zoning In:
Body/Parts

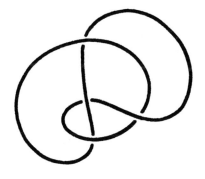

9

The Queen's Throat:
(Homo)sexuality and the
Art of Singing

Wayne Koestenbaum

As soon as the breath leaves the larynx, it is divided.

Lilli Lehmann, How To Sing

What do opera singers feel as they make sound? What do audiences imagine vocalists are experiencing? What ideologies of muscle, liquid, air, discipline, and sublimation, fill the opera house? No mere musicological curiosity drives me to ask these questions; rather, I am motivated by the sensation of lacking a singing voice, and the conviction that my vocal impoverishment might hold the key to opera's inmost heart. From the vantage point of the voiceless, a singing instrument represents a copyrighted, veined articulation, a fingerprint (or larynx-print) impossible to steal. This ideology of "voice" as original and identity-bestowing took root in an era that Michael Foucault has defined—a time when sexuality evolved as the darkness we yearn to illuminate, a constitutive hiddenness. Concurrently, the belief spread that no two voices were exactly alike, that anyone could sing, and that finding a voice would set a body free. Taking "voice" to mean self-expression, contemporary gay subcultures have equated vociferousness with the refusal to remain closeted. But centuries before the era of sexual liberation, "voice" already carried the values that come with uncloseting: self-knowledge, self-portrayal, presence. In Western metaphysics, spoken or sung utterance has long been thought to have more authority than the merely written. Poststructuralism has convinced us that this privileging of the oral is delusional; and yet my inquiry into vocal magic depends on these outmoded ideologies of presence—fictions that remain compelling, even though we are supposed to know better.

Catherine Clément, in her important book, *Opera, or the Undoing of Women*, uses the example of Freud's patient, Frau Rosalia, a would-be singer who loses her voice, to draw connections between hysteria and operatic singing.[1] The failure to sing is hysterical (the vocal chords are paralyzed because they remember, as Rosalia cannot, a prior trauma); but singing itself is just as hysterical. Coloratura and muteness are each a form of conversion hysteria. Because Clément focuses on the plots of opera and not on the semiotics of vocalizing, however, she concludes only that nineteenth-century operatic libretti are misogynistic, and falls short of what I consider to be a more electrifying conclusion, which is that the physiological techniques of operatic vocalizing have social and cultural meanings distinct from the libretti or the music. By operatic singing, I mean what we commonly call the "classically" trained voice—a style of tone production (cultivated for religious and declamatory singing even before opera was invented) whose control, volume, and flexibility—its distance from speech, its proximity to the purely instrumental—is now closely linked to opera because opera composers made such protracted and inspired use of it. Whether trained for theater, concert hall, church, or parlor, and whether or not it is draped by plot, set, and costume, this kind of voice is suitable for opera, and thus it connotes all that the "operatic" has come to mean.

Operatic singing doesn't represent any single sexual or gendered configuration, but it is a metaphor for how our bodies stumble into sex and gender in the first place. Every psychic constellation—hetero, homo, male, female—has a price, hard to pay, and I am uncertain which fate is most costly, or which path most closely resembles singing. Is the acquisition of a voice as taxing as heterosexual femininity, achieved (according to Freud) only after the girl breaks her primal tie to the mother? Or is singing like *any* heterosexual identity: "natural" and exhausting, reached through scarring Oedipal struggle and debilitating compromise? Or is singing more like homosexuality? Of the several sexualities catalogued in the nineteenth century, homosexuality is the most conspicuously taxonomic—the one that looks most effortfully and perversely *sexual*; though we know "homosexuality" only means *sexual acts or desires passed between two of the same gender*, we see the word tremble and shiver as if it connoted the entire field of sexualities, strenuously contracted into this one abhorred and hence tacitly privileged term.[2] Like the essence that reputedly makes gay people what they always already are, the spark that produces a voice is natural and acquired, free and expensive, speakable and unspeakable, pathogenic and curative.

If the ideology of voice is not fixed to any one sexual position, how can I claim that it has adhered, with however a gossamer touch, to the modern coinage "homosexual," and in particular, to the "opera queen," that song-maddened dreamer? The opera queen's origin is a subject that I must bracket, much as I must postpone the question of imperialism: suffice it to say that the opera queen bears, in his name, a residue of the imperialist values that have burdened opera—whether specific Orientalist libretti, or the nature of opera itself as an Italian genre exported, like tea or gold, abroad.[3] The throat, for gay men, is problematized: zone of fellatio, alterior eroticism, nongenitality. The opera queen—the gay consumer of opera—has an inactive, silent throat while he listens to the diva; the singer's throat is queen. But agency, in opera, is blurred: the queen's throat resides in a vocal body intangibly suspended between persons, and between the separate acts of production and reception. Similarly, the homosexual body, whether silent or vocal, occupies a crossroads where anatomies and institutions collide. Like voice, homosexuality appears to be taking place inside a body, when really it occurs in a sort of outerspace (call it "discourse") where interiorities converge; the vocal body and the homosexual body each appear to be a membraned box of urges, when actually each is a looseleaf rulebook, a ledger of inherited prohibitions.

The codification of singing techniques goes back to Aristotle's *De Anima* and *De Audibilibus*; there were several Renaissance students of the larynx (Codronchi, Fabricius, Bauhinus, Casserius); the genre of the singing manual, including Giovanni Camillo Maffei de Solofra's 1562 *Discorso della voce* (the first secular vocal treatise) precedes opera's invention. Evidently, opera did not, at its birth, initiate a radically new method of voice production, but tapped existing modes.[4] Because anatomy responds to history, however, methods of forming a singing voice have changed over time. For example, in 1836, when French tenor Gilbert Duprez carried his "chest register" up to a high C, he reshaped the way tenors have sung since.[5] The complicated history of operatic singing exceeds my grasp; I will concentrate, instead, on a few bizarre books written to teach the techniques of singing. A kind of conduct book, the voice manual has as much to do with social as with musical history. Though these texts cannot be entirely trusted to say what actually happens in a vocalist's body, they have a certain musicological legitimacy, for they draw on traditions that *have* influenced opera singing. Lilli Lehmann and Enrico Caruso wrote manuals;

so did a renowned castrato and teacher, Pietro Francesco Tosi, whose *Observations on the Florid Song* (1723), translated into English in 1743, epitomizes styles of tone production linked to Italian opera. Voice manuals, symptomatic of wider cultural purposes, don't solely reflect the quirks of their authors—whether practitioner or pedagogue. These instruction books—at least in the nineteenth and twentieth centuries—intend to spread "culture," to civilize. Sometimes, as if incidentally, they fulfill their stated function, which is to protect secret skills from vanishing. Like any literary text, a voice manual carefully imagines and shapes the body of its reader. And it is the *nonsinger* whose body the voice manual most effortfully exhorts. Studying the manuals, I locate the discourse of "voice" not merely in sonic vibrations and operatic history, but in the subjectivity of the outsider to opera, the aspirant who will never become a singer, and who reads voice manuals as field guides to the unobtainable.

The undercurrent of voice manuals—and of opera itself?—is an ideologically fraught distinction between speaking and singing. Though some pedagogues consider that singing is speaking intensified, others believe that speech endangers the singing mechanism: as twentieth-century diva Maria Jeritza put it, "So many girls do not seem to realize that the speaking voice is actually the enemy of the singing voice."[6] Much earlier, in 1774, Giambattista Mancini claimed that the vocal organs were "quiet and natural" during speech, but subject to fatiguing toil in singing.[7] Some manuals, attending to details of phonation and diction, imply that singing and speaking are the same[8]; but I am happiest with Jeritza's definition of "voice" as speech's enemy and opposite. "Voice," though it includes words, is also immune to them.

In the mid-nineteenth century, "voice" underwent a crisis of definition; one event that crystallizes this shift in vocal bodies is the invention of the laryngoscope, in 1854, by singer-teacher Manuel Garcia II (brother to divas Maria Malibran and Pauline Viardot). Garcia was hardly the first to look into the physiological sources of singing. For example, in the eighteenth century, scientist Antoine Ferrein discovered the so-called *cordes vocales* by experimenting on a cadaver's larynx. But what made Garcia's endeavor different was that he experimented on himself: seeking the cause of his cracked voice, he assembled a contraption, involving a dentist's mirror, and peered into his throat to see his glottis. The laryngoscope's influence may have been limited, but its invention coincided with the rise of scientific vocal methods, and the fall of the castrato, who, by 1800, had begun to disappear: the last decade of the eighteenth century represented the peak of his popularity and prominence. (It has been estimated that in eighteenth-century Italy, four thousand boys a year were castrated.[9]) Once the castrato fell, he fell quickly; 1844 marked a castrato's last performance in London, and castration—in Italy at least—absolutely stopped in 1870, coincident with the Italian risorgimento. With the castrato's demise came a vague fear that vocal art was declining. These fears of decadence were given a name: *bel canto*.

According to musicologist Philip A. Duey, the term *bel canto*, in its current sense—defined as a golden age of singing, a style of opera, and a technique of voice production—only entered discourse *after* that era (embodied by the castrato) had ended; specifically, the word took on its present meaning in the 1860s in Italy, and was taken up by other countries in the 1880s. The phrase itself, hardly new, had been used for centuries, but its present significance only appeared in dictionaries after 1900, and that meaning was itself a product of nationalistic struggle between Italian and German styles of singing.

So it appears that *bel canto* (as a nostalgic retrospective discourse) was invented in the 1860s. Another term was coined in the 1860s—in 1869, to be exact: "homosexual."[10] Imagine for a moment that this is not a coincidence, and consider that the discourses of *bel canto* and "homosexuality" might be parallel crystallizations. "Homosexuality" and *bel canto* are not the same thing, but they had related contexts: they came embedded in pseudo-scientific, medicalizing, admonitory discourses. The tradition of the voice manual precedes by centuries this historical moment of *bel canto*'s and homosexuality's invention; but the interest in resonators, phonation, larynx, and glottis (including theories of a false vocal band and a so-called stroke of the glottis), flourished with particular vehemence after 1860, while the number of voice manuals published reached a peak in the 1890s and early 1900s—a torrent of advice literature, including singer Nellie Melba's *Melba Method* (1926), Charles Emerson's *Psycho-Vox* (1915), Julius Edward Meyer's *A Treatise on the Origin of a Destructive Element in the Female Voice as Viewed from the Register Standpoint* (1895), and Clara Kathleen Rogers's *My Voice and I* (1910). I hypothesize that the impulse to discipline the voice grew heightened during a historical moment that will dominate this essay—the period between (roughly) 1840 and 1940, in which "voice culture" arose as a discourse containing the competing claims of scientific and natural techniques. Furthermore, I suggest that voice culture (and, by extension, operatic singing itself) is inseparable from nineteenth- and twentieth-century discourses of the sexual body, a choral entanglement in which "homosexuality" was a major though taciturn player, drowned out by two more talkative sibling discourses—psychoanalysis and hysteria. When we hear the static of hysteria, or the drone of psychoanalysis, be confident that we are surrounded by half-audible overtones of homosexuality, too. The connections between voice culture and psychoanalysis are obvious. Both are hell-bent on vocalizing hidden material, and both take castration seriously; voice culture desires the castrato's scandalous vocal plenitude, while psychoanalysis imagines castration to be the foundation of male and female identity. All these sexual and vocal discourses, insisting that the missing phallus means everything, zealously cast the "castrato" as star in the epic of psychic reality.

Though the epoch of the laryngoscope is my focus, fantasies of a lost golden age of singing precede the rise of voice culture. *Cantabile* seems weighted, even during the reign of the castrato, with a forsaken, mourned past. Tosi's *Observations on the Florid Song* opposes ancient virtues to modern lapses that include female singers, poor intonation, and lost exquisiteness. "I am old," he sighs; "but were I young, I would imitate as much as possibly I could the *Cantabile* of those who are branded with the opprobrious Name of Ancients."[11] These "ancients" flourished a mere thirty years before Tosi wrote his treatise—hardly long enough ago to earn the name. (He considers opera itself—distinguished from the "manly" church style—to be symptomatic of a decline into theatrical effeminacy.[12]) Jeremiads against present vocal standards, coupled with nostalgic appeals to vanished *cantabile*, are common in the manuals; if Tosi was obsessed with the Ancients who preceded him by a mere thirty years, nineteenth- and early twentieth-century instruction books characteristically regretted a decadence that partially stemmed from the castrati's disappearance—which no voice culturist dared explicitly mourn. Francesco Lamperti, in 1864, wrote that "It is a sad but undeniable truth that singing is to be found today in a deplorable state of decadence,"[13] and Sir Charles Santley, in 1908, justifies writing a voice manual by saying that the "Art of singing is dying out."[14] Fears of singing's decline tap Darwinist, racist fears of pollution and of sapped strength; a voice—even if achieved at the cost of castration—was a valuable masculine possession, to be preserved against syphilitic degeneration and new-fangled vices.[15]

Voice manuals—like tracts against masturbation, or psychoanalytic case histories—reflect a culture's wish to enforce some and not other channelings of energy through the body; the voice box glitters like a sexual organ because writers of manuals are so disciplinary in legislating how breath must move through the larynx to resonators in the face—called, tellingly, the "mask," as if voice were never capable of uttering the truth. Because singing does more than woodenly recapitulate a prior system called "sexuality," let us consider "voice" to be the master-discourse, and "sexuality," its appendage; if "sexuality" seems to be the term on top, and "voice" the term below, let us reverse the hierarchy, if only to see the two concepts more clearly. Rapt in this reversal, we might discover that the ramifications of "voice" are more majestic and shattering than the effects of "sexuality." What if "voice" were, finally, a more useful rubric than "sexuality"? Dispense with our sex rhetorics, and think of desire as articulated air, a shaped column of breath passing through a box on its way to a resonator. Are we experiencing "voice" or "sexuality" when we greet or hold a controlled shaft of air moving from a dark place out into the world?

Looking into the Voice Box

It is difficult to avoid noticing that "voice" has been persistently coded as feminine. And it is difficult to know what to do with this information. If voice is feminine, what happens if it resides in a male body? Is it therefore the agent of a radical anti-essentialism? If voice is neither masculine nor feminine, is it the sign of an exotic, nonspecific, third gender?

One major reason voice has been coded as female is because the organs of its production are hidden from view. To those who wished to organize singing into pedagogic principles, voice seemed like an obscure, mysterious essence whose problematic physiological source needed to be seen but remained invisible. Pedagogue and singer Sir Charles Santley in 1909 noted that the male instructor "has to teach an instrument which cannot be seen except by an expert, and cannot be touched at any time."[16] "No one can yet say that he has watched the vocal cords during the natural and unconstrained performance of their duty," writes one voice culturist in 1894,[17] confirming the failure of the laryngologist's dream.

Is the invisible vocal organism an absence, or is it merely an obstruction to sight, a door concealing valued presences? The secret of good singing might consist in opening the throat's door so "knowledge" can come out. Such an open-door policy won't permit the auditor ever to *see* the throat's secrets, but it will release the flood of buried stuff; and openness only comes to the singer who ignores his or her own mechanism. The singer who knows too much sings badly. In *How To*

Sing, Enrico Caruso insists that the throat is a "door through which the voice must pass," and that the door must be left open lest the breath seek "other channels"—morally dubious detours.[18] Many writers insist that the passageway to the human voice's resonance rooms must be left open, as if singing were mostly a matter of sincerity and the willingness to confess.[19] Foucault defined modern sexuality as the secret we all want to talk about. At once an invisible fortress and an unhinged gate, the voice can't keep a secret, or if it can, only an open secret— D. A. Miller's term for homosexuality as what we name by not naming, know by not knowing. Like the closet, the throat must be kept open but no one is allowed to guess, in the first place, that such a door exists.

"If only I could see the glottis!," Manuel Garcia reportedly exclaimed, on the verge of inventing the laryngoscope.[20] Modern "scientific" photographs of the singing larynx and glottis show us what Garcia might have seen (fig. 1). Voice commentators describe the larynx as labial—a connection that may rest in part on visual analogy, but more substantially on the figurative association between women and invisible things. The larynx—as an object of theory, as something to be curious about—is "feminine," but it does not always inhabit a woman's body: the first living, singing larynx seen by naked eye was a man's—Garcia, who trained a sort of speculum on himself. Indeed, regardless of the singer's gender, it is arguable that "voice culture"— the science that arose around the desire to see, understand, and control the voice—has invested the spookily genderless vocal cords with a "feminine" aura.

Many voice manual writers vigorously attribute vaginal characteristics to the throat. Jean Blanchet, as early as 1756, rhapsodized about the glottis—and included drawings!—as "a horizontal cleft terminated by two lips."[21] Robert Lawrence Weer, in 1948, matter-of-factly characterizes the larynx as "two thick membranes," "two lips" like

> little shutters, lying horizontally, with their opening running from front to back. The opening between these lips is called "glottis." When a vocal sound is produced the edges of these shutters come together firmly.[22]

Female singers themselves described voice as full of mucus (Ernestine Schumann-Heink warns vocalists not to swallow phlegm or mucus, a "disgusting habit that is altogether too widespread"), or as tightly tensed: diva Maria Jeritza compared singing to the sensation of "a strong rubber band being stretched out full length."[23]

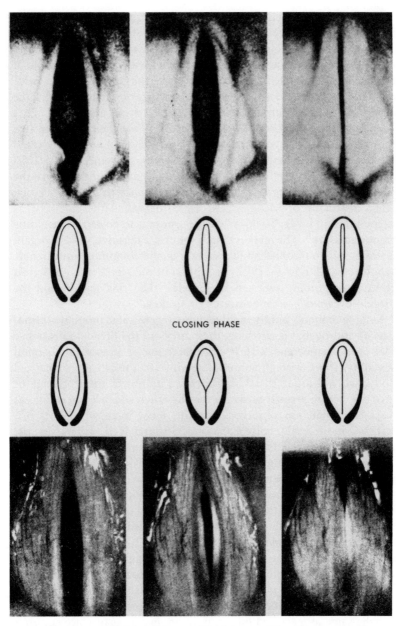

CLOSING PHASE

Figure 1. From D. Ralph Appleman, The Science of Vocal Pedagogy: Theory and Application *(Bloomington: Indiana University Press, 1967), 71.*

Though the voice culturist may zealously equate voice and vagina, it is possible that voice may be, in fact, a symbol of a separate pleasure zone that offers Edenic, imaginary alternatives to dominant cultural models of what sex means.[24] For the subtle, wily larynx is capable of embodying both male *and* female characteristics, or neither. In voice manuals, it is accorded the status of prehistoric anatomy, of some versatile, extinct species glamorously exempt from gender. In 1739, Johann Mattheson described the glottis as a "tonguelet" shaped like the "mouth of a little watering can." (Which gender is a watering-can?) He also finds a parchment-soft epiglottis, whose movement makes trills and mordents; it is tempting to consider trills as a pretext to give the epiglottis—a little organ of pleasure—the chance to speak.[25] French voice instructor B. Mengozzi, in 1803, described the epiglottis as shaped like an ivy leaf whose "chief purpose is to cover up the glottis when necessary"[26]: he implies that the glottis, a sensitive, modest organ, needs protection from chafing display. Equally voluptuous and archaic is Salvatore Marchesi's 1902 description of the glottis as a genderless vibrator containing two sets of muscles, the "ring-shield" and the "shield-pyramid"—able to stretch or slacken.[27]

Singing manuals hardly indulge, however, in some utopian affirmation of androgyny: if anything, they carry out the Freudian insistence that every tremor and wish is a displacement of an implicitly genital sexuality. If we wish to subordinate voice to the already sexualized body, we will argue that voice borrows its power from offstage or invisible bodily areas it seems to recall—much as voice in cinema, as Kaja Silverman has observed, acquires most force when it is off-screen.[28] Indubitably, voice's anatomical source is *always* outside the frame of the visible; and yet voice is hardly a simulacrum of the genitals. Rather than submitting to genital tyranny, the singing larynx declares itself sublimely independent of the place below.

For this independence, the throat must be punished; cathexis must be pushed down into the lower body, where it belongs. Voice emerges from the head, but the singer is often encouraged to forget—or lose—her head. Singer Emmy Destinn said, in the 1920s, "When I sing I feel as if I have no throat."[29] To sing, the head and throat must either vanish or suffer subtle symbolic injury. According to bass Herbert Witherspoon, Greek tragedians slashed the back of their throats to promote vocal projection[30]; though a sublimely unconscious throat is not the same as a slashed throat, both are instances of voice culture's tendency to scapegoat the throat for seeming to transcend the genital body. The female singer photographed in Millie Ryan's 1910 treatise,

What Every Singer Should Know, has learned her lesson, for she has neither throat nor head (fig. 2).[31] Do the photographs stop at her neck for heuristic economy, or to convince us that proper singing shoves the wandering uterus back down? The headless vocalist is encouraged to stand before an open window every morning, to take deep breaths and fondle her breast and ribcage as a "positive cure for all forms of nervousness"; like Freud's Dora, this singer now understands that sensation must *stay put* in the genitals. Diva Florence Easton commented in the 1920s that "You cannot make an omelet without breaking eggs," and you cannot make grand opera without "breaking voices."[32] Voice culture has a huge investment in the broken or missing voice: research into teaching the mute to speak—for example, the case of Helen Keller—overlapped with the voice manuals' detailed inquiry into phonation and laryngeal action.[33] Helen Keller was mute and Florence Easton was not, but in both cases, the throat was a site where expression and silence seemed eternally opposite, and magically the same—a place where a culture practiced making distinctions between liberty and captivity, intactness and rupture. Our throats bear greater discursive burdens than our genitals, and yet we lack a vocabulary for what the throat knows and suffers—perhaps because the throat is loath to speak about itself.

Hoping to define "voice" as nongenital, I turn to the mouth. Because voice is shaped there, might not singing recapitulate—at some distance—the pleasures of the oral stage? Witherspoon describes the mouth as a sexual organ, alive with easily excited "erective tissues," an organism containing "almost countless nerves": hence, "there is small wonder that things can go wrong very easily."[34] (Singing is *always* going wrong.) But singing's physiology is the opposite of sucking or swallowing, and thus is not a process of sexual or economic consumption. Isaac Nathan, in 1823, implies that singing transcends the mouth's desire to suck, and transports the singer away from the mother and toward a "friend," away from the passivity of shopping and toward the autonomy of production: "These pretty mouths, which at other times are watched with the anxiety of maternal vigilance, lest they should exceed the dimensions of a moderate-sized button-hole, are suffered, under the all-commanding sway of the singing-master, to distend wide enough to admit a friend."[35] Here, the friend is a finger: voice manuals consistently recommend that the mouth be opened wide enough so that "one can comfortably bring the little finger between" the teeth (according to Johann Adam Hiller in 1774).[36] This digit's arrival in the novice's mouth is portrayed as a sometimes unhappy rite

THE BREATH

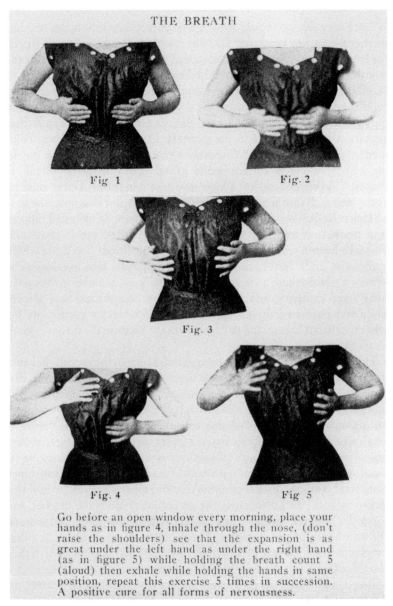

Go before an open window every morning, place your
hands as in figure 4, inhale through the nose, (don't
raise the shoulders) see that the expansion is as
great under the left hand as under the right hand
(as in figure 5) while holding the breath count 5
(aloud) then exhale while holding the hands in same
position, repeat this exercise 5 times in succession.
A positive cure for all forms of nervousness.

Figure 2. From Millie Ryan, What Every Singer Should Know *(Omaha: Franklin Publishing Co., 1910), 88.*

of passage. Lawrence Weer remembers his first voice lesson on "tongue control" taking place in his mother's kitchen; she told him to hold his tongue flat with a spoon while he sang scales. The spoon and other restraints brought on a kind of hysteria; he lost his voice and sought the aid of a specialist, who told him not to sing for six months.[37] Is it unnatural to open the mouth? Composer Jules Massenet told soprano Alice Verlet, in a rehearsal of his *Manon*, "You have the ideal singer's mouth; it opens naturally!"[38] But the mouth must not open too wide or admit too many friends. Sir Charles Santley says that for the lips to "fulfill their office," the mouth "ought not to open more than sufficient to introduce the tip of a finger"—not even up to the knuckle.[39] What severe regulation!

That so few writers have managed to describe the vocal mechanism as masculine suggests that there are indelible reasons to imagine the operatic singing voice as feminine, and to describe singing technique and laryngeal anatomy with imagery of female genitals. I am tempted to say this is merely imagery: but imagery reflects and induces ideology. The ideology underlying the voice box, then, is that voice and vagina are equivalent, and that, because the vagina is seen as an erring organ, a wanderer, singing itself always has the potential to be perverse, to deviate from its true path. I am uncomfortable with the singing manual's normative, punitive insistence that voice and vagina are analogous zones. I think that the manuals zealously enforce this equation because voice is so liable to be *thrown*, to disguise its agency, to hurl itself outside of the sex-and-gender field altogether and onto the sands of a signless, unremarkable, neuter shore. I want now to examine a specific case of voice escaping the genitals: falsetto. In falsetto, the contradictory demands that constitute the discourse of "voice" (that it must embody *and* transcend genitality) emerge. The falsetto is an instance of profound perversity. And I suggest that falsetto is not some freakish sideshow within operatic ideology, but is in fact central to the symbolic system of trained singing.

Finding the Falsetto

Codified voice production has never been happy with the falsetto: sylph-sheer embodiment of mystery, unnaturalness, absence. Isaac Nathan in 1823 called it the *fourth voice*—a fourth sex, not properly housed in the body: a "species of ventriloquism," "an inward and suppressed quality of tone, that conveys the illusion of being heard at a distance."[40] Like head voice in general, falsetto brings breath into the nose, where French styles of voice production often go: Antoine Bailleux, in 1760, warns that a voice must emerge straight from the chest "lest in passing into the head or into the nose it degenerate into falsetto by its muffledness."[41] The falsetto is part of the history of effeminacy—a compelling saga yet to be written. As long as there have been trained voices, there have been effeminate voices—tainted by affectation or "false" production. The ancients concurred in condemning such emissions: Plutarch disparaged "effeminate musical tattling, mere sound without substance"; John of Salisbury discouraged "womanish affectations in the mincing of notes and sentences"; and Saint Raynard insisted that "it becomes men to sing with a masculine voice, and not in a feminine manner, with tinkling, or as is popularly said, with false voices to imitate theatrical wantonness."[42]

The language used to condemn falsetto reflects—or foreshadows—the discourse of homosexuality, which, crystallizing in the late nineteenth century, affected in turn the antagonism to false tone production. One voice culturist, the English tenor Charles Lunn, even altered his theory of the falsetto between 1880 and 1888; in his earlier treatise, he did not explicitly disparage falsetto production, but in later works, in 1888 and 1904, he derided it as false and "utterly unemotional," a technique requiring no study and hence rarely used by a true artist.[43] In the same era, Sir Morell Mackenzie, Physician to the Royal Society of Musicians, described falsetto as a technique in which the two vocal cords push against each other "at their hinder part with such force as to stop each other's movement"—a retrograde, devolutionary motion; while chest tones emerge from the "natural aperture of the larynx," falsetto tones come through "an artificially diminished orifice, the chink becoming gradually smaller until there is nothing left to vibrate."[44] If vibration is civilization, falsetto represents its decline.

And yet in earlier times the falsetto was an asset—a secret—that singers sought and protected. Though the techniques of its production were scapegoated, and associated with degeneracy, detour, and artifice, the falsetto has long represented a resource, neighbor to more sincerely produced tones; the castrato Tosi speaks of the feigned voice as something "of Use" particularly when it is disguised by art.[45] If a modern voice culturist like Franklin D. Lawson, in 1944, saw it as a danger to both male and female voices—causing a "white," "blatant," and "effeminate" sound in the adult male, and a "colorless" tone in the female,[46] the castrato Tosi considered it a treasure to be discovered by a knowing master: "Many masters put their Scholars to sing the *Contr'Alto*, not knowing how to help them to the *Falsetto*, or to avoid the Trouble of finding it."[47] Falsetto is a skill, primarily male: a secret object or technique passed between pedagogue and student, it functions as patriarchal cultural lore. A sound at once false and useful, it may bring praise or condemnation to the singer who relies on it.

In the era of the castrato, young boys were sold to tutors or conservatories by parents who had detected musical (and monetary) promise, and wished to preserve the prepubescent voice, or who, in the absence of signs of inborn musicianship, gambled that inclination might arise after castration had taken place.[48] The castrato is an extreme case; but manuals suggest that puberty's onset is the signal event in every singer's vocal development, and that male voices stay high only because fathers and pedagogues insist. The generic biography of a male singer depicts puberty—the breaking of the voice—as a moment of Oedipal conflict with a father figure who insidiously wants tones that the son's voice can no longer produce. A headmaster wanted to profit from the young Caruso's voice—a relationship so consuming and problematic that when puberty hit, Caruso almost committed suicide; but he was rescued by a kindly baritone, who helped him place his voice.[49] Similarly, Sir Charles Santley's father insisted that the boy sing tenor, until the boy's "real register"—his natural inclination—emerged as incontrovertible evidence.[50] In puberty, the *real* erupts—an explosion that threatens the edifice of "voice." Singer Ernestine Schumann-Heink warns girls to postpone study until after their "physical development" is complete,[51] and Isaac Nathan cautions males not to sing during "mutation."[52] Only after puberty can a boy-singer "place" his voice, discover where chest voice ends and head voice begins; only then can he balance the irreconcilable symbolic values of "head" and "chest." It is the master's task to watch out for puberty's arrival in the student's body. If the teacher is himself a castrato, he may be particularly well schooled in masquerade; castrated or not, he must show his apprentice how to let the voice "pass" from one sexually resonant region into another.[53]

Puberty, always inscribed in the singing voice, is particularly invoked whenever a singer moves between registers. Are registers a fact of nature, or a figment of voice culture? They are, at least, a metaphorical way of describing and enhancing anatomical perimeters—of finding categories for a voice's uneven production as it moves from low to high. Some manuals say there are five registers, or one, or none. Some say men have two registers, and women three—or that each singable note is its own register.[54] However many registers a male or female voice possesses (and it is not clear whether a "register" represents a zone of opportunity or of prohibition), register-theory expresses two central dualities: true versus false, and male versus female. It is only loosely accurate to say that manuals privilege chest production as male and true, and dismiss head production as female and false; the two polarities—male/female, true/false—do not neatly correspond, for the discourse of voice thrives on categories other than gender. Like the system that divides the world into hetero- and homosexual, register-theory gives most weight to the difference between natural and unnatural: from this duality, all other, subsidiary distinctions (including gender?) derive.

Roughly speaking, there seem to be three bodily zones in which resonance occurs: chest, throat, and head. As the pitch ascends, the voice rises from one register to the next. The farther from the chest, the higher and falser the tone becomes, and the more one must exert vigilance in order to sing naturally. As early as the sixteenth and seventeenth centuries, voice manuals ascribed superior naturalness to chest voice: according to Domenico Cerone, in 1613, the "chest voice is the one that is most proper and natural."[55] Voice culturists are unsure whether head voice is, in fact, falsetto, or whether falsetto is an illegitimate subset of proper head production. Does every man and woman possess a falsetto? Falsetto is not, in itself, a liability; the sin is breaking into it undisguisedly. In 1782, when one "sopranist"—an uncastrated male who maintained a strong, working falsetto voice—fell out of falsetto and into his true, "robust," real tenor voice, Johann Samuel Petri observed that "my entire pleasure in his lovely soprano voice was utterly destroyed": a "loathsome harsh" note had interrupted the vocal masquerade, reminding listeners that the singer was a *he*.[56] One of the values most often associated with *bel canto* is the ability to prevent such loathsome eruptions by disguising the register breaks, and passing smoothly over them. (Musical passing, of course, recalls racial and sexual passing—as in Nella Larsen's 1929 novel, *Passing*, where a black woman, possibly lesbian, passes for white and straight.) I am not sure when the joining of registers was first valued, but it is clear that the break between them—fancifully called "Il Ponticello" (the little bridge)[57]—is the place *within* one voice where the split between male and female occurs, and that the failure to disguise this gendered break is, like falsetto, fatal to the art of "natural" voice production.

Singing is a matter of potential embarrassments. First: the male falsetto. Should that falseness be hidden, used, discarded? Is it a special case, or is it a natural extension of a singer's top notes? Second: the difficulty, shared by male and female singers, of the break between registers. Voice culture zealously disguises the register break and banishes the falsetto, but secretly knows that no body occupies, fulltime, the designation "unnatural"; a body merely moonlights there, seeking cover from danger, or relief from tedium. Falsetto is not an identity but a technique, a compromise, a way of working within a specific vocal situation. Because we lack sufficient paradigms to understand the discourse of homosexuality in its tangled variousness, and are left with ugly medical models, or severe theoretical ones, let me offer (in whimsy and seriousness) "head voice" or "undisguised register break" as two models of more lyrical, more pulsing, less punitive provenance. Though falsetto *seems* like the place where voice goes wrong, it is in fact a model for voice production in general, to the extent that vocalizing always imposes detours upon a blank and neutral column of air.

Forgetting its dependence on the feigned, voice culture homophobically overvalues the "natural." Most theorists of voice would agree with William James Henderson, who wrote in 1906 that "singing is nothing more than nature under high cultivation."[58] As long as singing is considered natural, however, there will darkly flourish a subculture of vocal techniques deemed degenerate. Nineteenth-century vocal manuals, in particular, resemble tracts against masturbation; both genres (pro-voice, anti-masturbation) inveigh against unnatural uses of natural gifts. For example, A. A. Pattou's *The Voice As An Instrument* (1878), relying on the discourse of degeneracy, offers scientific methods to remove the "defects of an unnatural voice." An opponent of slurring, Pattou strives to reform the throat, manage the larynx, and eradicate "all the faults or vices to which the human voice is subject." He even includes his own case history: because he sang wrongly—ignorant of "hygiene"—he suffered an inflammation of the throat, leading to "mental depression and a general distrust of society and all its belongings."[59] Sir Charles Santley's voice manual, too, ends with a confession: his throat grew inflamed from singing in rooms decked with imported flowers (including the hyacinth, clearly linked to homosexuality), and so he warns other singers not to let their "affection" overwhelm their "reason" in this dangerous matter of foreign blooms, lest a fondness for flowers ruin their careers.[60]

Of all vocal matters, vibrato and tremolo are the most potentially degenerate. Mozart criticizes a certain singer's vibrato as "contrary to nature"; one modern opera critic comments that anti-vibrato sentiment reached a peak in the nineteenth century—an instance of which is American laryngologist Holbrook Curtis's racist observation, in 1909, that vibrato is popular among the "Latin races," though frowned on by the Anglo-Saxons.[61] The trill, too, has been considered against nature, or at least effeminate: voice culturist de Rialp believes that though the trill was "very much in vogue" among nineteenth-century male singers, it should be confined to the female voice.[62] There seems, as well, to be an association between poor intonation and moral failure. Uncertain pitch reflects a cloudy cosmos: one Marchioness Solari wrote of certain castrati that "these degraded beings never sing in tune, when the maiming operation has taken place in bad weather."[63] Any affectation in singing is liable to be criticized as a symptom of degeneracy: Isaac Nathan warns in 1823 against lisping, drawling, or mouthing words so that "the singer appears dropping to the earth from the exertion."[64]

Degenerate singing can be traced not only to faulty tone, but to unattractive bodily gestures. According to Lilli Lehmann, "faces that are forever grinning or showing fish mouths are disgusting and wrong."[65] Singing in front of a mirror to ward off fish mouths is recommended by many nineteenth- and twentieth-century manuals. Castrati, too, were required to gaze in the mirror for one hour each morning while practicing; Tosi tells the singer that mirror-practice will help him avoid convulsive grimacing.[66] Mirrors play such a significant role in theories of self-invention that it is hard to avoid the conclusion that training the singing voice is a model for the more general project of training a subjectivity. Lacan suggested that identity is formed around a child seeing a whole self in the mirror, and wanting to become that seemingly coherent person. Manuel Garcia's laryngoscope—a device made of two mirrors—assured him that he had a larynx, and, by extension, a phallus and a self. A parallel assurance greets the male cinematic spectator, for whom, according to Kaja Silverman, the "acoustic mirror" of voice represents proof that he is not castrated. The mirror may be the silvery accomplice to the project of masculine ego-formation, but pathologized narcissism, embodied in mirror-practice, prevents "voice" from fully incarnating naturalness, and suggests that the singer practicing for a career occupies a dubious, unsanctioned position.

Self-listening is the sonic equivalent to mirror-practice; before the phonograph, could singers accurately hear themselves? As Arturo Buzzi-Peccia (teacher of Alma Gluck) remarked in 1925, "the singer cannot hear his own voice"; and for this reason, writes a voice culturist in 1899, the singer should not, in the early stages, practice alone.[67] Solitary, far from listeners, can a young voice fully occupy the plush but shameful designation "falsetto"? By itself, apart from mirrors, institutions, and audiences, can a body know itself as homosexual? Because rhetoric about unnatural singing precedes the nineteenth-century consolidation of "homosexual" as pathological identity, the discourse of degenerate voice (one of several models of the unnaturally produced self) enfolds and foretells the modern discourse of the homosexual.

Sing falsetto, now. (Are you alone as you read this?) Fill the room with a clear feigned sound, and ask yourself what act you have committed. Then produce the sound naturally, from the chest. Which of the two tones, chest or head, do you want your neighbors to overhear?

Singing and Self-Invention

"Voice" is a cultural myth as compelling, as naturalized, as hard to obtain distance from, as the myth of the sexual self. The image of sound as breath moving through the body relies on the hydraulic metaphor that dominated Freud's theories. Like id/ego/superego, or oral/anal/genital, voice is a three-tiered hierarchy. And the similarity between psyche and voice does not solely rest on the coincidental fact that both have been imagined as traveling through three zones. The categories "psyche" and "voice" do not simply record what actually happens; they persuasively prescribe what *should* happen.

The many maps of voice's trajectory differ on fine points—number of registers, where resonation takes place. . . . But the manuals agree that breath's movement is *upward*, and that the higher the sound goes (whether higher in pitch, or higher spatially, within the body), the more the sound risks becoming feminine or effeminate. Breath has no choice but to rise: breath turns into tone as ineluctably as unconscious desire changes to symptom, emotion, or deed. If trained "voice" is a dynamic ascent, like dreamwork or sublimation, then the singing body is either healthy (frugally expending breath) or sick (prodigal and digressive). Voice passes through a body as a toxin does, purgatively; singer and listener, seeking to judge a voice's quality, must ask, "Have all the poisons been flushed out?" Because voice operates hydraulically, as an essence, too fervid for storage, that escapes through whatever doors are open, then falsetto is breath that took the wrong exit out of the body.

I wonder, though, whether breath's movement from lungs to larynx to mask is always suspect. Though falsetto has the clearest links to homosexuality, a quintessentially perverse routing of libido, it is truer to say that all varieties of operatic voice are perverse. Even the dulcet, well-placed voice must move along the road of a dangerous double-bind. Within singing's illogic, air beguiled to a variant destination is as perverse as air that proceeds to the proper gate. Resonation *is* perversion.

A singer is an envelope of humors that need to be balanced and bled. Singing, like bloodletting, cures by restoring internal (gaseous, liquid) equilibrium. Voice culturist John Gothard, in his *Thoughts on Singing; with Hints on the Elements of Effect and the Cultivation of Taste* (1848), opens with a case history of a delicate neurasthenic man (subject to "continual sighing"), who was cured by befriending young men who indulged in glee-singing.[68] With equal optimism, Millie Ryan attests that "there is no tonic for the *nerves* equal to voice culture."[69] Singing is moral, psychological, and bodily housecleaning—even a form of surgery.[70] Neither sexologists nor voice culturists can tolerate a frigid, unresponsive mechanism: according to American teacher David Clippinger, in 1910, the singer's "lips, tongue, lower jaw and larynx should be free from all rigidity."[71] Singing is to this extent feminizing: after all, what codes of *masculine* conduct encourage men to free their larynxes from stiffness? Before training, the singer is tense, tight, nervous, delicate; afterwards, he or she unwinds. But such unwinding, hardly spontaneous, is as formulaic as a nineteenth-century hysteric's photographed *nature morte*. Yvette Guilbert, art and folk chanteuse of the early twentieth century, author of *How To Sing a Song*, offers guidelines for a kind of self-invention predicated on poses so stylized that they waver between "camp" and lunacy. She includes photographs of her own face in dramatic, comic, and pathetic attitudes recalling Hugh Welch Diamond's photographs of Victorian madwomen—a grammar of derangement: expressions named Ecstasy, Neutral Amiability, Moral Pain, Serenity, Gray, Red, Purple, and Vermilion, claim to be fixed and transhistorical codes that singers must master and reproduce. "Voice" is like phrenology—meanings mapped onto a body without regard for verisimilitude; the edifice called "voice" couldn't exist unless generations of singing bodies had complied with its strict correspondences. Guilbert indicates how grim this discourse can be when she insists that mimicry is every woman's natural endowment, regardless of class: "Whether it be the mouth of a great lady or mouth of a farm girl, large and red, thin and pale, every woman's mouth is a surprising accessory in the art of facial mimicry."[72] But will the discourse of "voice" accommodate a man imitating Guilbert's expressions?

Not if the manuals arbitrate the matter, for they hardly encourage self-invention. Voice, once taught, sings the story of its training: what a voice produces is the story of its labored production, the tale of the pedagogic structures that matured the sound. I suppose that any method of turning the body into a factory for expressivity inscribes the teacher's mark on the student's body: this is a fact of pedagogy, more than of "voice." But the trained singer bears the stain of tutelary institutions with peculiar precision.

Voice manuals staple the singer into the family, and into all the heterosexual and procreative moralities that the "family" as a prescriptive category implies: in 1839, H. W. Day writes that "singing has a refining effect on the moral feelings," and Lowell Mason, in 1847, comments that singing produces "social order and happiness in a family."[73] Fine musical sensibility and sterling voice production originate in a childhood free from strain, in a family where the "natural voice" is habitually used,[74] and where, according to Domenico Corri in 1811, there is opportunity to hear good music.[75] When a voice sings sweetly and successfully, it repeats the salutary childhood scenes that fostered it, and when it moves awkwardly between registers, it exposes an unnatural past. Opera singers sometimes took quite literally voice's power to re-enact its own aetiology. For example, in the era of the castrato, mothers of female divas often appeared with them on stage[76]; and Caruso mentions a prima donna who insisted that her mother stand in the wings during all her performances.[77] In both of these examples, the voice's origin (the on- or offstage chaperone) is the mother, and the female singer's debt to the mother is strongest.

Like any conduct book (whether for Renaissance courtier or modern teenager), the singing manual instructs how to secure class position, how to "shun low and disreputable company,"[78] and how—in the voice's bearing—to indicate "refinement."[79] Voice culture thrusts aristocratic values onto consumers perceived as passively waiting for uplifting instructions in the fine art of control: singing technique is imagined to be nothing less than the "correct management or the mis-management of the vibratory column of air" passing from vocal cords into mouth.[80] Homosexuality or voice—economies concerned with what might go wrong, or what has already gone wrong—are enfolded in dogmas of use and waste, retention and expulsion: matters of budgeting.

Like the arts of asceticism that, according to Foucault, constituted early modern sexuality, voice is a set of rules for withholding and dispensing a natural, numinous, and dangerously volatile substance; discharging sound, voice turns desire into money. Voice's emission is an image of the individual's body catapulting through society. And singing bodies are prized for moving up. High notes—associated with femininity as well as effeminacy—are expensive; in his satire, *Il teatro alla modo* (1720), Benedetto Marcello observes that the higher a castrato ascends in pitch, the more money he makes.[81] But wealth begins in stinting. The singer, according to Johann Mattheson in 1739, must let out the inhaled air "not at once nor too liberally, but sparingly, little by little, being careful to hold it back and save it."[82] And Caruso tells the singer to observe a similar economy over the career's whole length: the singer should limit the voice's output "as he does the expenses of his purse."[83]

In a singer's training, the conduct of the entire body—not merely the voice—is subject to punitive budgeting. Apparently, singing requires purity from top to bottom. Sexual abstinence and dietary moderation have been recommended since vocal instruction was first dispensed: Aristotle's *Problemata* insists that singing and digestion are intimately connected.[84] In the twentieth century, Millie Ryan recommends dried prunes for the throat; Herbert Witherspoon encourages the use of cathartics, and warns that the "mucous membrane of the pharynx and mouth is a 'tell-tale' of no mean value, and will often show clearly the troubles existing below."[85] "Voice" can't help but confess the state of a body's plumbing; singing, a flow chart, indicates if fluids and solids are circulating, if the waste system is functioning. Of course, voice not only describes the system, but makes the system sensational and sonic—encouraging us, thereby, to love (to quiver as we hear) the ideology of body-as-economy. Any nineteenth- and twentieth-century concern over regulating sexual or vocal flow evokes the specter of the "homosexual" as a site where control is gladly or unwillingly relinquished; even Foucault's discussion of a sexuality as a system of alimentary housekeeping relies on a Freudian assumption that male homosexuality is necessarily centered in anal pleasure, and thus connected to the anal (and paranoid) arts of budgeting.

"Red lines denote vocal sensations of soprano and tenor singers," writes Lilli Lehmann in *How To Sing* (fig. 3), admitting that singing is not a rock but a stream, not a target but an arrow.[86] (Incidentally, note the easy interchangeability of male tenor and female soprano!) The "self" has a bad reputation; we take "self" to signify every complacency we dare not interrogate. Describing subjectivity as mobile—as red hot lines—helps us to consider identities as evolving and combustible indecisions rather than fixed, leaden, foretold stations. It is impossible to describe or document what a singer—or a sexual self—*really* feels, though the path of its sentience may be mapped. Walt Whitman mapped it when he wrote "I Sing the Body Electric"—trumpeting the

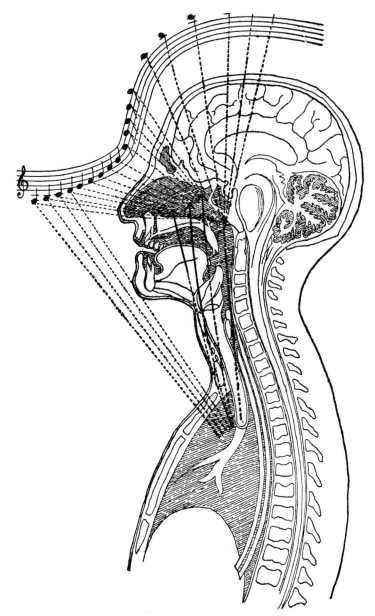

Figure 3. From Lilli Lehmann, How To Sing *(1902; reprint, New York: The Macmillan Company, 1960), 87.*

connection between trained voice production, and "voice" as a trope for homosexual self-inscription. Is singing's electricity a pleasurable charge, a natural light, like the firefly's? Or is singing a modern murderous technology, post-Edison, like electrocution?

Coda: Pleasure Coming Out

I wanted pleasure to suffuse this essay, and I am disappointed to note I have postponed pleasure until the end. Though "voice" may please the singer and gratify the listener, singing is not finally a question of delight. "Voice" builds a social identity; it doesn't fan the flames of private joy. In fact, rapture has no more place in a voice manual than in a guide to auto repair.

In valuing repair over rapture, "voice" and "homosexuality" are parallel: both are produced in order to bring pleasure, though the means of their production dampens the joy. The channeling of breath through the body's vocal factory is disciplinary, as the production of a homosexual identity may be pathologizing. There is no such thing as free expression; to express is to press out, by force (as in *espresso*). "Voice" aims to purify, to transcend; detergent, it seeks to scour the sodomitic dross that "homosexuality" has frequently embodied. In this sense, voice and homosexuality are adversaries: voice is evolutionary, homosexuality is devolutionary; voice is transcendent, homosexuality is grounded. But such a reductive division of labor between the two discourses does justice to neither. Voice and homosexuality are conductors of electricities not their own. They are *careers*, in the literal sense: vehicular undertakings. Toward what end does culture drive the "voice" and the "homosexual"? Even if destinations were clearly marked, bodies would not be particularly obedient in getting there. For bodies are neither predictable nor efficient; voice and homosexuality arise, as industries, to extract (or express) what no body, left to its own devices, would care to produce.

Finally, homosexuality and singing require decisions to be made about placement—verdicts the body comes to as if by itself, naturally. Where, on the map of registers, does the voice fall? Am I a tenor or a baritone? a soprano or a mezzo? Do I believe in these historical categories? What is the price of not believing in them? According to the manuals, placement should occur in puberty, when the male voice breaks, and when "mutation" commences in both sexes. But sexuality—homo or hetero—does not arrive only once, in that moment of self-discovery and self-articulation that we call "coming-out"; sexuality re-arrives in the body every time air moves through the larynx and into the mask. "Coming-out" is only the most narratively concise, politically expedient, and psychologically cleansing example of the vocalization underlying the concept of sexuality itself.

Whether or not one chooses to be vocal about sexuality, to be sexual is, in the first place, already to be vocal. Sexuality arrives in the body when it "comes out" in erection, lubrication, a racing pulse, a slow tremolo, or in the drier form of declarative (and defiant) speech. Are these manifestations pleasurable? We imagine sexuality as a visitation, annunciation, invasion—or we feel it as a molten predisposition that needs to be shaped by culture, good manners, and language. Is sexuality visited like plague on the body, or does it sprout from within, spontaneously? Breath's excursion through the body to produce a "voice" can hardly be called a pleasure trip. So I end, instead, with the vocabulary of pain: the arduousness that accompanies the ardor of training a voice, or voicing a sexuality.

Notes

1. Catherine Clément, *Opera, or the Undoing of Women*, trans. Betsy Wing (Minneapolis: University of Minnesota Press, 1988). The case of Frau Rosalia appears in Josef Breuer and Sigmund Freud, *Studies on Hysteria*, trans. James Strachey (New York: Basic Books, no date).

2. My understanding of the discourse of "homosexuality" has been significantly shaped by Eve Kosofsky Sedgwick, *Epistemology of the Closet* (Berkeley and Los Angeles: University of California Press, 1990). For an account of the evolution of "homosexuality," see Ed Cohen, *Talk on the Wilde Side* (New York: Routledge, forthcoming).

3. Opera and its image-repertoire are often troublingly reactionary, Eurocentric, racist, and elitist. And yet opera contains other meanings. In the larger project which this essay initiates, I aim to discover how a form so apparently entangled with oppression should have struck me and others similarly situated in modern gay culture as a form of liberation and speaking-out. My subjectivity—that of a gay white Jewish male raised in a middle-class North American family—has been substantially constructed by the "operatic," and I can't help but take my subjectivity, and hence the "operatic," seriously. I hardly insist that opera engenders political change; but I do not wish to mistake opera-culture's *phantasmal representations of aristocracy* for actual class position, or to forget that opera was once a popular art.

    I particularly wish to separate the gay male relation to opera from the kind of "camp" appropriation and revaluation that Andrew Ross describes in *No Respect: Intellectuals and Popular Culture* (New York: Routledge, 1989). According to

Ross, the effete intellectual recycles discarded artifacts in order to acquire cultural capital, to convert a civilization's trash back into marketable gold. But I would argue that when a minority gravitates toward a putatively "high" art form, more is at stake than the mere desire for upward mobility. In any case, opera is malleable, and attractive to marginal groups other than gay men; for example, African-American divas are central to any assessment of contemporary operatic practice. It is not clear whether Leontyne Price, Kathleen Battle, or Jessye Norman have the power to reshape the meaning of opera, but these divas are crucial modern instances of operatic vocalizing as a process imagined to be enfranchising, cathartic, and transformative, at the same time as it remains an art of social control, sublimation, and prohibition. And though I am using metaphors of vocal physiology to forward an inquiry into the lived experience of certain gay men, this essay's material could also be marshalled as evidence for a lesbian history of opera, a history which includes Gertrude Stein's (and Virgil Thomson's) *The Mother Of Us All*, the lesbian diva Olive Fremstad, and film star/diva Geraldine Farrar's legion of female fans (called "Gerryflappers").

I am concerned, here and elsewhere, with certain modern sissy subjectivities (in this regard, I have been inspired by Eve Kosofsky Sedgwick's recent work on gay youth). Admittedly, despite pressures of homophobia, the sissy drawn into opera's embrace is often privileged by virtue of race and class. I place this essay, therefore, in the context of a relative enfranchisement. And yet I would like to argue that the sissy's affection for opera, though enabled by privilege, is not solely a reflection of it. I started listening to opera, as a child, because it embarrassed me. The last thing I thought opera meant was cultural capital or glamor. Rather, announcing a love of opera would have been a badge of shame. I thought there was nothing nakeder, more obscene, than vibrato. I approached opera (warily, at first, and only in solitude) because it filled me with a kind of uncanny discomfort that I grew to call "pleasure." I wanted opera in my life because it seemed to me the sound of undiluted anger.

4. My knowledge of the history of singing depends entirely on a few voice manuals, and most particularly, on several compendiums of the vast literature of singing instruction. See Sally Allis Sanford, *Seventeenth and Eighteenth Century Vocal Style and Technique*, diss., Stanford, 1979 (Ann Arbor: UMI); Philip A. Duey, *Bel Canto in Its Golden Age: A Study of Its Teaching Concepts* (New York: King's Crown Press, 1951); Edward Vaught Foreman, *A Comparison of Selected Italian Vocal Tutors of the Period Circa 1550 to 1800*, diss., Graduate College of the University of Illinois, 1969 (Ann Arbor: UMI); Brent Jeffrey Monahan, *The Art of Singing: A Compendium of Thoughts on Singing Published Between 1777 and 1927* (Metuchen and London: The Scarecrow Press, 1978); Robert Russmore, *The Singing Voice* (New York: Dembner Books, 1984).

My source materials are Italian, French, German, British, and American, but I have read them all in English translation; it is arguable that this essay takes place in *the idea of Europe* as it entered America, a phantom Europe most crucially crystallized, for me, in the novels of Henry James. Opera is a continental European and Eurocentric art form that took on some of its most peculiar and indelible social meanings in Britain and the Americas.

I present my speculations in order to unsettle disciplinary boundaries; of course, these divisions have already been effectively challenged by other critics. I am not, however, a historian or a musicologist, and I cannot claim that my speculations are watertight, or that I have followed traditional scholarly methodology. Rather, I have attempted a lyric-historic (as in *lirico-spinto*) approach to the writing of cultural criticism. Though sometimes an essay on the history of singing, this is more often an exercise in positioning a critical voice. Where on the map of registers, of methodologies, might a writing voice fall? Somewhere in between poetry and musicology, history and literary criticism. Opera itself questions the division between word and music, between singer and listener. In the spirit of opera, then, this essay is dedicated to the space in between.

5. Foreman, *A Comparison*, 5.

6. Quoted in Frederick H. Martens, *The Art of the Prima Donna and Concert Singer* (New York: D. Appleton and Company, 1923), 195.

7. From Mancini's *Pensieri, e riflessioni pratiche sopra il canto figurato* (1774), quoted and translated in Foreman, 52.

8. For example, Francis Charles Maria de Rialp writes in 1894 that "Song is nothing more than speech upon a musical tonality." See de Rialp, *The Legitimate School of Singing* (published by the author, New York, 1894), 8.

9. Duey, *Bel Canto*, 46. For the history of the castrato, see Duey; see also Angus Heriot, *The Castrati in Opera* (reprint, New York: Da Capo Press, 1975).

10. Jeffrey Weeks, *Sexuality and Its Discontents: Meanings, Myths and Modern Sexualities* (London: Routledge & Kegan Paul, 1985), 66.

11. Pietro Francesco Tosi, *Observations on the Florid Song*, trans. John Earnest Galliard (1742; New York and London: Johnson Reprint Corporation, 1968), 87.

12. Tosi, *Observations*, 76.

13. Francesco Lamperti, *Guida teorica-pratica-elementare per lo studio del canto* (Milan: Ricordi, 1864); quoted in Duey, 5.

14. Sir Charles Santley, *The Art of Singing and Vocal Declamation* (New York: The Macmillan Company, 1908), ix.

15. On the discourse of degeneration, see Sander L. Gilman, *Disease and Representation: Images of Illness from Madness to AIDS* (Ithaca: Cornell University Press, 1988), particularly chapter ten, "Opera, Homosexuality, and Models of Disease: Richard Strauss's *Salomé* in the Context of Images of Disease in the Fin de Siècle." See also Klaus Theweleit, *Male Fantasies*, Volume 2: *Male Bodies: Psychoanalyzing the White Terror*, trans. Erica Carter and Chris Turner in collaboration with Stephen Conway (Minneapolis: University of Minnesota Press, 1989). Herbert Witherspoon, condemning the laryngologist, acknowledges that the "laryngologist proclaims a desire to reclaim a degenerate vocal art." Herbert Witherspoon, *Singing: A Treatise for Teachers and Students* (New York: G. Schirmer, 1925), 12.

16. Santley, *Art*, 11.

17. Francis Charles Maria de Rialp, *Legitimate School*, 27.

18. Enrico Caruso, *How To Sing* (reprint, London: The John Church Company, 1973), 28.

19. Critic and librettist William James Henderson in 1920 observed that "the whole neighborhood of the throat should be kept quiet," and Robert Lawrence Weer writes in 1948 that tone will resound in "all resonance rooms of the human vocal

instrument: *provided the doors to these rooms remain open!*" W. J. Henderson, *The Art of the Singer: Practical Hints about Vocal Technics and Style* (New York: G. Scribner's Sons, 1906), quoted in Monahan, 87; Robert Lawrence Weer, *Your Voice* (published by the author, Los Angeles, 1948), 80.

20. Quoted in (and fabricated by?) Russmore, *Singing Voice*, 177.

21. Jean Blanchet, *L'art, ou les principes philosophiques du chant*, 2nd ed., (Paris: A. M. Lottin, 1756); quoted and translated in Duey, 135.

22. Weer, *Your Voice*, 49.

23. Schumann-Heink quoted in Martens, *Art*, 266–67; Jeritza quoted in Martens, 202.

24. In my search for these Edens, I am helped by Henry Abelove's innovative work on foreplay. Abelove, "Some Speculations on the History of Sexual Intercourse during the Long Eighteenth Century in England," *Genders* 6 (November 1989): 125–30.

25. Johann Mattheson, *Der Volkommene Cappellmeister* (Hamburg: 1739), quoted and translated in Sanford, *Vocal Style*, 58.

26. B. Mengozzi, *Méthode de chant du Conservatoire de Musique* (Paris, 1803), quoted and translated in Duey, *Bel Canto*, 137.

27. Salvatore Marchesi, *A Vademecum for Singing-teachers and Pupils* (New York: G. Schirmer, 1902); quoted in Monahan, *Art*, 136–37.

28. Kaja Silverman, *The Acoustic Mirror: The Female Voice in Psychoanalysis and Cinema* (Bloomington: Indiana University Press, 1988). Reading Silverman helped to provoke some of my own speculations on voice's significance.

29. Quoted in Monahan, *Art*, 30, and in Pasqual Mario Marafioti, *Caruso's Method of Voice Production: The Scientific Culture of the Voice* (New York: D. Appleton and Co., 1922), 79.

30. Witherspoon, *Singing*, 1.

31. Millie Ryan, *What Every Singer Should Know* (Omaha: Franklin Publishing Co., 1910), 89.

32. Quoted in Martens, *Art*, 69.

33. Monahan, *Art*, 270, guides us to Frank Ebenezer Miller, *Vocal Art-science and Its Application* (New York: G. Schirmer, 1917), which includes descriptions of tuning fork tests made with Helen Keller.

34. Witherspoon, *Singing*, 25.

35. Isaac Nathan, *An Essay on the History and Theory of Music, and on the Qualities, Capabilities and Management of The Human Voice* (London: G. and W. B. Whittaker, 1823), 63.

36. Johann Adam Hiller, *Anweisung zum musikalisch-richtigen Gesang* (Leipzig, 1774); quoted and translated in Sanford, 94.

37. Weer, *Your Voice*, 5.

38. Quoted in Martens, *Art*, 286.

39. Santley, *Art*, 56.

40. Nathan, *An Essay*, 47.

41. Antoine Bailleux, *Solfèges pour apprendre facilement la musique vocale* (Paris, 1760); quoted and translated in Duey, 108.

42. Plutarch, *De Musica*, quoted and translated in Duey, 29; John of Salisbury quoted in Paul Henry Lang, *Music in Western Civilization* (New York, 1941), also quoted in Duey, 34; Saint Raynard quoted and translated in Duey, 41.

43. Charles Lunn, *Vox Populi: A Sequel to The Philosophy of the Voice* (London: W. Reeves, 1880), and Lunn, *The Voice: Its Downfall, Its Training and Its Use* (London: Reynolds and Co., 1904); quoted in Monahan, *Art*, 149.

44. Sir Morell Mackenzie, *The Hygiene of the Vocal Organs* (London: Macmillan & Co., 1886); quoted in Monahan, *Art*, 149–50.

45. Tosi, *Observations*, 24.

46. Franklin D. Lawson, *The Human Voice: A Concise Manual on Training the Speaking and Singing Voice* (New York: Harper & Brothers Publishers, 1944), 46.

47. Tosi, *Observations*, 23.

48. See Heriot, *Castrati.*

49. Caruso, *How to Sing*, 9–11.

50. Santley, *Art*, 17.

51. Martens, *Art*, 265–66.

52. Nathan, *Musurgia Vocalis: An Essay on the History and Theory of Music* (London: Fentum, 1836); quoted in Monahan, *Art*, 21.

53. James Nares, in his 1780 *Treatise on Singing*, observes that it is the Master's duty to show the Scholar how to join—"so as to be imperceptible"—the *Voce di petto* and *Voce di testa*. James Nares, *A Treatise on Singing* (London, ca. 1780); quoted in Sanford, *Vocal Style*, 23.

54. See Monahan, 140–8, for a succinct summary of the register war.

55. Domenico Cerone, *El Melepeo y Maestra* (Naples, 1613); quoted and translated in Sanford, *Vocal Style*, 34.

56. Johann Samuel Petri, *Anleitung zur praktischen Musik* (Leipzig, 1782); quoted and translated in Sanford, *Vocal Style*, 43–44.

57. Nathan, *Musurgia Vocalis*; quoted in Monahan, *Art*, 159.

58. W. J. Henderson, *The Art of the Singer*, 67–68; quoted in Monahan, *Art*, 33.

59. A. A. Pattou, *The Voice As An Instrument* (New York: Edward Schubert and Co., 1878), 4, 9, 28, 57.

60. Santley, *Art*, 143.

61. For this information on the vibrato I am indebted to Russmore, *The Singing Voice*, 190.

62. de Rialp, *Legitimate School*, 76.

63. Quoted in Heriot, *Castrati*, 46.

64. Nathan, *An Essay on the History and Theory of Music, and on the Qualities, Capabilities and Management of the Human Voice*, 67.

65. Lilli Lehmann, *How To Sing*, trans. Richard Aldrich (1902; reprint, New York: Macmillan Company, 1960), 169.

66. Heriot, *Castrati*, 48; Tosi, *Observations*, 88–89.

67. Arturo Buzzi-Peccia, *How To Succeed in Singing: A Practical Guide for Singers Desiring to Enter the Profession* (Philadelphia: Theo. Presser Co., 1925); quoted in Monahan, *Art*, 179. George E. Thorp and William Nicholl, *A Text Book on the Natural Use of the Voice* (London: R. Cooks & Co., 1896); quoted in Monahan, *Art*, 178.

68. John Gothard, *Thoughts on Singing; with Hints on the Elements of Effect and the Cultivation of Taste* (London: Longman and Co., 1848), iv.

69. Ryan, *What Every Singer Should Know*, 23.

70. Pasqual Mario Marafioti, in his treatise, *The New Vocal Art* (New York: Boni and Liverright, 1925), 251, compares singing's difficulty with the complexity of performing a surgical operation. See Monahan, *Art*, 39.

71. David Alva Clippinger, *The Head Voice and Other Problems; Practical Talks on Singing* (Boston: O. Ditson Co., 1917); quoted in Monahan, *Art*, 30.

72. Yvette Guilbert, *How To Sing a Song; The Art of Dramatic and Lyric Interpretation* (New York: Macmillan, 1918), 129. (See also photographic inserts.) For a discussion of hysteria and photography, see Elaine Showalter, *The Female Malady: Women, Madness, and English Culture, 1830–1980* (New York: Pantheon Books, 1985), 84–97.

73. H. W. Day, *The Vocal School: or, Pestalozzian Method of Instruction in the Elements of Vocal Music* (Boston: Otis, Broaders & Co., 1839); quoted in Monahan, *Art*, 17. Lowell Mason, *Manual of the Boston Academy of Music for Instruction in the Elements of Vocal Music on the System of Pestalozzi* (Boston: J. H. Wilkins & R. B. Carter, 1836); quoted in Monahan, *Art*, 17.

74. George Antoine Brouillet, *Voice Manual* (Boston: Crescendo Publishing Company, 1936), 42.

75. Domenico Corri, *The Singer's Preceptor, or Corri's Treatise on Vocal Music* (London: Chappell & Co., 1811), quoted in Duey, *Bel Canto*, 100.

76. Heriot, *Castrati*, 75.

77. Caruso, *How to Sing*, 57.

78. Tosi, *Observations*, 144.

79. Ryan, *What Every Singer Should Know*, 65.

80. Louis Arthur Russell, *The Body and Breath Under Artistic Control for Song and Fervent Speech: A Text Book for Private or Class Instruction* (Newark, N.J.: Essex Pub. Co., ca. 1904); quoted in Monahan, *Art*, 62.

81. See Heriot, *Castrati*, 57.

82. Johann Mattheson, *Der Vollkommene Capellmeister*; quoted and translated in Duey, *Bel Canto*, 79.

83. Caruso, *How to Sing*, 39.

84. Duey, *Bel Canto*, 19–20. For a summary of opinions on vocal hygiene during the *bel canto* era, see 139–51.

85. See Ryan, *What Every Singer Should Know*, 39, and Witherspoon, *Singing*, 45.

86. Lehmann, *What Every Singer Should Know*, 86–87.

10

Below the Belt: (Un)Covering
The Well of Loneliness
Michèle Aina Barale

The difference is comfort. *Hush Puppies® Shoes*

One of my students recently argued that history is a process of
progress, that as a species we continue to grow towards ever wiser
insights and ever better behaviors. As an example of what he meant,
he cited our changing treatment of the insane over the span of the
last two hundred years. When I asked if he thought that the use of
psychotropic drugs to permit the insane the privilege of sleeping in
doorways was an instance of our progress, he responded in quite a
wonderful way: "No. What I meant is, *before they used to think the
insane were different. Now we know that we're all a little bit crazy.*"

It is not surprising that previous to the articulation of something
generally called Gay Rights, lesbian texts nevertheless were written.
What is surprising is that they were published by mainstream presses
for an audience also presumably mainstream. When a subculture's
texts become an offering by and for dominant culture, one is tempted
to surmise that a change is taking place and further tempted to interpret
such change as progress. This notion of progress assumes that the
existing ideology has permitted entrance of the previously unspeakable
because a new and uncensored discourse has begun. Such cultural self-
visioning proceeds from a larger and more encompassing vision of
history itself as a process of ideological liberation, and provides a
means of appropriating the subcultural text so as to enable it to seem
consonant with existing ideology. The text, in other words, is colonized; and it is colonized precisely because it is useful in maintaining
the colonizer's structure. What my student forgot, when giving his

235

argument for history as progress, is that while we now know that we're all a little bit crazy, we can also identify the *real* lunatic—and it's not us. But because we can believe that we are all slightly nuts, we are able to presume that we therefore have some knowledge of what it means to experience the world insanely—that the lunatic's private experience of the world has been, can be, perhaps even should be admitted by us as one we, too, have shared. By enabling a democratic theory of madness, the dominant ideology can encompass self-deviation but still not modify itself. Furthermore, dominant culture can maintain the belief that the colonized Other remains unmodified as well. It is as though it were possible for a python to swallow a rabbit whole—and yet not digest it—even as the python supplements its own organic structure. The rabbit begins as a bulge in the python but concludes as python itself, while the python is no more like a rabbit after its meal than before.

It is not my intention to make the snake disgorge its dinner. That would be a real trick, and I am no charmer. What I am interested in doing is demonstrating the process by which rabbit heart and blood, eye and ear become python sinew: I want to look at how dominant culture can make marginalized texts read as its own. To do this, I shall examine four covers—two composed of illustrations (1951, 1964) and two using photographs (1974, 1981)—issued for the American paperback editions and reprints of Radclyffe Hall's *The Well of Loneliness*.[1] These covers provide visual and dictional representation of the dominant sexual ideology within which the novel has been published, marketed, and read over the last nearly forty years. The cover art, I will argue, invites heterosexual readers to engage with a narrative of a sexuality not their own, thereby encouraging the experience of the lesbian Other as friendly rather than alien. In so doing, the covers buttress and enlarge heterosexuality's domain.[2] But even as the covers promise the heterosexual reader the experience of homosexuality, they also enable the reader to make the important distinction that although we are all a little bit nuts, a little bit Other, that person over there is the one to watch out for. Homosexuality—lesbianism—is "good" just so long as it is useful in maintaining heterosexuality. Lesbian sexuality is permissible only when it is available for heterosexuality's consumption.[3]

Because the covers of this novel fashion how we perceive the text beneath, they can be understood as functioning as a kind of textual garment. Like all clothing, these garments reveal some parts and conceal others. But the fashion's physical revelations—what its necklines and hems, bodices and backs *bare*—are of neither more nor less interest than what fashion chooses to drape. The former is the stuff of vision, the latter the material of fantasy and dream. *Haute* and *bas coutoure* consist in endless refabrications of exposure and concealment by which the boundaries between the public and the private body, between the visually accessible and the only imaginable, are continually re-drawn. Each half of the binary demands the existence of the other for its own effects to work their magic. What fashion exposes offers a promise of what it covers up: that the unseen conforms to the expectations that the visible gives rise to; that the obvious provides analogical knowledge of the hidden; and that the secret places will therefore offer pleasures similar to but possibly even more delectable than the already known. All surprises will serve to stimulate; none will threaten. Thus, the ways in which this novel's covers enable lesbian sexuality to enter into the dominant sexual ideology also enable the fantasy that what the covers neglect to portray and what the heterosexual reader can now know firsthand—a lesbian body and its experience of desire—are nonetheless apprehendable, able to be possessed and enjoyed. The covers assure heterosexual readers that both the seen and the secrets of lesbian sexuality will enrich their heterosexual desire.

In order to appropriate the Other, it is represented as the Similar. Heterosexuality thus seeks to create lesbians whose desires are as apprehensible as its own. And what I will argue is that the lesbian body itself is made the site for such self-depiction. To make the Otherness of same-sex desire familiar, lesbians are depicted as bodies whose genital configurations visibly represent the nature of their desire. By according lesbians the Butch's assumed "male" body or the Femme's supposed "female" body, the Otherness of same-sex desire is rendered knowable. A desire posited upon genital difference is thus inscribed on bodies that are, in fact, genitally alike. And a way is found by which the female dyad neither excludes nor forbids male entry and enjoyment.[4]

Of course, even as the covers succeed in their attempt to make the alien and Other familiar and utilizable ("user friendly" is not an altogether unapt term here), something yet evades acquisition. *The* lesbian, with the desire and body heterosexuality has imputed to her, is not *a* lesbian. In solving the "mystery" of lesbian desire by creating the myth of genital difference, heterosexuality has acquired only its own projection. The lesbian body below the belt, like the lesbian narrative beneath the cover, continues to elude total depiction. Whatever access the covers and text may provide the heterosexual reader, the very difference that heterosexuality has needfully inscribed upon a female body in order to inflect it as recognizably lesbian results in the creation of a body—*the* lesbian body—that resists sure and certain paralleling with a real, palpable lesbian body. This creation of a third anatomical category, the non-heterosexual female, is the creation of a space that can be filled-in as cultural desires demand; but its distinctness from the genital anatomy of actual, non-representational lesbians— lesbians whose sexual desire and practice play themselves out in the Other world, the non-textual one—is utterly complete. Heterosexuality's dream of the lesbian's genitals offers no knowledge of a lesbian's reality.

The four covers from mainstream presses are quite distinct from one another, yet each finds some means of inscribing heterosexuality upon the story beneath. All four use copy to advertise that what is beneath the cover is a love story that has been "denounced, banned, and applauded" (1951, 1964), or that might be termed "classic" (1974), or that might have been "censored" as well as "classic" (1981). In any case, the covers' copy announces that what is here is "the strange love story of a girl who stood midway between the sexes" (1951, 1964), a "love that dared not speak its name" (1974 [back cover], 1981). Mainstream publishers, it would seem, could not be certain that mere visual representation of difference was sufficient to enable the general reader to perceive that the novel was a love story *and* that it was a lesbian love story. Verbal clues were also necessary to make explicit what might be otherwise ambiguous. Thus on the back cover of the 1951 Perma Book edition, in bright blue script, "Why can't I be normal?" rides above the more serious black type that informs us that Stephen Gordon is "a sensitive girl whose parents ardently desired a son in her place. How Stephen developed a natural tendency toward masculinity [note how nurture constructs nature], her tortured adolescence, and her love that the world—even her mother—condemned, is the theme of this extraordinary book." The back cover copy for the 1974 *Well* assures the reader that the novel deals "sympathetically" with its subject, that it makes "poignant the tortured existence of a girl at odds with her conscience and her world," and that her "only crime against society was a painful and hopeless longing. . . ." We are further assured that the novel is frank and sincere in its "treatment of a delicate subject" (1951) as well as "artistic and honest" (1974). It seems clear that the florid copy is meant to justify the novel's publication and its readers' interest in it. It is also clear that such justification is intended for a non-gay audience who need the sexual Other both distinguished for them and then made into a subject suitable for their interest—an interest assuredly not lascivious since it is shared by "millions who have already read" the novel (1954).[5]

Iconographically, the 1964 *Well* is the simplest of all the covers (fig. 1). On a white background, a green hand and forearm reach up to clasp a descending blue hand and forearm. The hands are genderless, the nails of both short, the fingers neither tapered nor emphatically blunt, and the forearms neither muscular nor noticeably slender. They could be both male or both female, but they clearly are not male *and* female. All that makes them different are their differing colors, and those colors are not even the usual gendered pairing of pink and blue. Green arm links blue arm; this, on a superficial examination, seems obvious. Hue thus provides the representation of difference.

The clasped hands and arms, genderless in this depiction, are instead, by means of color, inscribed with racial difference. Although green and blue themselves are colors neutral enough not to suggest which race each represents, such stipulation is unimportant. Racial inscription is more than able to imbue the image with dense sexual meaning. As Sander L. Gilman points out, as early as the Middle Ages the black body of both sexes was associated with concupiscence and, throughout the eighteenth century, served in the visual arts not only as a marker of "the sexualization of the society in which he or she was found" but as an icon for all deviant sexuality.[6] By the nineteenth century, the visual use of the black male body had dwindled and only the black female body was used to signal aberration. Moreover, a centrally focused white female figure could be paired with a black female in such a way "as to imply a similarity between the sexuality of the two."[7] The presumption of deviance in all blacks was reassigned solely to the black female body, and then, by association, was shared in by white women as well.

While the pairing of the two races on the cover thus signifies a mutual, deviant sexuality, the choice of placement of the arms upon the cover—vertical rather than horizontal—also hints of inequality and power imbalances. Someone is on top and someone is not. Such social hierarchy easily translates into an erotic one, calling forth fantasies of dominance and submission that in the context of Western racial history become fantasies of master/slave relations and possibly even fantasies of varieties of rape.

Such fantasies are most easily lodged in a heterosexual paradigm. This is not to deny the existence of either historical acts or pornographic depictions of female-to-female sexual abuse, nor is it to deny fantasized scenarios of such activities. Rather, I would suggest that within main-

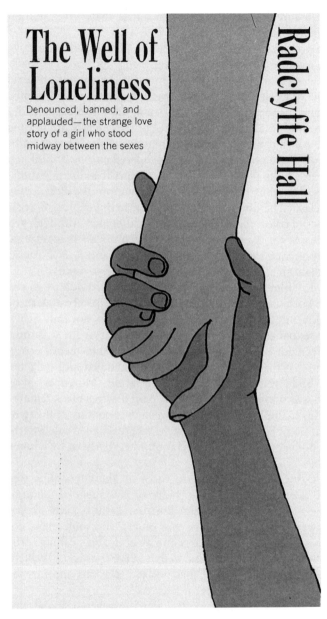

The Well of Loneliness

Denounced, banned, and applauded—the strange love story of a girl who stood midway between the sexes

Radclyfe Hall

Figure 1.

stream representation there is usefulness in suggesting the familiar— the heterosexual power imbalance—thereby safely allowing the forbidden its secret possibility. It is not surprising, then, that the genderless hands and arms are made to sign heterosexuality as well as race. What the cover copy promises, a "strange love story . . . midway between the sexes," is that a specific kind of narrative and a specifically unusual female body will be found within. The copy is, evidently, necessary lest the illustration, with only its ambiguous title and possibly unknown author, imply that this is a story about a Salvation Army General who extends a caring hand to the lonely down-and-out. In case neither the differing hues nor the explicit copy is sufficient to encourage the browsing buyer to read desire, gender difference is overtly supplied by means of the hands. The hand that thrusts up from the cover's bottom edge has its index finger extended beyond the hand it holds, while the hand on top has its index finger separated from the rest of its hand, thereby forming a curving-sided V. One hand has a protuberance, the other an invagination. Who needs pink and blue?

What is missing in the cover's visual synecdoche are the accompanying bodies with their genitals. But what is below the belt is nevertheless at hand. The cover's handy (mis)representation of genital difference is powerful enough to inscribe even what we cannot see, what in film theory would be termed *space-off*—the area "not visible in the frame but inferable from what the frame makes visible."[8] What we are invited to infer is that the unseen genitals of one of these missing figures—it hardly seems farfetched to presume the Butch—has genitals more male than female. To be specific, the implication is that one woman's clitoris functions as a penis for both herself and for her partner, since it gives and receives pleasure as a protuberance that can fill the other's available space.

As Gilman makes clear in his analysis of the nineteenth-century's fascination with black women's genitalia, dominant culture's interests in the lesbian "below the belt" cannot be separated from its interest in the sexual anatomy of all "other" women.[9] The scientific discourse that focused upon the supposed hypertrophy of black women's buttocks, clitorises, and labia reflected a broader cultural understanding of all female sexuality as pathological, Gilman argues. Hence, it was a short step to the "discovery" that both prostitutes and lesbians manifested similar genital malformation, especially clitorally.[10] The genital "abnormalities" that signaled the racial inferiority of black women signaled moral degeneracy in the too sexually active or the non-heterosexually interested woman.

Sexual literature about the "abnormal," literature that was intended for a general audience and that was easily available in the decades during which the four covers under discussion were published, indicates that an interest in lesbian genitalia, and the myth of clitoral overdevelopment, continued well past the nineteenth century.[11] Frank Caprio, M.D., states not only that some lesbians have an "unusually elongated" clitoris but provides the datum of "about six centimeters,"[12] while the ever-knowledgeable David Reuben, M.D., informs his public that a clitoris "as much as two or more inches in length when erect" was possible, and that "lesbians with this anatomical quirk are in great demand."[13] Even the not at all vainglorious Charlotte Wolff, M.D., notes that in lesbians it is not infrequent to find "a habitually enlarged clitoris" that in extreme conditions resembles "a small penis."[14] Exactly how these measurements were made, especially those of the erect clitoris, is troubling to speculate upon, particularly since Masters and Johnson report that "clinical mensuration of the clitoral shaft length has been so unreliable that results will not be reported."[15] The tone of both Caprio's and Reuben's discussion might well be termed medico-erotic and, when linked with their statements of vaginal penetration by enlarged clitorises, strongly suggests not only the heterosexualizing of lesbian activity but the inferiorizing of it as such: remarks Reuben of the two-or-more-inched clitoris used for penetration, "What would be a disgrace to a man is a delight to a woman."[16] Yet, while Masters and Johnson make a case for "marked variation" in clitoral structure, they also note that there are "reports of African tribes" who not only measure female sexuality in terms of clitoral length and labial hypertrophy, but who practice manipulation of the genitalia of infant and young girls to assure "the development of these artifacts."[17] (To be fair, Masters and Johnson do not believe that there is any reliable information connecting genital hypertrophy to female hypersexuality.) Thus, by 1981 the medical literature appears to have come full circle—right back to the nineteenth century's focus upon "other" women's genitals—and even further back, to classical reports of excessive genital development in non-European women.[18]

I would suggest that the inferred clitoral enlargement of *only one* of the cover's implied bodies serves as a mechanism whereby the heterosexual gazer can claim for him or herself the differing pleasures of *either* lesbian body: either the Butch's ability to penetrate or the Femme's ability to receive. Furthermore, the cover's ostensible lack of gender differentiation in its depiction of hands and arms allows each gazer, whether male or female, to align her or himself with whichever pleasure-receiving body he or she prefers. The male gazer—hetero- or homosexual—can as easily identify with the Femme as the female gazer—homo or heterosexual—can identify with the Butch. All is enabled by this invitation to fantasies of the omni-sexual.

But at the same time, this invitation to fantasy's secret dramas is safely inscribed with the proper markings of heterosexual difference, thus insuring that while gazers can have their hidden pleasures they can have their socially proper ones, as well. The Butch can be represented as desiring in ways that are like, but measurably less than, those enacted by a penetrating, heterosexual male; the non-Butch woman can, in turn, be heterosexualized as a woman who seeks the penis. In a phallo-centric logic, the Butch and the Femme are represented so as to provide differing sites where each sex can locate itself, and the heterosexual gazer can thereby "know" the "lesbian body" by his or her imaginative, but gender differentiated, proximity to it. The male can "know" the Butch and the female the Femme. But in neither situation, neither that of the secret, omni-possible nor that of the gender-regulated alignment, is *the* lesbian fantasized *a* lesbian. Except when providing a site for a lesbian gazer's imaginative pleasure, the cover invites heterosexuals and gay males to play as and with a desiring lesbian, a role whose content and a body whose desire is a heterosexual product.

The covers from the 1951 and 1974 *Well* offer the gazer two sets of female couples whose bodies, in three instances, do exist below the belt. The figures on the crudely drawn 1951 cover appear seated to the right of a fireplace (fig. 2). A fair-haired figure is located behind and above a dark-haired figure who is placed in the far right foreground of the cover. In fact, the dark-haired figure is so far to the right that all we see of her body is one shoulder (her right), a portion of her upper right arm, and one breast. None of her body below her breasts is visible. Because she is in profile, we see only half her face, and her single eye is hidden by its lid as she gazes down in the direction of her lap. The other figure inclines toward her and looks down at her. This fair-haired figure's face is turned for a three-quarter view and, like the figure in the foreground, has one shoulder and one breast visible. Unlike her partner, however, her lap can be seen to some extent, since we can observe what appear to be the flounces of her dress. Her bare arms rest upon her lap, the hands meeting palm to palm.

The figures are not highly oppositional in general appearance, al-though the decision to give one figure longer, looser hair and a flounced frock represents her as the more feminine of the two. What is significant is that the less stereotypically feminine woman is also the most physi-

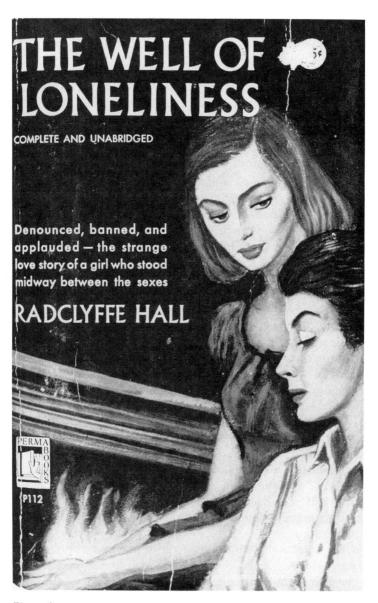

Figure 2.

cally absent. Nor does she look toward her partner nor at us. We, in turn, cannot read her eyes or ascertain the object of her gaze. She is present but mysterious. What it is like to desire as she does lacks representation; she is a closed system, and no information is forthcoming. The other woman, however, *is* present and forthcoming, almost stereotypically so. Her head is bent toward the other woman and her eyes are focused upon her. Her mouth seems about to speak. We know this feminine position: it is that of a woman seeking engagement with someone who is in the dominant position, a someone who is most often male. Furthermore, the shape of her breast is accentuated and her throat and neckline are exposed. This woman's body, unlike that of the dark-haired woman whose shirt's collar and fullness obscure neck and breast, is allowed both to emerge from her clothing and imprint her shape upon its cloth. Although the fabric hides her private body, public knowledge can supply what is missing. But then, what's missing, as in the first cover, is represented by her hands and her arms.

Those disproportionately long forearms that come together at her meeting palms form a V. The dark cloth of her dress is gathered up into that V. The curve of her white arms with the dark material between looks very like a woman's legs and hips with the dark pubic mound between. I would hesitate to insist upon such a reading of these details were it not for the location of the fireplace's flames. They appear above but they seem actually to arise from her arms, which represent her thighs. In addition, the fireplace's mantle forms a strong, thick bar that moves at a slight diagonal from left to right and concludes contiguous to the woman's breast and upper arm. Although well above the V, the phallus-finger points our gaze, directing our vision to the unmistakable curve of a female breast whose very tip it touches.

This figure is thus present both above and below the belt, as well as beneath her clothing. What is revealed is that she is, in all visible ways, like other—known—women. Moreover, there is every reason to believe that what is beneath her belt is pretty "hot stuff." It is no wonder if the other woman desires what can be found there, since it is exactly what would be desired by any "normal" man.

The difference that is being inscribed here is not so much that of anatomical opposition as it is that of familiar versus unknown female genitals. The gazer cannot see what lies between the thighs of the half/hidden woman. And it is not even clear that her genitals exist in space-off—that her genitals can be inferred—since we are given no visual clues by which to imagine them. There is only half a picture, a quarter of a woman. Because she is so genitally unrepresented, the gazer is free to fill her in. Unlike the overly present clitoris of the Butch, this figure's genitals are almost not there. So much is missing and so little is implied that any vulva might be imputed to her; any genital configuration would have validity. She can be dismissed, or she can provide more of the same delights as the other figure, or she can provide any shape or size the imagination desires. She is the most socially acceptable of lesbians—hardly there unless the gazer wants her.

But what is here for the heterosexual female gazer since she, too, must have been assumed to be a possible book browser/buyer? I would suggest that the more obviously feminine figure provides a "legitimate"—that is to say, an appropriately gendered—site for the non-gay woman to enter the cover's text. Through that more feminized figure, the heterosexual woman is encouraged to experience the desire that is signified when a woman inclines her focus and exposes her body to another who, by means of self-concealment, assumes a dominant position. It might be more difficult for a non-gay woman to align with the dark-haired figure of whom so little is present, although her nearly obscured face might well call up images of film's veiled female face and thereby invite identification. Certainly it might also be the case that this figure's clearly marginalized position on the cover (she is the focus of the gaze, but it is the gazer who occupies the center) provides a space that is cinematically designated female and so offers a place where a female gazer of any desire might suitably lodge herself. On the whole, however, the cover provides little space for the non-gay female spectator's erotic fantasizing, fewer possibilities for imaginative play. I would argue that the cover's producers do not take into consideration her presence as a gazer because they presume that as long as a heterosexual male can project *his* desire upon the illustration, his female (potential) partner could find her satisfaction. In other words, she can see her desires mirrored by observing his, since her sexuality is created in response to his. Her proximity to the site of his desire would be sufficient to stimulate her own: she would thus buy the book because its cover excited him. The most that is offered her—or perhaps I should say, the most that is offered her *if she is to fantasize heterosexually*—is the opportunity to imagine herself presenting herself to a man, hoping that her attentive posture and flaming thighs will encourage a response. But were she to fantasize gayly, then the dark-haired woman with her hidden eyes might offer a heterosexual woman a most tempting sight of alignment, a site where the shuttered gaze denies vision yet provides the locus for imagination's private display.

What is especially interesting is that it is the semi-presence of this same figure that makes the cover enticing for a lesbian gazer, although I feel certain that this was hardly the cover artist's intent. The included and missing details that make the figure unreadable and uninferable for a heterosexually fantasizing browser serve to make her a possible means of imaginative entry for gay women. This figure keeps her own counsel, it appears; she hides her thoughts, and possibly her desires as well, even when another woman makes gestures of intimacy. Because she seems to signify self-concealment, she creates a locus for homosexual existence, a site for self-mapping. Both despite and because of her semi-obscurity, her figure represents a real and marginalized sexuality whose safety derives from its ability to remain only partially visible and figuratively male. She will not reveal her secrets even though her presence gives notice that they exist.[19]

The 1974 cover uses a photograph of two women, both blond, both wearing a great deal of eyeshadow, conspicuously false eyelashes, heavy lipstick, and bright pink polish on long fingernails (fig. 3). As in the 1951 cover, the figure standing in the foreground is seen in profile, and she, too, gazes down—but at a bouquet of pink roses that she holds, her eyes hidden beneath the her thickly blue-shadowed lids. The other figure, standing at a ninety-degree angle to her, also has her eyes downcast and appears to be looking at either the roses or the breast of the woman holding them. Both figures can be seen from approximately the hips up. The foregrounded woman wears a lace patterned blue dress with a deep neckline and adorned by a kind of peplum hemmed in a plain fabric that curves over one hip and descends to the now-familiar V in front. In contrast, the other woman wears a brown pinstriped, very tailored walking suit with a deeply ruffled jabot and high collar. The femininely attired woman wears her hair in an elaborate coiffure; a cameo on a velvet ribbon tightly encircles her bared throat. The other figure's hair is short and swept tightly back from her face except for a large spit curl in front of her ear. Behind the women is either wallpaper or a mural with the stylized depiction, in vague shades of brown, of a leafy tree. The effect is to locate the figures indoors, in a room too formal to be comfortably contemporary. And although the tree does not look, to my unbotanical eye, to be apple, it surely suggests that of Biblical fame, implying that we are about to witness another, and possibly even quite original sort of, sin.

The use of so much fussily detailed dress and background seems noteworthy. While it is possible that photography can more easily reproduce minutiae that would entail costly effort for an illustrator, I do not think that this difference is sufficient to explain the prominence

Figure 3.

of such detail, nor does it account for why a photograph was chosen for the cover. I want to argue that the presence of heavily ornamented costumes and decor, as well as the use of photography, serves to inscribe the scene with a sense of "historical realism." We perceive *real* women, not some artist's rendering, wearing fashions that are clearly from another era.[20] The gazer is invited to experience a *tableau* that photography makes *vivant* in a way that illustration can not. Although the historicizing of the scene might distance the viewer from it and make the figures historical Others, it also lends it a kind of validity or authority. As the cover copy assures, this is *"the* classic story" (emphasis mine) of "Lesbian love." The cover solicits an educational scopophilia; furthermore, the voyeuristic pleasures that the scene provides will have pedagogic significance. The lesson, however, will be an erotic one—as any faithful reader of "classic" Victorian and pseudo-Victorian erotic narratives incorporating lesbianism well knows. Even though the scene itself is not "pornographic," it nonetheless suggests that genre to one who is its aficionado.

But one need not be a reader of the so-called pornographic novel to note this cover's eroticism. The pinstripe-suited woman is perceptibly more tailored than her partner. She is not only posed so as to be taller, but she is the gazer, whatever—rose or breast—may be her object. She represents, therefore, the dominant figure, the male, as she fingers a single, upstanding rose in the other woman's bouquet. The more femininely attired woman looks shy but also enrapt in the flowers, if not that particular flower. The lips of both figures are parted, and between the lips of the tailored woman can be seen her tongue as she inclines her head towards her partner and observes her own gesture, her own touch upon the flower. As we have seen before, the genitals represented are not of the same sex: one has a finger and the other has a rose.[21]

The use of the rose serves to establish more firmly oppositional gender and eroticizes the fingering and fingered women. Furthermore, while the unrevealed body of the masculine woman on the previous cover invited speculation concerning her genital configuration, the revealed rose of this cover encourages erotic fantasy about the feminine lesbian's genitals. The backgrounded, gazing lesbian can be ignored, or she can provide a focus for the male gazer's self-situating. *Without her*, the erotic significance of the scene nonetheless remains; *as her*, a man can watch himself as he watches himself touching a woman's genitals. The invitation to enter such a moment of doubly-distanced self-vision seems particularly enticing since the watched self need not remain in gender parallel with the watching self. The watcher may be male, but the watched, desired self may be imagined as wearing any anatomy beneath that costume. It is a moment when transvestic, transsexual, even androgynic pleasures can be had. But whether the masculine woman is removed or supplanted, the focus of our gaze is directed to the rose, the passive object of another's action. In fact, the rose appears to be the focus of interest for not only the fingerer but for the fingered, since the bouquet's holder is modestly casting her eyes upon it rather than upon her partner. It would seem that a "classic story of Lesbian love" can be read as a narrative of the vulva, that it can offer the same reading pleasures as do heterosexual tales about adventures with a vulva. The superfluity of details on this cover includes both female bodies: all that is important here is a rose and an appendage.

Although I was hesitant (but willing) to suggest earlier that the 1951 cover might permit a lesbian reading of and self-situating in its Butch figure, I am not at all uncertain here. The eroticizing of the one figure's hand, and in particular the eroticizing of her finger(s), is laden with lesbian significance since her hand can function as a means of sexual pleasure for another woman. Although the rose signifies the female genitalia, that finger is still a finger in a lesbian reading of the cover. Once again, I do not think that the lesbian book browser is being welcomed to the text, but rather that dominant culture knows and uses for its own ends representations and codes whose significance for sexual subcultures it cannot always foresee or control. In turn, subcultural readers can subvert these codes for their own meaning and pleasure, thereby finding within a heterosexually controlled image an unregulated representation of themselves.

And here, as before, a lesbian site offers entry for the female gazer in general as well as the specifically non-gay woman. The touch of female finger on female vulva can be read as autoerotic, the two figures coalescing into one by means of their gender similarity. Or, whether gayly or heterosexually fantasizing, a woman can place herself in the position of the bouquet holder, genitally caressed but unpenetrated (at least as yet). In this role she is utterly self-involved, concentrating, it would seem, upon her own pleasures rather than another's. What does it mean that the lesbian site is also the female site of alignment? Just as a lesbian is not the cover artist's intended reader, neither is a self-pleasuring or self-involved woman. Except when entering the cover as heterosexual women seeking the phallus, with concern for its pleasure, female self-situating must take place in sites of transgression. When the penis is not only secondary to enjoyment but not even necessary, the non-gay woman and the lesbian become similar in their sexual pleasure if not in the gendered object of their desire. For such non-phallic female pleasures there is no legitimate place.

The most recent *Well* cover (Avon, 1981) differs radically from those already discussed (fig. 4). It presents a single female figure and, although her fingers do indeed open to a V, there is no matching protuberance. Instead her attire itself signs masculinity in its man's hat, suit, tie, and white shirt. While the figure is discernibly present to the hips, it is only as a dark shape, since she is deeply shadowed. Only a portion of her face, her nose, and heavily lipsticked mouth can be seen beneath the slant of her dark hat's brim. Her throat and collar, the V-signing left hand of her crossed arms, and a small but very important triangular sliver of white cuff of the other crossed arm are also visible. Behind her, on an empty background, her hatted head and suited shoulder cast a large shadow. The novel's title is superimposed in pink upon her darkened body at the approximate height of her crotch.

I do not think there is any room for doubt here; this is a crossdressed woman and not an appropriately dressed man wearing lipstick. This is not to deny that a similarly made up, attired, and posed male could not achieve the same effect. This could even *be* a man, for all we know. But that possibility is immaterial, since the figure signals female even as it is enwrapped in male garb from which only a few of her parts emerge. The arched and elegant shading of her cheekbone, the graceful elongation of her fingers, the small, perfectly modeled mouth: these are part of the female iconography of *Vogue*'s women. Even her pose—the crossed arms denying visual access to her chest/waist but the sternly closed mouth nonetheless cosmetically accentuated so as to locate there the face's significance—is borrowed from that of the *haut monde* mannequin. The figure is as clearly female as her clothes are male. And the cover's design furthers this reading. That right arm whose white triangle of cuff shines in her body's dark interior points downward, toward the title and towards, equally important, the pubis. The left arm may bar access to her body's center, but the very stuff of her male attire points quite clearly to its hidden interior and to the title word, *Well*. Well, what we have here is what the book cover copy assures us is a "censored classic of a woman's love that dared not speak its name" but is not, it would seem, above pointing. This constitutes, I think, not only an invitation to find out what censored classics of lesbian love are all about, but a promise that light will be shed on dark, female interiors. Such an invitation need not be given to lesbians since they, presumably, know all about loving women and their concealed bodies.

But I do not want to drop too quickly the fact that the cover presents

Figure 4.

us with a woman in drag. Annette Kuhn, remarking on the crossdressed "dandy," points out that acts of crossdressing "denaturalize" what culture holds fundamentally natural—sexual difference—and in so doing reveal the "artifice" by which difference is constructed.[22] Kuhn suggests, therefore, that acts of crossdressing subvert cultural conventions of fixed and stable gender and provide "ironic comment" upon it.[23] Kuhn is correct when offering such a reading of gay "drag shows," costume balls, and the like, or when someone, usually a woman, is revealed to have played the part of a male for a number of years, accepted as such by wife, children, co-workers, and so on. But when the act of crossdressing is directed in its performance by capitalistic ideology and intended for consumption by heterosexual culture, neither subversion nor irony is the outcome. They occur only when the gazer is lured into an aesthetic and even erotic acknowledgment of the beautiful woman this man becomes or the enchanting man this woman makes. I would deny that the cover provokes such a moment, and instead contend that we never get to experience so delicious an error. The figure's male costume never succeeds in contradicting the female body beneath it. In fact, given contemporary fashion's advertisements, we might easily surmise that beneath the tailored jacket beats a lacy, pink-bra'd breast, "compliments of Olga."

However, while I do not believe that we are ever deceived by the cover, I cannot dismiss its ineluctable gayness. The cover allows the non-gay male or female to presume that the figure's hidden but alluded-to center will be available within the text. And the photographic conventions of high fashion posit that this center will offer no threatening surprises: the *well* of the figure's body, and even of her loneliness, is a waiting emptiness that is situated exactly where the "well" of the female body usually lies. The non-gay male can entertain fantasies of dipping in, and the non-gay female, as in the 1974 and 1951 covers, can imaginatively locate herself as well: her own body, which she knows intimately and erotically as indisputably female, will continue to exist as such, whatever costume she dons. (Nor do I want to impute a passive character to such heterosexual female musings. Imaginative self-locating on this cover would seem to call for fantasies of teasing playfulness, of I-dare-you-to-peek and can-you-guess-what-I've-got?) But even as the cover codes the male-clad figure female and provides suitable matter for heterosexual erotic speculation, it also draws on covert homoerotic interest in the non-gay viewer.[24]

In discussing the previous three covers, I have noted ways in which two of the covers provide sites for a specifically lesbian reading, but I cautioned against any assumption that such provision was intentional. Instead, I proposed that the covers' designers had unwittingly depicted instances of lesbian self-perception, of closeted self-knowledge. Neither the fingering lesbian nor the nearly hidden and therefore very private lesbian was intended to entice the gay female, much less gay male, viewer. Nor am I suggesting that the 1981 cover implies that the gay male or lesbian book browser will find a simpatico heroine beneath its cover. The gay appeal of this cover—its use of drag—is there for the heterosexual viewer, and not simply as a pedagogical adjunct to his or her already broad fund of sexual knowledge, as I argued the 1974 cover virtuously hinted.

Moreover, a possible reading-at-a-glance of this cover's hat-tilted figure as a detective, as the P.I. of *film noir* and Chandler's fiction, only serves to further inscribe the crossdressed woman with both regulatory and regulated significance.[25] While the private investigator of this cinematic and literary genre works independently from the explicit institution of the police, his detection functions to correct their blindness or ineptitude or to overcome their legally enforced impotence in curbing evil (their need for search warrants, for instance, is not an obstructive nicety that gets in the way of the private "dick"). As *adjunct* to the police, the private investigator implies that there is a clear distinction between heterosexuality and homosexuality, between male and female, since his inquiry has as its context the established binary system of good and evil. As an *extra*-legal investigator, however, the private eye suggests that there is a far murkier area that needs examination where, when the distinctions of binary difference become nebulous, the "real" facts of the matter can emerge. What such detection thereby uncovers can then be brought back to those institutions of justice that best maintain and enforce the binary system of sexual governance. When the detective upon closer inspection is revealed to be a crossdressed woman, the darkened figure offers a hint of a deeply hidden ideology that creates "outlaw" sexualities only to better regulate them, and regulates them only to enlarge—and to control—what it deems to be "legitimate" sexuality.

This cover figure elicits the hidden homoerotic in the public heterosexual who need not, therefore, come out of the closet to possess the experience. The non-gay female can indulge her forbidden attraction to male-garbed women or can be one herself. The non-gay male can indulge in fantasies of a non-phallic man, or he can reverse the gender hierarchy of sexual dominance and imagine himself as both sexual and non-phallic. Might not the half-hidden lesbian and the rose-proffering lesbian, and even the "dark" lesbian of the racially inscribed cover offer appeal equal to those of this cover? Recall this figure's looming shadow: it is the Other/self, cast behind and unavoidably present.

Notes

For their encouragement and good counsel/humor during the various drafts of this essay, I wish to thank Andrew Parker and R L Widmann. Diana Fuss asked all the questions one could wish for from an editor. Caroline Hinkley kindly put aside her own art projects in order to photograph this piece's cover art. And I am indebted also to the Lesbian Herstory Archives, which provided important historical material, and to Barbara Grier, who not only dug up documents when she herself was pressed for time, but whose bibliographic work has made visible the presence of the lesbian reader and her subject.

1. *The Well of Loneliness* has undergone numerous editions and reprints since its first British publication by Jonathan Cape in July 1928, and its American edition by Covici Friede (New York) in December of the same year. The 1951 paperback edition was issued by Perma Books; the 1964 edition and its 1974 reprint were published by Pocket Books, Inc.; the 1981 reprint is Avon's, photograph by Kathie A. McGinty. See Michael Baker, *Our Three Selves: The Life of Radclyffe Hall* (New York: William Morrow, 1985), 204–6 for a discussion of *The Well*'s early publication history. For a general history of paperback publication and cover art, see Thomas L. Bonn, *Under Cover: An Illustrated History of American Mass Market Paperbacks* (Middlesex and New York: Penguin, 1982).

2. See Sue-Ellen Case, "Towards a Butch-Femme Aesthetic," in *Making a Spectacle: Feminist Essays in Contemporary Women's Theatre*, ed. Lynda Hart (Ann Arbor: University of Michigan Press, 1980), 282–99; "Contemporary theory seems to open the closet door to invite the queer to come out, transformed as a new, post-modern subject, or even to invite straights to come into the closet, out of the roar of dominant discourse. The danger incurred in moving gay politics into heterosexual contexts is in only slowly discovering that the strategies and perspectives of homosexual realities and discourse may be locked inside a homophobic 'concentration camp' " (288).

3. Although this essay is focused on appropriations of lesbian sexuality, it is important to point out that dominant culture consistently endeavors to reposition all subcultures within its own ideological system, as in the recent film *Rain Man*, where a member of Idiot Savant culture becomes the means by which both capitalism and heterosexual intimacy are achieved. Of course, one can view this film from a gay-subversive perspective, in which case an Other manages to interrupt heterosexual love-making, gain an all-expense paid cross-country trip, finagle a kiss from his brother's woman, and dance in panoramic splendor in his brother's arms. I am not at all arguing that such a perspective was intended by the director, but rather am suggesting that there are ways of reading the film that allow us to see the python being consumed by the rabbit.

4. Because *The Well* is, in fact, precisely about a woman whose body and behavior correspond to that of the Butch, one might argue that its covers had to display the

Butch-Femme dichotomy. It is not fortuitous but explicable that the novel supplies dominant ideological needs; *The Well*'s reflection of the sexologists' depiction of the female "invert" as a man trapped in a woman's body is the culturally called-for homosexual narrative. Nor am I arguing that the covers are at odds with the text, but rather that both covers and text allow an Other's desire to be read heterosexually. After all, it was not Hall's presentation of the lesbian subject *per se* that elicited charges of indecency; it was her refusal to punish the lesbian for her sin of desire as well as Hall's reversal of the expected natural/unnatural paradigm: in Stephen Gordon's final peroration, the "invert" names herself as God's creation and as, therefore, natural.

5. Mention should be made of these publishers' decisions to continue to print Havelock Ellis's single paragraph commentary praising the novel directly after the Dedication page, as though it were a Preface (see Baker, 203–6). If the publishers' copy is not sufficient to justify indulging one's pleasure in reading such a text, then surely a learned sexologist's words can be.

6. Sander L. Gilman, *Difference and Pathology: Stereotypes of Sexuality, Race, and Madness* (Ithaca and London: Cornell University Press, 1985), 79.

7. Gilman, *Difference*, 81.

8. Teresa de Lauretis, *Technologies of Gender: Essays on Theory, Film, and Fiction* (Bloomington and Indianapolis: Indiana University Pres, 1987), 26. De Lauretis makes clear the ways dominant ideology seeks to invade all space, to infiltrate even absences (21–24).

9. Gilman, *Difference*, 83–90.

10. Gilman, *Difference*, 94–101.

11. See Frank Caprio, M.D., *Female Homosexuality: A Psychodynamic Study of Lesbianism* (New York: Grove, 1954); David Reuben, M.D., *Everything You Always Wanted to Know about Sex (But Were Afraid to Ask)* (New York, Toronto, and London: Bantam, 1970); Charlotte Wolff, M.D., *Love Between Women* (London: Duckworth, 1973).

12. Caprio, *Female Homosexuality*, 20.

13. Reuben, *Everything*, 270.

14. Wolff, *Love between Women*, 48.

15. William H. Masters and Virginia E. Johnson, *Human Sexual Response* (New York, Toronto, and London: Bantam, 1981), 48.

16. Reuben, *Everything*, 270.

17. Masters and Johnson, *Human Sexual Response*, 47–58.

18. See Thomas W. Laqueur, " 'Armor Veneris, vel Dulcedo Appeletur'," in *Zone 5: Fragments for a History of the Human Body, Part 3*, ed. Michel Feher (Cambridge and London: MIT Press, 1989), 91–131. Nor can I help but point out the ideology present in Reuben's use of "quirk," Wolff's "habitually," and Masters's and Johnson's "artifacts" and "excessive."

19. See Teresa de Lauretis, "Sexual Indifference and Lesbian Representation," *Theatre Journal*, 40, no. 2 (May 1988): 155–77, in particular 158–73, for a discussion of the difficulties in elaborating a theory of lesbian spectatorship.

20. Despite the costumes, the cover is historically inaccurate. The method of cosmetic application is fairly modern, and the costumes are from two different eras, as are the hairstyles. I suppose that the spit-curled coiffure is meant to be a bob or shingle, but the other resembles a cross between French Regency and early June Allyson.

21. The use of a rose to represent the vulva is part of a lengthy tradition, from the *Roman de la Rose* to *Rubyfruit Jungle*, whose title, the novel makes clear, is vulval and whose early Daughters, Inc. and later Avon covers display a single vivid rose on a white background.

22. *Annette Kuhn, The Power of the Image: Essays on Representation and Sexuality* (London, Boston, Melbourne, and Henley: Routledge and Kegan Paul, 1985), 49–54.

23. Kuhn, *The Power*, 54.

24. See Dean MacCannell and Juliet Flower MacCannell, "The Beauty System," in *The Ideology of Conduct: Essays in Literature and the History of Sexuality*, ed. Nancy Armstrong and Leonard Tennenhouse (New York and London: Methuen, 1987), 206–38, whose discussion of the Jane Fonda body demonstrates how a female body can call upon "the substantial homosexual reserves in the general male population" (232). See also de Lauretis, "Sexual Indifference and Lesbian Representation," in particular 155–57, and Laqueur, " 'Armor Veneris," 113; both posit an historical discourse of mono-sexuality by which the female body (Laqueur) and its desire (de Lauretis) are represented as male. De Lauretis is especially useful in noting how such signification appropriates the female and how its construction of femininity "had the effect of securing the heterosexual social contract by which all sexualities, all bodies, and all 'others' are bonded to an ideal/ideological hierarchy of males" (158).

25. I am indebted to Cathy Lynn Preston and Michael J. Preston for their observation of the detective lurking in the cover's shadow.

Figure 1.

11

Rock Hudson's Body

Richard Meyer

The Starbody

Rock Hudson's was a body to fill, even to overflow, the enlarging film screen of the 1950s. In response to its new competition of television, Hollywood touted and technologically reinvented the spectacular size of its image.[1] And Rock Hudson's body, featured in five cinemascope productions, seemed writ in particularly large-screen proportion. At 6'4" and 200 pounds, Hudson was physically the largest male star of the day and his hunky physique was emphasized, even pumped up, by his films and fan magazine photographs (fig. 1). His 1956 film *Giant*, for example, was promoted as a "big story of big things and big feelings."[2] In it, Hudson, as (big) rancher Bick Benedict, iconized both the state of Texas and the film's own delirious grandeur: "Rock Hudson is gigantic, relaxed, rocklike indeed, and right for the part,"[3] exclaimed *Newsweek*'s reviewer at the time.

According to an article in the 1957 *McCalls* magazine entitled, "Why Women Are In Love with Rock Hudson," the executives at Universal Studios decided that in all Hudson films "there would be at least one scene in which [Rock] overflows a normal sized doorway,"[4] as though to demonstrate that the scale of daily life was too diminutive for the Hudson body. This motif of Rock outstripping or barely fitting into the frame appeared not only in his films but in his publicity photographs as well. The March 1954 *Photoplay*, for example, offered Hudson's body as one so expansive that it must crouch to fit into the visual field of nature (fig. 2). And *Photoplay*'s 1958 image (fig. 3) seems equally insufficient in its effort to enframe the star's bending body, which is once again figured in a quiet communion with the outdoors. As these images suggest, Hudson's body was often set against a natural surround—even the patently inauthentic name, gleaned respectively from the Rock of Gibraltar and the Hudson River,[5] was meant to locate him in (and as) an expansive landscape of the masculine.

In his publicity images, Hudson was often photographed from below so as to increase the already prodigious proportions of his body. Consider, for example, a photograph of Hudson which was published in the October 1953 *Photoplay*. The image is part of a larger spread called "Meet the Champs" (fig. 4) which presented twelve beefcake stars, each with the ("vital") measurements of his height, weight, chest and waist. Hudson, the largest champ on display, is also the only one favored by a full-length, color portrait. In contrast to the close-up or ¾ length shots of Marlon Brando, Kirk Douglas, Ricardo Montalban and the rest, Hudson's full-length, low-angle photograph marks (and in a sense makes) the unique scale of his body. So too does the accompanying text which asserts that "Rock towers over even such lanky stars as Jimmy Stewart"[6] and "Rugged Rock 6'5", 190, 44", 32" has an appetite to match his size so he resorts to swimming, riding, tennis, and golf to stay in shape. And an eye-pleasing shape it is . . ."[7] Notice that *Photoplay* has added an extra inch to Rock Hudson's height, something that happened with some frequency in the fanzine reporting on him, as though his size were so impressive as to be indeterminate or expandable.

The insistence on Rock's stupendous proportions was meant, I think, to secure his manhood as similarly well-endowed. In the 1959 bedroom farce *Pillow Talk,* for example, when size-conscious Thelma Ritter warns the less knowledgeable Doris Day that "six foot six inches of opportunity doesn't come by every day. When you see it, grab it,"[8] she leaves little doubt that the length of Hudson's body is to be measured as phallus. Here again, the imagined dimensions of Rock's body are expanded—now to 6'6"—beyond the somatic limits of his anatomy.

Yet for all its emphatic bigness, Rock Hudson's (out-)size did not harden his screen persona into the 50s machismo of a Marlon Brando or even the rough readiness of a Kirk Douglas or a Robert Stack. What distinguished Hudson from the other male stars of his day was not just the fact (or fantasy) of his largeness, but the way he tempered that big body with a measure of safety, of "gentle giant" reassurance.[9]

Hudson's quieter masculinity may be traced, at least in part, to his roles in the domestic melodramas or "women's films" of Douglas Sirk. As Mary Anne Doane has observed, the "women's film"

> offers some resistance to an analysis which stresses the "to-be-looked-at-ness" of the woman, her objectification as spectacle ac-

cording to the masculine structures of the gaze . . . [It enacts] a
deflection of scopophiliac energy in other directions, away from the
female body.[10]

In Sirk's melodramas, one of the "other directions" in which scopophiliac energy is pointed is towards Rock Hudson's body. As the object of
a desiring, *implicitly female* gaze, Hudson's masculinity is at once less
aggressive and more eroticized than that of the conventional male hero
of Hollywood film.

Ironically, Hudson had himself embodied such heroic characters
before appearing in Sirk's melodramas. In the early 1950s, as a newly
signed contract player for Universal, Hudson was featured in a series
of frankly macho films—westerns, sports, and war pictures with titles
like *Gun Fury* (1951), *The Iron Man* (1953), and *Taza, Son of Cochise*
(1954). Important for our purposes is the fact that these films enjoyed
only limited success and that Hudson's shift toward domestic melodrama, beginning with his role in Sirk's *Magnificent Obsession* (1954),
marked the start of his major stardom and top box office status.[11] The
modification of Rock Hudson's masculinity as he switched from action
films to melodramas—from "men's movies" to "women's films"—
registered in his publicity photography as well. Initially domineering
(e.g. fig. 4), Hudson's body was gradually seen to slacken its stance
(fig. 5), to relax or lie recumbent, to more comfortably invite the look
of its (now female) viewer.

Within the context of Hudson's relaxed masculinity, I'd like to
consider a 1956 *Photoplay* spread called "Beefcake Kings" (fig. 6): On
the upper left of the layout, squinting while remaining seated, Kirk
Douglas looks resolutely past the camera. To the bottom right, Alan
Ladd concentrates on pruning a backyard tree, seemingly unaware of
the camera which catches his flexing deltoids *in medias res*. Both
Douglas and Ladd exemplify what Richard Dyer has called the instability of the male pin-up, "the contradiction between the fact of being
looked at and the model's attempt to deny it."[12] This denial usually
takes the form of the male model either ignoring the camera as though
unaware of its presence (as does the butch Alan Ladd) or acknowledging its gaze with a sort of phallic defiance, a looking past or through
its vision (as might be argued for Kirk Douglas). Douglas and Ladd—
all tense expression and improbable posture—stage their masculinity
as hostile to the stilling gaze of the camera.

But Rock Hudson, the third in this triumvirate of beefcake royalty,
submits rather more readily to the camera, anticipating, even inviting

Figure 3.

Figure 2.

its objectification. Hudson's frontal orientation and comfortable, contrapposto stance acknowledge the fact of self-presentation. And with his upward glance and slight smile he doesn't so much defy the camera as ethereally gaze beyond it. In contrast to Kirk Douglas's strained pool-side sitting and Alan Ladd's backyard pruning, Rock Hudson seems to be doing nothing except posing. Uniquely among these beefcake kings, Hudson could accommodate the intrinsic passivity of the pin-up stance, could visibly acquiesce to his position of "to-be-looked-at-ness."[13]

Part of the appeal of Rock Hudson's body, then, was that it seemed somewhat immobile, available as an object of erotic delectation but without the threat of male action. At a cultural moment when young women were often reminded of their "duty" to rebuff the erotic advance of their male companions,[14] Rock Hudson provided a less threatening, less sexual model of masculinity:

> Unlike Rudolph Valentino, who was the sex-boat of his day, Rock Hudson is not the lover type. He has sex appeal but the older fans want to mother him, young girls want to marry him, and men want to emulate him . . . He gives the appearance of great solidity.[15]

Consider the split between sex and domesticity here (it's the 1957 *Photoplay*), as Rock is aligned with marriage, mothering, and male identification and opposed to any fantasy—the lover, the sexboat—of heterosexual exchange. That his strapping male body should house this sort of (desexed) safety was promoted as the foundational reason "Why Women Are In Love with Rock Hudson":

> Through the magic of Rock Hudson's eyes and size, combined with his unaffected friendliness . . . he makes women feel they can count on him.[16]

McCalls will work the trope of Rock's reliability especially hard, repeatedly emphasizing his quiet compliance to the desires of a largely female audience:

> Rock is never cast as the heavy in movies, never appears drunk, and never, never makes a pass at a girl. His fans wouldn't stand for it.[17]

Hudson offered not only the visual pleasure of his form, his open-faced good looks and unparalleled large proportions, but the promise to control that big body, the promise not to pounce. And, as the 1958 *Look* magazine suggests, Hudson's promise of self-restraint extended

Figure 4.   *Figure 5.*

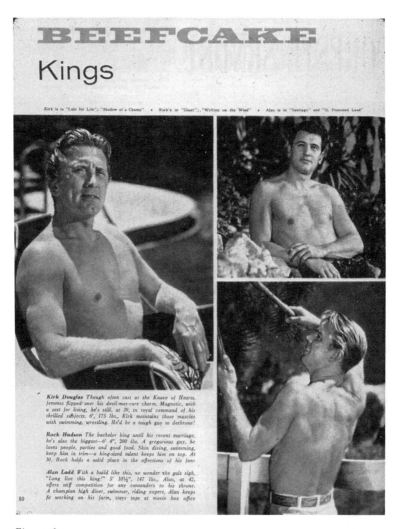

Figure 6.

not just to his romantic relations on screen but to the very surface of his starbody:

> In the past few years too many actors have been sensitive and spooky like Jimmy Dean; the public got tired of decay. So now here's Rock Hudson. He's wholesome. He doesn't perspire. He has no pimples. He smells of milk. His whole appeal is cleanliness and respectability—this boy is pure.[18]

Jimmy Dean's method actor angst and performative volatility (fig. 7) are figured as implicitly physical decay, to be set against Hudson's wholesomeness, which is here imagined as a kind of somatic wholeness. Rock Hudson's starbody will not break out or emit fluids; fantasmatically cleansed of pimples, pores, and perspiration, it serves as the consummate safe sex-object.[19]

Several of Hudson's fanzine photographs seem to play off this fantasy of sanitization: (figs. 8–11) washing his car in 1952, washing his hair or drinking from a spewing hose in 1953, relaxing in a bathtub in 1959—the fictions imagined in these beefcake shots are themselves ones of cleansing and purification. As opposed to the method actor body of "spooky" James Dean or "grubby"[20] Marlon Brando (fig. 12), Rock Hudson's body did not sweat or secrete emotion. Hudson's represented fluids were ones which had come from outside the body to cleanse it, rather than his own bodily fluids which had leaked and were soiling the surface. There were no layers of conflicted identity to be recovered beneath the serene surface of the starbody, no reason for it to break out into a sweat.

Rock's unflagging hygiene registered not only in the cleanliness of his fanzine photography but in the consummate health of the characters he played on-screen, particularly in the Sirk melodramas of the mid 1950s. During the course of these films, Hudson's body remains beautifully unmarked by the diegesis while the female characters combat any number of psychic and physical dysfunctions—blindness in *Magnificent Obsession* (fig. 13), migraine headaches and community ostracism in *All that Heaven Allows*, sexual insatiability in *Written on the Wind*.[21] Hence the paradoxical relation of the implied female spectator of the Sirk melodrama to Rock Hudson's body: while she could see and freeze Hudson's body in erotic delectation, her visual power was contested insofar as she identified with the look of the ailing female protagonist. "In films addressed to women," Doane writes, "spectatorial pleasure is often indissociable from pain."[22]

Figure 7.

Figure 12.

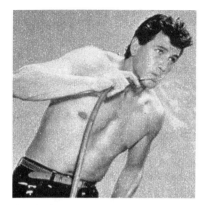

Figure 8.

Figure 9.

Figure 10.

Figure 11.

Of all Hudson melodramas, *Magnificent Obsession* is perhaps most pointed in the way it maneuvers both female spectatorial pleasure and (punitive) female pain around the pivot of Rock Hudson's body. In that film, the erotic spectacle of beefy Bob Merrick (Hudson) is repeatedly mediated through the desiring "look" of Helen Phillips (Jane Wyman). But because Helen is blind throughout most of the diegesis (figs. 14, 15), the spectator identifying with her—the spectator gazing at Merrick "through" Helen's eyes—draws a conflicted pleasure at best. And the spectatorial economy of Helen's "blind desire" for Bob Merrick is further complicated by the fact that it is his eroticized body which ultimately administers the cure for her blindness: After the three foremost experts on ophthalmology declare no hope for Helen's case (fig. 16), Merrick resumes his lapsed medical studies, becomes a neurosurgeon, and, at film's end, performs an experimental procedure which simultaneously saves Helen's life and restores her sight. The film's most explicit specularization of Rock Hudson's body occurs just before the sight-saving operation: a sustained ½ length shot catches a shirtless Dr. Merrick as he scrubs for surgery (fig. 17). Even as Helen is blind and comatose on the operating-room table, *Magnificent Obsession* takes time out to objectify Rock Hudson's body, "to freeze the flow of action in a moment of erotic contemplation."[23] It is as though the film can venture such an intense eroticization of Bob Merrick's body because Helen is at her most disabled point yet, her vision at its most impaired. And even after Dr. Merrick's strapping male body revives Helen to fully sentient womanhood, the camera does not take up her desiring gaze. Helen will see ("tomorrow," Merrick tells her in post-op) but the spectator will not see through her *functional* gaze, will not identify with her restored vision or spectatorial pleasure.

Where *Magnificent Obsession* manages the spectacle of Rock Hudson's body by blinding its female protagonist, Sirk's 1956 melodrama *Written on the Wind* diagnoses female desire for Hudson as a symptom of nymphomania (fig. 18). In that film, millionairess Marylee Hadley (Dorothy Malone) overproduces her libido because Mitch Wayne (Hudson), the one man she truly wants, will not reciprocate her desire: "Marylee . . . couldn't have Mitch, so she sought love when and where she could get it."[24] Because the film writes Marylee's active pursuit of Mitch as psychosexual pathology, Mitch's inert heterosexuality in the face of that pursuit is seen as necessary and normative.[25] As in *Magnificent Obsession*, the dysfunction and desire of the female character are here opposed to the immobile, immaculate masculinity of Rock Hudson. "In melodrama, it's of advantage to have one immovable

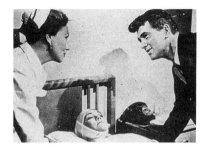

Figure 13.

Figure 14

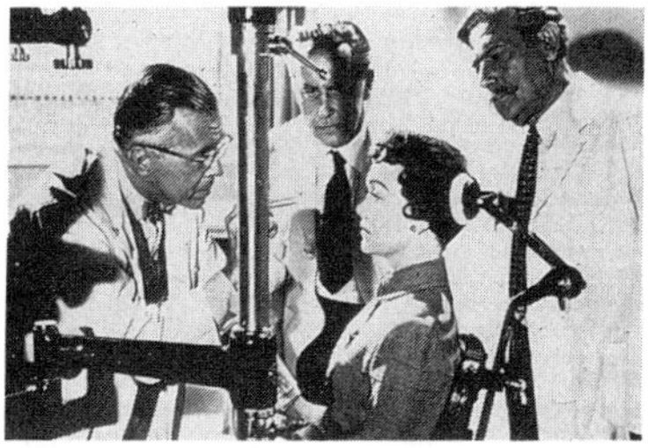

Figure 16.

Figure 15.

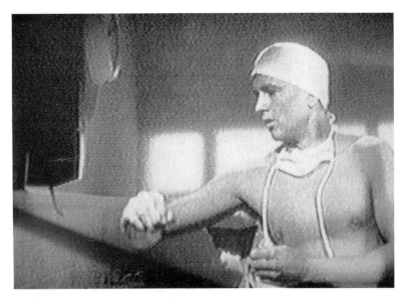

Figure 17.

Figure 18.

character against which you can put your more split ones," said Sirk, referring to Hudson's function within his films.[26] Pushing the point a bit further, I would argue that it was Rock Hudson's very "immovability" which fractured his female companion into sickness and desire, which, in effect, "split" her into the subject of melodrama.

The utter immobility of Hudson's characters came to frustrate the actor, however, and when *Written on the Wind* was being cast, he campaigned for the part of volatile, violently alcoholic Kyle Hadley—Marylee's brother and Mitch Wayne's best friend.[27] The role, and eventually an academy award nomination for it, went to Robert Stack while Rock was cast as geologist (!) Mitch Wayne. Barely veiling his resentment at the bland-boy typing, Hudson would accurately say of his performance in the film, "As usual, I am so pure I am impossible."[28]

In defense of the casting decision, one Dave Lipton, then head of Universal Studios publicity declared,

> Rock's fans won't accept his doing anything shoddy. . . . They like him because he's what they want their daughters to marry, or their children's father to be, or their childhood sweetheart. If we let him break out of that character, they'd howl.[29]

Once again, we hear a male narration of the heterosexual (and implicitly female) fan's power to keep Hudson grounded in his wholesome image. This *rhetoric* of determinant female desire—"they'd howl," "they wouldn't stand for it," "they won't accept anything shoddy"—was produced by a male-dominated publicity network to contain Hudson within his sanitized masculinity.[30] And when, as in the casting for *Written on the Wind*, Hudson attempted to transgress the boundary of that masculinity, the Hollywood rhetoric of "what women want" functioned to reinscribe him within it.

The indenture of Rock Hudson to the *purported* desires of his female fans reached its predictable extreme over the issue of his marital status. In 1955, as a still unwed Hudson neared the age of 30, the press exhorted him to marry. The title of a *Life* cover story, "The Simple Life of Busy Bachelor: Rock Hudson Gets Rich Alone," implied Hudson's duty to share his newfound wealth with a wife while the story inside reported that:

> since 1949 movie fan clubs and fan magazines have parlayed a $75-a-week ex-truck driver named Roy Fitzgerald into a $3,000-a-week movie hero named Rock Hudson . . . But now they are beginning to

grumble. Their complaints, expressed in fan magazine articles, range from a shrill "Scared of Marriage?" to a more understanding "Don't Rush Rock." Fans are urging 29-year-old Hudson to get married— or explain why not."[31]

A tabloid publication called *Movie/T.V. Secrets* fagbaited the bachelor star rather more overtly:

He is handsome, personable, intelligent, and a top-salaried actor— what's wrong with Rock where the fair sex is concerned, we ask?[32]

Adding considerable urgency to Hudson's "marriage question" was the fact that the tauntings of *Life* and *Movie/T.V. Secrets* were on the verge of becoming yet more explicit. According to several accounts, *Confidential*, a contemporary tabloid which billed itself as the publication which would "tell the facts and name the names," was threatening in 1955 to run a exposé on Hudson's homosexuality.[33]

And so, in November of that same year, Rock Hudson married Phyllis Gates, a woman formerly employed as the secretary of Hudson's agent Henry Willson. Although descriptions of the relationship between Hudson and Gates vary, it is clear that Willson, an openly gay man within Hollywood circles, masterminded both the match and the wedding, making certain that photographers would be on hand to record such seemingly intimate moments as (fig. 19) the couple in their wedding-night hotel room, the drinking of champagne on the conjugal bed(s), the sharing of joy, long-distance, with the bride's mother.[34] What lay behind this picture of nuptial bliss, then, was not only the explicit threat of homosexual exposure but Henry Willson's (gay) knowledge of how to construct an ideal heterosexuality for, and in, representation.

But why should Hudson's marriage have served as a foolproof defense against the tabloid threat of "outing"? Even after the wedding, might not *Confidential* have published an exposé on Hudson's *former* life as a homosexual, or on the Hudson-Gates marriage as a sham? Apparently not, as no such threat is mentioned following the nuptial moment. It is as though the images of Hudson's wedding and married home-life (fig. 20), working in conjunction with the domestic iconography of his films (fig. 21), signified a heterosexuality powerful enough to defuse any threat of homosexual exposure.

While the desire for Rock Hudson's marriage may have been orchestrated through the fictions of his films and fanzine stories, it was

Figure 19.

Figure 21.

Figure 20.

answerable in the contracts and rituals of his lived experience. Because there was no cultural space available for Hudson to "explain why not," his homosexual body was forced to enact the premier ritual of heterosexual identity. As Michel Foucault has famously observed,

> the body . . . is directly involved in a political field, power relations have an immediate hold upon it; they invest it, torture it, force it to carry out tasks, to perform ceremonies, to emit signs.[35]

In 1955, Rock Hudson's marriage was sufficient to secure and emit the sign "heterosexuality." Though the marriage would last less than three years, the sign would remain publicly affixed to Rock Hudson's body for the following three decades.

The Anti-Body

The star has no right to be sick or even to appear out of sorts.
—Jean Marais, preface to *Comment Devenir Vedette de Cinema?*[36]

Consider a publicity still from the early 1950s (fig. 22). Its fictive scenario suggests the characteristics of Rock Hudson's body which I have offered as definitive. The strapping star, nearly overflowing the door-jam, is called to the phone during a shower. Photographed from below so as to loom yet larger, Hudson embodies the codes of both hygiene and domesticity, both cleanliness and hetero-social communication. Now compare a news-photograph from the summer of 1985 (fig. 23), the moment of the public disclosure that Hudson was ill as a result of AIDS. Both photographs were published in a single layout (with the news photograph markedly larger than the publicity still) in the September 1985 *Life* magazine. The caption they shared reported that

> AIDS was given a face everyone could recognize when it was announced that Rock Hudson, 59, was suffering from the disease. The quintessential 1950's leading man . . . had looked ill when he appeared with Doris Day in July at a press conference.[37]

Implicit in the notion that Rock Hudson gave "AIDS a face everyone could recognize" is the unrecognizability, and in a sense, the un-reality of the 12,000 faces and bodies already diagnosed with AIDS in this nation by 1985, and the 6,000 faces and bodies already dead from it. Because those were primarily the bodies of non-celebrity gay men and intravenous drug users, they were either ignored by the media or constructed as radically other from the body of the Reader. Their death and dysfunction were not to be "recognized."

But is even Rock Hudson's illness recognizable in this before and after format, and if so, what have we been asked to recognize it as? The caption offers Hudson's as a familiar and universalized "face of AIDS," but the familiar face is the one attached to the hygienic body in the publicity still. Far from being asked to identify with Hudson's ailing body, the Reader is meant to view it as the contrast and contamination of his starbody, to view it as Rock Hudson's "anti-body:"[38]

> Tinged with the stigma of illness that dramatically destroys the body, what was usually absent from representation becomes spectacularly and consistently visible.[39]

What was absent from prior images of Rock Hudson's body but what is now meant to be visible—to be visibly leaking out—is his homosexuality. Within the economy of *Life*'s before and after circuit, the after image, the AIDS image, not only figures the physical signs of illness but proffers those signs as the evidence and horrific opening of Rock Hudson's closet. And what *Life* signified pictorially, *Time* would plainly state:

> to moviegoers of the 1950's and 60's no star better represented the old-fashioned American virtues than Rock Hudson . . . [but] last week as Hudson lay gravely ill with AIDS in a Paris hospital, it became clear that throughout those years the all-American boy had another life, kept secret from the public: he was almost certainly homosexual.[40]

In this scenario, homosexuality supplants HIV as the origin and etiology of Rock Hudson's illness. Closeted through all the years of his celebrity, Rock Hudson's secret finally registers, Dorian Gray-like, on the surface of his body. The physical repercussions of AIDS are here imbued with a heavy (and heavily homophobic) symbolism such that Hudson's moribund body becomes both signifier and symptom of his "almost certain" homosexuality.[41]

As I suggest above, Rock Hudson epitomized a particularly sanitized version of hetero-masculinity in American film culture of the 1950s

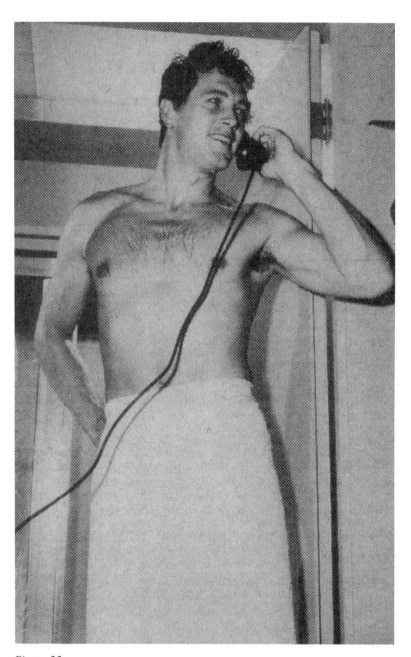

Figure 22.

Figure 23.

and early 60s. Because this image elided not just Hudson's homosexuality but the very fluids and functioning of sex itself, an extreme excess of signification obtained in 1985 to his AIDS body. Rock Hudson, once deeply overdetermined in his hygiene, became commensurately overdetermined in his sickness:

> The faceless disease now has a face. But it is not the ruggedly handsome face of *Giant* or *Magnificent Obsession* or even *Pillow Talk* that will be Rock Hudson's greatest legacy. Instead, that legacy will be the gaunt, haggard face of those poignant last days.[42]

Here again, the spectacular contrast of Rock Hudson's two bodies—before/after, well/ill, 1950s/1980s, and, implicitly, hetero-/homosexual—provides the central trope for the conceptualization of his AIDS.

The body/anti-body binary produced around Rock Hudson's illness may be usefully compared to the media's handling of the second episode in which a national celebrity was revealed to have contracted AIDS—the 1987 death of Liberace. Consider, for example, the covers which *People* magazine respectively devoted to each star's illness (figs. 24, 25). Published shortly after the July 1985 announcement of Hudson's illness but before his death that October, the Hudson cover features a contemporary image into which we are meant to read the visual evidence of AIDS. Image and text together signify that the "other life of Rock Hudson," his until-now covert homosexuality, has produced this, his ailing and "other" body. By contrast, the Liberace cover presents a familiarly flamboyant image of the star with the superimposed dates of his birth and (AIDS-related) death. Because Liberace, who became a star at roughly the same time as Hudson, was already situated outside the popular codes of heterosexual masculinity, *People* did not construct from his AIDS the kind of "other life" apparently required for Hudson. For *People*, Liberace's illness is iconized well-enough by his already (and flamingly) *other* image of masculinity. Hudson's illness, by contrast, must be produced as the very picture of his "fall" from ideal masculinity.

The tone of betrayal which underwrote many of the commentaries on Hudson's AIDS—though not on Liberace's—reflects an intensely fantasmatic investment in Hudson's particular image of hetero-masculinity. Theater critic Frank Rich, for example, speaking as (and for) a heterosexual audience, would write in *Esquire* magazine:

> Does Hudson's skill at playing a heterosexual mean that he was a brilliant actor, or was this just the way he really was, without acting at all? I suspect that most Americans believed that Hudson, who seemed so natural on screen, was playing himself, which means that in the summer of 1985 we had to accept the fact that many of our fundamental, conventional images of heterosexuality were instilled in us (and not for the first time) by a homosexual . . . everything that happened on screen was a lie, with the real content embedded in code.[43]

Homosexual panic here issues ("and not for the first time") from Rock Hudson's enactment of what was, for Rich, a most convincing, even an instructional masculinity. No matter that Hudson's screen-image was, as the star himself noted, "impossible" in its purity; Rich holds him accountable to it, to some imagined transparency of it.

In a similar if even more startling response to Rock Hudson's AIDS, sex-therapist Ruth Westheimer told *Playboy* magazine, "I feel sad for all the thousands of women who fantasized about being in [Rock Hudson's] arms, who now have to realize that he never really cared about them."[44] Because he has been revealed as homosexual through a spectacle of illness, Hudson is said to betray the projective fantasies of his heterosexual spectator, here a female one. Rather than scrutinizing the extreme over-investment of these spectators in Rock Hudson's starbody, Westheimer blames Hudson for not reciprocating their desire.

As Simon Watney has pointed out,

> Rock Hudson's death ... offered journalists an opportunity for particularly vicious revenge on a man whom they had casually taken to embody their own patriarchal and misogynistic values for more than three decades. To begin with we should note the practical impossibility of Hudson's "coming out" as gay in the American film industry of the 1950's ... given the intensely homophobic atmosphere of McCarthyite values in Hollywood.[45]

Watney inserts what Rich, Westheimer, and nearly all of the other mainstream commentators on Hudson's illness erase, namely the historical impossibility of any publicly homosexual identity for Hudson in the 1950s. In dehistoricizing Hudson's homosexuality, Rich, Westheimer, et al. suggest the actor's closet as a matter of personal agency and thus of deception. ("The Master of Illusion" and "The Hunk Who Lived a Lie" were among the titles of other articles on Hudson's illness). With Watney, we should recall that Hudson's closet was not an effect of individual choice but of homophobia and compulsory heterosexuality, systems of surveillance enforced with particular ferocity in 1950s America.[46]

And yet, when we consider the specific image of masculinity which Hudson embodied in the 1950s, we have proper cause to wonder precisely what kind of sexuality he was offering his film viewer. Recall the fanzine hype: "Rock Hudson is not the lover type" ... "his whole appeal is cleanliness and respectability" ... "he smells of milk" ... "he never, never makes a pass at a girl." Rock Hudson was a star fantasmatically defused of active (hetero)sexual desire, a man to marry or to mother but not to fuck. I would suggest that Hudson's homosexuality—however disavowed by Hollywood, by the film viewer, or by Hudson himself—registered in his star image, in the sexual immobility

Figure 24.

Figure 25.

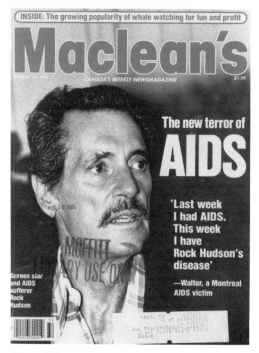

INSIDE: The growing popularity of whale watching for fun and profit

Maclean's

CANADA'S WEEKLY NEWSMAGAZINE $1.50

The new terror of

AIDS

'Last week
I had AIDS.
This week
I have
Rock Hudson's
disease'

—Walter, a Montreal
AIDS victim

Screen star
and AIDS
sufferer
Rock
Hudson

Figure 26.

of his masculinity, in the way that women really *could* count on him to maintain his erotic distance. Many of those who orchestrated Hudson's stardom were aware of his homosexuality—certainly his agent, probably his directors, photographers, and fanzine journalists and of course, Hudson himself.[47] It seems likely that the framing of Hudson's hunky but deheterosexualized masculinity worked off this knowledge, responded to it, *used* it as source and building block.

How then do we explain the heterosexual desire for Rock Hudson's body, the fact that he was the male star "men wanted to emulate" and "thousands of women" fantasized about embracing? As already discussed, Hudson promised straight women a space of sexual safety— he would acquiesce to domesticity without insisting on male domination. And Hudson's less typical straight male viewers (Frank Rich, for one) were no doubt relieved to find a role-model who did not require the exhaustive work of machismo to "measure up" to its masculinity. In Rock Hudson, then, a strapping gay male body closeted its explicit desire for other men while retaining its erotic neutrality towards women, thereby providing a sexual "safe place" for both sides of his heterosexual audience.[48] As D. A. Miller points out, the closet (and I would suggest Rock Hudson's closet in particular) might best be understood as ". . . a homophobic, heterosexual *desire* for homosexuality, and not merely a homophobic, heterosexual *place* for it."[49] There were things that heterosexual culture wanted from Rock Hudson's body (a safe date was one) but only under the proviso that the homosexuality underwriting those things remain unspoken and precisely unspeakable.

In the summer of 1985, when Rock Hudson's homosexuality was finally spoken by the popular media, it was as the "New Terror of AIDS" (fig. 26). By rights, that headline should have been reserved for a death count of 6,000 Americans and the lethal indifference of a Reagan Administration faced with those deaths. Instead, it described the collapse of a particular fantasy of male containment and sexual safety—a fantasy once attached to Rock Hudson's body, a fantasy once embodied by Rock Hudson's closet.

Notes

Versions of this essay were presented at a panel on "Male Bodies" at the Conference of the Lesbian and Gay Studies Center at Yale in October 1989 and at "The Body Positive: AIDS, the State, and Immunological Politics," a session of the annual meeting of the International Association for Philosophy and Literature at the University of California, Irvine in April 1990. Alfredo Monferre and Diana Fuss were the respective organizers of those panels and I thank them both.

I am grateful to Carol J. Clover, and Abigail Solomon-Godeau for helpful criticism of earlier drafts of this essay. Above all, this work is indebted to the encouragement and example of D. A. Miller.

Sources of the figures are as follows: figure 1: *Movieland* Feburary 1955; figure 2: "Photoplay Picture Gallery," *Photoplay*, March 1954; figure 3: "Can Rock's Marriage Be Saved?," *Photoplay*, February 1958; figure 4: "Meet the Champs," *Photoplay*, October 1953; figure 5: "Photoplay Pinups-Number Two—Rock Hudson: How Far is a Star," *Photoplay*, July 1959; figure 6: "Beefcake Kings," *Photoplay*, June 1956; figure 7: Publicity still, James Dean in *Giant*, reprinted in *James Dean*, Jean Loup Bourget (Paris: H. Veyrier, 1983); figure 8: Publicity photograph, 1952, reproduced in *People*, "The Long Goodbye: Rock Hudson: 1925–1980," 9 June, 1986; figure 9: Publicity photograph, 1952, reproduced in *People*, "Rock Hudson: On Camera and Off," 12 August, 1985; figure 10: "Are Actors Sissies?," *Photoplay*, February 1953; figure 11: "Pin-Ups," *Photoplay*, December 1959; figure 12: Publicity still of Marlon Brando, "Hollywood's New Sex Boat," *Photoplay*, July 1952; figure 13: Still from *Magnificent Obsession*, reproduced in *Sirk on Sirk: Interviews with Jon Halliday* (London: B.F.I., 1971); figure 14: Still, *Magnificent Obsession*, reproduced in *People*, "Rock Hudson: On Camera and Off," 12 August, 1985; figure 15: Still, *Magnificent Obsession*, reproduced in Jean Louis Bourget, *Douglas Sirk* (Paris: Edilig, 1984); figure 16: Still, *Magnificent Obsession*, reproduced in *Sirk on Sirk*; figure 17: Still, *Magnificent Obsession*; figure 18: Still, *Written on the Wind* (1956), reproduced in Michael Stern, *Douglas Sirk* (Boston: Twayne Publishers, 1979); figure 19: Publicity photograph Rock Hudson's wedding to Phyllis Gates, Universal International, produced in "The Master of Illusion," *People*, 9 June, 1986; figure 20: Publicity photograph of Rock Hudson and Phyllis Gates, Universal International, reproduced in Rock Hudson and Sara Davidson, *Rock Hudson: His Story* (New York: Avon, 1986); figure 21: Film still, *All That Heaven Allows* (1955) reproduced in Bourget, *Douglas Sirk*; figure 22: "Faces," *Life*, September 1985; figure 23: "Faces," *Life*, September 1985; figure 24: cover, *People*, 12 August, 1985; figure 25: cover, *People*, 16 February, 1987; figure 26: "The New Terror of AIDS," *Macleans*, 12 August, 1985

1. Such innovations of the 1950s as cinemascope, panavision, and Warnercolor sought to exploit those elements of the cinema—the larger scale of its image, the intensity of its color—which the "small screen" of television could not match. See Robert Carr and R. M. Hayes, *Wide Screen Movies: A History and Filmography of Wide Gauge Filmmaking* (Jefferson, N.C.: Mcfarland, & Co., 1988) and William Kuhns, *Movies in America* (Dayton, Ohio: Pflaum/Standard, 1972), 189.

2. Original advertisement for *Giant*, *Photoplay* (December 1956): 6–7.

3. "Young Dean's Legacy," *Newsweek*, 22 October, 1956: 112.

4. Joe Hyams, "Why Women Are In Love With Rock Hudson," *McCalls* (February 1957): 52.

5. According to, among others, *Variety*, "Rock Hudson, Hollywood Star for Three Decades, Dies at 59," 9 October, 1985, 42. Hudson's agent Henry Willson, who created the star-name, offers this recollection of its coining: "I picked Rock because of the Rock of Gibraltar—big and rugged. Also, there was only one other Hudson in pictures—Rochelle—and she worked infrequently. The name sounded right, because he was six-foot-four and handsome, but awkward and rather shy." Whitney Stine, *Stars and Star Handlers: The Business of Show* (Santa Monica: Round Table Publishing, 1985), 206.

6. Hildegarde Johnson, "Meet the Champs," *Photoplay* (October 1953): 43.

7. Johnson, "Meet the Champs," 43.

8. Unpublished manuscript of *Pillow Talk* (author's possession), screenplay by Stanley Shapiro and Maurice Richlin, 66.

9. I borrow the term from Simon Watney, whose brief but extremely insightful discussion of Hudson in *Policing Desire* is unique for its address to Hudson's alternative image of 1950s masculinity: ". . . Hudson's starring roles in films such as *Written on the Wind*, *Magnificent Obsession*, and especially *All that Heaven Allows*, construct him as a figure quite removed from mainstream 1950's masculinity, as represented by Victor Mature and Clark Gable. On the contrary, Hudson's film persona frequently presented him as a sensitive figure, a gentle giant aligned with nature rather than masculine culture." *Policing Desire: Pornography, AIDS, and the Media* (Minneapolis: University of Minnesota Press, 1987), 88. The references to Mature and Gable are slightly anachronistic to 1950s culture and may be replaced by, for example, Gary Cooper (the top box office draw of 1952) and John Wayne (#1 for 1953).

10. Mary Ann Doane, *The Desire to Desire: The Woman's Film of the 1940s* (Bloomington: Indiana University Press, 1987), 16. Doane's is the definitive analysis of the structures of spectatorship in the woman's film and my reading of Sirk's melodrama, and of the circulation of Rock Hudson's body within it, is deeply indebted to her work. See also *Home is Where the Heart Is: Studies in Melodrama and the Woman's Film*, ed. Christine Gledhill (London: British Film Institute, 1987).

11. According to *Variety*'s annual list of "Boxoffice [sic] Champs," *Magnificent Obsession* earned $5 million in its first year of release, making it the seventh most successful film of 1954 (as well as Hudson's most popular film, by a wide margin, to that date). See "1954 Boxoffice Champs" *Variety*, 5 January,1955, 7. Following *Magnificent Obsession*, Hudson grew progressively more popular until in 1957, he was voted the top box office attraction in America by the *Motion Picture Herald* poll of exhibitors. See Martin Quigley, Jr. and Richard Gertner, *Films in America 1929–1969* (New York: Golden Press, 1970), 266 and Roy Pickard, *The Hollywood Studios* (London: F. Muller, 1978), 46.

12. Richard Dyer, "Don't Look Now," *Screen* 23, nos. 3–4 (September/October 1982): 66.

13. The erotic specularization of Rock Hudson's body poses a problematic which Laura Mulvey's classic division of spectatorial labor along gender-lines ("woman as image, man as bearer of the look") cannot accommodate. See Laura Mulvey, "Visual Pleasure and Narrative Cinema," *Visual and Other Pleasures* (Bloomington: University of Indiana Press, 1989), 14–26. For a helpful response to some of the elisions of Mulvey's argument, see Steve Neale, "Masculinity as Spectacle," *Screen* 24, no. 6 (November/December 1983): 2–16.

14. See, for one example, the 1950s "educational films" on dating and "social hygiene" included in the 1989 documentary *Heavy Petting* (Fossil Films). These educational films—with such titles as "How Much Affection?," "Dating: Do's and Don'ts," and "How to Say No"—instruct young women to restrain (politely) their male companions while admonishing young men to restrain themselves.

15. Joe Hyams, "The Rock Hudson Story," *Photoplay* (February 1957): 90.

16. Hyams, "Why Woman Are In Love With Rock Hudson," 52.

17. Hyams, "Why Women Are In Love With Rock Hudson," 85.

18. Eleanor Harris, "Rock Hudson, Why He's Number 1," *Look*, 18 March 1958, 48.

19. The opposition set up by the article—Rock Hudson's health vs. James Dean's decay—was no doubt informed by the fact that Dean had died in an automobile crash just over two years before. At the time of the crash, Dean was on location in Texas shooting *Giant*, a film in which he played Jett Rink, the rival of Rock Hudson's Bick Benedict.

20. See Hedda Hopper, "Hollywood's New Sex Boat," *Photoplay* (July 1952): 62: "He's no rose—a grubby Peter Pan, some call him. But in any group of women, the name Marlon Brando acts like a flash fire . . . 'Marlon Brando? He's exciting.' 'Marlon Brando! He's coarse, he's vulgar', 'Marlon Brando, he's male! High time someone like him came along. . . .' "

21. Although Hudson's characters do not suffer physical dysfunction or long-term disease in Sirk's melodramas, they do have severe accidents (Bob Merrick's motor-boat flip in *Magnificent Obsession*, Ron Kirby's cliffside-fall in *All That Heaven Allows*). These accidents are not, however, the central predicament of the melodramatic plot so much as its initial "motor" (in *Magnificent Obsession*) or its closure (in *All That Heaven Allows*). Moreover, Hudson's characters miraculously recover from these accidents and are not visibly disfigured by them. Unlike the long-suffering female protagonists in Sirk's melodrama, Rock Hudson is seemingly immune from permanent damage or serious disease.

22. Doane, *Desire to Desire*, 16.

23. I am paraphrasing Mulvey here, although against the (gendered) grain of her argument: "The presence of woman is an indispensable element of spectacle in normal narrative film, yet her visual presence tends to work against the development of story-line, to freeze the flow of action in moments of erotic contemplation" (19).

24. Advertisement for *Written on the Wind, Variety*, 24 October, 1956, 21.

25. For more on the character of Marylee Hadley and her relation to the larger psychosexual economy of *Written on the Wind*, see Christopher Orr, "Closure and Containment: Marylee Hadley in *Written on the Wind*," *Wide Angle* 4, no. 2 (1980): 29–35.

26. Quoted in Michael Stern, *Douglas Sirk* (Boston: Twayne Publishers, 1979), 135–36.

27. Jimmy Hicks, "Rock Hudson: The Film Actor as Romantic Hero," *Films in Review*, 26 no. 5 (May 1975): 276.

28. Hyams, "Why Women Are In Love With Rock Hudson," 85.

29. Quoted in Hicks, "Rock Hudson," 276.

30. Consider that Hudson's agent, directors, publicity photographers, and even the authors of some of his fanzine articles (including "Why Women Are In Love With Rock Hudson") were men.

31. "The Simple Life of a Busy Bachelor: Rock Hudson Gets Rich Alone," *Life*, 3 October, 1955, 129–32.

32. *Movie/T.V. Secrets* (undated clipping, purchased by the author at *The Magazine*, San Francisco, September, 1989). Although the clipping is undated, I am confident that it is roughly contemporary with the *Life* piece cited above since it includes a reproduction of a fan letter addressed to Hudson on which a May 1955 postdate is visible.

33. See, for example, "AIDS Strikes a Star," *Newsweek*, 5 August, 1985, 69: "Rock: A Courageous Disclosure," *Time*, 5 August, 1985, 51–2; "Rock Hudson: On Camera and Off," *People*, 12 August, 1985, 34–41; "Rock Hudson, Hollywood Star for Three Decades, Dies at 59," *Variety*, 9 October, 1985, 42; "The Double Life of an AIDS Victim," *Time*, 14 October, 1985, 106; Jerry Oppenheimer and Jack Viteck, *Idol: Rock Hudson, The True Story of an American Film Hero* (New York: Villard Books, 1986), 55, and Sara Davidson and Rock Hudson, *Rock Hudson: His Story* (New York: Avon, 1986), 93.

34. Phyllis Gates, Rock's former wife, has recently attested to their relationship as a romantic and (rather) sexually active one in *My Husband Rock Hudson: The Real*

Story of Rock Hudson's Marriage to Phyllis Gates (New York: Jove Books, 1987, 1989). Other accounts (including most of those in the note above) claim the marriage as pure Hollywood cover, as Rock Hudson's heterosexual "beard." All the accounts agree, however, on the determinant importance of Henry Willson in setting up the marriage and on the fact that the union was exploited to secure Hudson's heterosexuality in the face of threatened homosexual exposure.

35. Michel Foucault, *Discipline and Punish: The Birth of the Prison*, trans. Alan Sheridan (New York: Vintage Books, 1979), 25.

36. Guy Gentilhomme, Pref. by Jean Marais, *Comment Devenir Vedette de Cinema?*, cited in Edgar Morin, *The Stars*, trans. Richard Howard (New York: Grove Press, 1960), 44–45.

37. *Life*, September 1985, 63.

38. My particular use of the term "anti-body" is borrowed from Timothy Landers's excellent essay, "Bodies and Anti-bodies: A Crisis in Representation," *The Independent* 11, no. 1 (January/February 1988): 18–24, reprinted in *Global Television*, ed. Cynthia Schneider and Brian Wallis (New York and Cambridge: Wedge Press and MIT Press, 1988), 281–299. Landers writes:

> Commercial media representations in general are informed by a variation on the normal/abnormal paradigm—one better suited to a visual medium: that of Bodies/Anti-Bodies. The Body—white, middle class, and heterosexual—is constructed in contrast to the Other, the Anti-Body (frequently absent from representation)—blacks, gay men, lesbians, workers, foreigners, in short, the whole range of groups that threaten straight, white, middle-class values. . . . Applied to the subject of AIDS, oppositions revolve around the nexus of health. The Body is, above all, healthy. The Anti-Body becomes, specifically, gay, black, Latino, the IV drug user, the prostitute, in other words, sick. (19)

39. Landers, "Bodies and Anti-Bodies," 19.

40. "Rock: A Courageous Disclosure," 51.

41. This economy of blame, apparent in the initial reporting of Hudson's illness, was most blatantly enacted in the 1990 ABC television docudrama "Rock Hudson" when a moribund Rock (played by Thomas Ian Griffith) makes the following "confession":

> I spent my whole life keeping everything inside, denying everything, and now everybody knows anyway. You know what's so damn funny, all the time I kept pretending that I wasn't gay, I kept on thinking I was the perfect man, the perfect star; [that] if it ever came out that I was gay it would kill me. And look, it has.

For an insightful discussion of the film, see Mark Gevisser, "Rock in a Hard Place," *Outweek*, 28 January, 1990, 58–59.

42. Neil Miller, "Personally," *Boston Phoenix*, 8 October 1985, 2 (Lifestyle Section).

43. Frank Rich, "The Gay Decades," *Esquire* (November 1987): 99.

44. Cited in Oppenheimer and Viteck, *Idol*, 175.

45. Watney, *Policing Desire*, 88.

46. On the cultural terrorism facing lesbians and gay men in 1950s America, see John D'Emilio, "The Homosexual Menace: The Politics of Sexuality in Cold War America," in *Passion and Power: Sexuality and History*, Kathy Peiss and Christina Simmons with Robert A. Padgug, eds. (Philadelphia: Temple University Press, 1989), John Gerassi, *The Boys of Boise: Furor, Vice and Folly in an American City* (New York: MacMillan, 1966), and Jonathan Katz, *Gay American History: Lesbians and Gay Men in the U.S.A.: A Documentary* (New York: Thomas Crowell, 1976).

47. Hudson's homosexuality was apparently an open secret within Hollywood circles. See, for example, "The Double Life of an AIDS Victim," *Time*, 14 October, 1985, 106, and "Rock Hudson: On Camera and Off," *People*, 12 August, 1985, 35–41. According to the latter, for example,

> Behind the doors of Universal, where he was a contract player, "we all knew Rock was gay, but it never made any difference to us," says actress Mamie Van Doren, who went on studio-arranged dates with Hudson. (36)

The extent of the knowledge of Hudson's homosexuality outside Hollywood is a complex issue which remains unresolved by this paper. At the very least, one can say that the media reports of Hudson's illness elided whatever public knowledge (or hunch or rumor) existed about his homosexuality so as to pathologize more dramatically his closeted homosexuality as disease(d).

48. The issue of the (historical) gay viewer's response to Rock Hudson's starbody must remain, at least for the time being, an open question. One would very much like to determine, for example, whether the defused heterosexuality of Hudson's masculinity held resonance for gay viewers, and particularly gay men, in its contemporary moment. Yet because of the enforced muting of gay voices, and of gay desire, during the 1950s, it is extremely difficult to mount a convincing reading of a gay male reception of Rock Hudson's stardom.

49. D. A. Miller, "Anal Rope," in this volume.

IV

Acting Up:
AIDS, Allegory, Activism

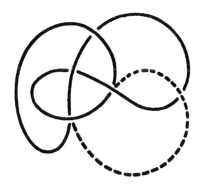

12

AIDS in America: Postmodern Governance, Identity, and Experience

Thomas Yingling

Do justice, cost what it may.   *Thoreau*

In a much-cited essay, Neil Hertz notes how the explosion of academic publishing in recent years induces in the subject enjoined to "keep up" a vertigo that recalls Kant's category of the mathematical sublime: an overwhelming series of numbers and/or sheer magnitude of information defeats comprehension and induces an abysmal intellectual and epistemological encounter that we mark as the sublime.[1] Any one interested in AIDS must suffer from a similar vertigo: the number of books, essays, pamphlets, and articles, the kinds of information, issues, and events that occur are so overwhelming in sheer number as to defeat any attempt at comprehensive incorporation by one person; the ever-increasing number of written responses to the history of representation of the disease makes it impossible even to survey recent literature much less to comprehend the totality of discourse about HIV since its appearance as GRID in January 1982. In addition, the exponential increase in cases and costs plus rapidly changing medical research and protocols challenge the intention of any individual to do intellectual and/or ethical justice to the various realities of the illness. As Sarah Schulman said at the Spring 1990 OUT WRITE conference in San Francisco, the field of AIDS and HIV continues to be transformed so rapidly that those who write about it do so with the understanding that by the time their words appear in print, they will be largely obsolete. Inscribed since its appearance as profoundly unimaginable, as beyond the bounds of sense, the AIDS epidemic is almost literally unthinkable in its mathematical defeat of cognitive desire.

But already we have here begun to make sense of AIDS, even if only in noting how it defeats our usual academic practice of careful, inclusive analysis. And we have also here assumed AIDS as an ongoing event, as something that moves within a history that is only partially *its* history. The mathematical sublime thus quickly gives way in the case of AIDS to what we might call the historical sublime, for even more than the mathematical, the historical sublime marks reading—and our stake in it—as an activity framed equally by demand and defeat, as the ground on which we are condemned to negotiate the difference between that which can be comprehended by the capacities of the intellect and that which can only be apprehended as beyond, in excess, or pitted against such capacities.[2] AIDS, for instance, can be apprehended—on bodies, in friends, in news reports, in changing populations, behaviors, and rituals: we know that it is in some undeniable sense "real," whether its reality be outside or within us. But the frames of intelligibility that provide it with even a meager measure of comprehensibility are notoriously unstable. This is evident not only on the macropolitical level, where intense battles over the meaning of AIDS have accompanied every stage of research and treatment in the history of the disease, but also on the micropolitical level, down to the level of the everyday (as anyone touched by it will tell you, the quotidian meaning of AIDS seems to change almost as often as the virus itself replicates—in wildly varying, if never quite random patterns). The gap between the apprehension and the comprehension of the disease is thus an asymptotic space where allegory persistently finds itself at play and where the ongoing histories in which AIDS unfolds (variously comprised of the viral, the personal, the communal, the national, and the global) are referred to larger and more masterful or authoritative histories that guarantee interpretation of its meanings and restabilize (sometimes ironically) those values it places at risk.

Like the systemic depletion that allows AIDS to appear as a seemingly endless number of symptoms and thereby remain both the same as and different from itself, the material effects of AIDS deplete so many of our cultural assumptions about identity, justice, desire, and knowledge that it seems at times able to threaten the entire system of Western thought—that which maintains the health and immunity of our epistemology: the psychic presence of AIDS signifies a collapse of identity and difference that refuses to be abjected from the systems of self-knowledge. Susan Sontag has noted that AIDS has surpassed cancer as the stigmatized term *par excellence* of contemporary culture, but her contention that it has the "capacity to create spoiled identity,"[3] to alter how we know ourselves, is remarkably tame. Because it provides only negative structures of identification, AIDS is most notable for its capacity to produce non-identity or internalized abjection. Unlike the collapse of subjectivity noted in narratives of postmodernism that celebrate the simulacrum of inscription or the break with an oppressive history of metaphysics, the finality marked as and by AIDS includes an undeniably literal death, a death so irretrievably literal that its figurality must be continually exposed *as figuration*, as cultural critics like Simon Watney, Jan Zita Grover, and Douglas Crimp have been doing for more than half a decade; *and* (to reverse the burden of literality and figurality) the finality of AIDS is so inwrought with configurations of cultural anxiety and dread that its literality must also be continually addressed in strenuous, referential narratives of victimization, punishment, resistance, and healing.

But in addition to offering us a focal point for analysis of the social and political intricacies of signification, AIDS also focuses for us numerous questions central to the current vogue for academic research and writing on the question of sexual minority. Who is the subject "at risk" in discourse about AIDS, in the homophobias attached to those discourses? Certainly it is not only those infected with HIV, and certainly not all those are gay men. But of particular interest here are two phenomena not perhaps to have been expected at the beginning of the epidemic: the appearance of large numbers of lesbian activists and post-liberation-generation gay men and women on the front lines of AIDS work. Let us ponder first of all how the two terms "lesbian" and "gay," driven apart by rapidly accelerating differences in visibility and privilege marking them through the supposedly halcyon decade of the 70s, have been brought together in this discourse—and how they remain apart. Surely it is not some lesser gift of generosity or conscience essential to gay men that leads to the oft-repeated assertion that, were the gay medical crisis of the 80s a woman's health crisis gay men would not be working for the cause with the fervor or numbers with which lesbians have responded to the crisis of AIDS. There are two important factors here: first, lesbians—as women—are marked in our culture in such a way that their "difference" is inescapable; gay men, on the other hand, are marked different in a way that does not preclude their "passing" or their negotiation of many of the privileges of masculinity even if known to be gay. Thus, the heartening lesbian response to AIDS may be due in large part to a heightened politicization of lesbian subjectivity (historically and personally) *before* the appearance of AIDS. Moreover, in its unyielding equation of value with white, male-embodied masculinity, American culture imprints a double-bind on those on its margins: gay people of color and lesbians, for instance, may well find themselves alienated from white gay male culture but they may also recognize that their own political future and visibility are bound in complex and equivocal ways to the struggle of gay white men. The dialectic of that recognition does not often work the other way: gay white men are less likely to see their own political fortunes at stake in what happens for people of color or women. It remains to be seen whether the numbers of younger gay men and women who have joined the battle against AIDS will continue their political work. Certainly they, too, know people infected and dying, dead or at risk, but *as a generation* they could choose to avoid AIDS, to see it as the issue of an older generation of gay men. Yet they continue to see their own subjectivity and freedom implicated in this battle. They have been politicized under the banner of AIDS precisely because one of the vigorously recurring allegories grafted onto AIDS has been its use as a mechanism for policing same-sex desire. These younger activists rightly perceive that what is at stake in public responses to the disease—from confusing, obscurantist, and moralistic safe sex recommendations to violent Congressional eruptions of homophobia tied cruelly to denials of public health—moves far beyond questions of public health. AIDS has provided a site for surveillance of the most private bodily practices, and where subjectivity is framed through sexual orientation and preference, such surveillance calls the question on any complacent desire for a comfortable "private life" (now read as the inadequate goal of gay liberation).

The political and the personal are, of course, so densely written *as intertexts* in the more recent history of minority discourse that it would be wise to say that it is only for purposes of analysis that we even begin to think of them separately here; AIDS is a late and agonizing—but by no means singular—moment of crisis for a culture bent on maintaining the fiction that the personal is not in any way political. When we return to the question of experience below, we will reforge the personal and the political in a more dialectical practice of reading, but let us begin with a consideration of how AIDS has been inscribed as an issue in the public forum. Perhaps the most visible and incontestable site of such inscription (and for that reason the site of the most vehement contestations) has been the apparatus of government, and while AIDS has forced a confrontation with government on virtually all levels, the apparatus of the nation-state seems most appropriate to our discussion here, for from the beginning of the epidemic in the United States the federal government has housed the broadest powers of identification and intervention, and has therefore been at the center of debates about public response.[4] In fact, municipal and state governments, with varying but usually lesser powers in this regard, have become the target of so much political work in part because of the vacuum created by federal irresponsibility. The failure to use their power (effectively) to intervene in the disease constitutes the continuing charge against all levels of government by AIDS activists, and Randy Shilts's narrative of its history, *And The Band Played On*, is—for all its faults—one of the most successful texts to date to document the colossal magnitude of bureaucratic indifference and ineptitude up to 1985 (Shilts's history, and not that ineptitude or indifference, stops in 1985).[5] Shilts's writing makes a convincing case for reading the early history of AIDS as determined by a remarkable lack of concern, communication, and cooperation on many fronts, much of that from within federal agencies and among organizations like the Centers for Disease Control and the National Institutes of Health. As baffling, however, was a similar lack of cooperation among nations working to isolate agents and treatments; as Shilts writes the history of AIDS, it would have followed a far different trajectory in a world not structured by competitive national economies that had in turn spawned competitive nationalistic communities and practices in supposedly transnational areas such as scientific research (scientists in the United States and France were unable—due largely, as Shilts tells it, to the vanity of Robert Gallo at NIH—to share research during the crucial first years of AIDS). In accounts such as this, the government is charged with criminal neglect of its people,[6] and the invocation of crime seems appropriate given the liberal philosophy that has historically constructed the nation-state as protector of citizen's rights by law and citizen's property and health through institutional intervention.

The allegory of value framed by the politics of the nation-state is a modern one, of course, its roots in the liberal politics of the nineteenth century. But despite our current need for such a model of government and for the needs-determined allocations it continues to promise if not deliver, it is not clear that an institutional framework developed during the imperialist excursions of bourgeois Europe remains a salient paradigm for political organization and analysis in a moment of multinational or postmodern capitalism. Ronald Reagan's simulation of same notwithstanding, postmodern governance is not based in the political representation of subjects under the beneficent gaze of a paternal presence. Jean Baudrillard, for instance, suggests that "the political and the social seem inseparable to us, twin constellations, since at least the French Revolution, under the sign (determinant or not) of the economic," but that "for us today, this undoubtedly is true only of their decline."[7] For Baudrillard, the entire politics of representation has eventuated in the implosion of meaning and the rise of a silent majority that functions to deny the meanings of the social; the masses are no longer potentially revolutionary, in need/search of some adequate self-knowledge, empowerment, or representation. The masses are not some "term which serves as universal alibi for every discourse" (66); rather, they

> no longer belong to the order of representation. They don't express themselves, they are surveyed. They don't reflect upon themselves, they are tested. The referendum (and the media are a constant referendum of directed questions and answers) has been substituted for the political referent. Now polls, tests, the referendum, media are devices which no longer belong to a dimension of representation, but to one of simulation. They no longer have a referent in view, but a model. (20)

The only political energy not bent to the implosion or denial of meaning in our era in the West comes from what Baudrillard terms "microgroups," those social forces that do not move passively and with fascination in the face of spectacle but insist on resistance, on decoding and recoding messages, "contrasting the dominant code with their own particular sub-codes. . . [by] way of redirecting, of absorbing, of victoriously salvaging the material diffused by the dominant culture" (42–43). The actions of "fringe" groups in response to the AIDS crisis, therefore—not only their seizure of signification, for instance, but their absolute insistence on it, their insistence on the political, social, collective, and individuated meaningfulness of AIDS—might be read as working against the annihilating but passive power of the silent majorities (ACT UP's first motto: "Silence = Death"). Baudrillard's critique also suggests that AIDS activism has not been coopted into the great institutional machinery of culture that currently recodes sign value as use value (found in the society of spectacle and its explosion of semiosis) but instead insists upon forcing spectacle itself into political use—hence the resurrection of agit-prop, street theater, poster art, etc.[8]

Also crucial here, however, is our recognition of a tension in American political and institutional life between the nation-state as a political entity and "America" as a term that ceases to designate the state and signifies instead a Platonic ideal of social consensus, homogeneity, and historical transcendence. Hannah Arendt describes the nation-state as claiming "to be above all classes, completely independent of society and its particular interests, the true and only representative of the nation as a whole,"[9] but the illusory quality of that claim has never become as broadly apparent in America as it has, for instance, in Europe, due in part to much stronger anti-state traditions and movements there. In fact, the term "America" functions with such slippery teleological power that all critique of the state's over-invested interests ends only by invoking a more originary value for the same term (thus Reagan was elected partly on a platform of appeal to end state domination yet that appeal was framed as a return to "America").[10] In American political discourse, "America" and the nation-state are not synonymous, and while the slippage between the terms is ever conveniently manipulated, the mythic term virtually always takes precedence and value over the more material one; conservatives may thus not only ignore the need for the nation-state to respond to population groups not visible within "America" (predominantly gays and IV-drug users in the early years of the AIDS epidemic) but may even cast those needs as anti-American, as a danger *to* rather than *within* the state. In addition, we encounter in American political discourse a rather unbreakable convention that the materiality of history disappear before the myth that America represents the end of (Western) history, what Jean-Philippe Mathy has noted as "the paradigm of posthistorical experience."[11] Long before Francis Fukuyama's recent apologia for the triumph of democracy as the end of history,[12] America was conceived as the achievement of a radical break with the European past and—in its claim to utopian fulfillment and modernity—with time itself. According to Mathy, "the American mission, because it is conceived in *moral* terms, is the exact opposite of realpolitik" and Americans evidence "an inability to think in historical terms."[13] Thus, Reagan's wax-museum performances could borrow indifferently from Jefferson, Lincoln, Roosevelt, or Kennedy, stripping their words of historical context and of any ideological difference from his own use of them, producing a spectacle that *invoked* American history only to collapse it into the supposed timelessness of America *as idea*. AIDS, on the other hand, is not intrinsically historical (unless we mean by history the appearance of that which moves within myths unable to contain it), but discourse on AIDS invariably invokes the notion of history: research suggests a "natural history" of the virus (ten-year-plus incubation periods); gay and lesbian rhetoric links the fight against AIDS to Stonewall and to the entire question of gay and lesbian history; PWA rhetoric states that the ethics of our historical moment will be judged by its response to AIDS; journalists and experts alike project "the next ten years" or rehearse the present and past in a narrative behind which always hovers a specter of apocalypse in which AIDS functions as the demonic counterpart to the beneficent "end of history" coded in myths of America. In *Borrowed Time*, his elegiac memoir of the deaths of his lover and other friends, Paul Monette suggests that AIDS is inherently historical for the individuals it effects: gay men, condemned according to Monette to seek their history in "mythic fragments, random as blocks of stone in [Greek] ruins,"[14] find that "the magic circle" of health and denial they were "trying to stay within the borders of" during the early days of the AIDS epidemic was "only as real as the random past."[15] AIDS thus becomes a rhetorical or epistemological nightmare as well: history, personal and/or collective, which should reveal pattern, reveals only a deadly but determining arbitrariness.

The other tenacious public discourse around AIDS, and one that is inseparable from the practices of the nation-state, is framed as science. From my latest T-cell count to Robert Gallo's theft of viral agents from French cultures, we have understood AIDS not only as a political crisis but also as a mystery to be solved by the power of science (understood as a pure domain of human knowledge wherein "nature" progressively submits to the power of human intellection and technological advance). Part of what baffles about AIDS, of course, is its resistance *as an illness* to this scenario of empowered science, but I am more interested here in the morality or politics of science, and in the failure of scientific communities to respond more fully and quickly to the demands of the disease. We may develop a method for reading the medical fiasco of AIDS in terms also suggested by recent philosophy and theory, particularly by Lyotard's notion of postmodernism. In what has become something of a touchstone, Lyotard suggests that the grand religious, political, and economic narratives of the past on which were premised the knowledge and totality of culture have fractured in an era of information (hence, "the postmodern condition"); as a result, "the temporary contract [elsewhere, "language game"] is in practice supplanting permanent institutions in the professional, emotional, sexual, cultural, family, and international domains."[16] As Mathy suggests in his comments on Lyotard, the major contention in *The Post-Modern Condition* is that "the proliferation of autonomous and heterogeneous universes of discourse and behavior separated, and protected, by incommensurable differences [is] the social and political counterpart to the generalized disbelief in . . . 'grand narratives.' "[17]

Translating this to the question of AIDS, we find a true incommensurability of discursive universes: as disciplines, medical and scientific research have indeed become separate, autonomous realms of knowledge and power unprepared to meet the emergency social conditions of the AIDS epidemic. Perhaps more sharply, the discursive universe in which gay men move and operate—a universe of open and various sexualities and (now) a universe of political rage—seems completely foreign if not still perverse to the medical community, the media, and the "mainstream" Americans constructed by that media.[18] Most costly among these incommensurabilities, however, is that between the nation-state and the populations most decimated by AIDS: still a cornerstone of the official "grand narrative" of American political and social life, the Platonic ideal of a classless, homogeneous State named "America" is incongruous with gay culture and the medical crisis AIDS forced upon it. Hence, as is suggested by Shilts's comments on the government's virtually immediate response to two other dramatic health crises of the 1980s (toxic shock syndrome and the Tylenol tampering case), the deaths of thousands of homosexual men did not solicit *any* government response for so long in part because homosexual men were not recognized as constituents of the (now infamously phrased) "general population," and in part because homosexual men did not constitute a rights-group in the eyes of a nation-state determined to read its population according to nineteenth-century demographic categories such as geography, age, ethnicity, labor, and gender rather than by behavioral patterns such as anal intercourse and intravenous drug use—*and* concerned mostly to guarantee the "health" of consumer culture, the non-toxicity of purchasable goods. Thus, AIDS becomes a rather obvious site on which to interrogate the beneficence of that autonomy granted within the postmodern, and this is perhaps one way to think the shift in gay male political needs and strategies pre- and post-AIDS: autonomy is desirable except as crises arise wherein the incommensurability of one site of culture with another (minority culture with medical, political, and scientific establishments) is written along lines of power that effectively prevent one of the parties in the "temporary contract" from partaking in the formation of the language game that constructs their social and political relations. This is the imperative of groups like ACT UP: to shift the language game, to speak, demonstrate, and demand in ways that are seen as inappropriate to the game when that game erases them or excludes them from its continual reformulation.[19]

If up to now our analysis has focused on rather conventional public or political sites, we must acknowledge that politics is not limited to the apparatus of the nation-state and its official mythologies. Critics

who have turned their attention to other ideological sites in culture—
and there have been many, particularly in the realm of the media and
its construction of AIDS—have sought to enable resistance through
critique and counterdiscourse. Simon Watney, Cindy Patton, and Jan
Zita Grover are exemplary among those who have treated AIDS itself
as a symptom, producing strong ideological readings in which AIDS
discourse is exposed as thick with political meaning.[20] Unlike the media, which have tended to mystify the disease (and to literally mystify
it: continuing, for instance, to identity it as "mysterious" long after its
epidemiological paths had been established),[21] these writers seek to
demystify both the disease itself and the apparatus through which
the media produces its mythologies of AIDS. Watney, for instance,
contrasts the notion of "AIDS in Africa" to "African AIDS," pointing
out how racist, colonialist residues function in the latter designation
to obscure "the specific characteristics of the different AIDS epidemics
in these countries [of Africa], constructing them in a spurious unity . . .
which is immediately denied any of the cultural, social, economic, and
ethnic diversity . . . taken for granted in Europe and North and South
America."[22] In his earlier, trenchant analysis of British homophobia
and AIDS, *Policing Desire*, he had suggested not only how "a particular
virus, one of the simplest life forms on the planet, has been used by a
wide variety of groups to articulate a host of issues and concerns,
consciously and unconsciously"[23] but also that many of those concerns
were tangential rather than central to questions of illness and public
health. For instance, homosexuality has been so insistently at issue in
the discourse on AIDS not because the disease occurs naturally as a
result of homosexual activity but precisely because the structure and
stability of contemporary configurations of heterosexuality require the
invisibility and interdiction of same-sex desire while the fight against
AIDS historically required that the lives of those framed by such desire
be made both visible and legitimate.[24] Similar analyses of the ideological invisibility of black and Latino cultures in America suggest that
AIDS is also spread by power imbalances between those communities
and a governmental structure not concerned with them in any instance
and therefore without the requisite knowledge and apparatuses for
education and provision of services in this particular, severely costly
instance.[25]

If such media analysis implies that some representational practice
adequate to the political, ethical, and semiotic demands of AIDS ought
to be found, this writing also opens a critique of the media as an
industry, as a commodifier of spectacle and information rather than as
a facilitator of some more genuine or analytical understanding. Here,

a postmodern critic (Baudrillard) and a modern one (Walter Benjamin) would agree that Western culture has reached the limit or the end of representational practices as they have traditionally functioned in alliance with knowledge of the social.

Baudrillard reads the media as destroyer of social meanings and as producer of information-as-spectacle and Benjamin marks this distinction as one between information and experience. But at stake in both analyses is history and the dialectic between the subject and her/his culture. Baudrillard may consider the curious passivity of the masses a sign of their denial of their own historicity while Benjamin's analysis is more clearly wagered on classical Marxian claims, but both fundamentally mistrust what Horkheimer and Adorno termed "the culture industry." Benjamin writes, "with the full control of the middle class, which has the press as one of its most important instruments in fully developed capitalism, there emerges a [new] form of communication . . . information."[26] Baudrillardian speculation on the collapse of meaning would reject *any* appeal to the meaningfulness of internalized process as anachronistic; we will take up below Benjamin's complicated and peculiar use of the term "experience" as a signifier for collective, dialectical knowledge. For now, let us see that information is not so much for Benjamin a representation structured by false consciousness and open therefore to ideology critique as it is a mode of semiotic circulation directly opposed to the cultural and subjective valuation of experience expressed in the following:

> Man's inner concerns do not have their issueless private character by nature. They do so only when he is increasingly unable to assimilate the date of the world around him by way of experience. Newspapers constitute one of many evidences of such an inability. If it were the intention of the press to have the reader assimilate the information it supplies as part of his own experience, it would not achieve its purpose. But its intention is just the opposite, and it is achieved: to isolate what happens from the realm in which it could affect the experience of the reader. The principles of journalistic information (freshness of the news, brevity, comprehensibility, and, above all, lack of connection between the individual news items) contribute as much to this as does the make-up of the pages and the paper's style. . . . The replacement of the older narration by information, of information by sensation, reflects the increasing atrophy of experience.[27]

Each item, each piece of data refers only to itself; "news" is the reification and sale of event, and this becomes even more apparent when AIDS appears in contiguity to—and hence as the scandal of—a culture of celebrity (the "shame" that inverts its "fame"). The deaths of Rock Hudson, Liberace, Willi Smith, and Amanda Blake are reported for their tremendous salability, but no connection between these deaths and the more political or even medical "facts" of the disease are encouraged in the reportage itself.[28] One need not subscribe to a fully Marxian theory of history and culture to recognize that any reading practice failing to link supposedly autonomous events and universes of knowledge—scientific research, op-ed pieces, the visible deaths of stars and the invisible deaths of so many others, public demonstrations, treatment advances, hospital overcrowdings, insurance and legal issues—is condemned to a limited understanding if not to a simple repetition or invocation of myth. Nor ought such issues remain isolated in a frame marked "AIDS": they take place and meaning in more inclusive allegories of value that determine when, how, and if they will signify at all.[29]

But how do we reconcile the fact that the genocide of AIDS continues to take shape in the United States both as deliberate public policy and more privately in the lives and on the bodies of millions of individuals, especially when the invocation of "individual," like Benjamin's appeal to "experience" or "inner concerns," would seem to many to operate within a discredited paradigm of subjectivity that locates meaning in interiority? More generally, what valence do we wish to assign subjectivity in our analysis of AIDS? Diana Fuss succinctly states in her inquiry into identity politics in gay and lesbian culture that "to the extent that identity always contains the specter of non-identity within it, the subject is always divided and identity is always purchased at the price of the exclusion of the Other, the repression or repudiation of non-identity."[30] If identity is not only a fiction but a particularly fragile, chiasmatic, and contradictory fiction at that, what is the value—political, personal, or ontological—of that identity marked "person with AIDS"? Has the prostitute who identifies herself as such merely accepted a false coherency in her life, and is it possible to read the subject marked "person with AIDS" as coherent in any case? Is the man who denies that his HIV positivity allies him somehow with "them" (those "people with 'full-blown' AIDS") both politically reprehensible *and* accurate in his sense that "person with AIDS" constitutes a distinct category of being?

Susan Sontag's *AIDS and Its Metaphors* provides one avenue into answering such questions, for it rightly suggests that one of the numerous differences between the constructions of meaning written onto

AIDS and those written onto earlier epidemics in history inheres in the fact that unlike AIDS, which is persistently interpreted as a judgment on the individual for sin or excess, "Diseases, insofar as they acquired meaning [in the past], were collective calamities, and judgments on a community."[31] Myths of identity *have framed* the interpretation of AIDS, and it remains a disease that attaches—rightly or wrongly—to identities: gay, IV-drug user, African, hemophiliac, infant, transfusion patient (the "guilty" and "innocent" "victims" are labeled through some category of identity that promises—falsely—to explain their contraction of the disease). Because AIDS has been read so persistently within a paradigm of group and/or individual identity, one of the continuing tasks facing those who respond to it has been to insist on it as a collective calamity. But one of those tasks has also been— because "person with AIDS" would otherwise signify non-being in a culture founded in and devoted to myths of being—the validation of any individual or collective identity threatened by the illness with erasure. We must think AIDS not only as a public issue of ideology, apparatus, and representation but also *as it is internalized and expressed* by those infected and effected, and we must do this not because disease is a matter of privacy nor because individual experience provides unmediated authority and knowledge but because "AIDS" as a signifier lodges in deep subliminal zones of memory, loss, and (im)possibility, zones that in the end are among the most crucial sites on which disciplinarity is inscribed and therefore potentially disrupted. Only because experience is material, dialectical, and collective can a critic like Benjamin be concerned about its atrophy, and we can employ "experience" as a signifier to mark not private and interior knowledges but the intersection between such knowledges and the collective, public structures that frame them.

When we turn to the inscription of AIDS in the discourse of private or personal experience, we find a number of powerful literary texts in the genre of memoir and confession, and a number in the conventions of domestic and family-crisis drama that establish the "likeness" of AIDS to—and its difference from—other social problems. Not all of those texts offer a dialectical understanding of AIDS as experience. It would perhaps be useful here to say something about the work attached to the name "Louise Hay." Hay is only one in what we must call a boom industry (those providing spiritual solutions or guidance in the face of the radical alterity AIDS introduces into a life), but her name has come almost to signify that industry, and her work ranges from books and tapes to seminars (weekly group sessions, attended by hundreds in L.A., are called "Hayrides"). Hers is, indeed, a labor based in and seeking the "affirmation" of people with AIDS, and for some Hay's work is truly transformative. Clients are encouraged to work with a mirror, to talk to themselves, to release rather than express anger, to love themselves; gay men taught to hate themselves or people with AIDS who internalize shame due to their illness can achieve a more positive self-recognition in these practices.[32] But the most pragmatically compelling aspect of Hay's work is also its most troubling, for it slips rather precariously from psychoimmunology to something closer to moralistic nonsense. Moving from a relatively nonjudgmental inquiry into the role of representation or mental imaging in physical well-being to a completely interiorized discourse in which illness, death, and even exposure to the virus are read as the free, "deep" choice of the individual, Hay's discourse has been attacked for its implication that those who fall or remain ill are incapable of effectively loving themselves, and for its mystification of AIDS as a gift to the self necessary to some crucial spiritual healing (not surprisingly, one available in her practice). There is nothing intrinsically wrong, of course, with any private experience, nor with private experiences of AIDS. But AIDS has required a continual vigilance against secrecy, shame, and repression, the hallmarks of that same (perhaps bourgeois) privacy that polices homoerotic desire: in that respect, completely private responses—while probably inevitable—seem insufficient for understanding the full cultural significance of the disease. The emphasis in Hay's work finally falls on an improved narcissistic relation as a cornerstone of cosmic harmony, and such transformations as result from it remain wholly contained within the individual's psyche. In framing this empowerment of the individual, Hay relies on a model of identity where the self is relatively stable, identifiable, and whole, where one recovers through meditation and spiritual growth an originary plenitude. The valence of purity and integrity of self in her discourse is clearly based in an epistemological imperative to keep the self separate from its others, something Donna Haraway has noted as the burden of most immune system discourse.[33] Hay is not alone in producing as a response to immune system disease a discourse where nothing foreign invades the self, but her work is open to a number of critiques. More recent theorists of gay and lesbian subjectivity, for instance, read the political subversiveness and radical marginality of gay and lesbian culture as the direct result of their situation outside the ordinary structures of patriarchal culture, including the structure of stable, transparent ego that would seem to be Hay's model of subjectivity. Unstable and psychically eccentric in ways interpretable as politically transgressive rather than pathological, the ego structured by same-sex desire in post-structuralist paradigms of-fers—in the words of Jonathan Dollimore—"the paradox of a marginal-ity which is always interior to, or at least intimate with, the center" yet not itself centered, and therefore key to the development of "new strate-gies and conceptions of resistance."[34] Judith Butler claims that "the gen-dered body" itself is "performative" rather than substantive, with "no ontological status apart from the various acts which constitute its real-ity."[35] That body, for Butler, "is not a 'being,' but a variable boundary, a surface whose permeability is politically regulated."[36] While the subjec-tivity constructed by AIDS should not be equated to gay or lesbian sub-jectivity, the paradigm of marginality and regulation would seem more than accidentally appropriate.

What we encounter in the field of AIDS—and of only marginal concern to someone like Hay—is the political regulation of the body around what is encoded as *the* supremely private site of accommoda-tion to discipline: death. In her refusal to read the collective dimension of AIDS as a death which is at least in part an act of political regulation, Hay would return us to what Edith Wyschogrod has termed the authen-ticity paradigm of death, the equation of a "good death" with moral value: "Nothing so palpably illustrates the refinement and self-control of a person as the fearless and noble management of his dying,"[37] the classic example being Socrates, in whose soul "is writ small the class virtues of the well-ordered state" (4). Wyschogrod offers a postmodern paradigm of authentic death as well, one where authenticity eventuates not through rational transcendence of death as an event but through acknowledgment of that death already represented in objects, persons, time, and desire. In the incorporation of death into life (her example here is Rilke), "the reciprocal relation between the acceptance of death and the profundity of the person holds: we redeem experience, render ourselves worthy of it, and it of us, by living up to the death in it" (10). But "neither the older nor the newer version of the paradigm can any longer provide meaning," Wyschogrod claims; they have been superseded by more recent histories of genocide and nuclear holocaust, by the intentional construction of death-worlds where the mimetic relation between an individual and his/her death is broken and "the living are forced to exist as if already dead" (34). The meaning of the death-world for Wyschogrod turns on intention, and although it arises from a technological society, its most profound function is mythical:

> The death-world is not the extreme expression of technological
> society itself, for what characterizes that society is its rationality, its
> divorce from mythic consciousness, its uprootedness from the life-

world. Instead the death-world is an attempt to make whole the
broken cosmos by an imaginative act of radical negation ... by
consigning to itself all that seems worthy of death. (28)

Plague will not do for this analysis because it seems to belong to a life-
world "of indeterminate horizons from which phenomena arise" (17)
rather than to the deliberate annihilation of vast numbers of people;
the Holocaust, on the other hand, will serve as an example, and the
point for us is that AIDS shares more, finally, with genocide than with
plague. Like the death-worlds Wyschogrod investigates, there is only
one signified in AIDS: all signifiers point to "death," and do so not as
a site of the validation of the life-world but as its negation. And as in
the death-worlds, it is the power of others to inflict dying that continues
to shape the history of AIDS: the benign neglect of government agencies
makes the epidemic a passive-aggressive act on the part of rational
society (the institutionalization of power as indifference). AIDS shares
many of the features of that man-made mass death that destroys the
authenticity paradigm, and it is the promise of metaphysical redemption, of a repair of that identity-confirming experience of death that
"healers" like Hay hold forth to those people with AIDS who desire—
among other things—a meaningful death.

But not all invocations of the "experience" of AIDS need turn on
this repair of broken subjectivity—or need not frame such repair as
the reconstruction of a free, rational, and ultimately singular psyche.
In an essay entitled "At Risk in the Sublime: The Politics of Gender
and Theory," Lee Edelman narrates his participation in the October
1987 Lesbian and Gay March on Washington, constructing it as his
"nearest approach to an experience of the sublime" (the sublime, of
course, can only ever *be* approached), claiming that "the multitudinous
unity and the mathematical sublime produced by our seemingly incomprehensible mass served to reconstitute our identity in the face of all
our devastations."[38] Noting, finally, that such reconstitution is "theoretically regressive" through the constitution of "a coherent locus of
subjectivity under the suspect banner of unity, idealism, and empowerment" when in fact the gay and lesbian community is often "painfully
incompatible" even with itself, Edelman nevertheless reads the march
as a "powerful and progressive force within the politics of gender."[39]
While AIDS does not appear in Edelman's essay as one of the "devastations" inflicted by "homophobic America" on its gay and lesbian
community, it is there as an unspoken devastation, and Edelman's
comments might be taken as a gloss on that other powerful experience

of collective identification in recent years that does in fact address the question of AIDS: the AIDS memorial quilt.

Although numerous reports of the experience of viewing the quilt mark its complex and overwhelming demand on apprehension and comprehension as a sublime rupture eventuating in unity, the object under consideration in this case seems to successfully resist the last move of the sublime (re-incorporation) precisely because the unity it allows and constructs, the identity it offers through its collective scope, remains outside all of our corporate structures of knowledge. As in evidentiary encounters with the Holocaust, AIDS in this concrete memorial induces a contemplation in which all systems of signification seem inadequate. Ultimately, of course, some repair overwrites this abysmal grief, but as an artifact the quilt continues to challenge our understanding, and any cognitive accommodation that is forthcoming remains marked as radically by difference as by identity. Even as *labor*, the quilt is in some profound way disturbing (handicraft in an era of consumer goods, and motivated neither by profit nor beauty; handicraft where the trace of labor and its social referent remains visible, where that is indeed what defines its value—an unreifiable practice; labor seeking to intervene in an appalling alienation and both out of a love and anguish encoded on the surface of the object). It would seem almost to fulfill some of the folkloric function of narrative as Walter Benjamin describes that in pre-industrial culture. Produced anonymously yet binding the culture together, the telling of stories during group activities and labor brings the "soul, eye, and hand . . . into connection"[40] and constructs a communal reference system of knowledge and value in which experience becomes recognizable through collective frameworks and becomes therefore communicable *as experience* rather than abbreviated or atrophied in a world of information and industrial alienation. It is only in structures such as the quilt or, to a greater or lesser extent, in any demonstration or performance— in the making of artifacts about AIDS—that the disease can become meaningful in a way that allows those affected and infected by it to secure it as an experience and not merely as information. It allows as well an affirmation of identity not fated to succumb to the traps of affirmative, bourgeois culture in its determination to seal that identity and those meanings in a world of alienation and death. Only in such artifacts may the collective experience of AIDS be encountered, and only in encountering that collective knowledge may the gay and lesbian community continue to become visible to itself as something quite other than the site *par excellence* of social atrophy and alienation.

Notes

1. Neil Hertz, "The Notion of Blockage in the Literature of the Sublime," *The End of the Line: Essays on Psychoanalysis and the Sublime* (New York: Columbia University Press, 1985), 40–60.

2. See the exchange between Neil Hertz and Paul de Man at the end of "Conclusions: Walter Benjamin's 'Task of the Translator'," Paul de Man, *The Resistance to Theory* (Minneapolis: University of Minnesota Press, 1986), 73–105.

3. Susan Sontag, *AIDS and its Metaphors* (New York: Farrar, Straus, and Giroux, 1988), 16.

4. AIDS is not, of course, a disease that occurs only in the United States—and its effects are far more devastating in non-metropolitan sites, whether that be the Ivory Coast, Brazil, or (within the metropole) Harlem. Nevertheless, my focus here is on how AIDS has inscribed itself in American culture. Similarly, AIDS is not a gay disease, but its history is so densely interwritten with the more recent history of gay culture that I take up both in this essay.

5. Randy Shilts, *And the Band Played On: Politics, People, and the AIDS Epidemic* (New York: St. Martin's Press, 1987).

6. One of the more powerful visual pieces produced by ACT UP represents the trace left by a bloodied hand and the written text: "The government has blood on its hands."

7. Jean Baudrillard, *In the Shadow of the Silent Majorities* (New York: Semiotext(e), 1983), 15. Subsequent references are cited in the text.

8. Douglas Crimp has written about "the graphic response to AIDS" in "Art Acts Up," *Out/Look* 9 (Summer 1990): 22–30. Also see the introduction to a book he has co-edited with Adam Rolston entitled *AIDS Demo Graphics* (Seattle: Bay Press, 1990).

9. Hannah Arendt, *The Origins of Totalitarianism* (New York: Harcourt, Brace, Jovanovich, 1951), 17.

10. For an analysis of the history and ideology of this practice see Sacvan Bercovitch, *The American Jeremiad* (Madison: University of Wisconsin Press, 1978).

11. Jean-Phillipe Mathy, "Out of History: French Readings of Postmodern America," *American Literary History* 2, no. 2 (Summer 1990): 272.

12. Francis Fukuyama, "The End of History?," *The National Interest* 16 (Summer 1989): 3–18.

13. Mathy, "Out of History," 273.

14. Paul Monette, *Borrowed Time: An AIDS Memoir* (New York: Harcourt, Brace, Jovanovich, 1988), 22.

15. Monette, *Borrowed Time*, 6.

16. Jean-François Lyotard, *The Post Modern Condition: A Report on Knowledge*, trans. Geoff Bennington and Brian Massumi (Minneapolis: University of Minnesota Press, 1984), 66.

17. Mathy, "Out of History," 292.

18. For superb analyses of the construction of media audiences through the negation of homosexual desire and representation see John Leo, "The Familialism of 'Man' in American Television Melodrama," *South Atlantic Quarterly* 88, no. 1 (Winter 1989): 31–52; and Simon Watney, *Policing Desire: Pornography, AIDS and the Media* (Minneapolis: University of Minnesota Press, 1987).

19. Thus, when ACT UP interrupted U.S. Secretary of Health and Human Services Louis Sullivan at the Sixth International AIDS Conference in San Francisco in June 1990, many felt their actions an "inappropriate" silencing of the speaker; the point in that intervention was multiple, but among the strong reasons for pursuing it was the continuing non-representation of those most directly effected by the epidemic in the very apparatuses (such as that convention, such as the Department of Health and Human Services) supposedly designed to address their needs, and supposedly doing an admirable job in that. The "game" in this case had failed to include all of its players, and some of those players—the ones with less power in the situation—decided to halt the game.

20. Here again we are confronted by the mathematical sublime, this time making it impossible to indicate all of the excellent work done in this field. In addition to those writers discussed here, see Douglas Crimp, *AIDS: Cultural Analysis/Cultural Activism* (Cambridge: MIT Press, 1988) for an introduction to some of the central issues.

21. James Kinsella, *Covering the Plague: AIDS and the American Media* (New Brunswick, New Jersey: Rutgers University Press, 1989), 134–36.

22. Simon Watney, "Missionary Positions: AIDS, 'Africa,' and Race," *differences* 1, no. 1 (Winter 1989): 90.

23. Watney, *Policing Desire*, 9.

24. Even though the media have aggressively sought to recolonize and commodify traditional Others in American culture (just as one may now sample endlessly from exotic cuisines and cultures in the marketplace), this cannot be accomplished for gay and lesbian people. As George Yudice suggests, "the mainstream media have launched a campaign to demarginalize, decolor [and] degender[, but] gays and lesbians, much harder to demarginalize, are either stigmatized as the 'sinful' AIDS-ridden Other or are left unrepresented." George Yudice, "Marginality and the Ethics of Survival," *Universal Abandon?: The Politics of Postmodernism*, ed. Andrew Ross (Minneapolis: University of Minnesota Press, 1988), 221.

25. See Ana Maria Alonso and Maria Teresa Koreck, "Silences: 'Hispanics,' AIDS, and Sexual Practices," *differences* 1, no. 1 (Winter 1989): 101–24.

26. Walter Benjamin, *Illuminations* (New York: Schocken Books, 1969), 88.

27. Benjamin, *Illuminations*, 158–59.

28. When Halston died in March 1990, for instance, *People* (April 9, 1990) made his death a cover story: "He put American fashion on the map. He dressed Jackie, Liz and Liza. He died last week of AIDS, a broken man." Although his business failure is the biographical referent of the last phrase, it signifies redundantly as the "truth" of any AIDS story (AIDS = broken), and while the magazine contains a four-page spread entitled "Fashion—An Industry Dressed in Mourning" and references to Michael Bennett's death from AIDS on its book review pages, there is nothing in it to suggest how these deaths are linked, linked to other social and political

questions—nothing, for instance, to link it to the story on George Bush's refusal of broccoli (nothing on his refusal to speak about AIDS) or the story on a woman basketball player at Wellesley who "escaped China's brutal crackdown." Much less is there any attempt to shape the reporting of the disease as more than a series of single deaths and private tragedies. This is not, of course, true in the non-mainstream—especially gay/lesbian—press.

29. The first weekly news magazine to put AIDS on its cover (*Newsweek*, April 18, 1983) featured a tube of blood marked "Caution: KS/AIDS" below the graphic, "Epidemic: The Mysterious and Deadly Disease Called AIDS May Be the Public-Health Threat of the Century. How Did It Start? Can It Be Stopped?" Above this are two small headers for other stories: "Challenger's Men Take a Space Walk" and "Russia's Spies Get the Boot." The final indifference to AIDS during the Reagan years cannot be separated from what were national priorities of the political right—increased militarism, a renewal of Cold War hostility with the Soviet Union, a flat denial of funding for domestic issues—and the *Newsweek* cover remains uncanny in its framing of AIDS by these other two stories.

30. Diana Fuss, *Essentially Speaking: Feminism, Nature and Difference* (New York: Routledge, 1989), 103.

31. Sontag, *AIDS and Its Metaphors*, 45.

32. See Louise Hay, *The AIDS Book: Creating a Positive Approach* (Santa Monica, California: Hay House, 1988).

33. See Donna Haraway, "The Biopolitics of Postmodern Bodies: Determination of Self in Immune System Discourse," *differences* 1, no. 1 (Winter 1989): 3–43.

34. Jonathan Dollimore, "Different Desires: Subjectivity and Transgression in Wilde and Gide," *Genders* 2 (Summer 1988): 37.

35. Judith Butler, *Gender Trouble: Feminism and the Subversion of Identity* (New York: Routledge, 1990), 136.

36. Butler, *Gender Trouble*, 138.

37. Edith Wyschogrod, *Spirit in Ashes: Hegel, Heidegger, and Man-Made Mass Death* (New Haven: Yale University Press, 1985), 3. Subsequent references are cited in the text.

38. Lee Edelman, "At Risk in the Sublime: The Politics of Gender and Theory," *Gender and Theory: Dialogues on Feminist Criticism*, ed. Linda Kauffman (London: Basil Blackwell, 1989), 220–21.

39. Edelman, 'At Risk,' 227.

40. Benjamin, *Illuminations*, 108.

13

"All the Sad Young Men":
AIDS and the Work of Mourning

Jeff Nunokawa

On April 15th 1985, Margaret Heckler, then Director of the Department of Health and Human Services, defined with bracing clarity the
extent of the Reagan administration's concern about acquired immune
deficiency syndrome: "We must conquer AIDS before it affects the
heterosexual population . . . the general population. We have a very
strong public interest in stopping AIDS before it spreads outside the
risk groups, before it becomes an overwhelming problem." Heckler's
now famous caveat, which prompted wags within the AIDS movement
to rename the department she directed Health and *Heterosexual* Services, doesn't appear to require much analysis. The reluctance of the
Reagan administration, as well as most state and city governments, to
furnish significant funding for research, treatment, or effective education, their reluctance indeed, to do anything other than develop testing
apparati for quarantining so-called risk groups, draws even the least
suspicious observer to conclude that they didn't and don't care very
much about saving the kinds of people who were and are dying by the
tens of thousands.

But such genocidal insouciance about *non*-heterosexuals already
dead, dying, or endangered registers more than simply a hatred of
homosexuals, or, more precisely, more than a simple hatred of homosexuals. I want to suggest that a kinder, gentler, and perhaps more
pervasive homophobia also counsels acquiescence to the catastrophic
effects of AIDS, namely a deep cultural idea about the lethal character
of male homosexuality. If, as Simon Watney remarks, "the spectacle
of AIDS calmly and constantly entertains the possible prospect of the
death of all . . . gay men . . . without the slightest flicker of concern,
regret, or grief," this is partly because the culture that watches this

311

spectacle, even with, perhaps especially with, concern, regret and grief, sees a population doomed to extinction, anyway.[1]

Our culture's inclination to regard gay men as *marked* men continues to play an important role in the current health crisis, helping to determine popular opinion, government policy, medical research agendas, and officially endorsed therapeutic strategies, or, more precisely, the dearth of officially endorsed therapeutic strategies. The aura of doom that surrounds gay men helps to explain why the energetic and multifronted response of the gay community itself to the current crisis has gone largely unnoticed. Douglas Crimp remarks that despite all the achievements of such activism, "the dominant media still pictures us only as wasting deathbed victims."[2] This may be in part because the dominant media has *always* pictured gay people as "deathbed victims." Captivity to such pictures has contributed to the remarkable tenacity with which the dominant imagination persists, even now, in rendering the crisis visible as a kind of gay plague—in the eyes of many, gay men suffering from HIV-related illnesses remain, despite overwhelming epidemiological evidence to the contrary, not only people with AIDS, but *the* people with AIDS. This confusion tends at once to cooperate with the various works of marginalization that render invisible the burdens that AIDS has imposed on other disproportionately affected groups in this country, not to mention in other countries, and, at the same time, to encourage our culture's sometimes lethal distaste for, and anxiety about, homosexuality. Moreover, if the notion that gay men are subject to extinction encourages the continued homosexualization of AIDS, it may also help to account for the continued resistance to the idea that the Human Immunodeficiency Virus is not uniformly fatal, the persistent failure to perceive HIV-related infections as things that people live with, as well as die from. AIDS is a gay disease, and it means death, because AIDS has been made the most recent chapter in our culture's history of the gay male, a history which sometimes reads like a book of funerals.

To trace this morbid delineation of gay identity in current constructions of people with AIDS, we need go no further than Randy Shilts's enormously popular novelization of the crisis, *And The Band Played On*. Through its chronicle of the French Canadian airline steward, Gaetan Dugas, or Patient Zero, *And The Band Played On* recirculates and renders explicit the rumor that gay men are fated to die early. James Miller's arresting nickname for *And The Band Played On*, "The Death of Little Nelly," works well to describe the story of Gaetan Dugas in Shilts's novel, but even this characterization fails to describe the full extent of its death drive: the bathhouse boy's progress proceeds with even less hesitation than that most necrological of narratives, Nell's journey to the grave in *The Old Curiosity Shop*. From his first appearance in Shilts's book, Dugas's character is framed by the prophecy of his death: "Gaetan Dugas examined his face closely in the mirror. The scar, below his ear, was only partly visible . . . He had come all the way from Toronto to enjoy this day, and for the moment he would put aside the troubling news the doctors had delivered just a few weeks before."³ And as his effort to put off the prophecy of doom in this passage suggests, any delay in the lethal movement that defines Dugas only strengthens the promise of its end.

Of course, the story of doom in which Shilts's character is inscribed, a story which casts the realization of lethal catastrophe as just a matter of time, in Shilts's words, "a nightmare waiting to happen," is hardly the exclusive experience of gay men. Anyone at risk who has submitted to the narrative discipline of the HIV test, or to any test that may predict death, knows the hollowing anxiety inscribed in the feeling that any doubt about the prospect of a positive result is an effort to delay a certain outcome. But Shilts's text identifies this death driven narrative as the definition of the gay subject, specifically, by casting Gaetan Dugas as paradigm for gay desire and identity, generally: "At one time, Gaetan had been what every man wanted from gay life . . . the ideal of the community; by the time he died, he had become what every man feared" (439). His unique role in the crisis, as the "man who gave us AIDS" is the paradoxical individuality of the exemplum.⁴ The story of Dugas singlehandedly infecting an entire community with HIV serves to narrate his status, in Shilts's novelization, as reflection of that community. There is little difference in Shilts's account between the man in the mirror that Dugas inspects for kaposi's sarcoma, and the men that he fucks to get even:

> when the moaning stopped . . . Gaetan Dugas reached up for the lights, turning up the rheostat slowly so his partner's eyes would have time to adjust. He then made a point of eyeing the purple lesions on his chest. "Gay cancer," he said, *almost as if he were talking to himself*. "Maybe you'll get it too." (198, my emphasis)

This is an old story; the lethal prophecy that confronts Dugas's partners and Shilts's readers was predicted a century ago, in the doom that defines an inaugural image of gay identity, the image of homosexual desire inscribed in and on *The Picture of Dorian Gray*. Saturated with metonymic markers of the love that dares not speak its name, the novel prompted nearly universal opprobrium when it was first published, as a tale fit for "outlawed aristocrats and perverted telegraph boys," and was adduced as evidence against its author during the trial of his homosexuality.[5] And if, as Richard Ellmann notes, *The Picture of Dorian Gray* furnished unprecedented literary publicity for an "uncelebrated form of love," in the ambiguous lineaments of its eponymous hero, it helped give such forms a human face.[6] Published in the last decade of the nineteenth century, just in time to participate in the construction of homosexual identity in England,[7] *Dorian Gray* casts the homosexual intensities it pictures as signs of an essential attribute, lodging the desire that dares not speak its name in the deepest grounds of the self. When Lord Henry's "low, musical voice" campaigns against the repression of "desire for what . . . monstrous laws have made monstrous and unlawful," and praises those "feelings," "thoughts," and "dreams" whose manifestation will revivify "the Hellenic ideal," Dorian Gray is

> dimly conscious that entirely fresh influences were at work within him. Yet they seemed to him to have come really from himself. The few words . . . said to him . . . had touched some secret chord that had never been touched before, but that he felt was now vibrating and throbbing to curious pulses.[8]

Lord Henry approaches Dorian Gray on behalf of "the Hellenic ideal," "[he]e came close to him, and put his hand upon his shoulder," and the consequence for the boy so addressed is an apocalypse of self-knowledge: "The lad started and drew back. . . . There was a look of fear in his eyes, such as people have when they are suddenly awakened. . . . Why had it been left to a stranger to reveal him to himself?" (44).

The most comprehensive framing of homosexual identity in *The Picture of Dorian Gray* is, of course, the picture of Dorian Gray, the portrait of the hero painted while the musical effects of Lord Henry's hellenistic eloquence "were at work within him." Basil Hallward's picture describes more than Dorian Gray's own homosexual desire; if the portrait describes the longings within Dorian Gray that Lord Henry has managed to arouse, they also comprehend the erotic interest of the artist and the tutor who draw, and draw out, those desires. For Basil Hallward, "every flake and film of colour" of the picture "seem[s] to reveal" the "secret" of his "fascinat[ion]" with Dorian Gray: "I felt

. . . that I had told too much, that I had put too much of myself into it" (145). Hallward's painting is also the portrait of Lord Henry's hellenistic sympathies, the "project[ion]" of his "soul into [a] gracious form" (60). The picture of Dorian Gray, Lord Henry declares, is "entirely due to me" (48).

And like Gaetan Dugas, whose first appearance is marked by a scar that prophesies his doom, the "self" expressed by hellenism's advocates is shadowed by the prediction of its impending cessation; the advent of the new Antinous merges with the announcement of his demise when Lord Henry, reading in the boy's beauty the sentence of his mortality, is compelled to a double disclosure: "There was so much in you that charmed me that I felt I must tell you something about yourself. I thought how tragic it would be if you were wasted. For there is such a little time that your youth will last—such a little time . . . we never get back our youth. . . . Our limbs fail, our senses rot" (46). If this inaugural characterization of homosexual identity pictures the hellenistic ideal as beautiful youth, this is another way of saying that it pictures the hellenistic ideal as the prospect of inevitable death.

This morbid identification is intensified, rather than cancelled, by the negotiation between Dorian Gray and his painting, in which the two exchange fates. Rather than excising the prospect of his death, this transposition drives it deep into his character, and thus into the generic homosexual subject concentrated there; lethal doom is transported from his body to his "soul" (186), from physical accident, to metaphysical essence; it ceases to be an external event, or eventuality, and becomes instead the closeted content of homosexual identity. The *secret* of Dorian Gray, the concealed referent that lurks beneath and defines a public surface crowded with the signs of male homosexuality, is not perverse desire, or not perverse desire, *per se*, but rather a spectacle wrapped in a cloth that "had . . . served often as a pall for the dead," a spectacle defined by a figure of death: "What the worm was to the corpse, his sins would be to the painted image on the canvas. They would mar its beauty, and eat away its grace" (149).

Now what exactly is so special about Dorian Gray? After all, the fate that defines him is the most pervasive sentence in the world. "There is a fatality about all physical and intellectual distinction. . . . It is better not to be different from one's fellows" (120). Such a declaration may puzzle us: if there is a fatality about that which is physically and intellectually distinct, there is also a fatality about that which is not. Fatality, like the fear induced by a test that predicts it, is *indistinct*. But Wilde's novelization of the homosexual male subject casts this most common sentence as the gay signature, concentrating fatality in the figure of a male homosexual identity, *as* the figure of male homosexual identity.

The lethal characterization that I have attempted to isolate has a complicated etymology; it arises from a range of pressures and conceptions.[9] What interests me here, though, is to assess the burden that this characterization imposes today on the gay community itself, as it takes up the work of mourning its own. The rumor of gay doom isn't restricted to the lurid heterosexism of Randy Shilts, whose book reminds us just how articulate, not to mention prolix, internalized homophobia can be. This rumor is broadcast further than we may know; it appears as well in labors of mourning that take place closer to home. To suggest this, I want to turn now to one of James Merrill's elegies for David Kalstone, who died recently of complications arising from acquired immune deficiency syndrome:

Investiture at Cecconi's
For David Kalstone

Caro, that dream (after the diagnosis)
found me losing patience outside the door of
"our" Venetian tailor. I wanted evening
clothes for the new year.

Then a bulb went on. The old woman, she who
stitches dawn to dusk in his back room, opened
one suspicious inch, all the while exclaiming
over the late hour—

Fabrics? patterns? those the proprietor must
show by day, but now—till a lightening insight
cracks her face wide: *Ma! the Signore's here to
try on his new robe!*

Robe? She nods me onward. The mirror triptych
summons three bent crones she defracted into
back from no known space. They converge by magic,
arms full of moonlight.

Up my own arms glistening sleeves are drawn. Cool
silk in grave, white folds—oriental mourning—
sheathes me, throat to ankles. I turned to face her,
uncomprehending.

Thank your friend, she cackled, *the Professore!*
wonderstruck I sway, like a tree of tears. You—

miles away, sick, fearful—have yet arranged this
heartstopping present.[10]

Seeking evening clothes, the speaker is sheathed instead in mourning
garments, stitched by the mythical three fates, the "three bent crones"
in *Macbeth*, the three fates who emerge here from the panels of the
mirror tripych, and merge in the Italian seamstress, "the old woman,
she who stitches dawn to dusk." As his encounter with this figure
suggests, the speaker of the poem, as well as the subject he mourns, is
involved in the predictions of fate: the robe that he wears, the dream
that he entertains, and the words that he speaks are fabrics and forces
that enfold him without his consent. Sheathed "throat to ankles" in a
garment drawn over his arms, the speaker's submission is deepened in
the next stanza when the arms over which the robe is drawn become
the limbs of a tree, swaying "wonderstruck," helpless limbs which
wear tears now, rather than garments of grief. Similarly, the mourner
is drawn into the dream-scene of the poem, just as the shroud is drawn
over him. His movement is determined by motions decided elsewhere,
decided by the figure of fate, who "nods me onward." Beginning with
the first line of the poem, where "that dream found me," the force of
the dream that draws the speaker on in the poem is weaved into the
structure of its sentences, which place him from the start as their object,
rather than their subject. Thus, Merrill's elegy not only records the
content of a dream: in the station it assigns its speaker, the poem also
recapitulates the place or plight of the dreamer, a figure drawn forth
by a script which someone else has written, rather than the author of
the action.

And these fabrics of Fate, the robe that is drawn on the speaker, the
dream and the poem that draws him on, are the same as the fate that
he mourns. The robe, the dream, and the poem do not merely outline
the inexorable progress of death; these heartstopping presents also
perform it. If at the beginning, the speaker is like a doctor, distanced
from the patients he loses after the diagnosis, the cool silk in grave,
white folds that sheathes him from throat to ankles—the robe—as well
as the dream and the poem that move him to the heartstopping end,
cause the speaker to converge finally with the lost patient.

Of course, the submission to mortal fate—what Freud calls "defer-
ence for reality"—that Merrill's poem performs is a constitutive aspect
of any work of mourning. But just as Wilde and Shilts cultivate the
confusion of gay identity with a death-driven narrative, Merrill's poem
characterizes the doom as the specific fate of gay men. We can begin

to see this by noticing that the title of Merrill's poem connects the lethal garment that enshrouds mourner and mourned with the sartorial trappings of papal induction. Among the rumors of Dorian Gray's homosexuality, none is more acute than his attraction to the Church and its paraphernalia: "It was rumored of him once that he was about to join the Roman Catholic communion; and certainly the Roman ritual had always a great attraction for him . . . He had a special passion, also, for ecclesiastical vestments, as indeed he had for everything connected with the service of the Church" (163, 171). The venerable tradition of sacred drag extends from Cardinal Newman's infamous penchant for holy crossdressing, to the well-publicized foibles of Cardinal Spellman, the twentieth century's most famous Catholic clothes queen.[11] The clothes queen reappears in secularized fashion within the body of the poem itself, when, in the second line, Merrill speaks of "our" tailor. "Our" tailor is, *mutatus mutandis*, the Italian designer who caters first to a gay coterie, and whose clothes eventually enwrap unsuspecting heterosexuals in an unspoken embrace that has supplied generations of homosexuals a certain passing amusement. "Our" tailor stitches the garments that enfold the figures of John Henry Newman, Francis Spellman, Perry Ellis, Halston, James Merrill, and David Kalstone, fond as they are, or were, of sometimes elaborate decorums of clothes and meter. Thus the lethal robe of necessity, the lethal robe that the dominant media now calls AIDS, stretches to cover a century of gay fashion.

"Our tailor" defines the sexual identity of this morbid garment; so do the details of its circulation, which begins when "she who / stitches dawn to dusk in his back room, opened / one suspicious inch." "[H]is back room" alludes unmistakably (if with characteristic quiet) to a site of subterranean gay sexual activity sufficiently well known within and outside our community to qualify as a textbook example of the open secret. And if the "back room" traces the architectural interstices of sexual opportunity housed by porn theaters and after hours clubs, the "open[ing]" of "*his* back room" "one suspicious inch" describes, *sotto voce*, one form of such opportunity: it intimates the action of "his" anus as it prepares to receive a penis. The outlines of anal eroticism introduced here at once confirm, and are confirmed by, another rumor of backside sexuality that appears in the next stanza, when the keeper of the robe recognizes its recipient, and the ceremony of its passing begins: "a lightening insight cracks her wide face."[12] Thus the ceremony of investiture commences in Merrill's poem as the figure of anal intercourse gains resolution, as the clarity of its picture, and the progress of its trajectory advance; the passing of the lethal garment from the mourned to the mourner starts as the figure of anal sex is brought out almost explicitly, and a hesitancy to dilate overcome. Just as the fateful, fatal robe itself is invested with various fabrics of homosexual history, its transmission takes place through the backrooms and backsides of gay sexual culture.[13]

I realize that all this may appear vexatiously aloof from the most immediate perplexities encountered by those within the gay community who have found it necessary to undertake the work of mourning, and met with the expurgation of the letters A I D S from newspaper obituaries, memorial services, and family circles, or with the reluctance of employers, parents, and the State to extend them the same rights of grief accorded heterosexuals with analogous affiliations to the dead. Homophobia has seldom been more obtrusive than in its current disinclination to allow the gay community to grieve its own publicly; seldom more annoying than in its refusal to honor an exigency of expression as compelling as hunger, anger, or fear; seldom plainer than in the harassment and repression, variously violent and squeamish, institutional and intimate, by which it has worked to make the casualties of the present crisis disappear. The understated, understood, remedial urgency of efforts of remembrance such as the Names Project, efforts of remembrance that emerge from the gay community itself, describes a pressure that persistently attends the work of remembering such casualties, a pressure to mark deaths that the majority culture is simply not disposed to notice.

I am suggesting however, that the savage indignity of censorship is not the only form of homophobia to confront the gay community today, as it takes up the task of counting its losses. At the same time that a virulent or embarrassed distaste for homosexuals functions to silence the mourning of gay culture, a softer homophobia helps to incite it. If a homophobic reticence helped to prompt the Names Project in the first place, a different homophobia has contributed to its canonization in the dominant media; if the majority culture is not inclined to recognize the death of the male homosexual, it is also not inclined to recognize anything else about him; if the majority culture grants no notice to his death, it also inters him from the start. The gay community is thus taxed during its sad time by a double burden: the variegated regime of heterosexism not only inhibits the work of acknowledging the loss of a gay man, it also exacts the incessant reproduction of this labor, by casting his death as his definition.

My aim here is not to condemn the participation of elegies such as

Figure 1.

Merrill's in the rehearsal of this definition; it is not to campaign for the censorship of this figure from our own performances of loss. Such a censuring would resemble other, at best unrealistic efforts at rectitude, like a simple condemnation of erotic forms that appear to recapitulate our oppression. Surely, this unsafe figure can't be simply banned from our theaters of mourning, any more than a taste for humiliation can be banned from our theaters of sexuality. Indeed, the very eloquence of Merrill's poem furnishes a measure of just how deeply insinuated the figure of preordained doom may be in our own work of mourning. The question with which I want to end is not how to expel the figure of the doomed homosexual when it appears in the midst of our own labors of mourning, but instead how to confront it?

A recent video by Tom Kalin entitled "They Are Lost to Vision Altogether" stages such a confrontation. Drawing together various conceptions of gay men, conceptions that have encouraged, and in turn, been encouraged by the dominant media's representation of the current crisis, "They Are Lost to Vision Altogether" reminds us that no form of mourning can help but participate in such constructions. Thus, for example, Kalin quotes a scene from *Dark Victory*, in which

Bette Davis, a queen of the gay gaze, with whom generations of gay men have identified, through whom generations of gay men have identified themselves, dies a spectacular, preordained death (fig. 1).[14] But now, the retroactive identity of the actor who played opposite Davis in the scene that appears in "They Are Lost to Vision Altogether" impeaches the spectacle of gay doom at the moment of its greatest force. If *Dark Victory* makes a heartstopping present still, Ronald Reagan's supporting role in this scene compels the viewer to look again; if Kalin's quotation pays heed to the figure of the doomed homosexual, it does something else as well. Reagan's appearance here works less to cancel the power of that figure than to crowd it with an alternate obituary, a competing account of gay morbidity. In the double vision of this image, the rumor of our doom is invoked and, at the same time, displaced by a different story, the story of a catastrophe made partly by accident, and partly by political forces which cast an awful actor as their star.[15]

Notes

This essay is dedicated to John Bommer Murphy, who died in 1986 from illnesses associated with acquired immune deficiency syndrome: *ave atque vale.*

1. Simon Watney, "The Spectacle of AIDS," *October* 43 (Winter 1987): 85.

2. Douglas Crimp, "Mourning and Militancy," *October* 51 (Winter 1989): 16.

3. Randy Shilts, *And The Band Played On: Politics, People, and the AIDS Epidemic* (New York: St. Martin's Press, 1987), 11. All subsequent quotations from *And The Band Played On* refer to this edition and are cited in the text.

4. The *New York Post*, October 6, 1987, 1.

5. *Scot's Review*, July 5, 1890. The reference is to Lord Arthur Somerset, and the Cleveland Street scandal, respectively. In "Writing Gone Wilde: Homoerotic Desire in the Closet of Representation," Ed Cohen argues for the generative significance of *The Picture of Dorian Gray* in the production of homosexual identity. *PMLA* 102 (October 1987): 801–13.

6. Richard Ellmann, *Oscar Wilde* (New York: Random House, 1988), 305. My discussion of the part that *The Picture of Dorian Gray* played in the formation of homosexual identity is not, of course, meant to imply that Wilde's text was solely responsible even for the literary construction of the homosexual during the nineteenth century.

7. See Regenia Gagnier, *Idylls of the Marketplace: Oscar Wilde and the Victorian Public* (Stanford: Stanford University Press, 1986), 140; Jeffrey Weeks, *Coming Out: Homosexual Politics in Britain from the Nineteenth Century to the Present* (London: Quartet Books, 1977); Michel Foucault, *History of Sexuality, Volume One: An Introduction*, trans. Robert Hurley (New York: Random House, 1980), 4; David M. Halperin, "One Hundred Years of Homosexuality," in *One Hundred*

Years of Homosexuality and Other Essays on Greek Love (New York and London: Routledge, 1990).

8. Oscar Wilde, *The Picture of Dorian Gray* (New York: Penguin, 1988), 41–2. All subsequent quotations from *The Picture of Dorian Gray* refer to this edition and are cited in the text. Wilde's invocation of the term "hellenistic" is, of course, imprecise, since the term indicates, specifically, a period ranging from 323 to 31 B.C. By this term, he (and I) refer to a more general rubric constructed in the nineteenth century to signify a collection of proclivities and practices associated with homosexuality. The widely acknowledged status of "hellenism" as synecdoche for homosexuality during the Victorian period becomes visible when we recall Henry Hallam's anxiety that Tennyson's devotion to Shakespeare's sonnets expressed a "sympathy with Hellenism." See Louis Crompton, *Byron and Greek Love: Homophobia in 19th-Century England* (Berkeley: University of California Press, 1985), and Halperin, *One Hundred Years of Homosexuality*, 1–40.

9. Jeff Nunokawa, "*In Memoriam* and the Extinction of the Homosexual," forthcoming in *ELH*.

10. James Merrill, *The Inner Room* (New York: Alfred A. Knopf, 1988), 92.

11. W. G. Ward's famous dream, in which a woman removes her veil, and reveals herself to be Newman, condenses a long train of rumors that intimate at once the Cardinal's homosexuality and his fondness for the sartorial extravagances of Catholicism. Charles Kingsley castigated Newman and his school for "an element of foppery" which expressed itself "even in dress and manner; a fastidious, maundering die-away effeminacy, which is mistaken for purity and refinement; and I confess myself unable to cope with it, so alluring is it to the minds of an effeminate and luxurious aristocracy." Quoted in Robert Bernard Martin, *The Dust of Combat: A Life of Charles Kingsley* (London: Faber and Faber, 1959), 239–40. The anecdotes about Spellman are legion and legend. One especially exemplary piece of apocrypha places Tallulah Bankhead in the balcony of Saint Patrick's Cathedral, watching Spellman as he proceeds towards the alter, clad in long robes and bearing incense. "Love the drag, aunt Fran," Bankhead is purported to have exclaimed, "but your purse is on fire." (I am grateful to Michael Cadden for this morsel of oral history.)

12. The gender of the figure through and upon whom the outlines of the anus are projected in Merrill's poem may be characterized as an instance of the confusion of gay and feminine sexualities that Leo Bersani detects in many dominant media representations of AIDS. For Bersani, the "startling resemblance" between the stories about the promiscuity of gay men which gained new prominence with the current health crisis, and the depiction of female prostitutes in the nineteenth century, revolves around their common reputation for "a sexuality physiologically grounded in the nonclimactic climax":

> The accounts of . . . gay men having sex twenty to thirty times a night, or once a minute, are much less descriptive of even the most promiscuous male sexuality than they are reminiscent of male fantasies about women's multiple orgasms. The Victorian representation of prostitutes may explicitly criminalize what is merely a consequence of a more profound or original guilt. Promiscuity is the social correlative of a sexuality physiologically grounded in the noncli-

mactic climax . . . the similarities between representations of female prostitutes and male homosexuals should help us to specify the exact form of sexual behavior being targeted in representations of AIDS, as the criminal, fatal, and irresistibly repeated act. This is of course anal sex. . .

See Leo Bersani, "Is The Rectum a Grave?," *AIDS: Cultural Analysis, Cultural Activism,* ed. Douglas Crimp (Cambridge: Mass: MIT Press, 1988), 211.

13. I am grateful to my students in the 1990 Telluride summer program at Cornell for getting me to think about the significance of the figures of erotic activity in Merrill's poem.

14. Davis's status as an icon of gay doom in *Dark Victory* is underwritten by the specific form of her death: a disease which, like one of the prominent opportunistic infections associated with AIDS, entails her loss of vision (altogether).

15. The double vision of gay doom, the double gesture of invocation and resistance that appears in Kalin's video is concentrated in Leo Bersani's "Is The Rectum a Grave?" Here, the coincidence of these things is radicalized to the point of identity: to submit to the sentence of death that defines the subjectivity and subjugation of gay men is also to evade it. According to Bersani, this condensation takes place in a self-shattering that Georges Bataille calls "communication," "a kind of nonanecdotal self-debasement . . . in which, so to speak, the self is exuberantly discarded" (217–18). Bersani locates the scene of this utmost act of self-denial in the rectum, at once "the grave in which the masculine ideal . . . of proud subjectivity is buried" (222), and the grave in which the gay man puts to rest an identity which is before all else the mark of death. Bersani's morbid troping of gay men's self-dissolution in anal intercourse as a kind of death subscribes, of course, to the lethal tradition that I have considered here, but his imagination of this fatality is a renaissance conceit, in which the casualty is death itself: " 'AIDS,' [Simon] Watney writes, 'offers a new sign for the symbolic machinery of repression, making the rectum a grave.' But if the rectum is the grave in which the masculine ideal (an ideal shared differently by men *and* women) of proud subjectivity is buried, then it should be celebrated for its very potential for death . . . It may, finally, be in the gay man's rectum that he demolishes his own perhaps otherwise uncontrollable identification with a murderous judgment against him" (222).

14

Undead

Ellis Hanson

Heckling from the Pit

> This was the shocking thing; that the slime of the pit seemed to utter cries and voices; that the amorphous dust gesticulated and sinned; that what was dead, and had no shape, should usurp the offices of life.   *Robert Louis Stevenson*[1]

In 1984, having known about AIDS for little more than a year, I began to realize that there is language that can kill me or, more insidiously, language that can persuade me to kill myself. Writing now, in 1989, I cope with the truism that AIDS has helped to concretize a mythical link between gay sex and death. But beyond the truism, I have a suspicion that notions of death have been at the heart of nearly every historical construction of same-sex desire.

Typically, in media representations of AIDS, I find neither people who are living with AIDS nor people who have died with AIDS. What I find, rather, are spectacular images of the abject,[2] the dead who dare to speak and sin and walk abroad, the undead with AIDS. I find a late-Victorian vampirism at work, not only in media constructions of AIDS now, but in the various archaic conceptions of same-sex desire which inform the present "Face of AIDS." We have not yet broken our bizarre link with the undead, even though this link found its most profound manifestation nearly a hundred years ago in the concomitant appearance of literature's two most notorious vampires: Bram Stoker's Dracula and Sigmund Freud's homosexuals.

I realize that the man with the cape and the funny accent has in this century become sanitized into a camp figure in B-movies, popular fiction, and commercial advertisements. From Bela Lugosi to John Holmes, Frank Langella to Count Chocula, the Dracula image has been heterosexualized and domesticated to sell everything from break-fast cereal for small children to rape fantasies for straight men.[3] What I am suggesting, however, is that while vampire films and novels may have lost their original capacity to excite homosexual panic, this collapse arrived just in time for a replacement genre: the AIDS documentary.

Whether by strategy or by error, the media have a commonplace tendency to collapse the category of "gay man" with that of "person with AIDS" within a convenient discourse of "high risk."[4] In this way, myths about gay sex serve to amplify myths about AIDS; and so when I speak of the vampire as the embodiment of evil sexuality, I speak of gay men and people with AIDS in the same breath. I am talking about the irrational fear of PWAs and gay men who "bite." I am talking about essentialist representations of gay men as vampiric: as sexually exotic, alien, unnatural, oral, anal, compulsive, violent, protean, poly-morphic, polyvocal, polysemous, invisible, soulless, transient, superhu-manly mobile, infectious, murderous, suicidal, and a threat to wife, children, home, and phallus.

I am talking also about the suspenseful quest to destroy gay life: the quest of lawyers, politicians, scientists, journalists, teachers and, at times, gay critics, to silence gay people, to identify and immobilize them, to expose their "secret" and define their characteristics, and at last (after a fashion) to impale them as with a stake. I mean the pop-science magazine that seeks to re-map my body in order to sell terrifying images of my blood and semen. I mean the policeman who is gloved and armed to the teeth, my teeth, for fear I might bite or scratch or spit. I mean the psychoanalyst who has defined me in terms of his own repugnance for feminine sexuality, who has made me not so much *vagina dentata* as *anus dentatus*. Rectum, urethra, mouth, tear ducts, a gash in my skin. All my orifices are one and the same, and all my orifices have teeth.

To comprehend the vampire is to recognize that abjected space that gay men are obliged to inhabit; that space unspeakable or unnameable, itself defined as orifice, as a "dark continent" men dare not penetrate; that gap bridged over or sutured together, where men cease to play dead and yet cease to accept the normative sexual role. I am seen as the caped one, who hovers over the dreaming body of Jonathan Harker and exclaims, "This man belongs to me!" and "Yes, I too can love."[5] I dare to speak and sin and walk abroad; and so like Lucy Westenra in her bed, Renfield in his cell, Dracula in his castle, I inhabit the space of all vampires, caught between our two twin redemptions: conversion and death. Conversion in every sense: psychological, biological, religious, sexual. Death in the sense of silence and peaceful burial.

Fixing the Gaze

Even in a strict sense, then, vampirism and psychoanalysis can be seen as rival sciences of the undead.   *Laurence Rickels*[6]

I always thought Renfield performed the ideal sickrole of the homosexual hysteric. He is a sort of gay male Anna O., passing perversely from semiotic howling to a polysemous formality.[7] He is for Dr. Seward a groundbreaking experiment. Renfield is fixed by the doctor's gaze. By "fixed," I mean transfixed, held in place and immobilized in his cell and in his straightjacket. He is pinned down with a gloriously oral-sadistic diagnosis: "zoophagous." By "fixed" I also mean repaired or cured, though with Renfield "fixing" takes on more the sense of punishment. By "fixed" I also mean castrated, as one might fix a dog, for it is only the threat of castration that stands between the would-be homosexual and his identification with the phallic mother. Insofar as homosexuality is caused by a seduction of innocence (frequently a hingepin in homophobic logic), Freud's phallic mother is that seducer abstracted into incubus. Dracula is to Renfield the embodiment of that incubus: the vulture-mother of Leonardo's dream.

That Dracula maintains a homoerotic master/maternal sway over Renfield is hardly doubtful. Renfield, "the naked lunatic," escapes from his cell, and at Dracula's gate is heard to say: "I am here to do Your bidding, Master. . . . I have worshipped You long and afar off. Now that You are near, I await Your commands, and You will not pass me by, will You, dear Master, in Your distribution of good things?" (118).

What is surprising is that Dr. Seward requires a similar relationship with his patient. Renfield's fawning might sicken him but, when Lucy's rebuff has left him with an "empty feeling" (72), Renfield apparently helps him to fill it. Seward refers to him as his own "pet lunatic" (261). He says that Renfield experiences "periods of gloom, ending in some fixed idea which I cannot make out." But within the frame of Stoker's narrative, Seward (through his case study) commands an autonomous authorial frame of his own within which he enjoys an almost uninterrupted power to construct "Renfield" both medically and literally. As with "the homosexual" or "the AIDS patient," Renfield is defined and framed for us entirely by an inimical discourse outside his control. "I want to make myself master of the facts of his hallucination," Seward writes (72). As with Anna O., we have a doctor constructing a conflict between an evil dream-master who promises to satisfy a mad hunger and a good doctor-master who seeks to sweep that hunger away.

I do not wish here to dismiss Freud, but rather to examine how we are framed by him. Clearly, Freud's theories have considerable radical potential for gay studies. For his time, he was remarkably enlightened and sympathetic, and even referred to himself as homosexual, especially in his friendships with Fliess and Jung.[8] I would point out, however, as does Jeffrey Weeks (and others before him), that while Freud was a radical iconoclast, he was also paradoxically a model bourgeois with a strong (hetero)sexist "normative stance."[3] Freud could speak of the fluidity of sexuality and could conceive of different kinds of homosexuality; however, even where he criticized the terms "masculine" and "feminine," homosexuals are always fixed by him in terms of distinctly heterosexual binarisms.[10] I find a paradox here: like a palimpsest, Freud's conceptions of homosexuality presume a subtext of heterosexual difference. In the case of homosexual men, one of the two men desires or is desired as a woman either because he identifies with the (phallic) mother or because he is desired for his feminine attributes. For Freud, homosexuals are never more than failed heterosexuals. In this way, he fell short of any real theoretical challenge to certain familiar gender stereotypes.

These active/passive, masculine/feminine, mother/father binarisms, which same-sex desire would seem to challenge rather than reassert, become a "straight jacket" for gay men and lesbians subjected to the Freudian gaze. In Freud, I find an affirmation of the polymorphous fluidity of sexuality, and yet at the same time this dichotomous device which poses me unnaturally, which fixes me into a set power relation between men and women. Roland Barthes speaks of much the same device in his discussion of early photographic portraiture: it was "a kind of prosthesis invisible to the lens, which supported and maintained the body in its passage to immobility: this headrest was the pedestal of the statue I would become, the corset of my imaginary essence."[11] As Guy Hocquenghem writes (to continue the photographic metaphor), the "homosexual" represents "an arbitrarily frozen frame in an unbroken polyvocal flux."[12] In short, suspended animation, a kind of death in life.

There are certainly far more obvious instances in which death appears as central to psychoanalytic notions of same-sex desire. For example, there is the homosexual as revenant, as the undead lover who interferes with the sexuality of the analysand, as in the case of Schreber's dead brother or the Rat Man's dead father. Near the end of his life, Freud suggested that a man's overcoming the terror of his homosexuality (his adopting a feminine attitude toward other men) is essential to his ascetic acceptance of the inevitability of death.[13] Ernest Jones informs us that anal-eroticism and infantile perversion, virtues generally reserved for homosexuals, are at the core of the necrophilous vampire myth. Then, of course, there is Jones's further equation of semen with blood in the unconscious, a theory which has the unfortunate consequence of rendering every cocksucker a kind of bloodsucker.[14]

Even the concept of narcissism which haunts much of Freud's work on homosexuality suggests an embrace of death. As Julia Kristeva writes, "Narcissus in love hides the suicidal Narcissus; the most urgent of all drives is death drive. Left to itself, without the assistance of projection upon the other, the Ego takes itself for a preferential target of aggression and murder."[15] This point is related to Freud's conservative impulse in *Beyond the Pleasure Principle* to distinguish death drive from libidinal instincts and to describe how death drive is sublimated (among other means) by aggression toward the other in the sexual act. Kristeva, drawing on André Green, sees narcissism as a screen for emptiness. For the homosexual narcissist, desire has at best only a spectral object, a gap veiled by a self-reflexive mirage, a mir(ror im)age; therefore, for the man who has identified with a phantasy of the phallic mother and taken himself as object of his own desire, the sexual act may be seen as both suicidal and murderous.

So the gaze of the psychoanalyst may be construed, but what of the gaze of the analysand? I am reminded of E. Ann Kaplan's work on film theory and the maternal gaze.[16] To her question, "Is the gaze male?," I would append a second question, "Is the gaze the gays'?" What could it mean for a man to engage the gaze of another man? In psychoanalytic terms, such a gaze would be a form of madness, an embrace of narcissism and death. The gay male gaze is the gaze of the male vampire: he with whom one is forbidden to identify.

The vampire is afraid of mirrors because his absence in them reminds him of his own unrepresentability, the fatal emptiness of the pleasure he embodies. Jonathan Harker is astounded by the Count's absence in the shaving mirror: "This time there could be no error, for the man was close to me, and I could see him over my shoulder. But there was no reflection of him in the mirror! The whole room behind me was displayed; but there was no sign of a man in it, except myself" (34). Dracula is the regressive dream, not the "sign of a man" but the unsignifiable phantasized, the phallic maternal, a threat that always approaches from behind. Dracula tosses the mirror-mechanism out the window and, as it shatters on the rocks below, he withdraws "without a word." He has replaced the word; he has become the mirror and will abide no "other." For Harker, he is no one "except myself," a mirror image, the imaginary collapse of self and other. When the gay vampire is the mirror, selves are lost in the fatal scrutiny of themselves. Paul Barber, in his book on vampires, likens the fear of mirrors to the fear of dead men's eyes:

> Just as mirrors are covered or turned to the wall, so are the eyes of the deceased closed or covered, perhaps because they too reflect an image and thus have a potential to capture the soul. . . . It becomes extremely important, in these circumstances, to avoid the gaze of the dead man.[17]

So too it becomes extremely important to avoid the gaze of the gay man. For a man, to fear the gay male gaze is to fear the Evil Eye or, rather, the Evil Not-I, the dissolution of self in narcissistic looking.

I can recall only one instance in which Freud speaks of the power of the gay male gaze. In the Leonardo essay he speaks of the androgynous painting of John the Baptist as an instance of sublimated homosexuality, and yet the mystery and intoxication in Freud's description belies the presence of something more powerful that remains unspoken and unseen:

> "Leonardo has turned the locust-eater of the Bible," says Murthèr, "into a Bacchus, a young Apollo, who, with a mysterious smile on his lips, and with his smooth legs crossed, gazes at us with eyes that intoxicate the senses." These pictures breathe a mystical air into whose secret one dares not penetrate. . . . They are beautiful youths of feminine delicacy and with effeminate forms; they do not cast their eyes down, but gaze in mysterious triumph, as if they knew of a great achievement of happiness, about which silence must be kept. The familiar smile of fascination leads one to guess that it is a secret of love. It is possible to see that in these figures Leonardo has denied the unhappiness of his erotic life and has triumphed over it in his art. . . .[18]

Is it not Freud who casts down his eyes? I detect an act of projection— a brief narcissistic daydream in which Freud is quick to express his aversion. He finds his own gaze turned back upon him. For a moment Freud is deposed, unfixed by the very unfixable gaze he recovers, then re-covers. His erotic fancy is sublimated through his very discussion of sublimation. Leonardo's art is not a triumph of art over eroticism, but a triumph of art as a reflection of eroticism: an incitement to gaze, an illicit act of seduction which Freud defensively declines. Same-sex desire remains for Freud mysterious and unnamed.

Of course, in classical cinema, the gaze is rarely gay. My gaze is reconstructed and heterosexualized by the camera so that I identify with man and desire fetishized woman.[19] Nowhere is this truer than in those vampire films in which the revenant as sexual deviant is neither to be identified with nor desired. In the heterosexualized gaze, the polymorphous is again relegated to its familiar abjected space. A case in point is Murnau's *Nosferatu* (1922), in which editing techniques vary every time the eye passes into the realm of the undead. As Laurence Rickels has described it, "Acceleration of the apparatus and deletion of individual stills produce the rapid, lurching movements of Nosferatu as he drives his carriage, piles up coffins, and rises from his crypt."[20] This sort of freeze-framing, a clumsy suturing of gaps within a more natural and fluid (sexual) narrative, is a familiar replication of the (Freudian) gaze that poses gay men artificially within a heterosexual context.

In *Nosferatu*, polymorphous sexuality is seen as the still photograph, normative heterosexuality as more natural and cinematic. I am reminded of Roland Barthes's discussion of photograph and film. The photograph is more akin to the cult of the dead. Like the homosexual's compulsion to repeat, the reproduction of the photograph is merely the hallucinatory repetition of a fixed point in time past. In Barthes's view, to love a photograph is to love a hallucination. Gazing at a photograph of a man condemned to die (an instance replicated in my own experience by photographs of people dying with AIDS), he writes, "I entered crazily into the spectacle, into the image, taking into my arms what is dead, what is going to die. . . ."[21] Cinema, however, takes part in the "domestication" of the photograph. Fictive film restores narrative and syntax and affirms the unreality of narcissistic phantasy. Like Freud's "heterosexuality," a highly suspect category even in his own opinion, cinema is itself merely a mundane illusion.

By directing attention to frozen frames within a film, *Nosferatu*, even within its own illusory space, fixes an Other space, that of the abjected Not-I, the vampire, Renfield's "hallucination"—the space immediately recognizable as unnatural by the masculine gaze.

Writing Patient Zero

Neither sun nor death can be stared at without blinking.
Francios, duc de la Rochefoucauld[22]

Mother, give me the sun.   *Henrik Ibsen*[23]

To return to the issue of AIDS, I would like to speak briefly of
Randy Shilts's docudrama, *And The Band Played On*. His book is an
indispensable journalistic recreation of the early years of the AIDS
pandemic, but as Douglas Crimp has pointed out, the book has a
dubious politics.[24] I single out Shilts's book first of all because it is a
bestseller and is perhaps one of the few coherent discussions of AIDS
many Americans ever experience. This book also interests me because
it is an archetypal instance of how the myth of the gay male vampire
got superimposed onto people with AIDS and how the whole package
was sold (by a gay journalist) to the American public.

And The Band Played On is a kind of vampire film. Like Stoker's
Dracula, in which newspaper clippings and case studies and bits of
diaries and journals, etc., are edited together to create a narrative, and
like Murnau's *Nosferatu*, with its self-conscious editing techniques,
Shilts's book takes part in that peculiar genre that freeze-frames images
of the gay vampire and cross-cuts them into a larger, "normal" social
narrative. Shilts tips us off to his intention fairly early: "It was November 1, 1980, the beginning of a month in which single frames of tragedy
in this and that corner of the world would begin to flicker fast enough
to reveal the movement of something new and horrible rising slowly
from the earth's biological landscape."[25] And the band played on . . .
and Bela Lugosi played the virus. The bourgeois genre itself, as Crimp
has shown, calls for a posse of good gays to triumph over a gang of
bad gays who, along with the government and the medical establishment, bear the brunt of responsibility for the pandemic. Doctors are
cross-cut with patients are cross-cut with politicians are cross-cut with
the creepy image of Gaetan Dugas in an attempt to motivate a continuous melodrama of gay male vanity and death.

Shilts's book is rife with vampire imagery. Take, for example, these
rather artful lines: "This was so African. Here was a man whose
intestines were being sucked dry by incorrigible amebic parasites, just
like some African bushman" (116).[26] Or "What a fucking nightmare.
The cold white fingers of the sea stroked the indifferent sand, littered
by a winter's worth of misshapen flotsam. Paul opened the box and

shook. The sea fingers reached to grab Jack's ashes and pulled them into the brine" (140). This happened. You were there.

Or compare the misty arrival of Dracula in Mina Harker's bedroom with the highly symbolic fog that is forever engulfing Castro Street. In *Dracula*: a "thin streak of white mist, that crept with almost imperceptible slowness across the grass towards the house, seemed to have a sentience and a vitality of its own . . . The mist was spreading now close up to the house, so that I could see it lying thick against the wall, as though it were stealing up to the windows." In *And The Band Played On*: "He saw the fog sweeping from the sea into the western half of San Francisco, its ghostly fingers creeping over the hillsides that guard Castro Street from the ocean breezes" (331).

Shilts also makes it clear that gay men are the embodiment of this ghostly threat. We have the bathhouse demons who share their methadrine needles (481). We have the requisite gay vampire with AIDS who purposefully poisons the public blood supply with his own blood (239). Every gay party becomes a *danse macabre* (40, 215, 377). Gay activists are suicidally stupid. Shilts cannot understand why they do not understand, even though doubting the media, doubting the clergy, and doubting doctors has always been a principal social activity of gay people who wish to do without self-hatred once and for all. The activists' irrational whining about civil rights can be heard just outside the house, always in the margins, like the monotonous hum of the zombies in *Night of the Living Dead*, a mindless chorus or mantra, the political rhetoric of the recently revived.

Then, of course, we have the very Dracula of AIDS, the flight attendant Gaetan Dugas, alias Patient Zero, who flits from coast to coast at "breakneck speed," remorselessly spreading the strange foreign illness of the blood. Whether Shilts intended it or not, Patient Zero, as the press releases for the book make clear, is the real selling point. What could it matter that the intimacy with which Shilts describes Dugas obscures the fact that the two men never met, or that earlier accounts of Dugas paint him as misinformed and regretful?[27]

Patient Zero is a pop-Freudian creation all Shilts's own. Critics have pointed out Dugas's fondness for mirrors and his narcissism. His notorious line, "I've got gay cancer. . . . I'm going to die and so are you" (165), reads like a parody of the old joke, "I'm a schizophrenic, and so am I," and recalls for us the link between gay sex, narcissism, and death as explored by Freud. Another disturbing connection with the Leonardo essay is Dugas's childhood trauma that Shilts dramatizes for us in a chapter called "Dirty Secrets." As Dugas examines himself in the steamy bathhouse mirror, he thinks back to, of all people, his mother. Like Leonardo, Dugas has two mothers and no father. Shilts writes:

> He had always been looking for someone, he thought. As a child he had searched for his mother, not the woman who had brought him up in Quebec City, but his real mother. . . . Now, as he searched the mirror, oblivious to the smiles aimed at his still handsome body, he was thinking about another search. Who had done this to him? Certainly somebody had. They had passed him the virus that meant he was going to die, and he couldn't get over wondering who it was, the way he once could not stop wondering what his real mother looked like. (196)

Looking in the mirror, looking for beautiful men, looking now for the sex partner that infected him, and looking for his "real mother," present a morbid and familiar correspondence. In mapping them one atop the other, Shilts has shown us that the real revenant in this book is Freud.

The mother theme is further exploited when Bill Kraus makes a desperate pilgrimage to Lourdes and, near death, winds up idolizing the Virgin as the enduring image of the "archetypal mother" (538). Another character soon to die has a similar Bernadette-like vision after discussing suicide with a good friend:

> Gary Walsh lay awake in his bed when she appeared to him, with long white hair and outstretched arms. Gary recognized the woman as the mother of a good friend; she had died just a few months ago. She was stunningly beautiful and beamed a spectacular smile as she assured him, "Don't worry, honey. I'll help you over that line. And it ain't bad at all here." (383)

The repeated motif of the death-mother mirrors Freud's misogynistic conception of mothers as somehow the cause of their sons' homosexuality: the mother vamps the son, and they engage in a sort of unspoken pre-Oedipal love-bond that is more like a suicide pact. The mother is made all the more insidious in the Leonardo essay by Freud's discussion of the vulture as the symbol for motherhood when, for most of us, the vulture is merely a bird that eats carrion. Freud finds the vulture not only (mistakenly) in Leonardo's homoerotic dream, but in the folds of the mantle around Leonardo's Virgin Mother. Even Freud's discussion of the Mona Lisa recalls Walter Pater's description of her as a vampire

who is older than the rocks among which she sits, a sort of gay male
madonna whose bambino is missing perhaps because she ate it (which
might at long last explain her mysterious smile). The gay vampire as
death-mother is certainly an aspect of *Dracula*. The Count "kisses" his
victims, killing them into a new life. Pressing Mina Harker's face to
his breast "like a child forcing a kitten's nose into a saucer of milk to
compel it to drink" (313), he force-feeds her his blood.

The image of the "mother" smoothing the way to death has become
a popular motif as thousands of gay men have found themselves at the
bedsides of friends who are dying. The image of Leonardo nursing and
mothering his male students had a similar appeal for Freud. As one gay
man wrote, "The closest model with which to compare my experience
during those seven months of life with Paul is the experience of mothering."[28] Is it unthinkable for men to look after men without lapsing
into a feminized or parental mode? Another question: why do images
of gay people as real mothers and fathers remain virtually non-existent,
despite the fact that at present in the United States gay men who are
natural fathers outnumber men, women, and children diagnosed with
HIV by at least three to one?[29] Could it be that the Freudian identification of gay men with the death-mother still appeals to the public eye?

Framing the Family

An empty castle, haunted by unappealing ghosts—"powerless" outside, "impossible" inside. *Julia Kristeva*[30]

Picture a gay man with AIDS going "home" to die. Picture his family,
they are all Mormons, their hatred for homosexuality is what drove
him away in the first place. Picture the religious crisis of the parents,
while their gay son lies in a hospital bed, elsewhere. Picture his gay
friends in San Francisco, for they are only pictures, photographs conjured by a voice-over. These friends appear once more: at the funeral,
seen from the distance of what seems a quarter-mile. Portrait of the
lover as no more than pallbearer.

Picture a gay man with AIDS confined to his hospital bed in Indiana.
No one gave a damn about him until they were sure he would die.
Picture a church group that comes to visit: they hug him, they talk to
him, they sing him the Gospel. Picture a bedside drama of the caliber
you thought went out of vogue with Little Nell.

Then picture you saw it all on PBS.[31]

Why can gay people and AIDS issues only enter living rooms in the guise of a crisis in Christian family politics? When AIDS hits the networks, gay lives cease to be valuable in themselves, but acquire relevance as a family comes to grips with tragedy and its age-old nemesis, The Homosexual. As Simon Watney has described it, the neo-conservative "family" starts to resemble something out of a 50s B-movie, a catastrophe flick in which horrendous natural forces threaten the heterosexual solidarity of the home. The very threat of child-molestation, a crime for which gay people have been falsely accused at least since Dracula bagged a baby and fed its mother to the wolves, obliges parents to "literally and metaphorically double-bolt the nursery windows night after night."³² Particularly with AIDS hysteria, "family" quickly becomes a metaphor for "nation," effectively rendering the citizenship and civil rights of gay people suspect. It is no mere coincidence that the plot of *Dracula* consists of a diseased alien invading a pure and manly England via a ship called *Demeter* (named for the goddess of fertility), all of whose se(a)men he has sucked dry.

The family photograph has always maintained a frame hermetically sealed against the gay vampire. Only one's procreative partner and procreative products are welcome within the frame. All sexuality that is not a part of this heterosexual nexus simply vanishes, so that one might have invisibly gay people in the picture, but never their lovers. To quote Simon Watney again, "Homosexuality can only enter this space as an intrusion, just as gay culture in all its forms will be given the spurious unity of a criminal environment, an infernal and bestial domain which is virtually non-human."³³ He gives the example of a man with AIDS whose lover is far from son-in-law: "The closing shot is thus all the more unfortunate since it shows a 'family album' picture of the Pierson family, united, after Michael's death—but of course without his boy friend. A traumatic episode is over. The family closes ranks, with the problem son conveniently dispatched."³⁴

I am reminded of the chapter in *Dracula* in which the Westenra home is sealed against the vampire. The doors and windows are locked, the cracks are rubbed with garlic, and Lucy (through whose veins Dracula will suck the blood of nearly every man in the book) is garlanded with a cross and garlic-flowers. Her house, like the frame of the photograph, is airtight; the home becomes a self-contained, self-justifying institution of normative heterosexuality. Only by seducing a wolf to shatter a window does Dracula finally break the frame.

Perhaps it is fitting then that so many people with AIDS are or become homeless. But even when a gay man does have a home, there would seem to be a taboo against filming him in it. You are more likely to see a gay man with AIDS on a park bench, in a doctor's office, or confined to a hospital bed, even though these places are not likely to be his usual habitats. The insularity of the gay domain was never more clear than when gay people were threatened with quarantine. In fact, Dennis Altman recalls letters to the press in Australia in 1984 which called for the confinement of "all homosexuals" to particular islands,[35] a strategy Rosa von Praunheim satirized in his film, *A Virus Knows No Morals*, in which people with AIDS are confined to an island called Helgoland, a sort of postmodern medical themepark with robots for sexual partners. I am reminded of the hydrophobic vampire who cannot cross large bodies of water, and the advice of vampire legends that the dead should be buried on islands.[36]

But do gay men have *homes* of their own? If we abide by popular representations, we would have to conclude that a gay man does not live somewhere, he lurks somewhere. He has no home, he has a haunt. The image of the polymorphous vampire straying from his haunt appears to terrify the "general population," which may explain their need to fix him firmly to a hospital bed (after the fashion of Nicholas Nixon) or in a black-and-white mugshot (the strategy of *Time*). Perhaps his ultimate haunt is the grave, but even there he is not fixed. He carries his grave around with him everywhere he goes, as Dracula does his coffins. To Leo Bersani's question, "Is the rectum a grave?,"[37] I would append a second question: "Are gay men permitted any other home?" Are we allowed any other position from which to speak? Such a home is the seat of my "compulsion": like a vampire in a grave, if I should desire, if I should dare to turn or twist, it is presumed to be with neither volition nor human consciousness. In the popular imagination, the domain of the gay man is always a peculiar mixture of anal-eroticism and undeath, from gloomy gay dives in Chelsea to the rows of coffin-like cells in bathhouses.

This popular view is certainly mirrored in *Dracula*. The Count's dirt-filled coffins, from which he cannot stray, are only part of the link. Castle Dracula itself has a certain anal-retentive exoticism that smacks of home. Stoker has a sphincteral obsession throughout the novel with keys and locked doors, and he always requires a respectable and professional alibi for "going in."[38] Jonathan Harker observes upon entering Castle Dracula that the noises of the door belie its having rarely been opened to strangers. Once inside, however, he slowly realizes that he may never leave. The castle is not only retentive of Harker, but of time itself. The very furniture and draperies are "centuries old, though in excellent order" (27); like a photograph, like Dracula's body, like the infantile phantasy of the phallic mother, the furniture freeze-frames a fixed point in time past, never maturing. The Castle is even retentive of language: no "letter" may exit the castle without Dracula's censorship, indeed, without his rewriting it. Like the voice of the hysteric, the words that do escape are not Harker's own, they are not "like him."

The castle is full of dark passageways, locked rooms, and taboo areas. The description of the ruined chapel where Dracula lurks is especially suggestive of the anal-exotic:

> At the bottom there was a dark, tunnel-like passage, through which came a deathly, sickly odour, the odour of old earth newly turned. As I went through the passage the smell grew closer and heavier. At last I pulled open a heavy door which stood ajar, and found myself in an old ruined chapel, which had evidently been used as a grave-yard. (58)

A vision of the rectum as failed vagina, as dead end, as ruined chapel because it cannot fulfill the transcendent office of procreation. The chapel has become the anal orifice of castration and death, littered as it is with Dracula's fecal/phallic coffins. The castle, taken as a (w)hole, becomes the deadly sacrificial altar of Jonathan Harker's "masculinity," as he lies passive and mesmerized, desiring the fatal vampire kiss in spite of himself.

What more illustration could we require for the adage that a gay man's home is indeed his castle?

Coda

> Don't you know that I am sane and earnest now; that I am no lunatic in a mad fit, but a sane man fighting for his soul?   *Renfield* (275)

I think there is much more to be said about homophobia and AIDS hysteria under the paradigm of the vampire myth. I might have addressed issues of race, class, female sexuality, AIDS in Africa, and children who bite in public schools. I want to conclude here, however, with a more personal observation. I was reading *Dracula*, with all its macabre blood transfusions and its vampires run through with wooden stakes, when I was visited by a friend of mine, Richard, who was diagnosed with ARC about two years ago.

He has done everything in his power to maintain his health, and thus far he has succeeded. He is fortunate in that he has the resources to pay for the best medical care, and he is equally fortunate to have friends, family, and a lover who care about him. At this time, however, he was having frequent blood transfusions to counteract the anemia which is sometimes a side-effect of AZT. He was also afraid he might be going blind and might need a catheter implanted in his chest. He told me it was not so bad, he had seen them, someone in his support group had lifted his shirt to show him what it looked like.

Having spent the entire week immersed in *Dracula*, the image threw me for a minute. I have not always been able to distinguish clearly between illnesses, sexualities, and metaphors. Never before was I more aware of how a text could mediate between me and someone I love. I do not deny the fact that Richard's health is fragile. I only deny now the myths that designate us the abjected ones. To be gay and to speak is always to risk flirtation with the revenant, who inevitably rises from the grave in anticipation of our speech. But I hope within my own frame, one can distinguish my relationship with Richard from my relationship with the vampire: "Richard's medical treatment has been beneficial. He still works full-time, even overtime. He visits me, he flies around the country, he goes out at night. He and his lover, who is not seropositive, still have sex. In fact, Richard simply does not have what I was led to believe is the 'Face of AIDS.' Richard's face looks the same to me as it always has and always will. Rather charming."

Notes

1. Robert Louis Stevenson, *Dr Jekyll and Mr Hyde* (1886) (New York: Oxford University Press, 1987), 74.

2. My definition of "abject" here is drawn from Julia Kristeva's *Powers of Horror*, trans. Leon S. Roudiez (New York: Columbia University Press, 1982). Briefly, the "abject" is that which must be thrown out or expelled from the body in order to preserve the illusion of purity, identity, and order. For a discussion of abjection and AIDS, see Judith Williamson, "Every Virus Tells a Story," *Taking Liberties: AIDS and Cultural Politics*, ed. Erica Carter and Simon Watney (London: Serpent's Tail, 1989), 69–80.

3. The vampire lesbian, however, abounds explicitly in such films as *Blood and Roses, Vampyres,* and *The Hunger,* which may be related to the proliferation of "fake lesbianism" in straight male pornography. I am perhaps repeating the error of many male critics in by-passing lesbian issues in this essay. The amount of material on the female vampire, lesbian or otherwise, is mountainous and could not be contained in an essay that takes AIDS as its focus.

4. In homophobic minds, even so-called "innocent victims," such as infants and hemophiliacs, can trace their infection-lineage back only as far as a culpable gay man's sexual act.

5. Bram Stoker, *Dracula* (1897) (New York: Dell, 1978), 47. All further references appear within the essay. For a fuller discussion of this moment in the text, see Christopher Craft, " 'Kiss Me with Those Red Lips': Gender and Inversion in Bram Stoker's *Dracula*," rpt. in *Speaking of Gender*, ed. Elaine Showalter (New York and London: Routledge, 1989).

6. Laurence Rickels, *Aberrations of Mourning* (Detroit: Wayne State University Press, 1988), 318.

7. See Joseph Breuer's "Fräulein Anna O." in Breuer and Freud's *Studies on Hysteria*, (1895), in *Standard Edition*, ed. James Strachey (London: Hogarth Press, 1955), 2:21–47.

8. For a discussion of the sexual nature of Freud's friendships with Fliess and Jung, see Christine Downing, *Myths and Mysteries of Same-Sex Love* (New York: Continuum, 1989), 13–29.

9. Jeffrey Weeks, *Sexuality and Its Discontents* (London: Routledge & Kegan Paul, 1985), 155.

10. See, for example, "The Psychogenesis of a Case of Homosexuality in a Woman" (1920), *Standard Edition*, 18:147–72, in which what appears to be a perfectly healthy lesbian is accused of harboring a "masculinity complex" in defiance of her father. Freud writes, "But psycho-analysis cannot elucidate the intrinsic nature of what in conventional or in biological phraseology is termed 'masculine' or 'feminine': it simply takes over the two concepts and makes them the foundation of its work" (171). This is not one of Freud's more "iconoclastic" moments.

11. Roland Barthes, *Camera Lucida*, trans. Richard Howard (New York: The Noonday Press, 1981), 13.

12. Guy Hocquenghem, *Homosexual Desire* (London: Allison and Busby, 1978), 36.

13. Sigmund Freud, "Analysis Terminable and Interminable" (1937) *Standard Edition*, 22. Christine Downing (*Myths*, 50, 285), in discussing Freud and Dionysus, makes the curious suggestion that the sexual submissiveness of a gay man with AIDS might help to reconcile him with death.

14. Ernest Jones, *On the Nightmare* (New York: Liveright, 1951), 119.

15. Julia Kristeva, *Tales of Love*, trans. Leon S. Roudiez (New York: Columbia University Press, 1987), 124.

16. E. Ann Kaplan, "Is the Gaze Male?" rpt. in *Powers of Desire: The Politics of Sexuality*, ed. Ann Snitow, Christine Stansell, and Sharon Thompson (New York: Monthly Review Press, 1983), 309–27.

17. Paul Barber, *Vampires, Burial, and Death* (New Haven: Yale University Press, 1988), 182.

18. Sigmund Freud, *Leonardo da Vinci and a Memory of His Childhood* (1910), *Standard Edition*, 11: 117–18.

19. I am being reductive here and relying primarily on Laura Mulvey's "Visual Pleasure and Narrative Cinema," *Screen* 16, no. 3 (1975): 8–18. This basic model has

recently been revised and considerably complicated, not the least by Laura Mulvey herself.

20. Rickels, *Aberrations*, 323.

21. Barthes, *Camera Lucida*, 117.

22. Maxim 26, quoted in Kristeva, *Tales of Love*, 365; ironically, this line introduces her discussion of Georges Bataille's highly erotic novel, *My Mother*.

23. Osvald, in the final scene of *Ghosts* (New York: Signet, 1970). He has inherited an incurable illness and has asked his mother to assist him in committing suicide. (Trans. Rolf Fjelde.)

24. Douglas Crimp, "How to Have Promiscuity in an Epidemic," *AIDS: Cultural Analysis, Cultural Activism*, ed. Douglas Crimp (Cambridge: MIT Press, 1988), 240.

25. Randy Shilts, *And The Band Played On* (New York: St. Martin's Press, 1987), 41. All further references appear within the essay.

26. Epidemiologists do not agree on whether HIV originated in Africa. For an antidote to Shilts's racism, see Simon Watney on Africa as an ideological rather than geographical location, " 'knowable' in terms of a long racist legacy of colonial connotations of supposed depravity, dirt and disease." Carter and Watney, *Taking Liberties*, 37.

27. Crimp, "How to Have Promiscuity," 245.

28. Joseph Interrante, "To Have Without Holding: Memories of Life With a Person with AIDS," *Radical America* 20, no. 6 (1987): 57.

29. But who's counting? Precisely the question in statistics on gay fatherhood, which vary considerably. My estimate is conservative. See Frederick Bozett, "Gay Fathers: A Review of the Literature," *Journal of Homosexuality*, 18, nos. 1/2 (1989): 138.

30. Kristeva, *Powers of Horror*, 49.

31. The Winter 1989 edition of *AIDS Quarterly*. Ironically, this series is one of the best of its kind.

32. Simon Watney, *Policing Desire: Pornography, AIDS, and the Media* (Minneapolis: University of Minnesota Press, 1987), 23. See also 16 and 48.

33. Watney, *Policing Desire*, 26.

34. Watney, *Policing Desire*, 114.

35. Dennis Altman, *AIDS in the Mind of America* (New York: Anchor Press, 1986), 63.

36. Barber, *Vampires*, 181.

37. Leo Bersani, "Is the Rectum a Grave?" *AIDS: Cultural Analysis, Cultural Activism*, ed. Crimp, 197.

38. On inversion, locks, and keys in fin-de-siècle England, see Wayne Koestenbaum on "unlocking Symonds," *Double Talk: The Erotics of Male Literary Collaboration* (New York and London: Routledge, 1989), 43–67.

15

Shocking Pink Praxis: Race and Gender on the ACT UP Frontlines

Catherine Saalfield and Ray Navarro

A strategy suits a situation; a strategy is not a theory.
Gayatri Spivak[1]

A park in Montreal in June could have been the place for much celebration, colorful floats, dancing, and a cacophony of Caribbean drum beats. In a way, it was, except for the raindrops drowning out the music, forcing people to cluster under makeshift umbrellas. The Caribana parade route turned off of Rue Henri Julien as Montreal's black community thrived in a glorious cultural spectacle. The two of us, both AIDS activists and queer artists, traced our own path, reluctantly in the opposite direction, towards the side door of the Notre Dame Hospital on the street they had left behind. Having protested the cold, scientific distance of the Fifth International AIDS Conference in Montreal, we were en route to visit our friend, recently struck by PCP (pneumocystis) pneumonia. Our painful separation from the singing crowds was reinforced as we entered the doors of the hospital, where the music from the parade could no longer be heard. This is the reality of AIDS activism, where our militant politics usher us into the hospitals and the clinics themselves. Strangers in a strange land: foreigners to the streets of Quebec, "innocents" to the global AIDS crisis. But not for long. For us, street parades soon become street demonstrations, sometimes become street riots.

A week later and now we're apart, keeping the New York-Montreal phone lines scrambling. "It's not raining in the city . . . like it was there. . . . I'm hoping the weather keeps up for the weekend. . . . Wish you two could be here for it. . . ." The twentieth Lesbian and Gay Pride

Parade is happening in New York City, but there never has been one in Montreal. For a new Person With AIDS (PWA), his lover, and their friend, the phone becomes a veritable lifeline connecting us with each other and with our cultures, those which have affirmed us, prepared us, sustained us, moved us from being "innocent" to being armed. If you are hated in the U.S. as Mexican-Americans, you may be loathed in Quebec for not being able to speak French. Imagining the lesbians and black drag queens who fought in the streets for equality during the sixties, we're commemorating the Stonewall Riots twenty years later (and we weren't even in kindergarten yet).

But we're still afraid.

"During the demonstration they drove into people! We took Seventh Avenue! They can't get away with this. . . ."[2] We know by now that PCP pneumonia is like the drivers of those cars: fast, silent, stupid. The same homophobic institutions that did allow them to get away with striking lesbian and gay bystanders on the street, that did look the other way and miss the assaults, have let the AIDS epidemic become the AIDS crisis. An epidemic does not have to become a global disaster of governmental neglect and hypocrisy. Viruses do not discriminate, people in power do and as they do, they willfully transform a medical emergency into a social and political crisis.

Counter-Media, Counter-Memory

"ACT UP, Fight Back, Fight AIDS!" We've been chanting this for over three years now, but simply shouting in the streets won't end the AIDS crisis. We are also community educators, caretakers, videomakers, writers. A year ago, we were asked to write an article about ACT UP (the AIDS Coalition To Unleash Power)—the direct action AIDS activist group with which we are both involved.[3] We saw the invitation as an opportunity to perform an intervention (theoretical and political), to grapple with concepts such as erotic "safe" sex (at a time when sex is supposed to be dangerous and avoided), political theory and practice, civil disobedience for the street activist, bar etiquette, and motorcycle jackets.

The article finally appeared in *Downtown* magazine, a basically straight, artsy, clubsy, punko-hip type of rag which usually features some choice investigative reporting and entertaining chatter. A forerunner to this present essay, "Shocking Pink Politics: Race and Gender on the ACT UP Frontlines," appeared in a regular column for guest activ-

FROM LEFT FIELD

WE
DIE
—
THEY
DO
NOTHING!

WE
DIE
—
THEY
DO
NOTHING!

WE
DIE

Shocking Pink Politics:
Race And Gender On The ACT UP Frontlines

Figure 1.

ists of various kinds, called "From Left Field." Two photographs, made by a fellow ACT UP member, Lola Flash, accompanied our words. Lola's work involves reverse color, or negative images, and these two particular photos depicted activists and fighters: people acting on necessity, people fighting for their lives (fig. 1). Blacks appear as white, whites come out black, and words read as they always do, a subtle layering of representation. What we couldn't have anticipated at that time was that our "shocking" piece would have appeared right next to a stupid and ugly image of a person with AIDS (by the wannabe Modernist photographer Nicholas Nixon).[4]

The irony of this juxtaposition was hard to swallow, considering that ACT UP had articulated criticisms of Nixon's photographs, going so far as to "zap," with a small but powerful demonstration, the Museum of Modern Art where they were being shown.[5] Friends of ours showed up in the museum's galleries wearing photographs of PWAs—their own family and friends—underscoring the insensitive anonymity imposed by the vampiric gaze of Nixon's camera. Nixon's flashy portfolio, as it appeared in *Downtown*, would have subsumed our commentary were it not for the presence of Flash's graphic reversal of the decontextualized, objectified "AIDS victim." PWAs are not victims. PWAs are only patients when they are hospitalized. And in Flash's photographs, AIDS activists—HIV+ or not—are presented as AIDS warriors.

The person with the photographic apparatus has a choice of who and how to image the body of a person living with AIDS. Pictures of advanced stages of AIDS usually have a sensationalized quality, one that exaggerates kaposi sarcoma lesions at the cost of a person's dignity and vitality. Pictures of HIV+ people, their lovers, friends, and families, descending on the Food and Drug Administration—in protest of blatant neglect—read quite differently. On October 11, 1988, ACT UP joined with ACT NOW (AIDS Coalition to Network Organize Win, a nationwide coalition of AIDS activists)—to "Seize Control" of this heartless bureaucracy. Flash is one of the people who confronted the FDA, protesting there *and* picturing it. In her shooting, the aim is protest. Not only does she carry a camera, but she also puts her body on the line. What comes out is neither a documentary nor an art photograph, but instead a concrete image of that contentious space between the two. Provocatively, the pictured protestor becomes at once unrecognizable and familiar.

Lola Flash's work is a critical element of any thorough understanding of ACT UP aesthetics, since the body of her photographs as a whole contains key signifiers of the organization's relationship to sexuality, race, gender, and ethnicity. At this point, we will concentrate on two particular groupings of her photographs which employ color reversal. In the first, Flash produced a series of black and white pictures which posit themselves within a tradition of photojournalism-documentary. Since most ACT UP demonstrations are widely publicized and attract large numbers of press people, both in TV and print journalism, ACT UP members now expect to see images of themselves in what are the city's otherwise nebulous and silent headlines. However, by implementing the strategy of negative printing even in her black and white photographs, Flash produces an alienation effect, and thereby subverts classic codes of authenticity and objectivity in the "news photo."[6] At first Flash's viewers are placed in a position of aesthetic appreciation; the tones are striking, unfamiliar, and the compositions are asymmetrical, disruptive. But then the viewer looks again and, in that double take, is placed at a critical distance from which the action taking place within the photograph finally can be viewed. Are these actors represented in the photograph located in a recognizable time or space which is the theater of protest?

Daily papers rely on truncated photo captions to anchor the meaning of what they present, underwriting the dominant and repressive perspectives of corporate media. For example, one *New York Times* captions reads, "After marching without a permit yesterday from Greenwich Village to Central Park, more than 1500 people gathered for a rally to mark the 20th anniversary of New York's modern gay and lesbian rights movement" (*NYT*, June 25, 1989). What this statement conceals is that Saturday's march uptown cannot be assimilated into business as usual. ACT UP *didn't have a permit* and 2000 people walked from Sheridan Square to 83rd Street. *And activists were in the middle of Sixth Avenue blocking traffic the entire time.* For four hours New York City was thrown off course, literally. Furthermore, the *New York Times* coverage of the demonstration attempts to represent a cohesive queer rights movement which celebrates itself indifferently by foregrounding only ACT UP members in the photo accompanying the above caption. Both photo and caption ignore the very divisions and disagreements within the gay and lesbian community that led to this action in the first place. This "event" was more than a parade, it was a protest march organized partly in opposition to the kiss-ass tactics of the Lesbian and Gay Heritage of Pride civic group which earlier that week happily accepted a token proclamation from then-mayor of New York, Ed Koch.[7]

More evidence of the nationwide media attack upon progressive AIDS activists and the false representation of the movement screams across the headlines everyday. The *San Francisco Chronicle* writes, "Police carried an uncooperative demonstrator out of the KRON lobby" (*SFC*, December 14, 1988). Flanked by four cops in full riot gear, a single unidentified AIDS activist is being hauled out of a building. Struggle? Not evident in this photo. However, what we do see is someone performing civil disobedience, and when people don't want to walk, they get dragged. *And what was he demonstrating about anyway?*

A photograph is a message without a code, open to interpretation until it is captured or captioned.[8] For AIDS activists, the potentially dangerous effect of seeing ourselves on the cover of Newsday can be reminiscent of seeing ourselves at a demo. Have we succeeded in garnering our fifteen minutes of fame? Or are these images the final proof that we really are the "AIDS Victims," "Drug Addicts," "Homosexuals," "Gay AIDS Carriers," they claim we are? Mainstream control over the field of news images threatens to extinguish the power of our protest. Editorializations—be they in human interest stories or front page trumpets—generally attempt to erase the immediate effect of ACT UP's presence and the history of our actions, imposing "official memory" upon political activists.

However, tee-shirt graphics, hilarious signage, and visual puns on posters, often puncture even the cruelest oversimplification in the layout of a mainstream newspaper. ACT UP is a media organization and these images can themselves feed the protest. And it is with these self-determined signals that activists also recognize themselves in Flash's work. But to different ends. According to Flash, she began photographing ACT UP precisely because of her attraction to these designs. She says, "The graphics that Gran Fury [an art collective in ACT UP] and others make are really strong," adding, with deceptively simple candor, "But I have no problem changing the colors they so appropriately chose." (We will return to this idea later). Her work functions as counter-media, most importantly within the movement itself, serving indeed to "make strange" the experience of seeing oneself imaged in the act of protest. Activists are made to look twice at slogans which are already deeply seated in downtown queer fashions and New York City's landscape, tight shirts on taut bodies and stickers in every corner phone booth.

Regardless of this "other" opportunity, ACT UP often fails to resist the tendency to allow dominant media representations of struggle to become everyone's memory. Nevertheless, a Flash photo of a demo can not be assimilated on those terms. "After I ran out of the Ciba-chrome paper that I usually used to print my slides [or "positives"] on, I had images I still wanted to print, so I used some negative paper [C-Print paper used to print negatives on] and the colors came out wrong, or backwards. I understood that this new possibility makes people see more the way I do," recalls Flash. Speaking specifically of the FDA series, she says, "I lose detail in some things, usually facial details drop out. Except, people who have dreads or strong ethnic features are intensified." Resisting dominant memory, this work formulates a counter-memory which has less to do with any fixed idea of identity and more to do with revealing the mechanisms which enact a multiplicity of identifications. After seeing her depiction of "Seize Control of the FDA," one knows that Rockville will never look like *that* again. And AIDS activists don't look like those "AIDS Victims" on the cover of the *Washington Post*. Instead, Flash's depiction of the FDA corresponds with ACT UP's impact upon it.

Flash's photographs record a counter-memory of the FDA action. This counter-memory can be established as a form of oppositional practice (oppositional understood as different from the dominant order, and practice as the implementation of a project by the group), but not merely as a political practice. Here matters of sexual and transsexual power assert themselves. As the psychedelic photographer and her comrades confront the nebulous institution of the FDA, the culture of pleasure and the politics of desire are always threatening to explode the stability of "official" history or the police record. If the formation of counter-memory were the formation of merely an oppositional category it would fall neatly into the binary logic of history (even if it were the opposite of "History" itself). Instead Flash's counter-memory of activism establishes itself between the pages of official record. That is why activists do not escape the dualism us/them by superficially asserting, "Our photographs are better than yours."

What then is the "counter-memory" invoked by photographs such as Flash's? And to what end is it invoked? An internal critique of racism and sexism within ACT UP itself is embodied in the material subversion of race identification (black is white and vice-versa) in Flash's pictures. Importantly, this subversion is not a "loss" of identity, but an assumption of it within a context of visual signifiers that play with color. At PS 122, a downtown performance and art space, Flash exhibited another series, 13 staged images of revolutionary fantasies. Transformed in brilliant, arresting color, all the models are women and people of color toting red (read blue) squirt machine guns, sporting ACT UP and military paraphernalia (pants, hats, buttons, boots) (figs. 2, 3). These folks are prepared to "up the ante" and are strategically placed in front of various symbols of institutionalized benign neglect (i.e. *The New York Times* sidewalk rack, the NY Telephone Company, the U.S. Post Office). Says Flash, "Some people think the guns are too strong, too violent. But I think the people in the pictures are protective, not violent. They're holding post; not shooting, but guarding. They will shoot only when provoked." So, what has provoked these images of violence?

Although the stickers plastered around in the background of this series are ACT UP products, the colors are always inverted. "You won't find any pink triangles in my photos," reminds Flash, confident in her association of pink with light/white skin. Although whites may not immediately make this association, the identity of a lesbian or gay person of color comes into crisis when the symbol earmarked for the queer liberation struggle is an oppressively iconic "flesh tone." Furthermore, the black triangle, not the pink, was used to designate

Figure 2.

lesbians (as vagrants or anti-socials) in Nazi Germany; the pink triangle misrepresents not only people of color but also women.

Current use of the symbolic pink triangle has been criticized by some historians and activists alike for its imprecise reference to the tragic legacy of victimization during the Holocaust. Stuart Marshall's work, for example, investigates what might be, on a certain level, the histori-cal consequences of resurrecting this stigmatizing "brand" as a sign of resistance.[9] In Marshall's noteworthy discussion, the precarious history

Figure 3.

of homosexuals in pre-Nazi Germany is fastidiously documented. The interrelationships between the repression of reproductive rights during the Weimar years and its relation to the eventual classification of homosexuality are all keenly put forth. Yet, for Marshall, the retrieval for present-day homosexuals of this history yields particularly irresponsible and ahistorical results; he goes so far as to assert that the decontextualized use of the pink triangle as a sign of queer power has oppressive or dangerous effects. What Marshall fails to account for in his analysis of ACT UP's inscription of "Silence=Death" beneath the inverted triangle is any notion of style or fashion or, dare we say, trend. Although the logo reissued in the contemporary frame of the AIDS crisis does not "accurately" refer to the experience of homosexual men in Nazi Germany, it won't be the first time that a social or political movement has rallied around a slippery identification, or a reactivated, *re*contextualized historical event.

According to Marshall, queer power is diluted by engaging with a historical sign such as the pink triangle. But, the identity of a late twentieth-century faggot in the U.S. does not in most ways resemble the victimized European homosexual of World War II. Since the development of a gay male aesthetic influence on fashion and design in late capitalist societies cannot be overstated or ignored, this image/word conglomerate functions most precisely as logo, as aesthetic slogan. Nor can the complex crossovers of racial—and thereby cultural—hybrids be overlooked, as in, for example the progression of gay (black) disco music in its relationship to the fashion and music industries. It may be here, at the superficial and rather morbid level, that the "trend" of AIDS activism—the purchase of alternative lifestyles under a bloodthirsty system—has been and will continue to be incorporated under commercialism insofar as taste is defined by the market. Gay men and lesbians are part of a market. The question is not whether this crossover (and cross-generational trade) is right or wrong, but rather, how is it working, and toward what end?

Numbers Numbers Numbers Lives Lives Lives

The representational issues in Flash's photographs lead us into a specific discussion of race and gender in the constitution of late twentieth-century "dyke and fag" radical politics specifically committed to ending the AIDS crisis. In ACT UP, an organization that was originally dominated by white gay male sensibilities, women and people of color have created coalitions and their own style of participation in order to negotiate their own agendas. In a self-representational struggle, not unrelated to Flash's aesthetic strategies, this political organizing has led to a concrete analysis of a contradictory situation. As Risa Denenberg—an ACT UP member of the Women's Caucus and columnist for *Outweek* magazine—observes, "And no, we [lesbians] don't want to be left out of anything. But not because we're prone to hysteria or want to be victims. Without our woman-centered perspective, women's needs will never make it to the agenda. This crisis may be the one that will provoke a deeper desire in all of us to change the conditions we are living under. Lesbians want to be in on it, to shape its form so we can get something out of it too."[10]

We recognize that every death related to HIV/AIDS complications is an act of racist, sexist, and homophobic violence. Therefore, the foundation of ACT UP was built on direct action to "bug the hell" out of the government and federal service agencies, to improve conditions for PWAs, and to change the mainstream media's patronizing and ignorant attitude towards the AIDS crisis. Our goals: drugs into bodies; money for health care and treatments; testing of drugs not people. However, as individual members of ACT UP learned more and more about the government's process of approval for experimental drugs, this original agenda proved to be too nearsighted.

The specific experience of discrimination which gay men in the 1980s encountered as a result of AIDS is similar to a number of historical instances of discrimination based on race and gender in relation to disease and science. For example, over the years, poor women and women of color in particular have been subject to forced pregnancy and/or sterilization in this country. Birth control methods and funding for abortion have been intentionally kept from women who desperately need accurate and complete information to make their own choices. Likewise, black men infected with syphilis in 1932 were subject to inhumane scientific monitoring and were denied available medical treatment during the later stages of the disease.[11]

The "drugs into bodies" agenda needed to be broadened to include the specific manner in which sexism and racism, as well as homophobia, have been used to perpetuate the AIDS crisis. ACT UP—heretofore, a single issue, "non-partisan," activist group—would find itself embracing a characteristically leftist slogan: "Health Care is a Right." In preparation for the FDA protest, ACT UP members reviewed the disproportionate representation of women and people of color in government-sanctioned clinical drug trials. The design of the protocols themselves illustrated a disregard for human life. Their clinical trials entailed the use of placebos, the exclusion of women between the ages of 25 and 45, and the construction of all-white protocols. Poor people and people of color could not meet the rigid criteria (criteria which also excluded anyone located too far from a local hospital or test site, anyone without a primary physician, and anyone who was an IV drug user or a prisoner).

By analyzing the crisis as it affects intravenous drug users (IVDUs), we can see more correlates of historical oppression between these individuals and the queer community. First of all, 60% of the minimally estimated 200,000 IVDUs are infected with HIV; 60% of the minimally estimated 200,000 PWAs are IVDUs. Blacks and Latinos account for 70% of PWAs in NYC, 85% of the women with AIDS, and more than 90% of the children. But where the numbers seem static, the government's dismissal of entire groups of people remains quite palpable. For example, New York City has not opened a new drug treatment slot, let alone a new drug program, since 1972. The city stopped running drug addiction treatment programs during the mid-1970s fiscal crisis, leaving the burden of responsibility to the state, which has not assumed a critical response. Only 42,000 of New York City's 550,000 drug users can be accommodated in all of the State's public and private drug treatments programs combined. And the average wait to get into a program is ten months, although the State Division of Substance Abuse Services estimates that 80,000 IVDUs would seek drug treatment if it were available.

In addition, approximately 10,000 homeless people living in Manhattan have AIDS, according to the Human Resources Administration's Division of AIDS Services.[12] The number of AIDS cases and HIV infections due to IV drug use is rising faster than the number of cases and infections due to any other transmission route. The city health department admits that AIDS deaths among IV drug users may be underreported by as much as 130 percent. AIDS is the leading cause of death among women aged 25–34 and men 30–59. One out of every 8 New Yorkers with AIDS is a woman; and 7 out of every 8 women with AIDS is a woman of color. One in every 79 women giving birth in New York City is infected with HIV, according to recent seroprevalence data. And city-funded ad campaigns continue to suggest that women bear sole responsibility for safer sex.

From the beginning the CDC refused IVDUs any "luxury" of cofactors. Ignoring poverty, racism, and poor nutrition, the CDC determines "risk" only in terms of the most discriminated against mode of transmission: the sharing of HIV-infected needles. The type of compensation that drugs offer in the face of a lack of options perpetuates an underground community which for many is seen as the only escape from the harsh conditions of inner-city poverty. The post-colonial legacy of slavery and its tradition of economic deprivation and servitude contribute to the perpetuation of addiction in black and Latino communities in the U.S. The "war on drugs" with its dangerous fabrications of Columbian drug smugglers and black addicts must be recognized as an absolute attack on people of color (and consequently upon people with AIDS), since that "war" imposes the responsibility for addiction upon historically oppressed people through false notions of individual agency. The drug war and the AIDS crisis are spurred on by government, state, and institutional investments in personal, political, and financial profit. So, in fact, the importance of fighting AIDS under the conditions of the "drug war" is disavowed by our "leaders" (like NYC Health Commissioner Woodrow Meyers) as they separate and hierarchize the inseparable crises.[13]

Like other "memory losses" or elisions, epidemics, genocide, and crises as they affect women and people of color are never acknowledged as such within the dominant, self-centered culture which defines itself through the very exclusion of these communities. The extermination of Native Americans by smallpox is never cited in "American History" books as a disaster perpetuated by racism and greed. As Denenberg says in her *Outweek* article "Lesbian AIDS Activists: What Are We Doing?," "Women comprise the majority of mental health patients who are institutionalized for depression. But it's not named an epidemic."[14] Responding to this kind of critique, and examining their own cultures' relationships to HIV disease, individual gay men of color stepped apart from the body of ACT UP in late 1987. They found themselves combatting dominant perceptions within ACT UP that communities of color were more sexist than whites and were innately more susceptible to drug addiction. These perceptions flew in the face of a tradition in communities of color of organizing around the struggle for health care. Similarly, the feminist health care movement in the seventies left a critical legacy for progressive health activists in the eighties. So, like the Majority Actions Committee, women had organized themselves apart from the male body of ACT UP into a Women's Caucus.

However, the collective experiences of women and people of color doing community organizing within feminist struggles and civil rights campaigns contain memories of alienation, ostracization, and closeting of lesbian and gay identities. Because of the price queers pay for doing political work which demands the privileging of race, gender, or class over sexual preference, we are now at great pains to make ACT UP work for us. Why? Because the straight left incorporates lesbians and gays as bohemians while passively enforcing their daily invisibility. Because the Chicano liberation movement has erupted around debates concerning gender without recognizing the validity of same-sex relationships. And because the women's movement refused to acknowledge that abortion is about sexual freedom (non-procreative sex for everyone) and that "choice" includes the preference for lesbian (and gay) sex.

For all of these reasons the Women's Caucus of ACT UP and the Majority Actions Committee joined forces to prepare for the October 1988 action "Seize Control of the FDA." The possibility of exploring common experiences of discrimination in access to AIDS treatment allowed "WIC/MAC" (Women's Caucus/Majority Actions Committee) to form. At that time WIC/MAC was specifically interested in exposing the government's failure to include women and people of color in clinical trials for AIDS treatments. Some members produced a concise and informative "FACTS/REALITY" leaflet which outlined our specific issues, including AIDS-related, but unnecessarily misdiagnosed, deaths of women and IVDUs. We also pointed out the heinous refusal on the part of prison authorities to give prisoners access to treatment and information about experimental drugs.

Direct action at the Food and Drug Administration (fig. 4). "We Die They Do Nothing." Clear day, 7:30 a.m. Scoping for a vulnerable entrance to the building. Affinity groups caucusing behind the media table in the parking lot. "We Die They Say Nothing." Hundreds of AIDS activists from across the nation handing leaflets to employees explaining ACT UP's presence and informing them about their employers' mishandling of the AIDS crisis. Boys in mini-skirts, girls with drums. Changing FDA policy. Sex and (non)violence.

"Seize Control" doesn't only mean lay siege to a building. More than an imperative which functions as a rousing chant for energetic activists, the announcement presupposes a sustained intervention into the bio-medical discourse on AIDS. There's no contradiction between jeering at their doors and meeting with Anthony Faucci (director of research at the National Institute of Infectious and Allergic Disease— NIIAD) who eventually solicited ACT UP's critical position and research when he went to develop new AIDS policies. Indeed, ACT UP has improved the system of approval for new treatments (e.g.,

Figure 4.

aerosolized pentamadine, ancyclovir) by intervening in their otherwise murderously slow release. The significance of community-based research at places such as the Community Research Initiative (CRI) and Project Inform parallels this intervention.[15] When PWAs enroll in experimental drug trials being held by community physicians, they are not embracing some apolitical, or objective, option. Rather, they are all participating in the crucial decentralization of data, taking part in a community initiative that relies on them. Furthermore, PWAs are physically invested in this collaboration.

And PWAs do not only rely on doctors for this investment. In bedrooms and streets, activists have taken control of the treatment of their bodies. The juice of "safer sex" has been in seizing control of the "sex" in sexuality. And so, women must negotiate the stifling and discouraging signals we receive from an anti-erotic, anti-woman society. Not surprisingly, then, too little safer sex education has been provided for lesbians, and for other women as well. Moreover, the political challenge of "safer sex" runs deeper than the prevention of HIV transmission into various unexamined, untreated, and unknown areas of lesbian health. Thus, as Audre Lorde has written about her breast cancer and the wrenching, related decisions she had to grapple with, "Every woman has a militant responsibility to involve herself actively with her own health. We owe ourselves the protection of all their information we can acquire . . . and we owe ourselves this information *before* we may have reason to use it."[16]

But even more to the point in this case, lesbian sex panic (timidity, repression, and "feminine manners") existed long before AIDS (and regardless of some STDs), so dental dams (latex squares available at the dentist's office and used to keep cunt juice out of your mouth) are in fact a very minute part of "safe sex" for lesbians. Just saying "Use dental dams" doesn't begin to help women initiate or facilitate sex and orgasms with other women, or with men. Women have to be supported in their efforts to make sex work for them, to have it their way without alienation or threat of violence. And to have it a lot. How to seize control . . .?

Safer sex advice for gay men also falls short at the point of saying, "Don't fist." Condom use is one aspect of a safer sex campaign, but where are the limits drawn? Declaring certain sex acts wrong, such as fisting, because of their "high risk" implications is to strangle the possibilities of exploration under the new conditions in which eroticism will continue. The voice that declares fisting "better off gone" actually stifles the body politic of the AIDS movement.

AIDS activists must encourage responsibility in sexual relations while perpetually testing the limits on that pleasure. Is it a "safe" super-ego that oversees the potential power the movement unleashes when we critique the current laws binding bodies? Just what does *safe* "dangerous sex" look like? For example, how does one employ latex as a preventative measure for HIV transmission during some of the more precarious sexual acts? And just what dangers must be encountered in order to secure this territory?[17]

At the FDA demonstration, WIC/MAC members encountered tendencies within the affinity group itself which challenged its internal agenda. There could be no consensus among us as to the meaning of "nonviolence" during a demonstration. The specific intent of the action was to critique the FDA's murderously bureaucratic policies of review for experimental AIDS treatments and make them less discriminatory by streamlining them. But in the field, the group was forced to confront ethical questions about the role of the cops (are they repressive agents of the State or just plain folks?) and tactical issues ("How far should we go to enter a building surrounded by a wall of billy-clubs?").

ACT UP members may have strong principles but the cops have nightsticks, handcuffs, and guns. Direct action implies this type of limit as well. Activists must be aware of the limits of both the safer sex and direct action guidelines. The body that lies down in a street gets carried away to a jail. And some of the bodies are already fighting HIV infection. These bodies do not benefit from police brutality in the streets. So, to what ends can (or should) they go to put their bodies literally up against those in the "wall of blue"? This very question has produced a controversy over ACT UP's direct action procedure, over what can "reasonably" be considered nonviolence, and over what limits must be embraced in order, most constructively, to channel collective rage. We aren't satisfied to resurrect the old left trope about where the violence really lies: with the Pentagon, the CIA, or the capitalists. Activists can and do empower themselves by setting their own agenda and not only by reacting to the status the police allot them. In other words, we must understand how we play into the hands of the cops when we assume the responsibility of self-criticism and self-control.

Thus, "Seize Control of the FDA" also means challenge and refuse police brutality. Don't take responsibility for their violence or ignorance. ACT UP's Direct Action Guidelines say, "We cannot guarantee the safety of participants at our demonstrations." True. It continues, "We try to protect each other at demonstrations by setting up a support and advocacy structure that can react quickly if problems should arise or if arrests occur. We recommend that all people considering civil disobedience go to a direct action training and that they join an affinity group." Definitely. However, as the guidelines go on, they kind of go off. They say, "At our actions, demonstrators act according to the love and caring we have built for each other. Individual or group actions that endanger the physical well-being of other demonstrators should not be done. Generally, actions that might endanger the safety of others at the demonstration include . . . actions that cause panic such as running and throwing rocks." This last section of the guidelines can place blame and responsibility in the wrong hands. Activists are not the only ones capable of escalating violence. As Malcolm X says, "I myself would go for nonviolence if it was consistent, if everybody was going to be nonviolent all the time. I'd say, okay, let's get with it, we'll all be nonviolent. But I don't go along with any kind of nonviolence unless everybody's going to be nonviolent. If they make the Ku Klux Klan nonviolent, I'll be nonviolent."[18] As is true in the original context, in AIDS activism, Malcolm's "everybody" includes the police. If a protestor gets hit or hurt by a cop, it's the cop's fault. And if people must run from cops at a demonstration, all should be sure to note what they are running from. Basically, if cops are made to be nonviolent, activists won't have to run and the latter part of ACT UP's nonviolent guidelines suddenly makes sense.

Homo-Promo: Spreading the Word, Not the Virus

By the March 28, 1989, Target City Hall action, when ACT UP and other AIDS activists descended on City Hall, WIC/MAC had rearranged itself into two affinity groups: La Cocina and Bored of Ed. Notably, the FDA action had not only produced advances within the bio-medical industry, but also implemented a dose of expediency in the bureaucratic drug approval process. The FDA action advanced ACT UP's own agenda and forced the group to engage with the much broader, and more specific, social aspects of the crisis. Furthermore, the demonstration put ACT UP in the spotlight of the media stage. The group was consistently and thoroughly sensationalized as spectacle (politics) by the press. And at least one major ideological shift within ACT UP had taken place: women and people of color were to be considered in every oppositional formulation from then on.

At City Hall—a *local*, not federal, target—the demands of the group at large had compounded and shifted to include a stinging critique of then-mayor Ed Koch's failure to address adequately, among other things, the concerns of homeless PWAs in NYC, the collapsing city hospital system, NYC's lack of services for women with AIDS, and more. This new, up-dated perspective resulted from a number of direct interventions within ACT UP, perhaps most significantly from the Women and AIDS Teach-In.

Blasting the invisibility of lesbians and other women from the myopic vision of the discourse surrounding AIDS, the Women's Caucus of ACT UP (21 women at the time) organized two 6-hour long evenings of in-reach: prepared talks packed with statistics and analysis, conversation, and food. At the same time, these women collectively produced a handbook to accompany the presentation because so much information was being gathered and so few outlets existed for its circulation. The handbook opens with two epigrams. Part of Muriel Rukeyser's poem entitled "Käthe Kollwitz" reads, "What would happen if one women told the truth about her life? The world would split open."[19] The women of ACT UP are trying to wedge open the chink in that world. We are trying to crack open the world in which women live and allow themselves the space to change what doesn't work. Audre Lorde authored the second epigraph, from "A Litany for Survival": "And when we speak we are afraid/ that our words will not be heard/ nor welcomed/ but when we are silent/ we are still afraid./ So it is better to speak/ remembering/ we were never meant to survive."[20] Anyone's survival, given the current system of health care in the U.S., is a privilege. But as lesbians and gay men in particular, if we have learned anything from the AIDS crisis, it is to speak out for our own survival, and that silence equals death.

Since the teach-in had been advertised only for the at-large membership of ACT UP, the Women's Caucus wanted to spread their newly compiled information and analyses to people nationwide through the handbook.[21] Making the facts apropos to social change, the primary objective of the handbook was to contextualize the basis for developing actions and demands. For example, both the teach-in and the handbook included such groundwork as lessons from the Feminist Health Care movement: "Don't trust the government. Only negotiate from a position of power. Build viable coalitions which will give you strength when you're down. Take care of yourselves—we're in this for the long haul. Keep your ear to the ground and study the opposition—stop them before they stop you."[22]

The teach-in strategy, ever since its implementation during ACT

UP's preparations for the FDA demo, consistently proves to be an effective means toward self-empowerment. The City Hall demo teach-ins (consisting of the City Issues teach-in, the Women and AIDS teach-in, and the Holistic and Alternative AIDS Treatments teach-in) exposed the city AIDS care apparatus to examination and critique by diverse and politically divergent think tanks within ACT UP itself. These think-tanks were not politburos or steering committees. Rather, the function of the "teachers" was to expand ACT UP's focus by including the differing agendas of people who aren't gay-identified, white, male, or middle class, but are, in vast numbers, living with AIDS in NYC. The teach-ins covered housing and homelessness by including a vital analysis of the city's fiscal policy, while segments on adolescents made painfully clear the coercion and fear which surround the daily lives of lesbian and gay teens.

The teach-ins were expanded by other groups fighting AIDS who came to address ACT UP during regular Monday night meetings. ADAPT (Association for Drug Abuse Prevention and Treatment[23]) sent three representatives to present information on substance abuse, the specifics of street outreach to IVDUs and the barriers facing drug users to cleaning their needles and/or not sharing them. Representatives from Hospital Workers Union 1199 came to one meeting seeking support for their own picket lines and encouraging ACT UP members to move forward with them by recognizing that their push for higher wages and more staff hours were inextricable from demands for better AIDS care. "Health care is a right!" acquired more substance as the demo day drew nearer, and the slogan ultimately and successfully linked ACT UP's own history with numerous concurrent health care struggles going on in communities of color, among nurses, in the reproductive rights movement, and by protestors of Medicaid cuts which, among other things, seek to limit recipients' paid doctor visits.

ACT UP's overall outreach efforts were permeated by promotional strategies for what would be the biggest ACT UP demonstration to date in New York City. Yes, *promotion*—"homo-promo" to be more exact. Embracing the campy strategies of the city's most popular night club spots, crafty members fashioned "invitations" on small palm cards: date, time, place (but no dress code). The Target City Hall announcements came in another form as well: stickers to be plastered around the boroughs like instant graffiti. The less spontaneous, better organized actions such as "Target City Hall" and "Seize Control of the FDA" offer ACT UP room to hype.

Our hype, however, is never unqualified, but rather is defined in a vocabulary which speaks directly to the community and clearly asserts our demands. For example, one poster campaign (whose torn remnants are still peeling off walls around town) located 25 reasons to march on City Hall for better city-wide health care:

> "2: 5,000 People with AIDS deserve a better place to live than the sidewalk you're standing on."
>
> "3: Here's another building the city says it doesn't have for homeless people with AIDS."
>
> "5: Since the city cut AIDS education, more kids get to leave school early."

Also, ACT UP designed catchy posters for subway cars which wouldn't immediately be recognized as fake and thus taken down. A foolish looking Ed Koch sends a comatose glance toward the straphanger while asking, "10,000 New York City AIDS Deaths. How'm I Doin'?"

Although these bits of demonstration paraphernalia seem to appear from nowhere—anonymous artistic members putting down on paper what they may have quipped during a Monday night meeting—the group does need money and budgeting skills to sustain the flood of imagery produced for themselves and the city at large. The money from fundraising campaigns—direct mailings, art auctions, and underground club benefits—is usually earmarked for the bail fund or the office rent, but some capital secured during the outreach process for City Hall bought advertising space in local papers: *The Village Voice, El Diario, The Amsterdam News.* In U.S. society, that kind of conspicuous consumption *is* power. The print ad pictured a jovial Koch in front of a field of tombstones and read, "What does Koch plan to do about AIDS? Invest in marble and granite." ACT UP's Media Committee was surprised by the press' overwhelmingly positive response to these images and ecstatic that they clearly wanted Ed out as well. Notably, ACT UP didn't advertise in the *New York Times.* That would have demanded so much compromise, needless to say so much money, for the overrated sense of "being read by millions."[24]

Instead, an artist's collective within ACT UP, called Gran Fury, literally covered *The New York Times* in a fly sheet supplement called *The New York Crimes.* It looked like the original rag (as Flo Kennedy says, "All the shit that fits the print"), but on every other level it subverted the precedent of vacuous reporting. With no captions on the photographs, with headlines like "Koch fucks up again" followed by a rigorous and critical analysis of the city's negligent AIDS policies, and with articles on prisoners with AIDS, *The New York Crimes* literally put AIDS on the front page, proving that the inaccuracies and understatements normally presented by that paper twice a day are deliberately constructed to appear factual. More than the counter-media approach, this action resembles the "détournement" called for by the Situationists during May 1968.[25] Instead of providing a "new" object, Gran Fury redesigned an old, certainly "worn out," one. ACT UP members have taken on the challenge of how to slip in their own information to disrupt the daily routine of the newspaper reading straphanger.

However, does ACT UP know the difference between the effect of its own media and that of the dominant media? Can that difference honestly be expressed through a look at the commodities themselves? Is going to an ACT UP demo like buying Calvin Klein underwear? Maybe. Indeed, making sexy political statements takes many forms. But what has Calvin Klein done for queer visibility and straight people's acceptance of us in the last ten years except hide in a fake marriage and tout himself to the public as a hetero-stud? The back page ad in the trendy *Crimes* reminds the buyer that "This is to enrage you." But this is also to inform you. Without *The New York Crimes*, without ACT UP stickers city wide, without demonstrations occupying the first few minutes on the nightly network news, many people would be unaware that some people are fighting for their lives, and why. They may also not know that they can take part in that fight. Calvin's briefs may promote androgyny and satisfy a yuppie craving for permissible fetishes, but will they be clean for Eternity if you end up in the hospital? Or if you have them on when you are strip-searched in jail?

MTV Activism

It is precisely ACT UP's obsessive relationship with its own image in the media which primed the pre-Target City Hall creation of yet another affinity group. This particular cluster of activists has a focus on video. Previously, videomakers documenting demonstrations had been bumping elbows with each other and had shared space left be-tween the legs of the TV cowboys with their big, big cameras and large press passes. So, the ACT UP folks fashioned their own press passes and hit the sidewalks with the big boys. On the back of the pictures and signatures of these badges the videomakers state their actual purpose. Nothing to hide:

> This card identifies the person named on the reverse as an authorized representative of DIVA TV. Please extend to her/him all of the professional privileges and assistance normally extended to the press.
> DIVA TV (Damned Interfering Video Activist Television) is an affinity group within ACT UP (AIDS Coalition To Unleash Power).
> We are committed to making media which directly counters and interferes with dominant media assumptions about AIDS and governmental negligence in dealing with the AIDS crisis.
> We are committed to challenging a racist, sexist, and heterosexist dominant media which is complicit with our repressive government.

The collective (although DIVA resents the constraints of that word and functions more like a guerrilla video team) formed precisely to make quick and dirty media which both looks and feels as if it was made on location with activists, by activists, and for activists.[26] The particular model DIVA subscribes to is more like newsreel and less like documentary, more like music video and less like nightly news. This is MTV activism since it's "More Than a Virus" that is killing people with AIDS.

The form of counter-media that DIVA produces reminds us of what's at stake in Lola Flash's photographs: self-representation and the notion of a counter-memory. DIVA TV is propaganda on every level, and that includes questions about lifestyle, fashion, collectivity, reversal, and empowerment. This time the activists are intervening in television production and distribution, exploiting channels of public access, organizing community-based screenings, selling footage to network television produced with DIVA's point of view (and label), and operating within the politics of ACT UP itself. What DIVA has effectively done is to image the group itself in a positive, fashionable representation, by enhancing the issues, without diluting the political urgency of the moment. Unlike television's tendency to trivialize the activist presence on the political landscape, DIVA tapes empower individual ACT UP members in all their customized regalia. The fashion-TV-politics triangle is best exemplified when DIVA plays their tapes at bars and clubs. Invitations to the five story (including a roof barbecue) club-of-the-day, Mars, declare DIVA's presence on a Sunday night in the same way ACT UP's demonstration invitations brought out the fun aspect of screaming one's head off in public.

Figure 5. *DIVA TV still,* Target City Hall, *Jocelyn Taylor.*

So far, DIVA has produced a series of tapes organized around various demonstrations as well as short Public Service Announcements about safer sex and AIDS activism in general. *Target City Hall* was the first half hour show comprised of three team-produced segments (fig 5). The tape begins with a music video à la Lou Reed documenting a civil disobedience training and then going outdoors to put the theory into practice. The second part follows individuals in one brand new affinity group, made up primarily of "first-timers," as they scheme to block traffic and later as they discuss the jail experience. The third part, called LAPIT (Lesbian Activists Producing Innovative Television) weaves together footage of the Women and AIDS Teach-in with women activists testifying about being illegally strip-searched after the City Hall demo. The piece ends with ACT UP women at the March on Washington for Women's Rights and Reproductive Freedom, insisting on the connections between women's body politics and the AIDS activist agenda.

The tapes which result from DIVA's collaboration are unequivocally celebratory, but also function, in their making, as counter-surveillance for demonstrators. Arresting police officers have been heard saying things like, "There aren't any photographers around this time. We can do whatever we want, now, you fucking queer." Because the police and FBI have their own roving plain-clothes camera people to build thick files on ACT UP and its members, DIVA (like Testing The Limits) has assumed the responsibility of providing an archive with which to counter the oppressive potential of images compiled by the eyes of the state.

In our videos, DIVA produces counter-culture seen from the perspective of AIDS activists, many of whom shoot on consumer formats (VHS, video–8, V–1 compact cassette). Not only content (with a mediatized formulation of protest action as mere spectacle), DIVA is engaged in creating images as a form of collective direct action. The presentation of ACT UP's politics at the level of individual participation thus comes full circle, as modeling and self-recognition merge and are accelerated in a process of counter-media production. Then, the play of images in an oppositional strategy are provocative and propagandistic, but only in so far as DIVA's tapes reflect the varied and powerful sentiments of ACT UP members during a protest: anger, fear, love. These images are part of ACT UP's collective and counter-memory.

Now we are watching TV. It is DIVA TV, the video called *PRIDE '69–'89*, showing dykes and fags during New York's twentieth-anniversary weekend of the Stonewall rebellion. We fastforward in search of our own memories, ones that both overlap and suppress our memories from last year of the parade in Montreal, of the emergency room in Montreal. But the images don't match up yet; the AIDS crisis is not over. We turn off the set and walk to the window of a hospital room looking out onto Greenwich Village and the Hudson River, New York City, wintertime. AIDS, we think, is so unglamorous, so unfestive. That's why we are members of ACT UP. Why we are members of DIVA TV. Why we are fighting for AIDS treatments, health care—*free and comprehensive*—for everyone in this country.

Notes

Ray Navarro and I completed this essay—footnoted, revised, edited for grammar and the invariable last minute theoretical impasse, while Ray was hospitalized with toxoplasmosis, an opportunistic disease which affects many people with AIDS. On November 9, 1990, soon after we had sent off the final manuscript, Ray died.

Before Ray became ill, we sat in front of this tiny computer screen sharing soup, socks, and sex stories. We had been collaborators in writing and video production since the day we met, when we began writing the original version of this essay.

Writing while he was in the hospital was an arduous task since Ray could not see and was hearing-impaired. Plus the distance between the "window onto Greenwich Village" that we sat by and the one we wrote about was sometimes too hard to fathom, so we'd stop trying. Other times our situation was thrown into glaring relief, and although painful, solidified our commitment to explain our passions, our struggles, our personal stake. In either case, we were used to writing, reading and re-reading each other's words and finishing each other's sentences, so Ray managed to keep entire paragraphs fresh in his mind and one day we just decided the piece was done and sent it off.

We always resisted writing about AIDS alone. I now resist having to.

—Catherine Saalfield

1. Gayatri Spivak, "In a Word. *Interview*," *differences* 1, no. 2 (Summer 1989): 127.

2. On Saturday night, June 24, 1989, the night before the annual Gay and Lesbian Pride Parade in New York City, over 1,000 people reenacted the Stonewall Riot by throwing yellow foam bricks at each other and at friends impersonating cops. During the course of the celebration, homophobes in cars struck three people on the corner of Grove St. and West 4th St.

3. ACT UP was started in March 1987 as "a diverse, non-partisan group of people, united in anger and dedicated to direct action to end the AIDS crisis." The group has had a powerfully pro-active effect on changing government policies for access to drugs for People with AIDS. ACT UP also functions as a pressure group within the lesbian and gay community, pushing for the expansion of the definition of lesbian and gay rights, and often conflicting with less militant, more mainstream, lesbian and gay rights organizations.

4. See the work in: Peter Galassi, *Pictures of People* (Nicholas Nixon Exhibition Catalogue) (New York: Museum of Modern Art, 1988). Read the criticism in: Douglas Crimp, "Portraits of People With AIDS," in Laurence Grossberg, Cary Nelson, and Paula Treichler, eds., *Cultural Studies* (New York and London: Routledge, forthcoming 1991). Watch the analysis unfold in: "The Silence That Silences," Paper Tiger TV (Southwest) and Bob Kinney, video, 35 mins., 1989.

5. A "zap," or a quick response to a local outrage planned in a mere hour or two, usually reflects a singular and specific demand. As opposed to a major action which takes months to organize and involves long-term goals and masses of protestors, a zap involves bratty strategies like constant phone calls, postcards, fax messages, and office sit-ins. The Lavender Hill Mob appears to have institutionalized the now commonly queer strategy of "zapping." Marty Robinson, Bill Bahlman, Henry Yeager, Margaret McCarthy, and David Kirshenbaum, who later started the ACT UP Issues Committee (which was in existence for the first year of ACT UP), are best known for zapping/disrupting government hearings in various forms of drag. Also, they are known for having uncovered important documents and highlighted problems in a flurry of paperwork which they reorganized into impressive and accessible fact sheets.

6. In theater, the alienation effect was used "in such a way that the audience was hindered from simply identifying itself with the characters in the play. Acceptance or rejection of their actions and utterances was meant to take place on a conscious plane, instead of, as hitherto, in the audience's subconscious." Bertolt Brecht, *Brecht on Theater: The Development of an Aesthetic*, ed. and trans. John Willett (New York and London: Methuen, 1964), 91.

7. Having spent eight years with Ed Koch as the negligent mayor of New York City, ACT UP knew better than to celebrate this closet case who was killing us. During his administration more than 11,000 AIDS deaths occurred, mostly within the gay community.

8. "Naturally, even from the perspective of a purely immanent analysis, the structure of the [press] photograph is not an isolated structure; it is in communication with at least one other structure, namely the text—title, caption or article—accompanying every press photograph. Of the two structures, one is already familiar, that of language, while almost nothing is known about the other, that of the photograph. . . . Thus . . . the special status of the photographic image: *it is a message without a code.* . . ." Roland Barthes, "The Photographic Message," *Image, Music, Text*, ed. and trans. Stephen Heath (New York: Hill and Wang, 1977), 16–17.

9. Stuart Marshall, "The Contemporary Political Use of Gay History: The Third Reich," paper delivered at "How Do I Look? Queer Film and Video Conference," NYC, 1989.

10. Risa Denenberg, "Lesbian AIDS Activists: What Are We Doing?" (in her own monthly column on women's health), "In Our Own Hands," *Outweek* #17 (Oct. 15, 1989): 31.

11. Experiments were conducted by U.S. Public Health Service from 1932–1972 in Macon County, Tuskegee, Alabama. In the name of "higher science," these "Tuskegee experiments" denied seriously ill people any treatment even though it was available. For a wonderful poem about the role of a black woman who was a nurse during the experiments, see: "Civil Servant," Essex Hemphill, *The Pyramid Periodical* 1, no. 3 (Summer 1989).

12. Sources: *The Pilot Needle Exchange Study in New York City: A Bridge to Treatment*, A Report on the First Ten Months of Operations, New York City Department of Health, December 1989. "Report and Recommendations to the Mayor on Drug Abuse in New York City," Mayor's Study Group on Drug Abuse, May 1990. ACT UP fact sheets from 1989.

13. Woodrow Meyers said, "There's a higher goal than the reduction of transmission of HIV, and that goal is the elimination of use of illegal narcotics by injection, period." Because he implies that an enormous number of people are therefore expendable, Mathilde Krim, of the American Foundation for AIDS Research, was quoted in the same article saying, "It's difficult to believe that people who have an education in public health and medicine pay no attention to fact." See Meyers Picks His Battle: Drugs," Catherine Woodard, *Newsday*, May 6, 1990.

14. Denenberg, "Lesbian AIDS," 30.

15. New York City's Community Research Initiative (CRI) was begun in 1987 to work with the AIDS community on the design and implementation of clinical studies of experimental treatments for AIDS and HIV-related conditions. CRI is "PWAs, PWARCs and their physicians taking the initiative to seek promising interventions against AIDS in a responsible manner." Project Inform was started by Martin Delaney, in San Francisco, California, in 1985 to investigate new and promising AIDS therapies. They maintain a hotline and a mailing list in order to provide related information.

16. Audre Lorde, "Breast Cancer: Power vs. Prosthesis," in *The Cancer Journals* (San Francisco: Spinsters, 1980), 73.

17. These dangers refer to the criminalization of our very sexuality as queers, the resulting homophobic tenor of our society and queer bashings, and the government and police response to our protest form of civil disobedience. For example, the 1986 Supreme Court decision on the case of Bowers v. Hardwick upheld criminalization of sodomy. Michael H. v. Gerald C. privileged a biological father over a non-father husband in a custody case which carries dangerous ramifications for lesbian and gay non-biological parents in their own custody battles and struggles for legal recognition as such. The list goes on and on in terms of reproductive rights legislation and immigration laws (see Webster v. Reproductive Health Services and the prohibition against HIV+ persons legally entering the U.S.). Not to mention laws (and both successful and attempted amendments) against prostitution and phone sex ads, obscenity, pornography, safer sex AIDS campaigns, and so forth and so on. One would think those legislators were obsessed.

18. Malcolm X, "To Mississippi Youth," *Malcolm X Speaks*, ed. George Breitman (New York: Grove Press, 1965), 138.

19. Muriel Rukeyser, "Käthe Kollwitz," in *Rising Tides, 20th Century American Poets*, ed. Laura Chester and Sharon Barba (New York: Washington Square Press, 1973), 70.

20. Audre Lorde, *The Black Unicorn*, (New York: W. W. Norton, 1978).

21. The handbook was also produced as an outreach effort. After much revision, nationalizing, and up-dating, the Women and AIDS Handbook was published in Winter 1990 by South End Press under the name *Women, AIDS and Activism*. One self-criticism of the teach-in was the lack of participation by women of color which reflected the constitution of ACT UP as a whole. Notably, many women of color have contributed to the massive revisions that the South End version of the book reflects.

22. An active member of ACT UP, Marion Banzhaf has worked in the feminist health movement since 1975. These lessons emerge from her experience as co-director of the Tallahassee, Florida Feminist Women's Health Center. She also worked at FWHCs in Los Angeles, San Diego, Chicago, and Portland, and Atlanta.

23. The Association for Drug Abuse Prevention and Treatment (or ADAPT) began in 1980 as a drug treatment and advocacy program run by recovering drug users to provide informed outreach, counseling, and support. In 1986, they modified their program to focus on the AIDS crisis as it was devastating IVDUs city wide and demanded a particular response from recovering IVDUs many of whom were discovering (after being clean) that they were HIV+.

24. Furthermore, as Bob Lederer (an active member of ACT UP and its subcommittee, Alternative and Holistic Treatments) illustrates in "AIDS: A Medical and Journalistic Disaster," "The *New York Times'* coverage of AIDS is a catalogue of serious reporting lapses and imbalances." In his excellent exposé, he lists the major examples of this as: late, inadequate, or non-existent coverage of major developments; spotty conference coverage; journalism by government press release; and ignoring or minimizing major political demonstrations. See *Lies Of Our Times* 1, no. 1 (January 1990) Sheridan Square Press Inc., and the Institute for Media Analysis, Inc., 12.

25. "Détournement: short for: détournement of pre-existing aesthetic elements. The integration of present or past artistic production into a superior construction of a milieu. In this sense there can be no situationist painting or music, but only a situationist use of these means. In a more primitive sense, détournement within the old cultural spheres is a method of propaganda, a method which testifies to the wearing out and loss of importance of these spheres," *an endless passion . . . an endless banquet,* a situationist scrapbook, Situationist International selected documents from 1957 to 1962, ICA Verso. *Situationist International Anthology,* ed. and trans. Ken Knabb (Berkeley, CA: The Bureau of Public Secrets, 1981).

26. This type of collective video production of AIDS activism is not without precedent. Since the early days of ACT UP, a video collective called Testing The Limits has been documenting demonstrations and creating an archive. Not only do TTL and DIVA share some personnel and equipment, but together they are articulating the role of oppositional media within the movement. For an overview of their project, see "Interview with Testing The Limits," in *Afterimage* 17, no. 3 (October 1989): 4–7.

V

Speaking Out: Teaching In

16

Visualizing Safe Sex: When Pedagogy and Pornography Collide

Cindy Patton

Going Too Far

In the spring of 1989, I was asked to comment on a controversy over a sexually explicit advertisement which had been placed in the gay and lesbian community newspaper of Ottawa. The ad—which was, in my view, tasteful in the extreme—featured a frontal nude male sporting a condom on his not very hard cock. The ad had been produced by a local gay photographer in conjunction with the local AIDS education council. The photographer's work was widely known in the Ottawa community—portraiture, erotica, news photography, and recently, safe sex posters. In short, his work and his style were so eminently recognizable in the local gay and lesbian community that a Phillip Hannan photograph would seem "natural," would feel as vernacular as a Keith Haring drawing might in New York City.

But this particular photograph created controversy on two fronts: radical feminists were outraged by the appearance of a documentary dick in the pages of their local rag and the safe sex pedagogues were concerned that the dick wasn't hard *enough*. They feared that condom novices might try to apply a condom before a proper erection. Poor Phillip was caught in the middle: in order to make the ad more accept-able in the pages of a serious newspaper—in order to make the ad visually distinguishable from, say, pornography or bar ads—he had agreed to photograph a model at half mast.

The regionally distributed newspaper GO is published by the Gays of Ottawa, the local gay and lesbian council, but is governed by a somewhat autonomous editorial board. GO is somewhere between a house publication and an independent periodical—the latter a tradition in gay community newspapers.[1] The ad in question was approved by the lesbians and gay men of the editorial board, folks savvy about local political trends.

After publication of the ad, a group of lesbian feminists levied strong accusations: the ad was deemed pornographic and thus available to the wealth of controversial analysis about the role of such representations in the oppression of women. The women argued that the ad, as a depiction of male sexuality, was assaultive to women, especially to female victims of male sexual violence. Although the hardline anti-pornographers were a minority in the community and among the membership of Gays of Ottawa, other women felt torn by a more inchoate discomfort with the ad and wanted to maintain their allegiance to their sisters. These women weren't especially interested in having naked men in their newspaper, but had at least initially believed that the ad constituted valid risk reduction education.

The crux of the controversy, at least in terms of the politics of representation, became clear in my conversation with one of the hardline anti-porn women. The woman made clear that she did not oppose risk reduction education. (I was officially there to lecture on AIDS and during the question period we had a heated discussion about whether monogamy and working toward "deeper" relationships, her favored solutions, were effective. Her views on the ad were framed by two beliefs—that monogamy is equivalent to safe sex and that pornography promotes uncaring, promiscuous relationships.)

"What did you feel was wrong about the ad?," I asked.

"It had exposed male genitals," she said.

"Oh," I said, with an air of confusion. "I thought you said he was wearing a condom."

Sex/Text: The Polyglot of Sexual Languages

Significant differences exist within and between cultures in their interpretations of representations of the body and of sexuality. Historically, in the Euro-American context, sexual representation has been relegated to the categories of frivolous, bawdy, inarticulate, unspeakable. It is a source of humor that the language of sex is so imprecise, so polyvalent that it is "hard" to know when we are talking about sex and when we are talking about business or politics or other weighty matters. With the appearance of sexology in the late 1800s, sexual languages to some extent lost their metaphoric flexibility as "scientists" pressed the utterances of sexualities into a more precise language *about* sex. Sexual vernaculars somewhat recovered their status in the flagrant 1960s and 1970s as the women's sexual freedom, and gay liberation movements produced no-holds-barred texts that demoted the penis, debated the forms of female orgasm, and suggested that real men "take it," too. The underground pornographies of working-class homosexuals, male desire for female domination, and sexes made equal by the desire for raw visual slime howled at the edges of mainstream media institutions. "Art films" and hard core porn converged in cinematic style; *Blue Boy* made its way to the 24-hour store rack next to *Playboy*; and feminist women wrote confessions of desires for domination and for dominating.

Alongside these narratives of sexual desire, clinical studies by sexologists told us what our neighbors were doing and a range of typically U.S. how-to books promised to improve our technique. The disciplinary erotics of clinical description and the sheer anti-romanticism of Kegel exercises provided a template for language about sex which disavowed desire, even as it incited festishistic, perhaps masochistic pleasure in the mechanized body observed and improved. In popular culture, the appearance of real penises and vaginas, complete with wrinkles and wayward pubic hairs, created a documentary aura even in the most fantastically plotted XXX film. It is, of course, forbidden now to conclude that there was a sudden release from a "repression," but the transformation of sex into overt and self-reflexive texts not immediately tied to activities culturally designated as "sex" seems to have reached a level of noticeability or undeniability. In short, the reality-decentering effect of the proliferation of texts characteristic of postmodernity—especially text-commodities—finally broke a basic "statement" of the modern sexual episteme. The barrage of texts, from porn to science to how-to books and magazine columns, which made truth claims about sex evacuated any lingering pretense that there was a fixed essence in sexuality. Sex lost its reality (that is, its ability to reference a hegemonic form of practice or a transcendent subjectivity) and gender came tumbling after.

The language of sex and the contexts in which it was deemed appropriate to speak *of* sex were radically fractured and fragmented by the early 1980s. We could apparently speak more frankly than ever before, although the Right was making apocalyptic predictions of the consequences of all this talking. And there was not, apparently, an inverse relation between talking about sex and doing it. No indeed, in the 1980s, text and sex merge: we Americans were a tribe textually constructed through our love of one-hand reads. We blurred the line between reading a sexual text and being a sexual text. We were pornographic, masturbatory. The recognition of the demands of female pleasure (and the technical difficulties of traditional coitus in achieving it) recast sex from a transcendent *jouissance* specific to the domain of pairbonding to become instead a play of parallel and mutually incomprehensible *plaisir*. Increased economic and social power for some women, open discussion of bi- and homo-sexualities highlighted the realities of sexual competition in a widening market: performance anxiety and the technical how-to manuals which quelled them formed a new kind of erotic literature to replace the mystical invocations of *karma sutra* variations popular in the "free love" sixties and early seventies. Sex was drawn under the careful regression analyses of demographers who deciphered the shifts in market forces won through decreasing racial, gender, and sexuality penalties. On the individual level Kinsey statistics replaced Casanova-like tales as benchmarks of our sexual quest. The visual and narrative structures of pornography filled the gulf left void by the cultural lust for realism and by the blunt imaginations most comfortable with the truncated information-aesthetic of the three-second bite of the six o'clock news.

Convention and Intention: Media for a Polysexual World

I was recently talking with a young gay man about problems of using pornography in safe sex education. He told me that he had only seen a few films, but he was surprised that they all showed safe sex. I was equally surprised and said that I had seen only a few commercial porn films that demonstrated condom use.

"Oh, you couldn't see the condoms," the young man said. "But they all pulled out before coming."

I began to explain to him that this was a convention in pornography, that it was not *meant* to be safer sex. But then I realized that it *was* safer sex.[2]

Two unprecedented events are converging in the late 20th century: an epidemic of a strange new virus and the proliferation of remarkable forms of cultural mediation. The virus is unusual in its slowness; those infected with it are linked by acts of intimate proximity (sex, needle sharing, receipt of the strange gift of a stranger's blood in transfusion, fetal-mother symbiosis) that construct a dotted line map of physical contact. The new media—from music and cable television to home video and FAX machines—are remarkable for their speed and distortion of place. Paradoxically, against these extremes of speed and slowness, proximity and displacement, the media and the virus serve as mutual metaphors: scientists talk about messenger RNA and remark that the virus is "trying to tell us something." Postmodern cultural criticism sees the intricacies of communication illustrated in the virus, as in minimalist musician Laurie Anderson's performance piece, "language is a virus."

The metaphorical armament accompanying the virus and the media tears us away from the mundane, everyday reality of bodies, of *our* bodies. The virus pulls toward the microscopic, the media toward the global. The HIV epidemic is lived in the hyperspace—*hypo*space?—vacated by the body. Void and surfaceless, the *human*-scale body so necessary for understanding and incorporating risk-reducing sexual techniques meets only silence about safe sex outside gay and some teen sexual cultures.[3] After two decades of poststructuralism, phenomenology has a nostalgic appeal.

The Place of Pornography

Ironically, what is unique about 1980s pornography is not so much its "explicitness," but its willingness to treat the human body in medium range, to employ televisual techniques, however prosaic, which short-circuit the cynical postmodern viewer's collaboration with her/his own duping, and suture the viewer to the body in the film. The viewer gets off; the will to embody inverts the usual *out of body* experience of the television watcher.[4] Whatever the acrobatics involved, however huge the actor's penis, porn's televisual techniques construct—indeed its appeal in part hinges on—a "real" person performing within the limits of his or her body, unenhanced by special effects. But porn is not so much realist as it is a mirror for activities we imagine but cannot observe ourselves engaged in. Porn is not reenacted but mimicked, subverted; it is not a manual but a site of memory, a repository of the phantasmagoric history of the body defying convention.

Much pornography is, of course, bad art, perceived as offensive and degrading to some people. Porn is both highly stylized and standardized, mixing filmic and televisual conventions with production values reflecting low budgets and a narrative theory comprised of hack Freudian ideas about sexual desire. Nevertheless, the mechanisms and codes of production, *how* an image is narrativized, marketed, contextualized, *and decoded by a range of viewers* and not the *image in itself* nor some essential structure of a "pornographic imagination" is what has constituted "the pornographic." The issue for theorization and political debate is not any aesthetic value of pornography, nor any balancing of its relative transgressive anti-capitalist aspects against its misogynist, racist, repressive aspects. A materialist analysis of pornography would back all the way up to the representational differences required by the current, historically specific performance of things-designated-as-"sexual," to split arbitrarily the natural/bodily from the linguistic/textual, and only then to assess the effects of the "mediation" of "sexuality." Although this is a much larger project which the immediate requirements of safe sex work cannot wait to have completed, it is already clear that the special vernacular of porn can be used in efforts to reconstruct a language of sex to go along with the reconstructed sexualities that resist both potentially HIV-transmitting activities and the destructive effects of attempts to silence, once again, the eloquent voice of homo-sexualities. Cultural expressions that are successful in safe sex education, however, must accurately gauge the borders and modes of circulation within gay male and other sexual subcultures. Two common assumptions compromise the usefulness (and political defensibility) of pornographic safe sex representations.

First, it is generally assumed that viewers or readers interpret "pornographic" material as real stories or actual, filmed sex. The presumption of realism ignores the reasons and mechanisms viewers use to suspend their realization that porn actors are indeed acting. While the medium-view scale of pornography enables a unique and visceral relation between the viewer and text, clearly both the text and the range of decodings are open, as my vignettes suggest. There has been virtually no interest in the meanings viewers make of porn (quantitative analysis has related exposure to attitudes rather than discovering phenomenologically what interpretive modes viewers produce). In part because of critical disinterest, until recently, in the rigorous study of popular culture, pornography was located on an outside edge of such culture. But equally important, the idea that porn has no narrative or aesthetic pleasure beyond mere "getting off" has suggested the wrong criteria for evaluation of decoding skills or differences. Highly explicit visual material is probably interpreted by some decoders as closer to lived experience not because it is mistaken for "real," or because the viewer accepts the truth claims of documentary elements of style, but because porn contrasts obvious fantasy scenes with representations of the body unenhanced by special effects or stunt men, the body with all its scars, stretch marks, lopsided balls, and unmatched breasts. Porn is simultaneously fantasy and direct cinema; porn consistently oversteps the distance generally produced between the text and the producers (actors) of the text. The ambiguities about "faking orgasm" or sexual pleasure redouble the emotional duplicity of method acting; we cannot decide and are pushed beyond caring whether we can discern "good acting" from natural acts.

Second, there is an assumption that people—chiefly men—imitate what they see in a porn video or porn magazine. Anti-pornography feminist analysis views pornography as an important direct cause of violence against women, and as an indirect support of misogynist ideology, and thus in itself a mediated form of violence against women. While there are important and immediate strategic concerns about legal action against men who claim that their acts of violence against women were "caused" or accompanied by pornography (displacing responsibility onto unchecked "male" desire, or the power of "female" desire to override their usually controlled passions), this is not the same as demonstrating that pornography is a perversion of an "unmediated" sexuality. It is hard to find a moment in which sexuality (desire?) is not partially constructed through texts and mediations, if only of memory or the imaginary. There may well be a complex relationship between the genre of pornography and the systematic, largely negative representation of women in mass media. It seems unlikely, however, personal testimonials notwithstanding, that men widely imitate porn in any straightforward way. Such analyses must explain why some but not all pornographic images are imitated; for example, the come shot in traditional pornography involves the male pulling out of his partner and then spewing his semen. Clearly, few heterosexual men engage in this practice in real life. The men in porn, are paid to *control* their orgasm, their sexuality, not for their partner in the film but for the viewer; the mimetic aspects of porn are surely contingent on the hermeneutic of viewers.

Safe Sex: Visualizing the Moment of Transmission

In October 1988, Washington D.C.'s gay Whitman-Walker Clinic prepared an ad "aimed at the male porno industry"[5] which included an artsy cutup of a video screen and the following headline:

"Are we getting off watching men kill each other?"

The ad's text continued:

> How many times have we watched a video showing unprotected anal sex?
> And how many times have we actually seen another porn star becoming infected with the AIDS virus?
> Who can doubt the result of all this. More sickness very possibly leading to death.
> The difference here is that the transmission of the AIDS virus is in a sense witnessed by every viewer, every purchaser of the video.
> It's time to insist on videos which show safer sex with condoms.
> And, let's make sure our own actions speak as loud as our words.

The ad was bold, ostensibly designed to get porn viewers (for who else would be able to answer the questions?) to become militants against condomless pornographies. But the pretended concern for the safety of porn stars only thinly masks the attempt to displace moral responsibility for the epidemic from societal and scientific inhumaneness onto individual acts of consumption (desire). The linguistic slippages in this ad are numerous—the equation of watching porn with watching murder; the labeling as infection-inducing representations of sex that do not show condoms (in fact, numerous producers edit to avoid showing the condoms, and state this in a preface); reinforcing the shaky syllogism with "who can doubt the result"; leaving unclear the referent to "all this" (porn? "actually seeing"? voyeurism of this alleged moment of killing?); proposing a "difference" with no clear item of comparison (the difference "here" as opposed to occasions of unsafe sex we know of, but leave unchallenged among our friends? Is the "difference" caused by the vice of commercialism?) But the most chilling construction is the one underlying the ad as a whole: when we watch porn, are we watching an actual moment of transmission? Can we "see" infection occur in a moment of real time?

This is a compelling question which resonates for all of us who are aware that we may now be or soon might be having sex with an infected person. But this is also a question asked in a later stage of this epidemic, the second cultural question after "Could it have been him?," the dark, unspoken question of the first years of the HIV epidemic, before the promise of *cultural* change redrew the line of moral culpability for infection. These questions—Was it him? Is it now?—form the structure of basic terror around which circulate the daily practices of safe sex organizing.

The blaming of "Could it have been him?" was countered with the argument that the epidemic "spread silently" for seven, maybe ten years before anyone even knew that they would be well served to avoid taking cum. The moral logic implicit in the blaming ethos was reoriented by promoting safe sex not only as an individual risk reduction practice, but as a practice of community-building through resistance. Safety meant not only avoiding HIV and possible co-factors, but it meant protecting ourselves with anti-discrimination laws, with activism, with demands for better drug trials.

The disturbing sentiment of the Whitman-Walker ad replaces the project of safety-through-solidarity with *policing* individual change. Speaking from the admonishing community's point of view—"Are we getting off watching men kill each other?" (a charge more easily brought against network news)—the ad articulates a perverse concern: Can the panoptic community "see" the acts of transmission? Do we "get off" on this imaging of a moment of transmission? This worry subtly eroticizes transmission: transmission, not sexuality, becomes the object of voyeurism. The ad reinscribes safe sex as a personal, rather than a cultural experience, and suggests that the *suppression* of eroticism binds community. The incoherence in viewer identification with porn (is the viewer only a voyeur, or does s/he identify with one or multiple characters?) turns the ad into a meditation on "our" culpability in "our" own death (which of course mimics the hateful projection of the right wing). Porn viewing becomes a metaphor for *watching transmission* and evokes a childlike, narcissistic voyeurism that lets it happen in order to watch it happen. But certainly, this fascinated immobility does not describe the history of gay community response to the epidemic: it sounds rather more like the epidemiologists who coolly add up their numbers. If voyeurism of the epidemic is the crime, surely scientists should be the first to face the charge.

So, could this pornography be a moment of transmission?

Hardly. For one thing, these actors are paid to come outside. Paid to control their orgasms, paid to have perfect penises. Slow motion and intercut cum shots enhance the illusion of control over ejaculation. There has been great scorn accompanying the deaths from AIDS-related illnesses of various porn stars, "gay" and "straight." But the evidence from studies of women sex workers suggest that it is not while at work (where many women have long insisted on condom use) that most women sex workers become infected, but rather at home with husbands and boyfriends. Women sex workers are much less able to gain safe sex compliance while trading sex in the complex bargain of domestic partnering in a sexist culture than when engaging in overt acts of commerce that constitute their work in the "oldest profession."

Surface/Depth

Why this obsession with imagining that a moment, caught on film, could be a moment of transmission? This kind of thinking distorts the complexity of HIV illness and undermines the kind of multiple-level community organizing that has enabled so many men to adopt and/or maintain non-transmitting sexual practices. The attempt at visualizing HIV *infection* is a move away from representing the somatics of the opportunistic infections which qualify as AIDS and which are constituted as the "result" of an unrepresented (and unrepresentable) "act." Both the Whitman-Walker representation of "men killing each other" and the old-style "after" photos associated with 1950s VD films *allude* to transmission, and try to construct a "dangerous reality" for risky acts through a pictograph. But the allusion confuses critically important information about HIV and its relationship to AIDS.

While HIV can be acquired during some very specific acts of sex, HIV and its immune system sequelae are quite different from the traditional sexually transmitted diseases. HIV transmission is largely effected through ejaculation into a closed space, like a vagina or an anus. The virus then makes it way to a permeable point in the cervical lining or anal mucosa and floats around until it latches onto some T-cells, or perhaps some other basal membrane cells—it is not entirely clear. By contrast, the classic venereal diseases are diseases *on* the skin, diseases of the surface. Surface to surface contact, rather than penetration and ejaculation, are the requirements for movement of the respective "germs" of VD. Yet another category of what are now called sexually transmitted diseases are the parasites and viruses—giardia, hepatitis, etc.—associated with getting the flora of one GI tract into another GI tract, whether that is through rimming, or mediated via a penis, finger, or sex toy that carries "bugs" from one person's butt to another person's mouth. It is only a quirk of historical construction that we, in the 1990s, consider ejaculation into a vagina or rectum, crotch rubbing, and sticking your tongue in or near another person's anus to be sufficiently similar activities to create a coherent category of "sexual transmissions."

VDs in the mid-20th century are represented as being on the genitals, as in Navy-produced risk reduction films of World War II. While the display of penises infected with a wide range of VDs did not tell the whole story about more systemic manifestations of syphilis, gonorrhea, or chancroid, the phallic parade served, didactically, to identify signs and symptoms of infection in order to enable early self-detection and prevention, and, through a cathexis, to signify the surface discomfort of VD.

HIV cannot reasonably be rendered as a surface phenomenon, although the insistent portrayal of the KS-lesioned body pervades medical conferences and enlivens Randy Shilts's novel about Patient Zero. Culturally, we want a stigmata of AIDS—if it cannot plausibly be KS, the wasting figure of the person with AIDS will do. But since HIV cannot be visualized as "on the body," it is represented, in the photographic works of, for example, Nicholas Nixon, in the figure of the forlorn, wasted person with AIDS. What he does not capture in framing the frail body he brings out by focusing on the eyes, long conceptualized as the point of entry to the soul.

But this culturally overdetermined "AIDS-body"—and I use that term guardedly to mean the body represented in art or science that flattens out and disempowers the whole life of the person living with AIDS by reducing him or her to a vessel of pathos and pain—is a long way in time from any moment of transmission. Ten years or more. It is opportunistic infections and not HIV *per se* to which the somatic markers of a Nixon photograph or a scientist's slides refer. The visual terrorism that crosses seamlessly from science to art, art to science, collapses AIDS and the person living with HIV (in any form) back into the virus. It is a terrorism of silence that equates infection with AIDS instead of explaining the daily techné of prophylaxis, treatments, and life changes standing between infection and symptoms, or between symptoms and (allegedly rapid) death. And buried in the text of the Nixon photos and the scientist's slides is a linkage between AIDS and sex, AIDS and drug injection. This conjunction is accomplished and elided through a brash splitting of the audience between the "general public" who must learn compassion in relation to the pathos of the marked and diminished AIDS-body, and the "communities" for whom the person living with (but produced as "dying from") AIDS is held out as a lesson, as a consequence.

The equivocal position of both aesthetic/artistic and objective/scientific representations is inflected in the practice of safe sex educators, many of whom—community folk and public health officials alike—believe that "knowing a person with AIDS" is the best motivator for initiating safe sex. The voice of people living with AIDS who speak of their experience at once publicly constitutes their subjectivity and en-lists their energies in a subtle form of scare tactics. Under this logic, linking changes in the normative structure of sexual cultures means we must either wait until a critical mass of people with AIDS is living in proximity—and they must live badly in order for AIDS to seem scary—or we must use work like Nixon's voyeuristic and hypostatizing appro-priation of the "experience" of people living with AIDS to produce in the "recalcitrant" or isolated individual a near experience of impending danger. In short, the individualistic approach that seeks to check ill-directed desires rather than to rework polymorphous eroticisms re-quires visualizing disastrous consequences for acts that must be sug-gested but then erased from view.

Sex is Not Murder

To whom, then, is the question in the Whitman-Walker ad directed? Who is the "we" who might be "getting off watching men kill each other"?

Not, I dare say, the viewers or producers of pornography. Rather, the question is directed to a community numbed by death, terrified by a repressive representational politic that confuses the pragmatics of transmission with the erotics of new forms of sex. The question is posed by prudish educators who work from a behavioral, individualis-tic stance instead of working on the cultural level—including using pornography and other sexual languages accessible to gay men in order to transform rich and symbolically charged practices to meet the challenge of safe sex.

The "we"—the "we" who live within the domain of a besieged sexual community that is rapidly losing its members and its voice, not to mention the rich and resistant vernacular—can make at least two responses. First, that we are not the ones "getting off" while we slowly make our way through our culture to transform it, even if it is too late to keep some of our brothers and sisters uninfected. We are not the ones "getting off," getting moralistic, or acting as voyeurs. The obser-vations and speech (including "pornographic") of safe sex community organizers are attempts to rework the intimate details of our lives into complex and powerful celebrations of life worth living, even in a war zone.

Second, "we" can be clear that in sex—even in the incautiousness of condomless sex, for whatever reasons someone is having it—men are not "killing each other." It is simple, but must be stated over again that sex is not murder, even if we have not yet created a culture in which each person will be equally responsible toward every other person, even if we have not yet created a culture in which every person will have the power (or self-esteem) to take care of him/herself. It is a strange turn of history that a virus should become the battleground of moral courage, and that one of the most despised subcultures should be the first to be judged for their ability to reorganize their way of life in order to accommodate a new and deadly reality. If there is any objective truth in this epidemic, it must be that gay men have shown far more ethical conduct in their sexual relations with their brothers than the dominant (heterosexual) culture has ever exhibited between men and women.

We can certainly ask the pornographers to create a range of videos[6] that work through a variety of representational conventions—vernaculars which will be meaningful to and discursively in the control of micro-cultures that do not have to fear the Jesse Helms's of the world. But we should also re-examine the erotics of political voyeurisms and moralisms that locate the "killing" in individuals rather than in systems and institutions. The editorial in the 31 August, 1989 issue of *Nature* expresses concern that AZT may "ironically" "prolong" the lives of people who, as evidenced by their infection are, in the mind of the writer, irresponsible and will, in his view, necessarily "infect" others. A fascinated science and prudish society effectively withheld life-saving education. Will they now withhold potentially life-sustaining treatment? If there are voyeurs here, if there are some people not moving quickly enough, if somebody is "getting off" on this epidemic, that charge must be laid at the door of the hegemonic culture and its scientific body-counters. And when we knock at that door, it won't be Ronald Reagan alone who answers.

Notes

1. Newspapers for the lesbian/gay community have emerged worldwide since the early 1970s. There were a handful of news/feature (as distinguished from literary or avant-garde) publications devoted to gay/lesbian issues from the mid-century homophile movements in the U.S. and Scandinavia; luscious underground or coded "skin" magazines (largely physique magazines which only ambivalently acknowledged that their aesthetic was designed to be easily appropriated by working-class, subcultural homosexuals); and the long-standing *Advocate* from California which slightly pre-dates gay liberation. The increase in new periodicals stems from the inspiration of

gay liberation and from the importance of the radical and underground presses of the 50s and 60s new social movements. Newspapers linked geographically dispersed homosexual groups—some highly organized and long-standing, some little more than transient social networks—with little in common beyond the as yet unspoken scars of a shared history of oppression and a vague idea of a homosexual desire or essence. An "imagined community" (to extend Benedict Anderson's notion) rapidly emerged, which debated political strategy, the meaning of "being gay," and produced a set of core values and social mores that hypostatized a sense of "lifestyle," social (if not geographic) place, and accompanying identities. The importance and role of the gay media in generating the gay/lesbian subject in post modernity has yet to be theorized. On media, see John D'Emilio, *Sexual Politics, Sexual Communities: The Making of a Homosexual Minority in the United States, 1940–1970* (Chicago: University of Chicago Press, 1983); Michael Bronski, *Culture Clash* (Boston: South End Press, 1984). For a possible conceptual source on the relation between media, language, "nationalism," and community see Benedict Anderson, *Imagined Community* (London: Verso, 1983). For a fruitful materialist account of the relationship between lifestyle/community and cultural artifacts see Pierre Bourdieu, *Distinction* (Cambridge: Harvard University Press, 1984).

2. This is, of course, not a recommended form of safe sex because most men cannot completely "pull out" before ejaculation, and because some men have large quantities of "pre-cum," which are a potential reservoir of HIV infection. The point here is that conceptually, "pulling out" and "coming outside" meet a minimal requirement of the safe sex dictate "on me, not in me," It is rare in our culture and in safe sex discourse to separate penetration and ejaculation, even though they are conceptually distinct. Ejaculation by an HIV seropositive person in the anus or vagina of another person, and not penetration *per se* is required for transmission of HIV.

3. The appearance in 1988–89 of numerous rap songs about "jimmy hats" and the emergence of "posse" (rap vernacular from *posse comitatus*, and the preferred self-designation of urban youth "gangs") involvement in sex and drug education are critical examples of the resistance in some youth cultures to the taboos on conveying even the most basic information about the safe pursuit of pleasure.

4. For a semiotic phenomenologic study of television viewers physical experience of TV watching see Jenny Nelson, "Eyes Out of Your Head: On Televisual Experience," *Critical Studies in Mass Communication* 6, no. 4 (December 1989): 387–403.

5. This is the description contained in a covering memo to the National AIDS Network board of directors. Clearly, the gay porn industry is what is meant, and thus, heterosexual porn is reconstituted as somehow *not* a male industry, not an industry aimed at men, or not of concern to the unidentified "viewers." This is a curiously misogynist hijacking of anti-pornography feminist analysis implicit in the ad's text.

6. I explore some of the specific approaches taken by porn manufacturers and by educators using porn imagery in "Safe Sex in The Pornographic Vernacular," in *How Do I Look? Queer Film and Video*, eds. Bad Object Choices (Seattle: Bay Press, 1991).

17

School's Out

Simon Watney

How Childhood tries to reach us, and declares that we were once
what took it seriously.[1]   *Rainer Maria Rilke*

The most crucial aspect of psychoanalysis . . . is its insistence that
childhood is something in which we continue to be implicated and
which is never simply left behind. . . . It persists as something which
we endlessly rework in our attempt to build an image of our own
history.[2]   *Jacqueline Rose*

Introduction

The American artist Tim Rollins has recently argued that

> one of the most cherished ideas in America, the rationale for compul-
> sory education and public schooling in this country, is the belief that
> a genuine democracy cannot exist without the full education of all
> its citizens.[3]

Much the same could be said of most people's attitudes towards education in the United Kingdom. Yet when I was at school in the 1960s the
subject of homosexuality only existed as a pretext for sniggers and
insults. Little has significantly changed in either country. Two subsequent decades of debate and action in the direction of multi-culturalism
in the classroom has had, at best, only uneven results. But the question
of homosexuality remains in total abeyance. Which is to say that
the question of *sexuality* remains in abeyance, since our respective
education systems manifestly fail to acknowledge the actual diversity
of human sexuality within the curriculum or outside it. In effect,

children are taught that homosexuality is beyond consideration. This is bad for everyone in education, but most especially for lesbian and gay teachers, and lesbian and gay students. In this article I want to consider briefly the immediate legal and ideological circumstances that frame the subject of homosexuality in schools, for unless we understand the historical and institutional dimensions of anti-gay prejudice, we will not be able to develop effective counter-strategies.

Section 28 and the "Wolfenden Strategy"

On May 24, 1988, Section 28 of the Local Government (Amendment) Act came into force in the United Kingdom. The Act states that

(1) A local authority shall not
  (a) intentionally promote homosexuality or publish material with the intent of promoting homosexuality;
  (b) promote the teaching in any maintained school of the acceptability of homosexuality as a pretended family relationship.
(2) Nothing in subsection (1) above shall be taken to prohibit the doing of anything for the purpose of treating or preventing the spread of disease.

This was the culmination, to date, of more than a decade of increasingly polarized debate and controversy focused around so-called "family values," which has involved a special emphasis on education in the broadest sense, from the formal curriculum in schools, to plays, films, and art exhibitions housed or in any way financed or supported by local government. In other words, we are witnessing an increasing acknowledgment of the role that culture plays in the construction of sexual identities, and it is the field of cultural production that is ever more subject to frankly political interventions, in Britain as in the United States.[4]

Yet it would be a mistake to regard Section 28 as something entirely new. On the contrary, in many respects it may be seen to stand in the mainstream of modern British legislation concerning homosexuality, which has never aimed to establish or protect the rights of lesbians and gay men. Rather, it has always aspired to protect our imaginery victims—those whom the law regards as especially "vulnerable," including the feeble-minded, women, and above all children. However, the concept of childhood remains highly elastic in relation to all aspects of homosexuality, as in the most obvious example of the legal age of consent for sex between men, which is still firmly fixed at 21, five years more than the age set for heterosexuals.[5] Far from ushering in a new age of sexual enlightenment, the famous Sexual Offences Act of 1967 paved the way for the implementation of what Beverley Brown has named the Wolfenden Strategy, which has established ever more effective control of sex and sexuality by the State, but also by many other non-State institutions, from the mass media to clinical medicine. Indeed, the Sexual Offences Act of 1967 clearly enacted the legal moralism of the Report of the Wolfenden Committee on which it was belatedly modeled, which explicitly regretted the "general loosening of former moral standards."

Sadly, there has never been any question of English law turning its archaic attention to the rising tide of anti-gay prejudice and discrimination and actual violence in contemporary Britain. This is largely a result of the absence of any effective discourse of civil rights within Parliamentary politics in the U.K.[6] On the contrary, the workings of the Wolfenden Strategy have consistently, if unconvincingly, attempted to define "acceptable" human sexuality in strict relation to reproductive sex between married couples, and to contain all forms of non-reproductive sex, from homosexuality to prostitution, in a legally defined private sphere where they are permitted to exist, but not to be culturally validated in any way. Hence it is no surprise that British lesbians and gay men are at the very bottom of the line in terms of available police protection, way behind women or racial minorities. In 1989 the Metropolitan Police launched a major poster campaign in London to combat racism. Yet a parallel campaign against anti-gay discrimination remains entirely unthinkable. In the meantime, police prosecutions of gay men in Britain in 1990 have reached the worst levels of the notorious witch-hunts of the mid-1950s.[7] This wider question of anti-gay prejudice in Britain, and the United States, must also be related to the worsening tragedy of HIV/AIDS in both countries, which are distinguished in international terms by governmental refusal to establish proper national policies which would take the epidemic seriously, and by the constant harassing of health education and non-government AIDS service organizations whose work is deemed to "promote homosexuality" or "drug abuse."[8] And in both countries the political opposition party has equally failed to challenge official government policies, or their absence, for fear of association with the dreaded "electoral liability" of lesbian and gay issues. The assault against lesbians and gay men in the field of education, whether as students or teachers, must be viewed in this wider perspective if its full significance is to be understood, and if effective strategies are to be developed to remedy the situation. Section 28 simply put into law the previous recommendations of the Department of Education, which published an official Circular in November 1987 that badly stated

> There is no place in any school in any circumstances for teaching which advocates homosexual behaviour, which presents it as "the norm," or which encourages homosexual experimentation by pupils.[9]

These brief yet densely written clauses already speak volumes about the attitudes and beliefs that constitute anti-gay prejudice, and the laws it brings about and sanctions. Indeed, they provide a startlingly clear insight into the world that the prejudiced inhabit, a world that is mainly defined by *fear*—fear of gay couples being accepted just like other couples, a world in which homosexuality is a perpetual and terrifying menace, a world in which the young are always thought to be in danger of corruption, and in which they can never be sufficiently protected. If we want to understand the force of anti-gay prejudice, and the role that it plays across the entire field of modern education, we must begin by considering the ways in which heterosexual adults are encouraged to identify with children. This required a close understanding of the discourse of "promotion" that unites both Section 28 in Britain, and the Helms Amendment which banned Safer Sex education for gay men in the USA for several years in the late 1980s.[10] Yet at the same time, such laws also serve paradoxically to draw attention to the fact that fundamental definitions of sexual identity and sexual morality are historically contingent, and by no means "natural." They also further demonstrate the confidence of the institutions which insist that the existing power relations of sexuality and of gender must be vigorously defended, pre-emptively if necessary.

Certainly no area of social life has been subjected to more violent ideological contestation in the modern period than sex education, and the whole vexed question of homosexuality in schools. As we have already seen, this has now culminated in the State's claim to distinguish between supposedly "real" and "pretended" families. At a time when a third of babies in Britain are born into single-parent families, it would appear that underlying, long-term changes in the nature of adult sexual relations and patterns of child-raising are encouraging ever stronger patterns of resistance, retrenched around a powerful fantasy of how "family life" used to be, and should be in future. Sex is the central and heavily overdetermined focus of such fantasies, which involve a sharp distinction between the world of marriage and the home, and the lives of lesbians and gay men. Since homosexuality cannot be acknowledged within the ordinary workaday world, it must of necessity be thought of as the completely different inversion of the heterosexually known and familiar. Indeed, it is vitally important that lesbians and gay men should be able to understand the mechanisms of displacement and denial that inform heterosexual projections about us as people, for these projections determine the world in which we must live our lives. Furthermore, as public attitudes gradually change over time, it would appear that there has been a consolidation of prejudice at the level of institutional politics, where the subject of homosexuality can easily be exploited, or else ignored as a supposed electoral "liability." Hence the need for broad cultural strategies in relation to "public opinion," as well as specific strategies targeting the State, and the very concept of "politics."

Promoting Homosexuality

Throughout the long debate which accompanied the publication and the eventual passing into law of Section 28, journalists and other commentators frequently referred to the Bill's aim to prevent the promotion of homosexuality in schools. The concept of "promotion" behind the Bill was rarely questioned, except in legal opinions sought by the teaching trade unions and others in order to oppose it. Thus by analogy with British company law, Lord Gifford concluded his written Opinion with the observation that

> "promote homosexuality" involves active advocacy directed by local authorities towards individuals in order to persuade them to become homosexual, or to experiment with homosexual relationships.[11]

While Section 28 does not supersede the legal authority of previous legislation concerning sex education in Britain, it has nonetheless had a wide cultural impact—not least in establishing the notion of homosexual "promotion" as never before. In this respect it is helpful to note the way in which the wording of Section 28 binds together a theory of the formation of sexual identity with a theory of representation. On the one hand it is assumed, within the wider terms of the Wolfenden Strategy, that "the vulnerable" may be easily seduced into sexual experimentation, and into a rejection of supposedly "natural" heterosexuality. On the other hand it explicitly targets representations in any medium that depict lesbian or gay relationships as equivalent to heterosexual families. The unconscious logic thus runs that homosexuality can only exist as a result of the seduction of minors by predatory older perverts. This seduction may, however, be indirect, and effected via *cultural* means. In other words, there is a clear recognition that sexual identities are culturally grounded, and an acknowledgment that gay identity does not follow automatically from homosexual desire or practice. Something else is needed—the active presence of a confident, articulate lesbian and gay culture that clothes homosexual desire in a stable, collective *social* identity.

In this respect, the strategic significance of Section 28 lies in the way it harnesses a theory of (homo)sexual identity to a theory of representation which is remarkably like crude "copy-cat" theories concerning the supposed influence of pornography on its users, and especially on those who supposedly come across pornography "by accident." What in effect is acknowledged is the *pedagogic value* of gay culture in developing and sustaining gay identities. In all of this, it is the imagined vulnerability of heterosexuality that is most significant, together with the assumed power of homosexual pleasure to corrode the "natural" order of social and sexual relations. This is evidently a response to the long-term impact of gay culture in modern Britain, where the Government's Inspectorate of Schools concluded in 1986 that "given the openness with which homosexuality is treated in society now it is almost bound to arise as an issue in one area of another of a school's curriculum."[12] They therefore conclude that

> Information about and discussion of homosexuality, whether it involves a whole class or an individual, needs to acknowledge that experiencing strong feelings of attraction to members of the same sex is a phase passed through by many young people, but that for a significant number of people these feelings persist into adult life. Therefore it needs to be dealt with objectively and seriously, bearing in mind that, while there has been a marked shift away from the general condemnation of homosexuality, many individuals and groups hold sincerely to the view that it is morally objectionable. This is difficult territory for teachers to traverse, and for some schools to accept that homosexuality may be a normal feature of relationships would be a breach of the religious faith upon which

they are founded. Consequently LEA'S (Local Education Authorities), voluntary bodies, governors, heads and senior staff in schools have important responsibilities in devising guidance and supporting teachers dealing with this sensitive issue.[13]

In all of this it should be noted that there is no consideration of the consequences for lesbian and gay teachers or students. Indeed, it is the very open-endedness of the Inspectors' Report, published by the Department of Education, which seems to have been an immediate trigger behind the lobby that orchestrated Section 28. For the Report unambiguously recognizes a reality, "a marked shift away from the general condemnation of homosexuality," that the authors of Section 28 equally unambiguously wish to deny.

Section 28 thus exemplifies an extreme registration of the changing sexual politics of the past twenty years. In one sense it evidently belongs to the long tradition of anti-Freudian thought that denies infantile sexuality, whilst at the same time it is almost *too* eager to concede that sexuality may be "artificially" conjured into being via sexual "experimentation." This sense of homosexual desire as a kind of omnipresent potential contagion is wholly in keeping with Michel Foucault's prophetic observation in 1980 that, in the future,

> Sexuality will no longer be a form of behaviour with certain precise prohibitions but rather a kind of danger that lingers. . . . Sexuality will become the threat looming over all social bonds, relations among generations as among individuals. On this shadow, on this phantom, on this fear the power structure will assume control by means of a seemingly generous and blanket legislation thanks largely to a series of timely interventions that will probably involve judicial institutions supported by the medical profession. And there will arise a new order of sexual control. . . . Sex will be decriminalized only to reappear as a danger, and a universal one at that. There lies the real danger.[14]

Certainly we are presently witnessing an unparalleled struggle between values and identities forged within the sexual categories of the late nineteenth century, and rival values and identities that have emerged in the twentieth century. This struggle is waged with special ferocity in those areas of social life where sexual identity is most contested, of which education is perhaps the most significant. Education has clearly long been targeted by anti-gay traditionalists because it is identified as the site at which the supposed "threat" of homosexuality is most acute, and where pre-emptive maneuvers are most needed. Yet public opinion polls in both Britain and the United States suggest that broad levels of prejudice are actually in decline. For example, 71% of Americans recently polled thought that lesbians and gay men should have equal job opportunities to heterosexuals, compared to only 59% in 1982.[15] Meanwhile in Britain a still more recent survey suggests that 60% of heterosexual men and 62% of women think that gay men should be allowed to adopt children, while over 60% of men and over 80% of women think that no gay person should be barred from any job on the grounds of their sexuality.[16] It is thus far from clear that popular consent could actually be won in relation to any attempt to recriminalize homosexuality as such, and it is highly significant that there has been no serious attempt in either Britain or the U.S. to introduce legislation to proscribe specific "sexual acts," in the manner of pre-modern laws. The contestation that is currently being fought out in relation to education involves a fight to the death between the diverse forces of radical sexual pluralism, including single-parent families, pro-abortion campaigners, and all whose lives are invalidated by "family values," and those who devotedly subscribe and submit themselves to "family values." Insofar as school represents a double threshold, between the privacy of the home and public space, as well as between the categories of child and adult, it was inevitable that education would find itself caught in the cross-fire between fundamentally incompatible definitions of what it means to be a man or a woman in the late twentieth century, an adult or a child. In this context it is imperative that we appreciate the new significance of the discourse of "promotion," whether it is employed to justify attacks on gay culture as in Britain, or on Safer Sex education, as in the United States.[17]

For gay identity can undoubtedly be promoted, in circumstances where homosexual desire might otherwise have little opportunity of providing the ground for an integrated sense of self. Section 28 aims to restore a world of exclusively heterosexual values, identities, and institutions, in which homosexual desire could only be lived within the compliant, subservient terms of "homosexual" identity. "Homosexuals" are thus envisaged as a discrete number of invisible individuals, who preferably do not act on the basis of their desires. This is the picture of homosexuality and "homosexuals" that traditionalists wish to impose on young people and, as far as possible, throughout the rest of society. "Homosexuals" are thus depicted as a uniform type, an abstract, generalized, and thus dehumanized menace—especially dangerous because they cannot necessarily be readily identified. Unlike people of color, lesbians and gay men cannot immediately be recruited to constitute a visible, immediate definition of Otherness in relation to which Heterosexuality can be positively contrasted. It is therefore imperative that the cultural iconography of "the homosexual" has precedence over any representations that might reveal the actual diversity and complexity of sexual choice. Hence the traditionalists' obsession with the *representation* of family life, and their violent iconoclasm in relation to images that contravene their codes of "acceptable" gender imagery. It is precisely at this point that anti-pornography campaigners often unwittingly find themselves in alliance with another, parallel social-purity movement, rooted in anti-gay prejudice and strict patriarchal values. Ultimately, the conflict of contemporary sexual politics concerns the unreconcilable conflict between power relations that seek increasingly to define and divide people along the lines of sexual object-choice, and a politics which aspires to transcend the power relations of the categories of sexuality altogether, along with the identities they produce. This conflict is currently being waged with special ferocity around rival definitions of the meaning of Childhood. On the one hand, there is evidently a growing demand that sexual diversity should be acknowledged in schools, while on the other it is insisted that homosexuality should only be represented as a hideous perversion of heterosexuality, understood as a "natural" domain of unassailable, rigidly gendered characteristics organized around the prime purpose of sexual reproduction and the "protection" of asexual children.

Theorizing Childhood

In his celebrated *Introductory Lectures on Psychoanalysis*, Freud succinctly argued that

> to suppose that children have no sexual life—sexual excitations and needs and a kind of satisfaction—but suddenly acquire it between the ages of twelve and fourteen, would (quite apart from any observations) be as improbable, and indeed senseless, biologically as to suppose that they brought no genitals with them into the world and only grew them at the time of puberty. What *does* awaken in them at this time is the reproductive function, which makes use for its purposes of physical and mental material already present.[18]

Those who refuse to accept this "are committing the error of confusing sexuality and reproduction and by doing so you are blocking your path to an understanding of sexuality, the perversions and the neuroses."[19]

It is important at once to note that, for Freud, "perversion" was simply a descriptive term used to theorize all aspects of sexuality that do not have a reproductive aim, and one of the most productive tensions within his work concerns the way he often contradicts himself in relation to the supposed reproductive ends of adult sexuality. For elsewhere he insists that "in man the sexual instinct does not originally serve the purpose of reproduction at all, but has as its aim the gaining of particular kinds of pleasures."[20]

From Freud's perspective, it is above all *education* which serves to restrict the aim of sexual pleasure, and to channel it into socially and culturally acceptable directions—in other words, into the familiar patterns of marriage and, we must note, of homophobia. Nor is this aim simply that of sexual reproduction. On the contrary, for Freud education aims

> to tame and restrict the sexual instinct when it breaks out as an urge to reproduction, and to subject it to an individual will which is identical with the bidding of society. It is also concerned to postpone the full development of the instinct till the child shall have reached a certain degree of intellectual maturity, for, with the complete irruption of the sexual instinct, educatability is for practical purposes at an end.[21]

In other words, according to Freud, perhaps the central aspect of education is the inculcation of certain specific rules and attitudes towards sex, which will guarantee the subsequent sexual workings of (patriarchal) society, including the familiar double-standards of sexual morality in relation to women and men of which he was a particularly bitter critic. With the benefit of hindsight we can also recognize that attitudes towards homosexuality are also thus an indispensable target of education, since it is always at least potentially available as a site of alternative sexual satisfaction to heterosexual sex, a site moreover which must therefore be rigorously controlled. In all of this, however, we should also note that neither Freud nor his followers have ever demonstrated much concern for the fate of young lesbian and gay people within a pedagogic environment which has as its central business the production of compliant heterosexual identities, largely by means of demonizing homosexuality. This is precisely where we pick up psychoanalysis in the late twentieth century. For the vital point is that young people do not lack sexuality: what they are frequently *denied* is an identity in relation to their sexuality.

This is largely effected by means of the establishment of the widely pervasive belief that there indeed exists a distinct "world of childhood," quite separate from and independent of adult life. While this is generally felt to be in the child's own best interests, it actually dooms children— and especially gay children—to very considerable misery, since the ordinary relations between adults and children are arbitrarily severed. As Hannah Arendt has pointed out, this can easily have disastrous consequences for the child for, by being "emancipated" from the authority of adults, he or she

> has not been freed but has been subjected to a much more terrifying and truly tyrannical authority, the tyranny of the majority . . . either thrown back upon themselves or handed over to the tyranny of their own group, against which, because of its numerical superiority, they cannot rebel, with which, because they are children, they cannot reason, and out of which they cannot flee to any other world because the world of adults is barred to them.[22]

This strikes me as a peculiarly accurate depiction of the dilemmas facing most young gay people at school.

Nor can most gay children expect any understanding of this dilemma at home, where their marginalization and vulnerability is only likely to be reinforced. Hence the familiar strategies such children so frequently develop as self-defense mechanisms—the semblance of ultra-conformism to conventional gender roles, excessive zealousness in competitive sports or academic pursuits, and so on. Somehow we have to develop ways to defend young lesbians and gay children from the consequences of their own defensive strategies, with which they will often closely identify for obvious reasons. Much later unhappiness is undoubtedly rooted in such common childhood experience. This is one clear reason why we should not lie to children about the (homo)sexuality of historical or contemporary cultural figures, including scientists, writers, artists, and athletes. For good education involves helping children to learn how to make and exercise choices. This is not to say that one's sexuality is in any simple sense "chosen," at least in the same way that one might choose a career. However, the choices one makes on the basis of one's sexuality should be respected and encouraged, and this must include sexual experimentation, which in turn involves (for most of us) both success and failure. What we have to end is a world in which young lesbian and gay students often feel no real sense of belonging, and where they have precious little opportunity to develop a sustaining sense of their own self-esteem. Given the grotesque denial of Safer Sex education to young gay men in schools, and our increasing understanding of the role of self-esteem in relation to preventing the transmission of HIV, this is now more urgently important than ever. We must never forget that great violence is routinely perpetrated against all young lesbians and gay men in the name of "education," violence which is generally continuous with the emotional violence of heterosexual domesticity and "family values" which would deny our very existence, let alone the dignity and significance of our particular emotional and sexual needs, whether as young people or as adults.

From this perspective we may invert the usual question of what children supposedly want or need from education, and ask what it is that adults want or need of children in the name of "education." For it is in relation to theories of Childhood that the practices of adult power relations may be very productively analyzed, and nowhere more so than in the wholesale denial of children's sexuality. As Michel Foucault has pointed out:

> When it comes to children, the first assumption is that their sexuality can never be directed towards an adult. Secondly they are deemed incapable of self-expression. Thus no one ever believes them. They are believed to be immune to sexuality, and unable to discuss it.[23]

It is especially ironic that this position is generally presented within the context of a heavily vulgarized version of psychoanalysis itself, harnessed to the most reactionary (and anti-Freudian) purpose of denying children's sexuality altogether. In this respect we should recognize the high priority of targeting the domain of "educational psychology" that underpins so many aspects of the training of teachers. This in turn involves acknowledging the erotic component that plays so central part in *all* educational environments. As long as education is imagined to be entirely nonsexual, the actual erotics of the pedagogic situation can be displaced away in the imaginary likeness of the evil pervert, "promoting" his or her sexuality with "innocent" children. The question is *not* whether or not children are sexual beings, but how adults respond to children's sexuality, in ways that range from total denial to an untroubled acceptance.

Conclusion

Behind the rhetoric that identifies the supposedly widespread and perilous "promotion" of homosexuality lies a particularly dense core of fantasy and denial that needs to be carefully unpacked if the rhetoric is to be successfully countered. On a descriptive level we may easily detect deep-seated fears that cross over the familiar social barriers of class, gender, and culture. These fears constitute a narrative, according to the logic of which "vulnerable" (i.e., nonsexual) children are in constant danger of being seduced into homosexuality via sexual "experimentation" stimulated by the depiction of gay and lesbian relationships as fully equivalent to "family" (i.e., heterosexual) relations. The discourse of "promoting homosexuality" thus articulates real anxieties on the part of many people, as well as providing an imagined solution to the problem in the form of new laws and other extraordinary measures. These are rationalized as forms of defense against what is perilous, yet they are in fact transparently aggressive and preemptive, since powerful legislation already exists to deal with the complex realities of actual child abuse. We may therefore be justified in suspecting that the "reality" that this discourse addresses is not that of concrete social relations but of the unconscious.

In a sense this should already be apparent from the sheer tenacity of the ways in which the narrative returns to the imagined spectacle of the child's seduction, and his or her *acceptance* of the seducer, which is most dreaded. In other words, the narrative of "homosexual promotion" should be regarded as a powerful fantasy which permits some heterosexuals to legitimately dwell on the image of children's bodies as objects of (homo)sexual desire, and, moreover, as its active *subjects*. In this respect the narrative reveals significant parallels to other fantasy-narratives that also possess widespread contemporary currency, from those of Satanic child abuse, to demonic possession, and so on. All of these share a heavily overdetermined investment in the "innocence" of childhood, and the depravity of the surrounding adult world, from which it is considered to be the primary responsibility of parents to protect the young. In all these respects the discourse of the "promotion" of homosexuality should be recognized as an essentially pre-modern construction, that is only able to conceptualize homosexual desire in the likeness of sinister, predatory perverts, luring innocent victims to their doom, having corrupted them from within. It articulates "the homosexual" in the image of nineteenth-century Christian popular culture as an essentially *immoral* figure against which "the heterosexual" is left to define "morality." In these terms, homosexuality is to all extents and purposes a metaphysical force rather than a human characteristic, and the resurgence of the discourse of "promotion" may best be explained as a last-ditch attempt to resist the larger implications of the emergence of gay politics, which insist on giving lesbians and gay men ordinary human features. This perhaps is what is most terrifying of all to those who conceptualize themselves and other people in brutally archaic terms. For as long as "the homosexual" is not regarded as human, individual lesbians and gay men can continue to be marginalized and persecuted. The greatest threat that gay politics offers to this ideological formation is the risk of acknowledging that, on the contrary, we are as human as everyone else. It is precisely this threat that the discourse of "promotion" aims to forestall. What is new is the tacit recognition that there is no going back to the strategy of criminalizing sexual acts, and with this we witness a displaced concern with the role of *representation*, as in so many other areas of contemporary moralism. The discourse of "promotion" therefore aims to saturate the image of "the homosexual" with the traditional connotations of depraved sexual acts, and to prevent the cultural acceptability of gay identity, and sexual diversity rooted in the principle of sexual choice. It is choice that the discourse of "promotion" wishes to deny, and it is on this level and around these terms that gay politics will undoubtedly have to fight its major battles in the 1990s.

Notes

1. Rainer Maria Rilke, "How Childhood tries to reach us," *Selected Works Volume 2, Poetry*, ed. J. B. Leishman (London: The Hogarth Press, 1967), 322.

2. Jacqueline Rose, *The Case of Peter Pan, or the Impossibility of Children's Fiction* (London: Macmillan, 1984), 12.

3. Tim Rollins, "Education And Democracy," in *Democracy: A Project by Group Material*, ed. B. Wallis (Seattle: Bay Press, 1990), 47.

4. For example, see Lisa Duggan, "On Sex Panics," *Artforum* 28, no. 2 (October 1989): 26–27.

5. See Simon Watney, *Policing Desire: Pornography, AIDS, and the Media* (Minneapolis: University of Minnesota Press, 1989).

6. See Simon Watney, "Practices of Freedom: 'Citizenship' and the Politics of Identity in the Age of AIDS," in *Identity: Community, Culture, Difference*, ed. J. Rutherford (London: Lawrence & Wishart, 1990).

7. Indecency prosecutions against gay men in the UK have risen from 857 in 1985 to an astonishing 2,022 in 1989.

8. See Simon Watney, "Introduction," in *Taking Liberties: AIDS and Cultural Politics*, ed. Erica Carter and Simon Watney (London: Serpent's Tail Press, 1989).

9. Department of Education and Science, *Circular 11* (1987).

10. See Douglas Crimp, "How to Have Promiscuity in an Epidemic," in *AIDS: Cultural Analysis, Cultural Activism*, ed. Douglas Crimp (Cambridge, MA: MIT Press, 1988).

11. Quoted in Madeleine Colvin with Jane Hawksley, *Section 28: A Practical Guide to the Law and Its Implications* (London: National Council for Civil Liberties, 1989), 12.

12. *Health Education from 5 to 16* (London: Her Majesty's Stationery Office, 1986).

13. *Health Education from 5 to 16.*

14. Michel Foucault, *Semiotext(e) Special, Intervention Series 2: Loving Children* (Summer 1980), 41–42.

15. Michael R. Kagay, "Homosexuals Gain More Acceptance," *New York Times*, 25 October, 1989, A24.

16. "Is it still OK to be gay?," *New Woman* (October 1990): 16–20.

17. See Crimp, "How to Have Promiscuity," 10.

18. Sigmund Freud, "The Sexual Life of Human Beings," in *Introductory Lectures On Psychoanalysis* (Harmondsworth: Penguin, 1972), 353.

19. *Ibid.*

20. Sigmund Freud, " 'Civilised' Sexual Morality and Modern Nervous Illness," *Penguin Freud Library Vol. 12* (Harmondsworth: Penguin, 1977).

21. Freud, "The Sexual Life," 353.

22. Hannah Arendt, "The Crisis in Education," *Between Past and Future: Eight Exercises In Political Thought* (Harmondsworth: Penguin, 1977), 181–82.

23. Foucault, *Semiotext(e)*, 42.

Source Bibliography

Abraham, Nicholas and Maria Torok. *The Wolf Man's Magic Word: A Cryptonymy.* Translated by Nicholas Rand. Minneapolis: Minnesota University Press, 1986.

ACT UP/NY Women and AIDS Book Group. *Women, AIDS & Activism.* Boston: South End Press, 1990.

Adam, Barry D. "Structural Foundations of the Gay World." *Comparative Study of Society and History* 27 no. 4 (October 1985): 659–71.

———. *The Rise of a Gay and Lesbian Movement.* Boston: Twayne Publishers, 1987.

———. "Passivos y Activos en Nicaragua." *Out/Look* 1 no. 4 (Winter 1989): 74–82.

Adams, Parveen. "Of Female Bondage." In Teresa Brennan, ed. *Between Feminism & Psychoanalysis.* London and New York: Routledge, 1989.

Allen, Hilary. "Political Lesbianism and Feminism—Space for a Sexual Politics?" m/f 7 (1982): 15–34.

Allen, Jeffner. *Lesbian Philosophy: Explorations.* Palo Alto: Institute of Lesbian Studies, 1986.

———, ed. *Lesbian Philosophies and Cultures.* Albany: SUNY Press, 1989.

Allen, Paula Gunn. *The Sacred Hoop.* Boston: Beacon Press, 1986.

Allison, David, et al., eds. *Psychosis and Sexual Identity: Toward a Post-Analytic View of the Schreber Case.* Albany: SUNY Press, 1988.

Alonso, Ana Maria and Maria Teresa Koreck. "Silences: 'Hispanics,' AIDS, and Sexual Practices." *differences* 1 no. 1 (Winter 1989): 101–24.

Anzaldúa, Gloria. *Borderlands/La Frontera.* San Francisco: Spinsters/Aunt Lute, 1987.

———, ed. *Making Face, Making Soul—Haciendo Caras: Creative and Critical Perspectives by Women of Color.* San Francisco: Aunt Lute Foundation Books, 1990.

Ardill, Susan and Sue O'Sullivan. "Upsetting An Applecart: Difference, Desire and Lesbian Sadomasochism." *Feminist Review* 23 (Summer 1986): 31–57.

———. "Sex in the Summer of '88." *Feminist Review* 31 (Spring 1989): 126–34.

Bad Object Choices, eds. *How Do I Look? Queer Film and Video.* Seattle: Bay Press, 1991.

Barthes, Roland. *S/Z.* Translated by Richard Miller. New York: Hill and Wang, 1974. Originally published as *S/Z* (1970).

———. *A Lover's Discourse*. Translated by Richard Howard. New York: Hill and Wang, 1978. Originally published as *Fragments d'un discours amoureux* (1977).

Bataille, Georges. *Literature and Evil*. Translated by Alastair Hamilton. London: Marion Boyars, 1985. Originally published as *La Littérature et le mal* (1957).

———. *Erotism: Death and Sensuality*. Translated by Mary Dalwood. San Francisco: City Lights Books, 1986. Originally published as *L'Erotisme* (1957).

Beaver, Harold. "Homosexual Signs *(In Memory of Roland Barthes)*." *Critical Inquiry* 8 no. 1 (Autumn 1981): 99–119.

Bennett, Paula. *Emily Dickinson: Woman Poet*. Iowa City: University of Iowa Press, 1991.

Benstock, Shari. *Women of the Left Bank: Paris, 1900–1940*. Austin: University of Texas Press, 1986.

Berg, Elizabeth L. "The Third Woman." *Diacritics* 12 (Summer 1982): 11–20.

Bersani, Leo. "Pedagogy and Pederasty." *Raritan* 5 no. 1 (Summer 1985): 14–21.

———. " 'The Culture of Redemption': Marcel Proust and Melanie Klein." *Critical Inquiry* 12 no. 2 (Winter 1986): 399–421.

———. "Is the Rectum a Grave?" In Douglas Crimp, ed. *AIDS: Cultural Analysis, Cultural Activism*. Cambridge, Massachusetts and London: MIT Press, 1988.

Bérubé, Allan. "Caught in the Storm: AIDS and the Meaning of Natural Disaster." *Out/Look* 1 no. 3 (Fall 1988): 8–19.

Boffin, Tessa and Sunil Gupta, eds. *Ecstatic Antibodies: Resisting the AIDS Mythology*. London: Rivers Oram Press, 1990.

Boone, Bruce. "Gay Language as Political Praxis: The Poetry of Frank O'Hara." *Social Text* 1 no. 1 (1982): 59–92.

Boone, Joseph A. and Michael Cadden, eds. *Engendering Men: The Question of Male Feminist Criticism*. New York and London: Routledge, 1990.

Booth, Mark. *Camp*. New York: Quartet Books, 1983.

Boyers, Robert and George Steiner, eds. *Homosexuality: Sacrilege, Vision, Politics*. Saratoga Springs: Skidmore College, 1983.

Brittan, Arthur. *Masculinity and Power*. New York: Basil Blackwell, 1989.

Britton, Andrew. "For Interpretation: Notes Against Camp." *Gay Left* 7 (1978–79): 11–14.

Bronski, Michael. *Culture Clash: The Making of Gay Sensibility*. Boston: South End Press, 1984.

———. "Eros and Politicisation: Sexuality Politics, and the Idea of Community." *Radical America* 22 no. 1 (Jan/Feb 1989): 45–51.

Bulkin, Elly, Minnie Bruce Pratt, and Barbara Smith. *Yours in Struggle: Three Feminist Perspectives on Anti-Semitism and Racism*. New York: Firebrand Books, 1984.

Burstyn, Varda, ed. *Women Against Censorship*. Toronto: Douglas & McIntyre, Ltd., 1985.

Butler, Judith. "The Body Politics of Julia Kristeva." *Hypatia* 3 no. 3 (Winter 1989): 104–18.

———. "The Force of Fantasy: Feminism, Mapplethorpe, and Discursive Excess." *differences* 2 no. 2 (Summer 1990a): 105–125.

———. *Gender Trouble: Feminism and the Subversion of Identity.* New York and London: Routledge, 1990b.

———. "Lana's 'Imitation': Melodramatic Repetition and the Gender Performative." *Genders* 9 (Fall 1990c): 1–18.

Butters, Ronald R., John M. Clum, and Michael Moon, eds. *South Atlantic Quarterly* 88 no. 1 (Winter 1989). Special issue on "Displacing Homophobia."

Cadden, Michael. "Engendering F. O. M.: The Private Life of *American Renaissance*." In Joseph A. Boone and Michael Cadden, eds. *Engendering Men: The Question of Male Feminist Criticism.* New York and London: Routledge, 1990.

———. *The Body Theatrical.* New York and London: Routledge, forthcoming.

Camera Obscura 17 (May 1988). Special issue on "Male Trouble." Constance Penley and Sharon Willis, eds.

Card, Claudia. "Lesbian Attitudes and *The Second Sex*." *Women's Studies International Forum* 8 (1985): 209–14.

Carmen, Gail, Weeba, and Tamara. "Becoming Visible: Black Lesbian Discussions." In *Feminist Review*, eds. *Sexuality: A Reader.* London: Virago Press, 1987.

Case, Sue-Ellen. "Toward a Butch-Femme Aesthetic." *Discourse* 11 no. 1 (Fall/Winter 1988/1989): 55–73.

Castiglia, Christopher. "Rebel Without a Closet." In Joseph A. Boone and Michael Cadden, eds. *Engendering Men: The Question of Male Feminist Criticism.* New York and London: Routledge, 1990.

Castle, Terry. "Matters Not Fit To Be Mentioned: Fielding's *The Female Husband*." *English Literary History* 49 no. 3 (Fall 1982): 602–22.

Cavin, Susan. *Lesbian Origins.* San Francisco: ism press, 1985.

Cheseboro, James W., ed. *Gay Speak: Gay Male and Lesbian Communication.* New York: Pilgrim Press, 1981.

Citron, Michelle. "Films of Jan Oxenberg: Comic Critique." In Charlotte Brunsdon, ed. *Films for Women*, 72–78. London: British Film Institute, 1986.

Cixous, Hélène and Catherine Clément. *The Newly Born Woman.* Translated by Betsy Wing. Minneapolis: University of Minnesota Press, 1986. Originally published as *La jeune née* (1975).

Clark, Wendy. "The Dyke, the Feminist, and the Devil." *Feminist Review*, eds. *Sexuality: A Reader.* London: Virago Press, 1987.

Cohen, Ed. "Writing Gone Wilde: Homoerotic Desire in the Closet of Representation." *PMLA* 102 (1987): 801–13.

———. "Foucauldian necrologies: 'gay' 'politics'? politically gay?" *Textual Practice* 2 no. 1 (Spring 1988): 87–101.

———. "Legislating the Norm: From Sodomy to Gross Indecency." *South Atlantic Quarterly* 88 no. 1 (Winter 1989): 181–217.

———. "Are We (Not) What We Are Becoming?: 'Gay' 'Identity,' 'Gay Studies,' and the Disciplining of Knowledge." In Joseph A. Boone and Michael Cadden, eds. *Engen-*

dering Men: The Question of Male Feminist Criticism. New York and London: Routledge, 1990.

————. *Talk on the Wilde Side: Towards a Genealogy of Male Sexualities.* New York and London: Routledge, forthcoming.

Combahee River Collective. "A Black Feminist Statement." In Gloria T. Hull, Patricia Bell Scott, and Barbara Smith, eds. *All The Women Are White, All the Blacks Are Men, But Some of Us Are Brave: Black Women's Studies.* Old Westbury, New York: The Feminist Press, 1982.

Cook, Blanche Wiesen. "The Historical Denial of Lesbianism." *Radical History Review* 20 (Spring/Summer 1979): 60–65.

Cooper, Emmanuel. *The Sexual Perspective: Homosexuality and Art in the Last 100 Years in the West.* London and New York: Routledge & Kegan Paul, 1986.

Cornwell, Anita. *Black Lesbians in White America.* Tallahassee, Florida: The Naiad Press Inc., 1983.

Craft, Christopher. " 'Descend, and Touch, and Enter': Tennyson's Strange Manner of Address." *Genders* 1 (Spring 1988): 83–101.

————. " 'Kiss Me With Those Red Lips': Gender and Inversion in Bram Stoker's *Dracula.*" In Elaine Showalter, ed. *Speaking of Gender.* New York and London: Routledge, 1989.

Creet, M. Julia, "Speaking in Lesbian Tongues: Monique Wittig and the Universal Point of View." *RFR/DFR* 17 no. 4 (December 1987): 16–18.

Crimp, Douglas, "Fassbinder, Franz, Fox, Elvira, Erwin, Armin, and All the Others." *October* 21 (Summer 1982): 63–81.

————, ed. *AIDS: Cultural Analysis, Cultural Activism.* Cambridge, Massachusetts and London: MIT Press, 1988.

————. "Mourning and Militancy." *October* 51 (Winter 1989): 3–18.

————. "The Boys in My Bedroom." *Art in America* (February 1990a): 47, 49.

————. with Adam Rolston. *AIDS Demo Graphics.* Seattle: Bay Press, 1990b.

————. "Portraits of People with AIDS," In Cary Nelson, Larry Grossberg, and Paula Treichler, eds. *Cultural Studies Now and In the Future.* New York: Routledge, 1991.

Cruikshank, Margaret, ed. *The Lesbian Path.* San Francisco: Grey Fox Press, 1980, 1985.

————. *Lesbian Studies: Present and Future.* Old Westbury, New York: The Feminist Press, 1982.

Dannecker, Martin. *Theories of Homosexuality.* Translated by David Fernbach. London: Gay Men's Press, 1981.

Davy, Kate. "Constructing the Spectator: Reception, Context, and Address in Lesbian Performance." *Performing Arts Journal* 10 no. 2 (1987): 43–52.

de Beauvoir, Simone. *The Second Sex.* Translated and edited by H. M. Parshley. New York: Vintage, 1989. Originally published as *Le Deuxième sexe* (1949).

de Lauretis, Teresa. "The Female Body and Heterosexual Presumption." *Semiotica* 67 nos. 3–4 (1987a): 259–79.

————. *Technologies of Gender: Essays on Theory, Film, and Fiction.* Bloomington: Indiana University Press, 1987b.

————. "Sexual Indifference and Lesbian Representation." *Theatre Journal* 40 no. 2 (May 1988): 155–77.

Deleuze, Gilles and Félix Guattari. *Anti-Oedipus: Capitalism and Schizophrenia.* Translated by Robert Hurley, Mark Seem, and Helen R. Lane. Minneapolis: University of Minnesota Press, 1983. Originally published as *L'Anti-Oedipe* (1972).

Deleuze, Gilles. *Foucault.* Translated by Seàn Hand. Minneapolis: University of Minnesota Press, 1988. Originally published as *Foucault* (1986).

Dellamora, Richard. *Masculine Desire: The Sexual Politics of Victorian Aestheticism.* Chapel Hill: University of North Carolina Press, 1990.

D'Emilio, John. "Capitalism and Gay Identity." In Ann Snitow, Christine Stansell, and Sharon Thompson, eds. *Powers of Desire: The Politics of Sexuality.* New York: Monthly Review Press, 1983a.

————. *Sexual Politics, Sexual Communities: The Making of a Homosexual Minority in the United States, 1940–1970.* Chicago and London: University of Chicago Press, 1983b.

Derrida, Jacques. *Glas.* Translated by John P. Leavy and Richard Rand. Lincoln: University of Nebraska Press, 1987a. Originally published as *Glas* (1974).

————. *The Post Card.* Translated by Alan Bass. Chicago: University of Chicago Press, 1987b. Originally published as *La carte postale* (1980).

————, and Marie-Françoise Plissart. "Rite of Inspection." Translated by David Wills. *Art and Text* 32 (Autumn 1989): 20–97. Originally published as *Droit de regards* (1985).

DiCaprio, Lisa "*Lianna*: Liberal Lesbianism." *Jump Cut* 29 (1984): 45–47.

Doane, Mary Ann. *The Desire to Desire: The Woman's Film of the 1940s.* Bloomington and Indianapolis: Indiana University Press, 1987.

Dolan, Jill. " 'Lesbian' Subjectivity in Realism: Dragging at the Margins of Structure and Ideology." In Sue-Ellen Case, ed. *Performing Feminisms: Feminist Critical Theory and Theatre.* London: The John Hopkins University Press, 1990.

Dollimore, Jonathan. "The Dominant and the Deviant: A Violent Dialectic." *Critical Quarterly* 28 nos. 1–2 (Spring/Summer 1986): 179–92.

————. "Homophobia and Sexual Difference." *Oxford Literary Review* 8 nos. 1–2 (1986b): 5–12.

————. "Different Desires: Subjectivity and Transgression in Wilde and Gide." *Textual Practice* 1 no. 1 (Spring 1987): 48–67.

Donald, Adrienne. "Coming Out of the Canon: Sadomasochism, Male Homoeroticism, Romanticism." *The Yale Journal of Criticism* 3 no. 1 (Fall 1989): 239–52.

Duberman, Martin Bauml, Martha Vicinus, and George Chauncey, Jr., eds. *Hidden From History: Reclaiming the Gay and Lesbian Past.* New York: New American Library, 1989.

Duchen, Claire, ed. and trans. *French Connections: Voices From the Women's Movement in France.* Amherst: University of Massachusetts Press, 1987.

Duggan, Lisa. "The Anguished Cry of an 80's Fem: 'I Want to be a Drag Queen.' " Out/
Look 1 no. 1 (Spring 1988): 63–65.

Duyves, Mattias, et al., eds. Among Men, Among Women. Amsterdam: Grafisch Cen-
trum Amsterdam, 1983.

Dyer, Richard, ed. Gays and Film. London: British Film Institute, 1977.

———. "Getting Over the Rainbow: Identity and Pleasure in Gay Cultural Politics." In
George Bridges and Rosalind Brunt, eds. Silver Linings: Some Strategies for the
Eighties. London: Lawrence & Wishart, 1981.

———. "Seen to Be Believed: Some Problems in the Representation of Gay People as
Typical." Studies in Visual Communication 9 no. 2 (Spring 1983): 2–19.

———. "Male Gay Porn: Coming to Terms." Jump Cut no. 30 (1985): 27–9.

———. Heavenly Bodies: Film Stars and Society. New York: St. Martin's Press, 1986.

———. "Children of the Night: Vampirism as Homosexuality, Homosexuality as
Vampirism." In Susannah Radstone, ed. Sweet Dreams: Sexuality, Gender and Popular Fiction. London: Lawrence & Wishart Limited, 1988.

———. Now You See It: Studies on Lesbian and Gay Film. New York and London:
Routledge, 1990.

Edelman, Lee. Transmemberment of Song: Hart Crane's Anatomies of Rhetoric and
Desire. Stanford: Stanford University Press, 1987.

———. "At Risk in the Sublime: The Politics of Gender and Theory." In Linda Kauffman, ed. Gender and Theory: Dialogues on Feminist Criticism. Oxford: Basil Blackwell, 1989a.

———. "Homographesis." The Yale Journal of Criticism 3 no. 1 (Fall 1989b): 189–
207.

———. "The Plague of Discourse: Politics, Literary Theory, and AIDS." South Atlantic
Quarterly 88, no. 1 (Winter 1989c): 301–17.

———. "Redeeming the Phallus: Wallace Stevens, Frank Lentricchia, and the Politics
of (Hetero)sexuality." In Joseph A. Boone and Michael Cadden, eds. Engendering
Men: The Question of Male Feminist Criticism. New York and London: Routledge,
1990.

———. Homographesis. New York and London: Routledge, forthcoming.

———. "Tearooms and Sympathy, or The Epistemology of the Water Closet." In Patricia
Yaeger, Doris Sommer, Andrew Parker, and Mary Russo, eds. Nationalisms and
Sexualities. New York and London: Routledge, forthcoming.

Ellenzweig, Allen. The Homoerotic Photograph. New York: Columbia University Press,
forthcoming.

Epstein, Julia. "Either/Or—Neither/Both: Sexual Ambiguity and the Ideology of Gender." Genders 7 (Spring 1990): 99–142.

Epstein, Steven. "Gay Politics, Ethnic Identity: The Limits of Social Constructionism."
Socialist Review 7 nos. 3/4 (May/Aug 1987): 9–54.

Escoffier, Jeffrey. "Sexual Revolution and the Politics of Gay Identity." Socialist Review
15 nos. 4–5 (July–October 1985): 126–96, 133–42.

Faderman, Lillian. *Surpassing the Love of Men: Romantic Friendship and Love Between Women from the Renaissance to the Present.* New York: Morrow, 1981.

Farley, Tucker Pamella. "Lesbianism and the Social Function of Taboo." In Hester Eisenstein and Alice Jardine, eds. *The Future of Difference.* New Brunswick: Rutgers University Press, 1980.

Fassler, Barbara. "Theories of Homosexuality as Sources of Bloomsbury's Androgyny." *Signs* 5 no. 2 (Winter 1979): 237–51.

Feminist Review no. 34 (Spring 1990). Special issue on "Perverse Politics: Lesbian Issues."

Fenichel, Otto. *The Psychoanalytic Theory of Neurosis.* New York: Norton, 1945.

Ferenczi, Sandor. "On the Part Played by Homosexuality in the Pathogenesis of Paranoia," 131–56. In *Contributions to Psycho-analysis.* Translated by Ernest Jones. Boston: The Gorham Press, 1916.

———. "The Nosology of Male Homosexuality." *Sex in Psycho-Analysis.* Translated by Ernest Jones, 250–68. New York: Dover Publications, 1956.

Ferguson, Ann. "Lesbian Identity: Beauvoir and History." *Women's Studies International Forum* 8 (1985): 203–8.

Ferguson, Russell, et al., eds. *Out There: Marginalization and Contemporary Cultures.* New York: The New Museum of Contemporary Art, and Cambridge: MIT Press, 1990.

Finch, Mark. "Sex and Address in *Dynasty.*" *Screen* 27 no. 6 (Nov/Dec 1986): 24–42.

Finch, Mark, and Richard Kwietniowski. "Melodrama and 'Maurice': Homo is Where the Het Is." *Screen* 29 no. 3 (Summer 1988): 72–80.

Findlay, Heather. "Is there a Lesbian in this Text? Derrida, Wittig, and the Politics of the Three Women." In Elizabeth Weed, ed. *Coming to Terms: Feminism/Theory/Politics.* New York and London: Routledge, 1989a.

———. "Renaissance Pederasty and Pedagogy: The 'Case' of Shakespeare's Falstaff." *The Yale Journal of Criticism* 3 no. 1 (Fall 1989b): 229–38.

Fischer, Lucy. *Shot/Countershot: Film Tradition and Women's Cinema.* Princeton: Princeton University Press, 1989.

Foster, Jeannette H. *Sex Variant Women in Literature.* Tallahassee, Florida: The Naiad Press Inc., 1985.

Foucault, Michel, Guy Hocquenghem, and Jean Danet. "La loi de la pudeur." *Recherches* 37 (April 1979): 69–82.

Foucault, Michel. "L'Occident et la verité du sexe." *Le Monde,* Edition Internationale (Nov 4–10, 1976): 12–13.

———. *Herculine Barbin: Being the Recently Discovered Memoirs of a Nineteenth-Century French Hermaphrodite.* Translated by Richard McDougall. New York: Pantheon Books, 1980a. Originally published as *Herculine Barbin, dite Alexina B.* (1978).

———. "The History of Sexuality: Interview." Translated by Geoff Bennington. *Oxford Literary Review* 4 no. 2 (1980b): 3–14.

———. *The History of Sexuality Vol. I: An Introducion.* Translated by Robert Hurley.

New York: Vintage Books, 1980c. Originally published as *Histoire de la sexualité vol. I: La volanté de savoir* (1976).

——. "The Simplest of Pleasures." Translated by Mike Riegle and Gilles Barbedette. *Fag Rag* 29 (1981a): 3. (First published in *Le Gai Pied* 1 (April 1979): 1,10.)

——. "De L'amitié comme mode de vie: un entretien avec un lecteur quinquagenaire." *Le Gai Pied* 25 (April 1981b): 38–39.

——. "A Conversation with Michel Foucault." By Gilles Barbedette. Translated by Brendan Lemon. *Christopher Street* 6 no. 4, Issue 64 (1982a): 36–41.

——. "Des Caresses d'hommes considérées comme un art." *Libération* (June 1, 1982b): 27.

——. "Michel Foucault: An Interview: Sex, Power and the Politics of Identity." By Bob Gallagher and Alexander Wilson. *The Advocate* 400 (Aug 7, 1984): 26–30, 58.

——. *The History of Sexuality Vol. II: The Use of Pleasure*. Translated by Robert Hurley. New York: Vintage Books, 1985. Originally published as *Histoire de la sexualité vol. II: L'usage des plaisirs* (1984).

——. "Sexual Choice, Sexual Act: An Interview with Michel Foucault." In *Michel Foucault: Politics, Philosophy, Culture: Interviews and Other Writings, 1977–1984*. Lawrence D. Kritzman, ed. New York and London: Routledge, 1988a. (First published in *Salmagundi* 58–59 (Fall/Winter 1982/1983): 10–24).

——. *The History of Sexuality Vol. III: The Care of the Self*. Translated by Robert Hurley. New York: Vintage Books, 1988b. Originally published as *Histoire de la sexualité vol. III: Le souci de soi* (1984).

Franklin, Sarah and Jackie Stacey. "DYKETACTICS FOR DIFFICULT TIMES: A Review of the 'Homosexuality, Which Homosexuality?' Conference, Amsterdam, 15–18 December 1987." *Feminist Review* 19 (Spring 1988): 136–50.

Freud, Sigmund, *Three Essays on the Theory of Sexuality* (1905a). Vol. 7 of *The Standard Edition*. Translated by James Strachey, 125–243. London: The Hogarth Press, 1953.

——. *Dora: Fragment of an Analysis of a Case of Hysteria* (1905b). Vol. 7 of *The Standard Edition*. Translated by James Strachey, 3–122. London: The Hogarth Press, 1953.

——. "Leonardo Da Vinci and a Memory of His Childhood" (1910). Vol. 11 of *The Standard Edition*. Translated by James Strachey, 59–230. London: The Hogarth Press, 1957.

——. "Psychoanalytic Notes on an Autobiographical Account of a Case of Paranoia" (1911). Vol. 12 of *The Standard Edition*. Translated by James Strachey, 3–84. London: The Hogarth Press, 1958.

——. *Totem and Taboo* (1913 [1912–13]). Vol. 13 of *The Standard Edition*. Translated by James Strachey, ix–164. London: The Hogarth Press, 1955.

——. "The *Moses* of Michelangelo" (1914). Vol. 13 of *The Standard Edition*. Translated by James Strachey, 209–38. London: The Hogarth Press, 1955.

——. "A Case of Paranoia Running Counter to the Psychoanalytic Theory of the Disease" (1915). Vol. 14 of *The Standard Edition*. Translated by James Strachey, 263–72. London: The Hogarth Press, 1955.

——. *From the History of an Infantile Neurosis* (1918 [1914]). Vol. 17 of *The*

Standard Edition. Translated by James Strachey, 7–122. London: The Hogarth Press, 1955.

———. " 'A Child is Being Beaten': A Contribution to the Study of the Origin of Sexual Perversions" (1919). Vol. 17 of *The Standard Edition.* Translated by James Strachey, 179–204. London: The Hogarth Press, 1955.

———. "The Psychogenesis of a Case of Homosexuality in a Woman" (1920). Vol. 18 of *The Standard Edition.* Translated by James Strachey, 145–72. London: The Hogarth Press, 1955.

———. "Some Neurotic Mechanisms in Jealousy, Paranoia and Homosexuality" (1922). Vol. 18 of *The Standard Edition.* Translated by James Strachey, 223–32. London: The Hogarth Press, 1955.

Frontiers: A Journal of Women's Studies 4 no. 3 (Fall 1979).

Frye, Marilyn. *The Politics of Reality: Essays in Feminist Theory.* Trumansberg, New York: The Crossing Press, 1983.

Fuss, Diana. *Essentially Speaking: Feminism, Nature and Difference.* New York and London: Routledge, 1989a.

———. "Getting Into History." *Arizona Quarterly* 45, no. 4 (Winter 1989b): 95–108.

Garber, Eric. "Gladys Bentley: The Bulldagger Who Sang the Blues." *Out/Look* 1 no. 1 (Spring 1988): 52–61.

Garber, Marjorie. "Spare Parts: The Surgical Construction of Gender." *differences* 1 no. 3 (Fall 1989): 137–59.

———. *Vested Interests: Cross-Dressing and Cultural Anxiety.* New York and London: Routledge, forthcoming.

Garner, Shirley Nelson. "Feminism, Psychoanalysis, and the Heterosexual Imperative." In Richard Feldstein and Judith Roof, eds. *Feminism and Psychoanalysis.* Ithaca and London: Cornell University Press, 1989.

Gay Left Collective, eds. *Homosexuality: Power and Politics.* London and New York: Allison and Busby, 1980.

Geever, Martha and Nathalie Magnan. "The Same Difference: On Lesbian Representation." *Exposure* 24 no. 2 (1986): 27 – 35.

Geever, Martha. "Girl Crazy: Lesbian Narratives in *She Must Be Seeing Things* and *Damned If You Don't.*" *The Independent* 11 no. 6 (1988): 14–18.

Gilman, Sander L. *Disease and Representation: Images of Illness from Madness to AIDS.* Ithaca and London: Cornell University Press, 1988.

Grahn, Judy. *Another Mother Tongue: Gay Words, Gay Worlds.* Boston: Beacon Press, 1984.

———. *The Highest Apple: Sappho and the Lesbian Poetic Tradition.* San Francisco: Spinsters/Aunt Lute, 1985.

———. *Really Reading Gertrude Stein.* Freedom, California: Crossing Press, 1989.

Greenberg, David F. *The Construction of Homosexuality.* Chicago and London: University of Chicago Press, 1988.

Grosz, Elizabeth. *Sexual Subversions: Three French Feminists.* Sydney: Allen & Unwin, 1989.

Grover, Jan Zita. "Dykes in Context: Some Problems in Minority Representation." In Richard Bolton, ed. *The Contest of Meaning: Critical Histories of Photography.* Cambridge: MIT Press, 1989.

Gubar, Susan. "Sapphistries," *Signs* 10 no. 1 (Autumn 1984): 43–62.

Gutíerrez, Ramón A. "Must We Deracinate Indians to Find Gay Roots?" *Out/Look* 1 no. 4 (Winter 1989): 61–67.

Haggerty, George E. "Literature and Homosexuality in the Late Eighteenth Century: Walpole, Beckford, and Lewis." *Studies in the Novel* 18 no. 4 (Winter 1986): 341–52.

Hallett, Judith. "Female Homoeroticism and the Denial of Roman Reality in Latin Literature." *The Yale Journal of Criticism* 3 no. 1 (Fall 1989): 209–27.

Halperin, David M. "One Hundred Years of Homosexuality." *Diacritics* 16 no. 2 (Summer 1986): 34–45.

———, John H. Winkler, and Froma I. Zeitlin, eds. *Before Sexuality: The Construction of Erotic Experience in the Ancient Greek World.* Princeton: Princeton University Press, 1989.

———. *One Hundred Years of Homosexuality and Other Essays on Greek Love.* New York and London: Routledge, 1990.

Haraway, Donna. "The Biopolitics of Postmodern Bodies: Determinations of Self in Immune System Discourse." *differences* 1 no. 1 (Winter 1989): 3–43.

Heath, Stephen. *The Sexual Fix.* New York: Schocken Books, 1984.

———. "The Ethics of Sexual Difference." *Discourse* 12 no. 2 (Spring/Summer 1990): 128–53.

Hennegan, Alison. "On Becoming a Lesbian Reader." In Susannah Radstone, ed. *Sweet Dreams: Sexuality, Gender and Popular Fiction.* London: Lawrence & Wishart Limited, 1988.

Heresies 12, The Sex Issue. New York: Heresies Collective Inc., 1981.

Hoagland, Sarah Lucia and Julia Penelope. *For Lesbians Only: A Separatist Anthology.* London: Onlywomen Press, Ltd., 1988.

Hoagland, Sarah Lucia. *Lesbian Ethics: Toward New Value.* Palo Alto: Institute of Lesbian Studies, 1989.

Hoch, Paul. *White Hero Black Beast: Racism, Sexism, and the Mask of Masculinity.* London: Pluto, 1979.

Hocquenghem, Guy. *Homosexual Desire.* Translated by Daniella Dangoor. London: Allison and Busby, 1978.

Hokenson, Jan. "The Pronouns of Gomorrah: A Lesbian Prose Tradition." *Frontiers* 10 no. 1 (1988): 62–69.

Hollibaugh, Amber and Cherríe Moraga. "What We're Rollin Around in Bed With: Sexual Silences in Feminism." In Ann Snitow, Christine Stansell, and Sharon Thompson, eds. *Powers of Desire: The Politics of Sexuality.* New York: Monthly Review Press, 1983.

Hooks, Bell. "Reflections on Homophobia and Black Communities." *Out/Look* 1 no. 2 (Summer 1988): 22–25.

Hughes, Walter. " 'Meat Out of the Eater': Panic and Desire in American Puritan Poetry." In Joseph A. Boone and Michael Cadden, eds. *Engendering Men: The Question of Male Feminist Criticism.* New York and London: Routledge, 1990.

Hull, Gloria T. *Color, Sex, and Poetry: Three Women Writers of the Harlem Renaissance.* Bloomington: Indiana University Press, 1987.

Irigaray, Luce. *Speculum of the Other Woman.* Translated by Gillian C. Gill. Ithaca: Cornell University Press, 1985a. Originally published as *Speculum de l'autre femme* (1974).

———. *This Sex Which Is Not One.* Translated by Catherine Porter with Carolyn Burke. Ithaca: Cornell University Press, 1985b. Originally published as *Ce Sexe qui n'en est pas un* (1977).

Jardine, Lisa. " 'Girl Talk' (for boys on the Left), or Marginalising Feminist Critical Praxis." *Oxford Literary Review* 8 nos. 1–2 (1986): 208–17.

Jay, Karla and Joanne Glasgow. *Lesbian Texts and Contexts: Radical Revisions.* New York and London: New York University Press, 1990.

Jay, Karla. *The Amazon and the Page: Natalie Clifford Barney and Renée Vivien.* Bloomington: Indiana University Press, 1988.

Jones, Ernest. *Papers on Psycho-Analysis.* Boston: Beacon Press, 1912.

Jump Cut no. 16 (1977). Special section on "Gay Men and Film."

———, nos. 24–25 (1981). Special section on "Lesbians and Film."

Kaite, Berkeley. "The Pornographer's Body Double: Transgression is the Law." In Arthur Kroker and Marilouise Kroker, eds. *Body Invaders: Panic Sex in America.* New York: St. Martin's Press, 1987.

Kaufman, Michael, ed. *Beyond Patriarchy: Essays by Men on Pleasure, Power, and Change.* New York and Toronto: Oxford University Press, 1987.

Kehoe, Monika, ed. *Historical, Literary, and Erotic Aspects of Lesbianism.* New York: Haworth, 1986.

Kennard, Jean E. "Ourself Behind Ourself: A Theory for Lesbian Readers." *Signs* 9 no. 4 (Summer 1984): 647–62.

King, Katie. "The Situation of Lesbianism as Feminism's Magical Sign: Contests for Meaning and the U.S. Women's Movement, 1968–1972." *Communication* 9 no. 1 (1986): 65–91.

———. "Audre Lorde's Lacquered Layerings: The Lesbian Bar as a Site of Literary Production." *Cultural Studies* 2 no. 3 (1988): 321–42.

Kinsman, Gary. *The Regulation of Desire: Sexuality in Canada.* Montreal and New York: Black Rose Books, 1987.

Kitzinger, Celia. *The Social Construction of Lesbianism.* London: Sage, 1987.

Knopp, Sherron E. "If I Saw You Would You Kiss Me?: Sapphism and the Subversiveness of Virginia Woolf's *Orlando.*" *PMLA* 103 (1988): 24–34.

Koedt, Anne, Ellen Levine, and Anita Rapone, eds. *Radical Feminism.* New York: Quadrangle Books, 1973.

Koestenbaum, Wayne, *Double Talk: The Erotics of Male Literary Collaboration.* New York and London: Routledge, 1989.

———. "Callas and Her Fans." *The Yale Review* 79 no. 1 (Autumn 1989): 1–20.

———. "Wilde's Hard Labour and the Birth of Gay Reading." In Joseph A. Boone and Michael Cadden, eds. *Engendering Men: The Question of Male Feminist Criticism.* New York and London: Routledge, 1990b.

Kopelson, Kevin. "Wilde, Barthes, and the Orgasmics of Truth." *Genders* 7 (Spring 1990): 22–31.

Landers, Timothy. "Bodies and Anti-bodies: A Crisis in Representation." *The Independent* 11 no. 1 (Jan/Feb 1988): 18–24.

Ledes, Richard C. with the assistance of Martin G. Koloski. "AIDS and the Ninjas." *Copyright* 1 (Fall 1987): 133–45.

Lesselier, Claudie. "Social Categorizations and Construction of a Lesbian Subject." *Feminist Issues* (Spring 1987): 89–94.

Lewes, Kenneth. *The Psychoanalytic Theory of Male Homosexuality.* New York: Simon and Schuster, 1988.

Lilly, Mark, ed. *Lesbian and Gay Writing.* London: Macmillan, 1990.

Linden, Robin Ruth, Darlene Pagano, Diana Russell, and Susan Leigh Star, eds. *Against Sadomasochism.* San Francisco: Frog In The Well, 1982.

Lorde, Audre. *Sister Outsider.* Trumansburg, New York: The Crossing Press, 1984.

———. *A Burst of Light.* Ithaca, New York: Firebrand Books, 1988.

Mager, Don. "Gay Theories of Gender Role Deviance." *Sub-Stance* 46 (1985): 32–48.

Martin, Biddy and Chandra Talpade Mohanty. "Feminist Politics: What's Home Got to Do With It?" In Teresa de Lauretis, ed. *Feminist Studies/Critical Studies.* Bloomington: Indiana University Press, 1986.

Martin, Biddy. "Lesbian Identity and Autobiographical Difference(s)." In Bella Brodski and Celeste Schenck, eds. *Life/Lines: Theorizing Women's Autobiography.* Ithaca and London: Cornell University Press, 1988.

Martin, Robert K. *The Homosexual Tradition in American Poetry.* Austin: University of Texas Press, 1979.

———. *Hero, Captain, and Stranger: Male Friendship, Social Critique and Literary Form in the Sea Novels of Herman Melville.* Chapel Hill: University of North Carolina Press, 1986.

Matthews, Peter. "Garbo and Phallic Motherhood: A 'Homosexual' Visual Economy." *Screen* 29 no. 3 (Summer 1988): 14–39.

Mayne, Judith. *The Woman at the Keyhole: Feminism and Women's Cinema.* Bloomington: Indiana University Press, 1990.

McEwen, Christian and Sue O'Sullivan, eds. *Out the Other Side: Contemporary Lesbian Writing.* London: Virago Press, 1988.

McIntosh, Mary. "The Homosexual Role." *Social Problems* 16 no. 2 (1968): 182–92.

Mercer, Kobena. "Imaging the Black Man's Sex." In Pat Holland, Jo Spence, and Simon Watney, eds. *Photography/Politics Two.* London: Comedia/Methuen, 1986.

Mercer, Kobena and Isaac Julien. "True Confessions: A Discourse on Images of Black Male Sexuality." *Ten* 8 no. 22 (n.d.): 4–9.

————. "Race, Sexual Politics and Black Masculinity: A Dossier." In Jonathan Rutherford and Rowena Chapman, eds. *Male Order: Unwrapping Masculinity.* London: Lawrence & Wishart, 1988.

Merck, Mandy. "The Train of Thought in Freud's 'Case of Homosexuality in a Woman'." *m/f* 11/12 (1986): 35–46.

————. "Difference and Its Discontents." *Screen* 28 no. 1 (Winter 1987a): 2–9.

————. " 'Lianna' and the Lesbians of Art Cinema." In Charlotte Brunsdon, ed. *Films for Women,* 166–79. London: British Film Institute, 1987b.

Metcalf, Andy and Martin Humphries, eds. *The Sexuality of Men.* London and Sydney: Pluto Press, 1985.

Meyer, Richard. "Imagining Sadomasochism: Robert Mapplethorpe and the Masquerade of Photography." *Qui Parle* 4 no. 1 (Fall 1990): 62–78.

Mieli, Mario. *Homosexuality and Liberation: Elements of a Gay Critique.* Translated by David Fernbach. London: Gay Men's Press, 1980.

Miller, D. A. *The Novel and the Police.* Berkeley: University of California Press, 1988.

————. "Sontag's Urbanity." *October* 49 (Summer 1989): 91–101.

Minson, Jeff. "The Assertion of Homosexuality." *m/f* 5/6 (1981): 19–39.

Mohr, Richard. *Gays/Justice: A Study of Ethics, Society, and Law.* New York: Columbia University Press. 1988.

Montero, Oscar. "Lipstick Vogue: The Politics of Drag." *Radical America* 22 no. 1 (Jan/Feb 1988): 36–42.

Moon, Michael. "The Gentle Boy from the Dangerous Classes: Pederasty, Domesticity, and Capitalism in Horatio Alger." *Representations* 19 (Summer 1987): 87–110.

————. "Flaming Closets." *October* 51 (Winter 1989): 19–54.

————. *Disseminating Whitman.* Cambridge: Harvard University Press, 1990.

Moraga, Cherríe. *Loving in the War Years.* Boston: South End Press, 1983.

———— and Gloria Anzaldúa, eds. *This Bridge Called My Back: Writings by Radical Women of Color.* New York: Women of Color Press, 1981 and 1983.

Munt, Sally. "The Inverstigators: Lesbian Crime Fiction." In Susannah Radstone, ed. *Sweet Dreams: Sexuality, Gender and Popular Fiction.* London: Lawrence & Wishart Limited, 1988.

Murphy, Jeanette, "A Question of Silence." In Charlotte Brunsdon, ed. *Films for Women,* 99–108. London: British Film Institute, 1986.

Neale, Steve. "Masculinity as Spectacle: Reflections on Men and Mainstream Cinema." *Screen* 24 no. 6 (November/December 1983): 2–16.

Nelson, Jeffrey. "Homosexuality in Hollywood Films: A Contemporary Paradox." *Critical Studies in Mass Communication* 2 (1985): 54–64.

Nestle, Joan. "Butch Fem Relationships: Sexual Courage in the 1950's." *A Restricted Country.* Ithaca, New York: Firebrand Books, 1987. Originally published in *Heresies* 12 (1981): 21–24.

Newton, Esther. *Mother Camp: Female Impersonators in America.* Chicago: University of Chicago Press, 1972.

———. "The Mythic Mannish Lesbian: Radclyffe Hall and the New Woman." *Signs* 9 no. 4 (Summer 1984): 557–75.

O'Brien, Sharon. " 'The Thing Not Named': Willa Cather as a Lesbian Writer." *Signs* 9 no. 4 (Summer 1984): 576–99.

O'Rourke, Rebecca. *Reflecting on the Well of Loneliness*. New York and London: Routledge, 1989.

Owens, Craig. "Outlaws: Gay Men in Feminism." In Alice Jardine and Paul Smith, eds. *Men in Feminism*, 219–32. New York and London: Methuen, 1987.

Pacteau, Francette. "The Impossible Referent: Representations of the Androgyne." In Victor Burgin, James Donald, and Cora Kaplan, eds. *Formations of Fantasy*. London and New York: Methuen, 1986.

Parker, Alice. "Writing Against Writing and Other Disruptions in Recent French Lesbian Texts." In Linda Kauffman, ed. *Feminism and Institutions: Dialogues on Feminist Theory*. Oxford: Basil Blackwell, 1989.

Patton, Cindy. *Sex and Germs: The Politics of AIDS*. Boston: South End Press, 1985.

———. "AIDS: Lessons from the Gay Community." *Feminist Review* 30 (Autumn 1988a): 104–11.

———. "The Cum Shot: Three Takes on Lesbian and Gay Sexuality." *Out/Look* 1 no. 3 (Fall 1988b): 72–77.

———. "Hegemony and Orgasm—Or the Instability of Heterosexual Pornography." *Screen* 30 nos. 1–2 (Winter/Spring 1989): 100–12.

———. *Inventing AIDS*. New York and London: Routledge, 1990.

Phelan, Shane. *Identity Politics: Lesbian Feminism and the Limits of Community*. Philadelphia: Temple University Press, 1989.

Plummer, Kenneth. *Sexual Stigma: An Interactionist Account*. London: Routledge & Kegan Paul, 1975.

———, ed. *The Making of the Modern Homosexual*. London: Hutchinson, 1981.

Radical America 21 nos. 2–3 (March/April 1987). Special issue on AIDS.

Ramos, Juanita, comp. and ed. *Compañeras: Latina Lesbians (An Anthology)*. New York: Latina History Project, 1987.

Raymond, Janice. *The Transsexual Empire: The Making of a She Male*. Boston: Beacon Press, 1979.

Resources for Feminist Research/Documentation sur la recherche féministe. *The Lesbian Issue/Entre Lesbienne*. Toronto, 1983.

Rich, Adrienne. *On Lies, Secrets, and Silence*. New York and London: W. W. Norton & Company, 1979.

———. "Compulsory Heterosexuality and Lesbian Existence." In Ann Snitow, Christine Stansell, and Sharon Thompson, eds. *Powers of Desire: The Politics of Sexuality*. New York: Monthly Review Press, 1983.

———. *Blood, Bread, and Poetry: Selected Prose 1979–1985*. New York and London: W. W. Norton & Company, 1986.

Rich, B. Ruby. "From Repressive Tolerance to Erotic Liberation: *Mädchen in Uniform*."

In Mary Ann Doane, Patricia Mellencamp, and Linda Williams, eds. *Re-vision: Essays in Feminist Film Criticism*. Frederick, Maryland: University Publications of America and the American Film Institute, 1984.

Richardson, Diane. *Women and AIDS*. New York: Methuen, 1988.

Riviere, Joan. "Womanliness as a Masquerade." *International Journal of Psycho-Analysis* 10 (1929): 303–13.

Roberts, J. R. *Black Lesbians: An Annotated Bibliography*. Tallahassee, Florida: The Naiad Press, 1981.

Roof, Judith. "The Match in the Crocus: Representations of Lesbian Sexuality." In Marleen S. Barr and Richard Feldstein, eds. *Discontented Discourses: Feminism/ Textual Intervention/Psychoanalysis*. Urbana and Chicago: University of Illinois Press, 1989.

———. "Freud Reads Lesbians: The Male Homosexual Imperative." *Arizona Quarterly* 46 no. 1 (Spring 1990): 17–26.

———. *A Lure of Knowledge: Configurations of Lesbian Sexuality*. New York: Columbia University Press, forthcoming.

Roscoe, Will. "Making History: The Challenge of Gay and Lesbian Studies." *Journal of Homosexuality* 15 nos. 3–4 (1988): 1–40.

Ross, Andrew. "Uses of Camp." *The Yale Journal of Criticism* 2 no. 1 (Fall 1988): 1–24.

———. *No Respect: Intellectuals and Popular Culture*. New York and London: Routledge, 1989.

Ruehl, Sonja. "Inverts and Experts: Radclyffe Hall and the Lesbian Identity." In Judith Newton and Deborah Rosenfelt, eds. *Feminist Criticism and Social Change: Sex, Class and Race in Literature and Culture*. New York and London: Methuen, 1985.

Ruse, Michael. *Homosexuality*. Oxford and New York: Basil Blackwell, 1988.

Russo, Vito. *The Celluloid Closet: Homosexuality in the Movies*. New York: Harper & Row, 1981, 1987.

Sabatier, Renée. *Blaming Others: Prejudice, Race and Worldwide AIDS*. Philadelphia: New Society Publishers, 1988.

Safouan, Moustapha. "Contribution to the Psychoanalysis of Transsexualism." In Stuart Schneiderman, ed. and trans. *Returning to Freud: Clinical Psychoanalysis in the School of Lacan*. New Haven: Yale University Press, 1980.

Samois, ed. *Coming to Power*. Boston: Alyson Publications, 1982.

Sargent, Dave. "Reformulating (Homo)Sexual Politics: Radical Theory and Practice in the Gay Movement." In Judith Allen and Paul Patton, eds. *Beyond Marxism? Interventions After Marx*. Sydney: Intervention Publications, 1983.

Saslow, James M. *Ganymede in the Renaissance: Homosexuality in Art and Society*. New Haven: Yale University Press, 1986.

———. "A Veil of Ice Between My Heart and the Fire: Michelangelo's Sexual Identity and Early Modern Constructs of Homosexuality." *Genders* 2 (Summer 1988): 77–90.

Sedgwick, Eve Kosofsky. *Between Men: English Literature and Male Homosocial Desire.* New York: Columbia University Press, 1985.

———. "The Beast in the Closet: James and the Writing of Homosexual Panic." In Ruth Bernard Yeazell, ed. *Sex, Politics, and Science in the Nineteenth-Century Novel: Selected Papers from the English Institute.* Baltimore: The Johns Hopkins University Press, 1986.

———. "A Poem is Being Written." *Representations* 17 (Winter 1987): 110–36.

———. "Epistemology of the Closet (I)." *Raritan* 7 no. 4 (Spring 1988a): 39–69.

———. "Epistemology of the Closet (II)." *Raritan* 8 no. 1 (Summer 1988b): 102–30.

———. "Privilege of Unknowing." *Genders* 1 (Spring 1988c): 102–24.

———. "Purple Prose: Relations of Sentimentality, Relations of the Closet." In Jonathan Arac and Barbara Johnson, eds. *Consequences of Theory: Selected Papers from the English Institute.* Baltimore: The Johns Hopkins University Press, 1989a.

———. "Tide and Trust." *Critical Inquiry* 15 no. 4 (Summer 1989b): 745–63.

———. "Pedagogy in the Context of an Antihomophobic Project." *South Atlantic Quarterly* 68 no. 1 (March 1990a): 139–56.

———. *Epistemology of the Closet.* Berkeley: University of California Press, 1990b.

Seidman, Steven. "Transfiguring Sexual Identity: AIDS and the Contemporary Construction of Homosexuality." *Social Text* 19/20 (Fall 1988): 187–209.

———. *Romantic Longings: Love in America, 1830–1980.* New York and London: Routledge, 1991.

Shaktini, Namascar. "Displacing the Phallic Subject: Wittig's Lesbian Writing." In Jeffner Allen and Iris Marion Young, eds. *The Thinking Muse: Feminism and Modern French Philosophy.* Bloomington and Indianapolis: Indiana University Press, 1989.

Shepherd, Simon and Mick Wallis, eds. *Coming on Strong: Gay Politics and Culture.* London: Unwin Hyman, 1989.

Signs 9 no. 4 (Summer 1984). "The Lesbian Issue."

Silverman, Kaja. *The Acoustic Mirror: The Female Voice in Psychoanalysis and Cinema.* Bloomington: University of Indiana Press, 1988a.

———. "Too Early/Too Late: Subjectivity and the Primal Scene in Henry James." *Novel* 21 nos. 2–3 (Winter/Spring 1988b): 147–73.

———. "White Skin, Brown Masks: The Double Mimesis, or With Lawrence in Arabia." *differences* 1 no. 3 (Fall 1989): 3–54.

———. *Male Subjectivity at the Margins.* New York and London: Routledge, forthcoming.

Smith, Barbara. "Toward a Black Feminist Criticism." In Elaine Showalter, ed. *The New Feminist Criticism.* New York: Pantheon Books, 1985.

Snitow, Ann, Christine Stansell, and Sharon Thompson, eds. *Powers of Desire: The Politics of Sexuality.* New York: Monthly Review Press, 1983.

Sontag, Susan. "Notes on Camp." In *Against Interpretation.* New York: Dell, 1967.

Stacey, Jackie. "Desperately Seeking Difference." *Screen* 28 no. 1 (Winter 1987): 48–61.

Stambolian, George and Elaine Marks, eds. *Homosexualities and French Literature: Cultural Contexts/Critical Texts*. Ithaca: Cornell University Press, 1979.

Steakley, James D. "Iconography of a Scandal: Political Cartoons and the Eulenburg Affair." *Studies in Visual Communication* 9 no. 2 (Spring 1983): 20–51.

Stein, Arlene. "Style Wars and the New Lesbianism." *Out/Look* 1 no. 4 (Winter 1989): 34–42.

Stein, Edward, ed. *Forms of Desire: Sexual Orientation and Social Constructionist Controversy*. New York: Garland, 1990.

Steven, Peter, ed. *Jump Cut: Hollywood, Politics and Counter Cinema*. New York: Praeger, 1985.

Stimpson, Catharine R. "Zero Degree Deviancy: The Lesbian Novel in English." In Elizabeth Abel, ed. *Writing and Sexual Difference*. Chicago: University of Chicago Press, 1982.

———. *Where the Meanings Are: Feminism and Cultural Spaces*. New York and London: Routledge, 1988.

Straayer, Chris. "Personal Best: Lesbian/Feminist Audience." *Jump Cut* 29 (1984): 40–44.

Textual Practice 4 no. 2 (Summer 1990). Special issue on "Lesbian and Gay Cultures: Theories and Texts." Joseph Bristow, ed.

Thompson, Mark, ed. *Gay Spirit: Myth and Meaning*. New York: St. Martin's Press, 1987.

Treichler, Paula A. "AIDS and HIV Infection in the Third World: A First World Chronicle." In Barbara Kruger and Phil Mariani, eds. *Remaking History*. Seattle: Bay Press, 1989.

Tyler, Carole-Anne. "The Supreme Sacrifice? TV, 'TV,' and the Renée Richards Story." *differences* 1 no. 3 (Fall 1989): 160–86.

Tyler, Parker. *Screening the Sexes: Homosexuality in the Movies*. New York: Holt, Rinehart and Winston, 1972.

Valverde, Mariana. *Sex, Power, and Pleasure*. Toronto: The Women's Press, 1985.

Vance, Carole S., ed. *Pleasure and Danger: Exploring Female Sexuality*. Boston: Routledge & Kegan Paul, 1984.

Van der Meer, Theo and Anja van Kooten Niekerk, eds. *Homosexuality, Which Homosexuality?* London: GMP Publishers, 1989.

Van Leer, David. "The Beast of the Closet: Homosociality and the Pathology of Manhood." *Critical Inquiry* 15 no. 3 (Spring 1989a): 587–605.

———. "Trust and Trade." *Critical Inquiry* 15 no. 4 (Summer 1989b): 758–63.

Walters, Suzanna Danuta. "As Her Hand Crept Slowly Up Her Thigh: Ann Bannon and the Politics of Pulp." *Social Text* 23 (Fall/Winter 1989): 83–101.

Warner, Michael. "Homo-Narcissism; or Heterosexuality." In Joseph A. Boone and Michael Cadden, eds. *Engendering Men: The Question of Male Feminist Criticism*. New York and London: Routledge, 1990.

Watney, Simon. "Hollywood's Homosexual World." *Screen* 23 nos. 3–4 (Sept/Oct 1982): 107–21.

————. *Policing Desire: Pornography, AIDS, and the Media*. Minneapolis: University of Minnesota Press, 1987a.

————. "AIDS: The Cultural Agenda." *Radical America* 21 no. 4 (July/Aug 1987b): 49–53.

————. "The Subject of AIDS." *Copyright* 1 (Fall 1987c): 125–31.

————, and Erica Carter, eds. *Taking Liberties: AIDS and Cultural Politics*. London: Serpent's Tail, 1989a.

————. "Missionary Positions: AIDS, 'Africa,' and Race." *differences* 1 no. 1 (Winter 1989b): 83–100.

————. "Photography and AIDS." In Carol Squiers, ed. *The Critical Image: Essays on Contemporary Photography*. Seattle: Bay Press, 1990a. ·

————. "Practices of Freedom: 'Citizenship' and the Politics of Identity in the Age of AIDS." In J. Rutherford, ed. *Identity: Community, Culture, Difference*. London: Lawrence & Wishart, 1990b.

Waugh, Thomas. "Lesbian and Gay Documentary: Minority Self-Imaging, Oppositional Film Practice, and the Question of Image Ethics." In Larry Gross, John Stuart Katz, and Jay Ruby, eds. *Image Ethics: The Moral Rights of Subjects in Photography, Film and Television*. New York: Oxford University Press, 1988.

Weeks, Jeffrey. *Coming Out: Homosexual Politics in Britain from the Nineteenth Century to the Present*. London: Quartet, 1977.

————. "Movements of Affirmation: Sexual Meanings and Homosexual Identities." *Radical History Review* 20 (Spring/Summer 1979): 164–79.

————. *Sexuality and Its Discontents: Meanings, Myths, and Modern Sexualities*. London, Boston, and Henley: Routledge & Kegan Paul, 1985.

————. *Sexuality*. London and New York: Tavistock Publications, 1986.

Weston, Kath. *Families We Choose: Lesbians, Gays, and Kinship*. New York: Columbia University Press, 1991.

White, Patricia. "Madame X of the China Seas." *Screen* 28 no. 4 (Autumn 1987): 80–95.

Williams, Walter L. *The Spirit and the Flesh: Sexual Diversity in American Indian Culture*. Boston: Beacon Press, 1986.

Wilson, Elizabeth. *Hidden Agendas: Theory, Politics, and Experience in the Women's Movement*. London and New York: Tavistock Publications, 1986.

Wine, Jeri Dawn. "The Lesbian Continuum in Academe." *RFR/DRF* 16 no. 4 (December 1987): 27–29.

Winkler, John J. *Constraints of Desire: The Anthropology of Sex and Gender in Ancient Greece*. New York: Routledge, 1989.

Wittig, Monique. "The Straight Mind." *Feminist Issues* (Summer 1980): 103–11.

————. "One is Not Born a Woman." *Feminist Issues* (Fall 1981): 46–54.

————. "The Category of Sex." *Feminist Issues* (Fall 1982): 63–68.

————. "The Point of View: Universal or Particular?" *Feminist Issues* (Fall 1983): 63–69.

———. "The Mark of Gender." In Nancy K. Miller, ed. *The Poetics of Gender*, 63–73. New York: Columbia University Press, 1986.

Woodhouse, Annie. *Fantastic Women: Sex, Gender and Transvestism*. New Brunswick: Rutgers University Press, 1989.

Woods, Gregory, *Articulate Flesh: Male Homo-eroticism & Modern Poetry*. New Haven and London: Yale University Press, 1987.

Yingling, Thomas. *Hart Crane and the Homosexual Text: New Thresholds, New Anatomies*. Chicago: Chicago University Press. 1990a.

———. "How the Eye Is Caste: Robert Mapplethorpe and the Limits of Controversy." *Discourse* 12 no. 2 (Spring/Summer 1990b): 3–28.

Young, Robert. "The Same Difference." *Screen* 28 no. 3 (Summer 1987): 84–91.

Zimmerman, Bonnie. "The Politics of Transliteration: Lesbian Personal Narratives." *Signs* 9 no. 4 (Summer 1984): 663–82.

———. "What Has Never Been: An Overview of Lesbian Feminist Criticism." In Elaine Showalter, ed. *The New Feminist Criticism*. New York: Pantheon Books, 1985.

———. *The Safe Sea of Women: Lesbian Fiction 1969–1989*. Boston: Beacon Press, 1990.

Contributors

Michèle Aina Barale teaches English and Women's and Gender Studies at Amherst College. She is the author of *Daughters and Lovers: The Life and Writing of Mary Webb*. Presently she is at work on a book tentatively called *Below the Belt: Essays in Gay Reading*, from which the essay printed here is drawn, and (in conjunction with Henry Abelove and David Halperin) she is editing an anthology of lesbian and gay criticism.

Judith Butler teaches in the Humanities Center at Johns Hopkins University. She is the author of *Gender Trouble: Feminism and the Subversion of Identity* (1990), and she is presently working on a manuscript entitled *Bodies That Matter*.

Ed Cohen teaches Cultural and Gender Studies at Rutgers University. His book *Talk on the Wilde Side: Towards a Geneology of Male Sexualities* is forthcoming from Routledge. Currently he is working on the problems of inclusion and exclusion raised by identity politics.

Richard Dyer teaches Film Studies at the University of Warwick, Great Britain. He is the author of *Heavenly Bodies: Film Stars and Society* (1986) and *Now You See It: Studies on Lesbian and Gay Film* (1990). He is currently preparing two collections of articles on issues of entertainment and representation as well as a book-length project on the cultural construction of whiteness.

Lee Edelman teaches English at Tufts University. He is the author of *Transmemberment of Song: Hart Crane's Anatomies of Rhetoric and Desire* (1987). A collection of his essays on gay theory, titled *Homographesis*, is forthcoming from Routledge.

Diana Fuss teaches English and Women's Studies at Princeton University. She is the author of *Essentially Speaking: Feminism, Nature and Difference* (1989), and she is currently working on theorizations of gay and lesbian identities.

Ellis Hanson is a doctoral student in English at Princeton University. He is presently preparing a dissertation on decadence, desire, and religious conversion.

Wayne Koestenbaum teaches English at Yale University. He is the author of *Double Talk: The Erotics of Male Literary Collaboration* (1989) and *Ode to Anna Moffo and Other Poems* (1990). He is presently at work on a study of opera and homosexuality, tentatively entitled *The Queen's Throat*.

Judith Mayne teaches French and Women's Studies at Ohio State University. She is the author of several books: *Private Novels/Public Films* (1988); *Kino and the Woman*

Question: Feminism and Soviet Silent Film (1989), and *The Woman at the Keyhole: Feminism and Women's Cinema* (1990). A book entitled *Spectatorship* is forthcoming.

Richard Meyer, a doctoral student in art history at the University of California, Berkeley, has published in *Outweek* and *Qui Parle*. With Larry Rinder, he organized Group Material's *AIDS Timeline* at the University Art Museum (Berkeley). He is currently preparing a dissertation on competing discourses of masculinity in American art of the 1960s.

D. A. Miller teaches English at Harvard University. He is the author of *The Novel and the Police* (1988).

Ray Navarro was a freelance writer and media activist living in New York City. He contributed articles to *Outweek, The Independent, The Guardian*, and various other publications. He was one of the organizers of Media Network's AIDS video community-based screening project, and he spoke publicly on the subject of AIDS media and people of color.

Jeff Nunokawa teaches English at Princeton University. He is co-editor of *How Do I Look? Queer Film and Video* (1991) and has published widely on such topics as orientalism, tourism, imperialism, AIDS, and mourning. He is currently completing a manuscript on sexuality and economics in nineteenth-century narrative.

Cindy Patton teaches Women's and Gender Studies at Amherst College. She is the author of *Sex and Germs: The Politics of AIDS* (1985), *Making It: A Woman's Guide to Sex in the Age of AIDS* (1987), and *Inventing AIDS* (1990). Presently she is at work on a study of sexual vernaculars, from which the present essay is taken, as well as a study of the construction of race and gender in popular culture narratives.

Catherine Saalfield writes on AIDS and other lesbian and gay issues for various publications, including *Outweek, The Independent*, and *The Guardian*, and she is co-author of *Women, AIDS & Activism* (1990). She is a video curator and media activist in New York City and also collaborates on videos and video installations.

Carole-Anne Tyler teaches English at the University of California, Riverside. She is working on a book tentatively titled *Female Impersonation*, from which her essay is drawn. Portions of the book have also appeared in *differences* (1989) and in *Theory Between the Disciplines: Authority/Vision/Politics* (1990).

Simon Watney is the Assistant Editor of the National AIDS Manual in the UK. He has been actively involved in gay politics since the early 1970s, and was for many years Senior Lecturer in the History and Theory of Photography at the Polytechnic of Central London, and a member of the editorial board of *Screen*. He is the author of *Policing Desire: Pornography, AIDS, and the Media* (1987), and the co-editor (with Erica Carter) of *Taking Liberties: AIDS and Cultural Politics* (1989). His most recent book is *The Art of Duncan Grant* (1990).

Patricia White is a doctoral student in the History of Consciousness program at the University of California, Santa Cruz. She is currently writing on representations of lesbianism in classical and independent cinema and in feminist film theory.

Thomas Yingling teaches English and Textual Studies at Syracuse University. He is the author of *Hart Crane and the Homosexual Text: New Thresholds, New Anatomies* (1990). His areas of research interest include critical theory, American culture, and the imprint of modernity on conscious and unconscious life.